Soviet Intellectuals and Political Power

Soviet Intellectuals and Political Power

THE POST-STALIN ERA

Vladimir Shlapentokh

PRINCETON UNIVERSITY PRESS

PRINCETON, NEW JERSEY

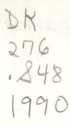

Copyright © 1990 by Princeton University Press
Published by Princeton University Press, 41 William Street,
Princeton, New Jersey 08540
In the United Kingdom: Princeton University Press, Oxford

Library of Congress Cataloging-in-Publication Data

Shlapentokh, Vladimir.
Soviet intellectuals and political power : the post-Stalin era /
Vladimir Shlapentokh.
p.   cm.
Includes bibliographical references and index.
1. Soviet Union—Intellectual life—1917– 2. Soviet Union—
Politics and government—1953–1985. 3. Soviet Union—Politics and
government—1986– I. Title.
DK276.S48   1990   947.084—dc20   90-36648

ISBN 0-691-09459-4 (cloth : acid-free paper)

This book has been composed in Linotron Sabon

Princeton University Press books are printed on acid-free paper,
and meet the guidelines for permanence and durability of the
Committee on Production Guidelines for Book Longevity of the
Council on Library Resources

Printed in the United States of America by Princeton University Press,
Princeton, New Jersey

10   9   8   7   6   5   4   3   2   1

To the memory of my dear friend Isaak Kantorovich, with whom I passionately discussed the role of the intelligentsia in socialist society at Kiev University from 1945 to 1951, and to his son, Vladimir, who has taken the place of his father as my friend

Contents

Preface

SINCE the 1970s practically all socialist countries have found themselves in a deep economic crisis associated with and exacerbated by ideological decay and demoralization in the population, particularly among the young people. In the 1980s this crisis has reached such proportions that the leaders of socialist countries, especially the USSR and China, have had to acknowledge the problem publicly. At the same time, they have promised to overcome these difficulties and put their societies back on the road to economic and social well-being.

Can the type of socialist societies that exists in the USSR, Eastern Europe, and a number of countries in other parts of the world truly cope with the profound problems with which they are faced? Are Soviet-type societies flexible enough to adjust their social, economic, and political structures to changing conditions in the world, particularly to the fast pace of technological change? Are they able to transform themselves into a modern society with democratic institutions and an economy capable of serving consumers? Few questions are as fascinating and important as these.

The difficulty of accurately predicting the potential for change in a social system is well known. Among the numerous variables that determine a society's potential for change is the importance placed by that society on the "national creative energy," that is, the position accorded the intellectuals, the highly educated people with special creative gifts, in any given society.

There are two different approaches to defining the intelligentsia and the intellectuals (the former being the term used in Russia, the latter being that used in the West). The first approach is normative and therefore subjective. It supposes that a member of the intelligentsia or an intellectual is one who possesses a cluster of intellectual, cultural, and, most importantly, moral virtues such as kindness and altruism, and who serves as a model for the rest of society. This approach was dominant in prerevolutionary Russia and continues to be very popular among dissidents in the Soviet Union (e.g., Altaiev 1970; Pomerants 1981; Solzhenitsyn 1974), as well as among official writers, especially during the period of glasnost (e.g., Dudintsev 1987b; Granin 1987, 1988a; see also the discussions in *Literaturnaia Gazeta*, August 17, 1988; September 21, 1988; November 23, 1988). Some Western authors also follow this approach (e.g., Aron 1955; Bell 1973; Besançon 1977; Brym 1980; Mannheim 1949; Merton 1949).

In the West, however, this subjective approach has also been combined with an emphasis on the cognitive role of the intellectuals as the interpreters and critics of reality and of ideologies. This interpretation and critique may be very positive, neutral, or extremely negative (Benda 1927; Bell 1973; Bodin 1964, pp. 11–13, 62–67; Gagnon 1987; Hayek 1960, pp. 371–385; Johnson 1988; Shils 1972, p. 3; Weber 1968, p. 925).

The second approach to defining the intelligentsia and the intellectuals utilizes formal criteria, such as level of education and involvement in creative work, that is, the production of either new ideas or new things. This approach is accepted by some Western scholars (e.g., Aron 1955, pp. 213–214; Brown 1982, pp. 7–12; Hofstadter 1963; Lipset 1959, p. 333), as well as by official Soviet statisticians and by Soviet sociologists (e.g., Shkaratan 1982; Zaslavskaia 1988, p. 17).

By utilizing such formal criteria, it is possible to arrive at approximate estimates of the number of educated people supposedly engaged in creative activity in the USSR. By the mid-1980s there were about 500,000 scholars with doctoral and postdoctoral degrees, about 10,000 writers (members of the Writers' Union), around 2,500 composers (members of the Composers' Union), approximately 73,000 actors and 7,000 filmmakers, about 19,000 architects, roughly 20,000 artists, and approximately 83,000 journalists—all members of their respective unions (Ivanova 1987, p. 173; Prokhorov 1987, pp. 1252–1253, 1256; *Ogoniok*, no. 45, 1987, p. 18; no. 2, 1988, p. 23; *TsSU*, 1987, p. 62). All told, there are approximately 700,000 highly educated people formally engaged in creative activity in the Soviet Union. Of these, probably about 10 percent are most highly qualified.

Throughout this work the second approach to defining the intelligentsia will be used. This approach is far from flawless, however, particularly because it does not allow truly creative individuals to be separated from those who merely imitate creative work. This distinction is of fundamental importance, particularly in light of the radical transformation of the intellectual community during the 1970s. As with any other professional group or social institution, "genuine" intellectuals in any society are accompanied by "bogus" intellectuals. The latter, through imitation of the former, survive as parasites, demanding public reward for work that has little or nothing to do with true creative activity. Given a modicum of relatively efficient consumer control, bogus professional groups will remain small and will exert relatively little effect on society. However, with the relaxation of such control, as often occurs in socialist society, the number of bogus intellectuals tends to increase. This was, in fact, what transpired in the USSR. In the 1970s bogus intellectuals, which were heavily comprised of party officials with scholarly degrees, took the upper hand in the intellectual community. According to some Soviet estimates, more than half of all Soviet scientific production is done by 5 to 10 percent of all Soviet scholars (*Izvestia*, April 14, 1989).

Of course, the division between the "wheat" and the "chaff," between the genuine and bogus intellectuals, is a division between two "ideal types." Throughout this work, when intellectuals are discussed without qualification, these will always be truly highly educated people engaged in genuinely creative activity.

Clearly, such a radical division between the two types of intellectuals is difficult to document. This is to be expected, of course, since the second group, by definition, will always strive to remain undistinguishable from the first.

Common sense dictates that, all other things being equal, a nation's technological and cultural progress depends heavily on its capacity to utilize the talents of its people, including those with special education and training that foster creativity. A society's capacity to capitalize on such talents depends very much, in turn, on the social status of intellectuals and, in particular, on the intellectuals' attitudes toward the existing social, economic, and political order. The greater the intellectuals' alienation from the society in which they live and create, the less they will contribute to the progress of that society.

Of special importance is the place of the intellectuals as political actors in any society. The intellectuals' political attitudes, political behavior, and social ideals directly influence the degree to which they are integrated into the dominant social system. Their position as political actors significantly influences their professional activities as well as the political stability of the society. The greater the intellectuals' hostility toward the system, the higher the probability that they will be involved in both the debunking of official ideology and the creation of organizations that present a serious threat to the regime.

The intellectuals' role in the political system in post-Stalin Soviet society is the main subject of this book. An analysis of this subject requires the examination of various issues related to the intellectuals' place in classical "socialist society" as it functioned prior to Gorbachev's revolution.

What are the attitudes of Soviet intellectuals toward their society, and especially toward the Soviet political order? To what extent do intellectuals' political views influence their professional work? How prepared are intellectuals to translate their views into open, public behavior? Which of the intellectuals' social ideals are opposed to official doctrine? How do intellectuals change their behavior and views under the direct pressure of the political elite? These and other questions will be discussed in this book.

I will advance the premise that the intellectuals and the political elite, as two political actors in a socialist society based on political power, exhibit dual and deeply contradictory attitudes toward each other. Indeed, it is this duality which determines the ambiguous place of the intellectuals in socialist society, and which makes the questions formulated above so difficult to answer.

In chapter 1 I will attempt to describe the relationship between the intellectuals and the political elite from the perspective of the latter. In chapters 2 and 3 I will first describe the value orientations of the intellectuals and their subculture, and then will examine the ways in which these values are manifested in the intellectuals' life-style.

Chapters 4 through 8 are devoted to the analysis of the main issue of the book: specifically, the political behavior and ideologies of Soviet intellectuals in the post-Stalin period. Chapter 4 is dedicated to the elaboration of a theory regarding the political activity of intellectuals, based on an understanding of the role of private and public life in Soviet-type societies. Chapters 5 and 6 are devoted to the empirical and historical substantiation of the theory put forth in chapter 4, via an examination of the political life and ideologies of intellectuals in the 1960s—the period of liberalization. Chapters 7 and 8 describe the intellectuals' political behavior and ideology in the 1970s and early 1980s—the period of political reaction. And finally, chapter 9 is committed to examining the condition of the intellectual community in the mid-1980s, following the new regime's proclamation of the necessity of revamping the economy and restoring public morals. The chapter will cover the developments between the installation of the new regime in March 1985 and the election of the new Soviet parliament in 1989, the event that marked the end of the first stage of Mikhail Gorbachev's political reforms.

But first, a few words about the methodological principles followed in the writing of the book. My focus is primarily on intellectuals in the Soviet Union, and especially those in Moscow, Leningrad, and other Russian cities and regions. In and of themselves, these intellectuals comprise an extremely complex and multifaceted subject. I discuss only casually the unique and distinctive issues specifically related to the intellectuals in the national republics.

Of course, the fruitful analysis of any significant social phenomenon is clearly impossible without a comparative perspective. Unfortunately, a lack of space precludes engaging in a strict intercultural study here. For this reason, the book includes few references to the lives of intellectuals in other societies and incorporates only a fragment of the pertinent data at my disposal, given their nonrepresentative and imprecise nature. Nevertheless, whatever the issue in question, intellectuals in two types of countries are generally discussed: those in socialist countries (primarily

China, Poland, Czechoslovakia, and Hungary), and those in Western countries (particularly the United States, but also France and England). When appropriate, the lives of intellectuals in nonsocialist countries with former or current repressive regimes (such as those in Latin America) are also discussed.[1]

Given this admittedly limited comparative perspective, this book can clearly be considered a case study sufficient to the task of shedding light on the political activity of intellectuals—not only (although primarily) those in socialist societies of the Soviet type, but to a considerable degree those in all societies with strong political power. It may also help one to better understand the position of the intellectuals in democratic, pluralistic societies. The degree to which the book succeeds in these ambitions is for the reader to decide.

In focusing on Soviet intellectuals, the book examines a gamut of sources of a diversity unbelievable only fifteen to twenty years ago. The arguments of the most conservative Soviet ideologues are contrasted with those of the most consistent enemies of the Soviet system. Similarly, Soviet publications that attempted to destroy dissidents are dealt with alongside materials distributed by the dissidents themselves. In addition, the last decade has been rich with the memoirs of Soviet intellectuals— memoirs that have been published by official Soviet publishing houses as well as by those in the West. These, too, have been incorporated in this study. Of course, Gorbachev's glasnost has significantly enriched the empirical basis of this book, making it possible to document many of the developments of the 1960s and 1970s—a task that was very difficult when the first draft of this book was finished in the early 1980s.

The book incorporates a great deal of quantitative information on the intellectuals in the Soviet Union. In writing this book, I had the distinct pleasure of being able to use information obtained from a number of surveys, including those of the readers of *Literaturnaia Gazeta* (Literary Gazette), which I directed while still working in the Soviet Union. Since the 1960s *Literaturnaia Gazeta* has been read primarily by the intelligentsia (one of the earliest facts to be established by these surveys). More so than any other periodical, *Literaturnaia Gazeta* reflects the mood and views of Soviet intellectuals.

In spite of my orientation toward sociological data and literature, I considered it necessary to use Soviet fiction as an important source of additional information. In addition, technological progress has been of

---

[1] Charles Kadushin's *American Intellectual Elite* (1974) is nearly identical to the current book in its attempt to grasp the life of the intellectual in the United States, while Roderic Camp's *Intellectuals and the State in Twentieth-Century Mexico* (1985) attempts to do the same for Mexican intellectuals. Also see Harish Srivastava's *Intellectuals in Contemporary India* (1978).

benefit to this work: thanks to recent developments, I have been able to examine a number of videotapes of recent Soviet movies, and since 1987 I have had the opportunity to watch Soviet television on a daily basis.

Finally, as a researcher and scientist, I am acutely aware of the influence of any researcher's political orientation on the results of a social study. In addition, I do not wish to conceal from my readers (and it would hardly be possible) that my sympathy lies with Soviet liberal intellectuals, among whom I was included. From the 1960s through my emigration in 1979, I was considered part of this group not only by my colleagues and Soviet readers, but by Soviet authorities as well.

What is left to an author who realizes that he takes sides emotionally in an intellectual conflict? Only to follow Weber's advice and to counter, as much as possible, his ideological predilections, thereby allowing his readers to make the final judgment on the merits of different views and different behaviors.

Acknowledgments

MANY ISSUES raised in this book have been discussed with my friends Aron Katsenelinboigen, Vladimir Kontorovich, Bob Solo, and Berni Finifter, as well as with my son Dmitri, my daughter Sasha, and my wife Luba. I am deeply indebted to all of them for their criticisms and suggestions.

My most sincere gratitude goes out to Blake Armstrong and especially to Tanya Chowdhury, for her help in checking the countless Russian names that permeate this work, and to Neil F. O'Donnell, not only for his extremely scrupulous editing of the manuscript before it went to the publisher, but for his numerous suggestions and comments, which greatly improved this book.

My special thanks go to Gail Ullman, for her sensitivity to the ideas which I developed in this book and for her cordial support in my endeavor; and to Alice Calaprice, for her perfect editing of the manuscript and her good-humored patience with the author.

Abbreviations

THE NAMES of Soviet journals and periodicals will be abbreviated if cited more than once in any chapter. Thus, when first cited in that chapter, the full name of the journal or periodical will be used, e.g., *Literaturnaia Gazeta*, July 19, 1986. Thereafter, the name of the journal or periodical will be given in abbreviated form, as follows:

DN	*Druzhba Narodov*
Iu.	*Iunost'*
Iz.	*Izvestia*
Kom.	*Kommunist*
KP	*Komsomol'skaia Pravda*
LG	*Literaturnaia Gazeta*
LR	*Literaturnaia Rossia*
MG	*Molodaia Gvardia*
MN	*Moskovskie Novosti*
Mos.	*Moskva*
NS	*Nash Sovremennik*
Ned.	*Nedelia*
NRS	*Novoye Russkoye Slovo*
NM	*Novyi Mir*
Og.	*Ogoniok*
Ok.	*Oktiabr'*
Poi.	*Poiski*
P.	*Pravda*
SK	*Sovietskaia Kul'tura*
SiM.	*Strana i Mir*
TsSU	*Tsentral'noie Statisticheskoie Upravlenie*
VS	*Vol'noie Slovo*
VF	*Voprosy Filosofii*
ZiS.	*Znanie i Sila*

Soviet Intellectuals and Political Power

Soviet Intellectuals in the Soviet Structure: Love-Hate Relationships with the Political Elite

DO INTELLECTUALS FORM A COHESIVE GROUP?

There are several schools of thought regarding whether intellectuals (or the creative intelligentsia) constitute a distinct and identifiable social group in modern society. Most analysts of U.S. society deny that its intellectuals constitute a distinct group with its own culture and interests. Numerous writers have suggested that American intellectuals came closest to forming their own social group between the 1930s and the 1950s, when a circle of leftist and radical intellectuals in New York City developed a reasonably cohesive ideology and subculture directed against the establishment (see recent publications on this issue by Abel 1984; Barrett 1982; Glazer 1984; Hellman 1976; Howe 1982; O'Neill 1982; Pells 1985; Perry 1984; Phillips 1983; Podhoretz 1979).

Numerous writers also dispute whether intellectuals in socialist countries comprise their own well-defined social groups (e.g., Hruby 1980). In my view, the degree to which intellectuals constitute a distinct social group is a function of both the nature of political power and the tensions among classes in a society. That is, intellectuals tend to form cohesive groups only in societies with strong, uncontrollable political power and in societies with deep class antagonism (see le Goffe and Köpeczi 1985, pp. 12–22).

From this perspective, it is questionable whether one can view intellectuals in the United States as comprising a distinct social group (Gella 1976, p. 20; Gouldner 1979). In authoritative states, however, one can expect intellectuals to develop their own distinct subculture, typically opposed to the existing regime.

Tradition also plays an important role in whether intellectuals form their own group. The Soviet Union, as well as other societies in which intellectuals represent a distinct group, has a long history of despotic regimes that have alienated the most educated and creative segments of society, driving them toward a common position in opposition to the state. Moreover, the distinctiveness of intellectuals as a social group is associated with the distance between the dominant class and the masses. The greater this distance, the more strongly the intellectuals oppose the dominant class and emerge as the spokespersons of the masses. Such class distinctions need not be associated with highly repressive regimes: it is possible to identify cohesive intellectual communities in Western European societies, where class boundaries are more clearly defined than are those in the United States.

Paradoxically, while opposing the dominant class and acting as defenders and spokespersons of the masses, intellectuals tend to become estranged from the lower classes. The intellectuals' subculture, which stresses education and creativity, distances its members from the majority of the population. The masses, in turn, with their egalitarian tendencies, often disdain intellectuals, suspecting them of being unfairly rich and of wallowing in luxuries, and equate intellectuals with the apparatchiks and with trade and service workers, who are notorious for their dishonest income (see Oleg Dmitriev's article in *Literaturnaia Gazeta*, January 20, 1988). And, while the rise of general education, the expansion of the mass intelligentsia, and the dissemination of mass culture have diminished the gap between the intellectuals and those they claim to represent, great distances remain. This important political fact is often used by the dominant class in its attempts to generate mass opposition to the intellectuals.

Nevertheless, these two characteristics of the intellectuals—their opposition to the dominant powers and their isolation from the masses— are not sufficient to describe the complex and contradictory position of the intelligentsia in the political structure of Soviet-type society. Another critical factor that makes the picture more intricate is that of power—a force that can both alienate and attract intellectuals, pushing them away from and into cooperation with the dominant class (about this, see Shils 1972).

In centralized society, where the political elite commands resources and where private support of intellectual activity assumes only very limited and illegal forms, intellectuals must cooperate with, and accept the roles imposed on them by, the state. That is, they are required to serve the political elite as creators of weapons, as ideologues, and as promoters of national prestige as musicians and artists. Those who accept these roles are handsomely rewarded by the authorities; those who do not face direct coercive means, which the state willingly uses against them. These two factors contribute to the readiness of intellectuals to collaborate with the state, and to accept the resulting privileges.

Whatever the underlying forces that drive intellectuals into cooperation with the state, more than a few members of this group see the political elite as their benevolent masters, or even as their partners in guiding a nation incapable of pursuing the rules of the democratic game. The same willing cooperation also takes place, although to a much lesser degree, in modern capitalist society, where the resources commanded by the centralized government or large corporations are significant, but not as great as those in socialist society (see Brym 1980, pp. 18–19; Coser 1965; Shils 1972, p. 13).

The collaboration between intellectuals and the state has led some scholars to regard intellectuals as a "new class" (Gouldner 1979; Parkin 1972), or as a part of the dominant class (Konrad and Szelenyi 1978). These concepts recall the early-twentieth-century ideas of Jan Machajski (1968), who argued that the intelligentsia would replace the capitalists as the exploiters in socialist society. Although there is an element of truth to these theories about the "new class," they should not overshadow another fact. Their authors confound proximity to the political elite with the capacity to make important political and social decisions. This privilege is totally withheld not only from intellectuals but from other groups in the population as well.

The dual attitudes of the intellectuals toward power are inextricably linked to the same dual attitudes of the dominant class toward the intelligentsia. This mutual duality in relations complicates the intellectuals' position in Soviet society, such that on some occasions they work with the political elite, while on other occasions they are diametrically opposed to the programs and goals of the political elite. These inconsistencies are the main source of internal conflict within the intellectual community, and account for a great deal of its heterogeneity.

While underscoring the inconsistencies in the intellectuals' social position and the dual character of their relations with the political elite, I take the position that, in general, the intellectuals are much closer to the masses politically and are best regarded as a segment of the ruled rather than of the rulers. In fact, in a society based on the Stalinist model, the intellectuals are deprived of any participation in political power, of any political freedom, and of any autonomy. They are almost entirely at the mercy of their rulers.

With very few exceptions, at the most critical periods in the history of the Soviet Union and other socialist countries, the intelligentsia as a whole has allied with the masses against the dominant class. In some cases, however, the intellectuals have become temporary allies of the political leadership in its conflict with the party apparatus. Such was the case, in particular, during the first Soviet "thaw" of the late 1950s and early 1960s, and during the period of glasnost, from 1985 to 1989.

The intellectuals' political cohesiveness is directly proportional to the extent of the repression in their society and the unity of the dominant class. In a society ruled by mass terror, where genuine communication between people disappears, the intellectuals as a group almost entirely cease to exist. They resuscitate only when socialist society enters a period of milder and more selective repressions. Then, with the nightmare behind them, they tend to unite strongly in their hatred of the party and of the state and begin, almost unanimously, to support liberal ideology.

The situation changes yet again if the regime makes progress toward liberalization and if the dominant class breaks into factions offering different programs for coping with society's crises. In this case, intellectuals begin to lose their unity and split into warring camps.

The question of the intellectuals' unity is further complicated by ethnic issues. Almost nonexistent in countries such as China or Vietnam, ethnic issues exert a powerful influence on intellectuals in other socialist countries. In the small nations under Moscow's control, nationalism and liberalism are usually allies, particularly if repressions are mild. In these cases, intellectuals are, in general, not strongly divided in their attitudes toward the question of nationalism. The role of ethnic issues is of extraordinary importance in a country as ethnically diverse as the USSR. In general, the sequence of events there has been the same as that in other socialist countries—transition from a unity based on liberal principles, during the initial post-Stalin period, toward periods during which nationalism increases significantly among intellectuals and begins to challenge liberal ideologies.

During glasnost, the resurgence of liberals and the new aggressiveness of nationalists has widened the gap between intellectuals. The dissension among them has become so strong that separation into two intellectual communities—liberal and nationalist—does not seem inappropriate for this analysis.

The political and ideological split among the intellectuals is also related to their various occupations. Because social scientists and those in the humanities are more prone to state manipulation, they tend to be more conservative than are natural scientists (Zaslavskaia 1988, p. 17). I suggest that the more radical political behavior of natural scientists and others in the technical intelligentsia is also related to the lower proportion of bogus and mediocre intellectuals among them—the result of the State's promotion of talentless and obedient people in the social sciences, literature, and the arts during the last seven decades. When the state adopted similar advancement policies for those in the technical intelligentsia, as happened in the 1970s, the differences between the two groups became much less clear.

The Composition of the Dominant Class and the Intellectuals

The specific status of the intellectuals in Soviet society puts them in relations with the dominant class that are radically different from those between the masses and the dominant class. In this respect, the division of the dominant class into the political elite and the apparatchiks (i.e., the bureaucracy) is of extraordinary importance to the intellectuals.

The political elite in Soviet society holds a monopoly on strategic decisions—those decisions that generate or block any significant change in social life—and expends considerable energy attempting to prevent the emergence of any competing center of power. This monopoly on strategic decisions should not, however, be confused with the efficacy of those decisions. The political elite may preserve its monopoly but remain incapable of implementing its policies or even of curbing processes that endanger its existence.

The majority of the dominant class consists of the apparatchiks, who implement the dictates of the political elite. No apparatchik, even one who holds the position of minister or regional party secretary, can make significant changes on his or her own initiative. While apparatchiks hold great power over their subordinates, they are effectively powerless in relation to the political elite, and can only sabotage orders issued by those above them.

The structure of the dominant class has a direct impact on the life of the intellectuals and the mass intelligentsia. For the most part, the intellectuals were under the direct control of the political elite until the late 1980s. This is particularly true with respect to intellectuals in Moscow. Virtually any action in favor of or in opposition to an intellectual must be endorsed by the political elite.

Iosif Stalin himself decided the fate of many Soviet writers, scholars, artists, and musicians. It was Stalin who ordered the arrest of Osip Mandel'shtam and later sanctioned his death. For his own personal reasons, Stalin chose to spare Boris Pasternak and Il'ia Ehrenburg and allowed Evgeni Zamiatin to go abroad, while sending Mandel'shtam and Isaak Babel' to the gulag. Stalin also permitted Mikhail Sholokhov to retain chapters examining dekulakization (the elimination of kulaks) in his novel *Soil Upturned* (Ehrenburg 1960; Khrushchev 1970, pp. 240–241; Mandel'shtam 1970; *LG*, June 25, 1986).

Stalin's successors have followed this pattern and have made official policy decisions regarding the most prominent, and even some "ordinary," intellectuals. Nikita Khrushchev initiated the persecution of Pasternak in 1960, but allowed Alexander Solzhenitsyn to publish *One Day in the Life of Ivan Denisovich*. Khrushchev also rudely attacked Ernst Neizvestnyi at the famous exhibition in 1957, but chose not to eliminate Neizvestnyi from public life (Neizvestnyi 1984). Khrushchev allowed the film director Iulius Raizman the freedom to name a new movie, against the wishes of the minister of the movie industry, and he also allowed the public presentation of Klimov's first movie (*Ogoniok*, no. 2, 1988, p. 16). It was Khrushchev who permitted pianist Vladimir Ashkenazy to settle abroad, and who revoked the prohibition of pianist Sviatoslav Richter and dancer Maia Plisetskaia from performing in the West (Ashkenazy 1985, p. 177; Khrushchev 1970, pp. 292–293). The fates of Andrei Sakharov, Solzhenitsyn, Iuri Orlov, and all other prominent intellectuals of the time were determined by Leonid Brezhnev and the Politburo.

Despite glasnost's expansion of the intellectuals' autonomy, practically all leading Soviet intellectuals were, until the late 1980s, under the direct control and supervision of the Central Committee (the staff of the political elite). All directors of academic institutions, as well as the chiefs of all organizations representing the creative intelligentsia (e.g., the Writers' Union, the Artists' Union, etc.) were appointed only after their candidacies were approved by the Politburo or the secretaries of the Central Committee. The same is true of their deputies.

To be appointed, department heads in academic institutions, and even leading fellows, must be endorsed by a department at the Central Committee. As Galina Vishnevskaia (1984, p. 326) witnessed, even top actors in the Bolshoi Theater secure their positions only with the permission of the Central Committee.

The Politburo's crucial decision-making role and the rivalry within it explain why the intellectual community is so concerned with information on events occurring "above." The intellectuals' interest in these matters is surpassed only by that of apparatchiks, whose fate is also dictated by shifts at the top of the hierarchy. Indeed, conflicts within the Politburo are often quite useful to the intellectuals, for one faction generally presents itself as advocating the active participation of intellectuals in the political life of the country and as supporting their freedom in professional activity. Such was the case in the USSR between 1965 and 1968, between 1985 and 1989, and in China in the late 1970s and the 1980s.

While the intellectuals are, as a rule, directly or indirectly controlled by the political elite and by the General Secretary, the mass intelligentsia is at the mercy of local party bureaucracies. Professionals such as teachers and cultural workers, as well as individuals holding low-level command positions, such as directors of hospitals or schools, are formally under the authority of local party committees who dictate their appointments and behavior.

While the political elite maintains ultimate control over the intellectual community, members of the elite cannot actually make all the decisions relevant to these matters. Such decisions involve a variety of issues, from approval of appointments and sanctions against improprieties, to the endorsement of a new branch of science or the creation of a new journal. These matters are far too numerous for the elite to deal with alone, for they must also be concerned with other developments in society. Thus, many of the decisions in this realm are made at lower levels of the hierarchy.

When the elite has established a clear policy on particular issues, the interaction between it and the party apparatus is relatively clear-cut. For example, the decisions on Solzhenitsyn and Sakharov were made at the highest levels of leadership and provided no difficulties for those expected to carry out these decisions. In other cases, the policies toward intellectuals and their activities are influenced by a number of sometimes conflicting goals and considerations. In these cases, the leadership itself may be unclear regarding the proper course. When this occurs, the interaction between the leadership and the apparatus can become considerably more complex and may produce unpredictable developments.

When the goals of the leadership are unclear or contradictory, the apparatchiks must make concrete decisions regarding specific matters. These situations often generate considerable uncertainty among apparatchiks, who must determine appropriate decisions using extremely vague guidelines. Apparatchiks faced with this uncertainty cannot ask a superior for instructions on making a decision, for fear of appearing incompetent. At the same time, improper decisions also cast doubt on an apparatchik's competence. Thus, when policies from above are unclear, members of the apparatus must move very cautiously, making minor decisions and waiting for repercussions from superiors. In the complex atmosphere of the party apparatus, some intellectuals develop the skills necessary to participate in party machinations, and may even compete with apparatchiks.

The Importance of Intellectuals for the Political Elite

Unlike its Western counterparts, the Soviet political elite considers its relationship with the intellectuals to be of primary importance. Soviet leaders manage problems with intellectuals far more often than do Western politicians. This difference stems from a fundamental distinction between Soviet and Western society—in the former, the political elite manages the economy and ideology on a daily basis, while in the latter, politicians influence these two realms in more indirect ways.

Soviet politicians have long recognized that their efficacy in economic and ideological matters depends strongly on the cooperation of the intellectuals. The Soviet leadership is well aware of the paramount role of science in both the modern economy and the military and even introduced a special amendment in Soviet Marxism recognizing science as an important part of the forces of production in society.

In addition, while political order is maintained via the coercive apparatus of the state, control over ideology is also considered very important.

Those in power conceptualize ideology very broadly and assume that they cannot influence the people effectively without the active participation of literature, the arts, and professional journalism, and without educated people as propagandists. In the areas of science and ideology, the political elite cannot survive without the active concurrence of intellectuals. Indeed, the leadership recognizes, at least in principle, the unique role of the intellectuals, and the impossibility of replacing them without damaging the interests of the state.

The political elite also recognizes intellectuals as a means of enhancing Soviet prestige, and thus their own prestige, in the international arena. As a result, the Soviet state expends considerable resources in the selection and promotion of young talent. In this respect, the Soviet system appears superior to that of the West, in which the future of gifted people depends mostly on commercial factors (about this see Ashkenazy 1985).[1]

Stalin's position toward the intellectuals is noteworthy in view of the relationship between the state and the intellectuals discussed above. On one hand, Stalin bore direct responsibility for the persecution and execution of thousands of intellectuals (see the list of outstanding intellectuals killed by Stalin in Medvedev 1989a, pp. 151–156). On the other hand, Stalin (unlike Mao) never lashed out directly against the intelligentsia as a group. Only in the early 1930s did the mass media attack "bourgeois" conservative engineers and scholars, going so far as to assign some of them the status of saboteur; by 1939, however, these overtones had vanished completely. Moreover, in various speeches of the late 1930s, Stalin demonstrated respect for the intelligentsia (Stalin 1952, pp. 550–551).[2]

Certainly, Stalin's deep enmity toward independent intellectuals was obvious. He was, however, compelled by economic and military considerations to behave quite differently toward some intellectuals, such as Sergei Korolev (who would come to organize the Soviet space program), Lev Landau (a future Nobel Prize winner in physics), and Alexei Tupolev (a leading figure in the development of Soviet aviation), who were released from the gulag. During World War II, Stalin created the famous *sharazhki*, a special prison camp where intellectuals were interned and treated much better than inmates in ordinary camps (for more about *sha-*

---

[1] In the mid-1930s, due to an effective educational system and active support from the state, Soviet musicians began to win competitions, thereby glorifying socialism. Even in concentration camps, actors and musicians enjoyed many privileges, since camp bosses delighted in having teams of talented performers at their disposal to entertain them and their guests (e.g., Shturman 1985).

[2] Stalin's statements regarding the intelligentsia in his reports on the 1936 constitution and to the Eighteenth Party Congress were regarded by many as recognition of the intelligentsia's important role and as exoneration from earlier allegations that the educated were servants of the old regime (see Chalidze 1981, pp. 20–21).

razhki, see Solzhenitsyn's *The First Circle*, 1968; see also *Moskovskie Novosti*, no. 48, 1987; Kopelev 1978).

Stalin's successors faced the same dilemma during their periods of rule. Whatever their attitudes toward intellectuals in general, they were forced to recognize the uniqueness of one or another scholar, especially those working for the military. Thus, when Soviet ideologues contended in the past that the party bestowed on the intelligentsia a major role in socialist society, what they really meant was a major role in accomplishing the tasks set by the political leadership (see, for instance, Fediukin 1983, or Stepanian 1983).

THE OFFICIAL PRIVILEGES OF SOVIET INTELLECTUALS

Since its inception, the Soviet state has considered the intellectuals a group deserving of special privileges and high status. Despite the strong equalitarianism of the Bolsheviks immediately following the Revolution, the government soon began treating the intellectuals as individuals who should be protected and who should enjoy a standard of living higher than that of the masses. It is well known that Lenin sought to aid scholars, writers, musicians, and artists suffering from the civil war, and that he sought to satisfy all of the intellectuals' requests for assistance.

One of the Bolsheviks' first steps away from egalitarianism was connected with the protection of intellectuals. Despite his proclamation that all incomes should be equal, written in *The State and Revolution* a few months before the October seizure of power, Lenin insisted on the introduction of larger incomes for "bourgeois specialists," the most qualified segment of the population.

Along with party bureaucrats and the political police, the intellectuals benefited from the stratification of Soviet society carried out by Stalin after the late 1920s. The material life of those who demonstrated loyalty to the system was significantly better than that of workers or clerks, not to mention that of peasants.

Of course, life in the 1920s and 1930s was quite harsh, and many intellectuals suffered from various deprivations (on the lives of Soviet scholars and writers during this period, see Berberova 1983). Life was particularly rough for intellectuals who were frowned upon by the state, as the experiences of Mandel'shtam and Mikhail Bulgakov demonstrate. But for those who were accepted by the leadership, living conditions were substantially superior to those of the masses during the 1930s (Grigorenko 1982; Kopelev 1978; Orlova 1983).

During World War II, intellectuals again received favorable treatment. Many were exempt from induction into the army and were among the first evacuated from more dangerous areas. As in the 1930s, intellectuals were favored in the procurement system, and their diet was much better than that of the working class (Berg 1983; Grossman 1980).

After the war, Stalin was particularly concerned with the United States' monopoly on nuclear weapons, which led to measures to improve the living conditions of intellectuals three- and fourfold. In 1946 Stalin substantially raised the salaries of scholars and professors, who for the next two decades were among the wealthiest of Soviet people. While the average city-dweller's monthly income during this period was about 50–60 rubles (at today's value), a senior fellow in an academic institute or a professor in a university received 400–500 rubles. Also during this time, intellectuals moved into the privileged stratum, with access to special hospitals, stores, and resorts.

Following Stalin's death, the favored position of the intellectuals did not diminish; in fact, their privileges increased during the late 1950s and 1960s. (About the material privileges of Moscow actors, see Vishnevskaia 1984, pp. 84, 206, 226, 326; about composers, see Gol'dshtein 1970, pp. 103–108; regarding musicians, see Ashkenazy 1985 and Reznikov 1984, p. 109.)

The organization of life in the "scientific towns" is representative of the privileges accorded the intellectuals. These towns were constructed in the late 1950s and 1960s, the most famous being Academic Town in Novosibirsk. Occupants of Academic Town enjoyed a much higher standard of living than did residents of Novosibirsk and other Siberian cities. When I lived there, the food supply and housing conditions available to scholars seemed almost miraculous in comparison to the other cities and villages where I had lived before. The privileges available in the other scientific towns, such as those in Dubno (about life there, see Polikanov 1983), Chernogolovka, and Pushchino, were essentially the same as those in Novosibirsk.

Conditions changed for the intellectuals in the late 1960s following the Czechoslovak invasion. They began to be considered a potential threat to the leadership's political dominance. In addition, in response to rising discontent in the working class, the difference in living standards between the intelligentsia and the workers was decreased. These developments contributed to the erosion of the relative privileges of the intellectuals, and an increasing number of occupations began to yield incomes equal to or greater than those of the intelligentsia.

Research by Ovsei Shkaratan illustrates this pattern of change. Between 1967 and 1975, the difference between the income of the creative intelligentsia and that of the working class shrank significantly. While salaries of the intellectuals in Kazan were about 57 percent higher than those of workers in 1967, by 1975 they were only 19 percent higher (Shkaratan 1982, p. 47). In 1984 two Soviet authors concluded that "the difference in income between skilled workers and the intelligentsia is very insignificant. Moreover, the work of some groups of skilled workers . . . is rewarded more highly than that of some groups of the intelligentsia" (Koval'chuk and Naumova 1984, pp. 92–93).

In addition, as corruption and the "second (i.e., illegal) economy" began to play a larger role in the 1960s and 1970s, those engaged in illegal activities enhanced their material position relative to that of the intellectuals. This new trend in Soviet society, whereby speculators and black marketeers live more comfortably than do scholars, has become a popular theme in literature in the 1970s and 1980s, such as Vladimir Arro's play, *Look Who Has Come*, or El'dar Riazanov's movies, *Railroad Station for Two* or *Garage*. Still, despite the declining privileges of the intelligentsia in the 1970s, many of them continued to enjoy a higher standard of living than did individuals from other segments of society.

The relative material stature of the intellectuals clearly deteriorated under Gorbachev's regime. Gorbachev's policies regarding privatization legitimized unlimited incomes in private business, and these incomes clearly surpassed the once-high revenues of scholars and writers—revenues that have remained unchanged since the 1940s. While university professors or senior fellows in an academic research institute continued to earn 400–500 rubles per month and a waitress in a cooperative café might earn the same amount, the incomes of many members of private cooperatives were greater than 700–800 rubles. In addition to these relative comparisons, rampant inflation has also lowered the absolute well-being of the intellectuals.

It is clear that bogus and mediocre intellectuals have been far more materially successful and prosperous than have true intellectuals. Prior to the mid-1980s, bogus intellectuals enjoyed the genuine support of the authorities and secured for themselves a standard of living unattainable for even the most talented scholars, writers, and film directors. With unlimited opportunity to publish whatever they wanted, regardless of demand, authors such as Sergei Mikhalkov and Georgi Markov became millionaires, complete with life-styles befitting their social positions.

On the other hand, quite a few true intellectuals, even those not formally considered dissidents, could scarcely make ends meet during the 1970s. In 1988 Vladimir Dudintsev recounted both the difficulties in material survival faced by him and his family across three decades, and his obligation to the many private citizens who helped him, some of whom remained anonymous (Dudintsev 1988a). No less dramatic is Alexander Askol'dov's story of material deprivation following the mid-1960s prohibition of his movie *Komissar* (see *Novoye Russkoye Slovo*, June 21, 1988).

Variations in the material well-being of intellectuals remain substantial.

While some Soviet writers have become millionaires, the average monthly literary income of the ten thousand writers in the Soviet Union was no more than 162 rubles in 1987, while the salary of the average Soviet worker was a little more than 200 rubles (*Nedelia*, July 17, 1988, p. 14).

The financial well-being of the intellectuals took an interesting twist in 1988 when the debate about the nomenclature's benefits reached its peak (in the Soviet Union, the nomenclature is a group of officially recognized VIPs). Party apparatchiks defended the nomenclature's benefits via reference to the high material status of intellectuals, writers, and scholars (see *Pravda*, August 1, 1988, for a detailed comparison of the lives of these groups).

It is interesting to note how the Soviet people perceive the well-being of the intellectuals. By all accounts, the masses, with their strong egalitarian tendencies ("Nobody should live better than I, whatever the importance of his work"), view the intellectuals' standard of living with a jaundiced eye, often exaggerating the number of people who enjoy increased privileges. Still, a 1988 *Moskovskie Novosti* survey indicated that the majority of Moscow residents considered the privileges of "famous actors, writers, and artists" to be far more justified than those of party apparatchiks (but less so than those of the leaders of the country, the military, and diplomats). On a scale from 2 to 5, with scores of 5 indicating privileges considered legitimate and scores of 2 indicating privileges considered illegitimate, Muscovites assigned the privileges of the intellectuals a score of 3.6, those of the leaders of the country a 4.2, and those of the apparatchiks a 2.8 (*MN*, July 3, 1988). During this period, intellectuals regularly and vehemently protested erroneous popular perceptions of their material status (see *Izvestia*, November 3, 1988).

THE OFFICIAL PRESTIGE OF SOVIET INTELLECTUALS

The prestige bestowed upon members of Soviet society by the political elite is a scarce and finite resource, such that an increase in the prestige of one group necessitates a decrease in that of others.

In the years immediately following the October Revolution, the intellectuals' official prestige was fairly low, due at least in part to the strong egalitarian tendencies of the Bolsheviks and the animosity of the old intelligentsia toward the new regime. At one point, the term "intelligentsia" was even considered profane (Chalidze 1981, p. 20). Yet, as the new system stabilized, its leadership increased the official status and public recognition accorded the intellectuals.

Although less privileged than bureaucrats materially, intellectuals have been favored in terms of public visibility. By the 1930s, the government had introduced the title of "People's Actor." In the mid-1930s, Stalin introduced scholarly degrees and undertook numerous measures to up-grade the status of the Academy of Sciences, as well as that of the unions of writers, painters, and actors. During this period, the government also introduced new titles for artists, musicians, and the like, and a variety of competitions were conducted in the cultural fields. The winners of these competitions were awarded the title of Laureate, as well as medals, finan-cial prizes, new apartments, and valuable musical instruments. By 1984 there were sixteen national titles for figures in the arts, and twenty types of medals used generously for decorating intellectuals.

The high official prestige of the intellectuals explains, to a considerable degree, their correspondingly high prestige among ordinary people. The first Soviet sociological surveys, conducted in the early 1960s, revealed that in the prestige hierarchy, the intellectual professions held practically first place, a condition unheard of in American society at any time.

According to Vladimir Shubkin's data from the early 1960s, on a 10-point rating scale of prestige, male graduates from secondary schools in Novosibirsk assigned scholars an average score of 6.61. Engineers re-ceived an average score of 6.55, workers in industry 4.01, and agricul-tural workers 2.50 (Shubkin 1970, pp. 280–286). Since that time, the prestige of the intellectual professions has declined (I will discuss this trend later), although in the early 1980s the intellectual occupations still ranked among the most prestigious. Of nineteen occupations selected for ranking by researchers, all five "intellectual" occupations ranked among the top ten in prestige (Cherednichenko and Shubkin 1985, pp. 71, 91; Chernovolenko et al. 1979, p. 205; Shubkin 1979, p. 50; Shubkin 1984, pp. 76, 80–81; Titma 1973, p. 253).

THE POLITICAL ELITE AGAINST THE INTELLECTUALS

The Soviet leadership regards the intellectuals as both a valuable segment of society and as a potential or actual enemy. The political elite tends to regard the intellectuals as the one group expected to oppose the existing order. Of course, other segments of society, such as the working class, deeply religious people (especially those belonging to illegal sects), and certain ethnic minorities, are also considered dangerous, but revolts by workers and nationalists have, until the mid-1980s, been relatively rare events, and normally the working class has been fairly loyal to the system.

It is well established that, in general, people much prefer a positive rather than a negative evaluation of the state of their lives. Rationaliza-tion and other powerful coping mechanisms usually push people toward satisfaction with their condition. The situation is different primarily in times of crisis, when basic needs are endangered, or when prospects of improving the standard of living emerge, bringing with them new aspirations. This latter situation was especially evident from 1985 through 1989, when, under glasnost, Soviets became much more aware of the condition of their lives compared to that of others.

Under normal circumstances, however, people's negative attitudes toward the outside world are rather weak. This is supported by numerous studies of their perceptions of their quality of life conducted in this and other countries, including the Soviet Union. These studies reveal not only that the majority of people tend to report satisfaction with their lives, but also that, regardless of the elements of life evaluated, the number of persons reporting dissatisfaction remains more or less constant (Campbell et al. 1976; Shlapentokh 1975).

At the same time, a great deal of data suggest that involvement in any form of critical activity steadily increases with a person's level of education and with the creative character of a person's work. In the opinion of the Soviet leadership (an opinion borne out by the facts), the intellectuals, and to a lesser degree the mass intelligentsia, are distinguished by their permanent critique of the state of affairs in society, a critique the intellectuals make public insofar as possibilities to do so exist. The political elite is well aware that its every move is carefully watched by the intellectuals, and that its activities are subject to constant criticism.

Among the most important domains of social life about which the intellectuals and the elite confront one another are ideology, culture, and cadres, as well as current policies, both domestic and international. However, the threat posed by the intellectuals is not limited to their criticism of the political elite. Even more threatening, from the perspective of the elite, is the tendency of Soviet intellectuals to create their own organizations in various spheres of social life, thus undermining the political elite's fundamental characteristic: its absolute monopoly on power. The developments during the first and second thaws (the 1960s and the second half of the 1980s, respectively) served to confirm these views. I will return to this critical issue in subsequent chapters.

THE PERMANENT CONFRONTATION

The history of the Soviet Union, as well as that of China, Poland, Hungary, other socialist societies, and of authoritarian societies in general, has demonstrated that conflict between the political elite and the intelligentsia is a permanent fixture in nondemocratic society. Of course, the specific nature of this conflict assumes different forms at different times.

It is noteworthy that the Russian intelligentsia, weary of the tsarist leadership's bureaucratic control, supported the February Revolution of 1917. As the Soviet historian Vera Ulanovskaia indicated, "the scholarly intelligentsia hoped . . . that the Provisional Government, and later the

Constituent Assembly, would give a number of rights and privileges to scientific institutions and higher schools, and that the state would cease its interference at least in the activities of scientists" (1966, p. 37).

For similar reasons, Russian intellectuals worried about the anti-intellectual nature of the Bolshevik Revolution and the incompatibility between the Revolution's aims and freedom of creative activity. As a result of these concerns, a large number of prominent Russian intellectuals fled to the West. With very few exceptions, all of those with liberal, creative minds—poets, novelists, critics, historians, philosophers, and so on—left Lenin's Russia. Among prominent scholars of the time, perhaps less than a dozen were truly enthusiastic about the October Revolution. As one Soviet historian noted (even before glasnost): "The majority of scholars, like the bourgeois intelligentsia as a whole, met the October Revolution with confusion, anxiety, and even animosity" (Ivanova 1980, p. 23; see also Arnol'dov 1980, p. 23; Krasil'nikov and Soskin 1985, pp. 120–131).[3]

Despite his brilliant education, highly developed creative faculties, and the generally high intellectual level of those in his government, Lenin's deep hostility toward the intellectuals and his suspicion of them as either potential or actual enemies of his cause were obvious from the very beginning of his rule. His use of the term "the intelligentsia" was exclusively pejorative, and, in 1922, he ordered about two hundred prominent intellectuals expelled from Russia. (Among those expelled were Nikolai Berdiaev and Pitirim Sorokin, who later became leading authorities in the West.) In 1922, five years after the Revolution, the leadership launched a campaign against two organizations of scholars: the Council of Scholars and the United Council of Scientific Institutions. When these organizations proved immune to outside pressure, they were simply dismantled (Ivanova 1980, p. 209). Although an alternative organization under the direct control of the leadership was established, it was largely ignored by scholars. In Moscow, teachers in the higher schools went on strike in 1922.

By 1927 Soviet scholars were convinced that the leadership held only hostile attitudes toward them. It was in this year that the Soviet authorities executed twenty professionals without a trial, and gave the Academy of Science the "choice" of "electing" three Marxist philosophers (who were also members of the party) as full Academy members or face the dismantling of the organization. The scholars' feelings were summed up that year at the Fourth Congress of Soviets by the academician Alexei

[3] The Bolsheviks at first received support only from a group of writers with strong nationalist, religious, and mystic tendencies, such as Alexander Blok, Sergei Esenin, Andrei Bely, and a few others. However, practically all of them either died, were executed, or emigrated in the early 1920s, thereby allowing only limited cooperation with the new authorities (Agurski 1980, pp. 15–50).

Bakh, who was among the few good scholars to become Soviet activists: "To our deepest regret, the overwhelming majority of our leaders of science and technology evaluated the October Revolution negatively." At about the same time, historian Mikhail Pokrovski, a party scholar, sent a letter to the government indicating that there was "a gloomy mood and anti-revolutionary feeling among scholars" (see Esakov 1971, pp. 50, 66).

The intelligentsia's attempts to maintain independence were shaken in 1928 with the first major "show trial," the Shakhtinskoie Delo (the Shakhty Affair), in which the defendants were prominent engineers. Efforts to preserve autonomy were damaged further in 1930 with the trial of Prompartiia (the Industrial Party), among whose defendants were the prominent scholars Leonid Ramzin and Nikolai Charnovski. The intense anti-intellectual character of both trials was fully recognized during glasnost, in Vasili Beliaev's sensational television documentary movie "Trial" (1988), as well as in many publications of 1986–1989 (see Alexeiev 1988, p. 6; Lel'chuk 1988, pp. 354–355; Medvedev 1989a, pp. 180–185).

Persecution of intellectuals and scholars peaked in the first half of the 1930s, following the Shakhtinskoie Delo and Prompartiia trials. The intellectuals became the second group, following the party apparatchiks and the old Bolsheviks, to be targeted in the Great Purges of 1935–1938, and then for the repressions of the 1940s and early 1950s. During this period, more than one thousand writers were sent to the gulag, where many of them died (see *Knizhnoie Obozrenie* 25, 1988).

In the first half of the 1930s, people were suspicious of the intellectuals simply because they were "mental" and not "manual" workers. This deeply rooted enmity, based on Marxist ideas, was not only evident in Stalin's Russia in the 1930s but was manifested in even more conspicuous and cruel ways during the Cultural Revolution in China in the 1960s and the Pol Pot regime in Cambodia in the 1970s.

During the 1930s zealous servants of the Stalin regime (including Ernest Kol'man, future defector from the USSR and author of the book *We Had Not to Live in This Way*, 1982) introduced the idea of "proletarian science" and looked for wreckers of the socialist state and carriers of reactionary theories. Examples were found in almost all disciplines: economists were represented by Nikolai Kondratiev and Alexander Chaianov, physicists by Iakov Frenkel (the author of the "big bang" theory) and Lev Landau, biologists by Alexander Gurvich and Lev Berg, eugenicists by Nikolai Kol'tsov, geologists by Vladimir Vernadski, mathematicians by Alexei Bogomolov and Dmitri Egorov, and historians by Sergei Platonov and Evgeni Tarle. Special "methodological teams" comprised of "true Marxists" roamed throughout scientific institutions and "set the brains of scholars" (to use the expression of Maximov, a leader of these teams and a future correspondent member of the Academy of Sciences).

Special magazines—*Varnitso* (the acronym for the National Associations of Scholars) and *Front of Science and Technology*—were assigned the mission of launching regular broadsides against the most respected of scholars. The former magazine called upon its readers to meet the challenge of one activist to "vie with OGPU [Soviet political police at that time] in the number of discoveries of saboteurs in science," while the latter magazine, headed by Bakh, actively applied the thesis of "the exacerbation of class struggles" to science.

It was also during this time that several true intellectuals who had no illusions about the new order (unlike those who were still true believers) decided to do whatever was necessary to save their lives, even if that meant sycophantically serving the regime at the expense of their own colleagues. The famous philosopher Abram Deborin was among those who chose to do so (Alexeiev 1988).

Subsequent stages of Soviet history reveal continued conflict between the state and the intelligentsia. And, contrary to the argument that most intellectuals hostile to the Soviet system were those with prerevolutionary backgrounds, this conflict has persisted well into periods when most intellectuals had been born and educated in the Soviet system. Prior to the mid-1980s, every leader since Lenin, including Khrushchev and especially Brezhnev, has been associated with some form of hostile action against the intellectuals, even if in the 1960s and the 1980s the nature of anti-intellectual activity has become less severe, and the outright imprisonment and extermination of the 1930s has been replaced by such measures as dismissal from positions, bans on publication, restrictions on travel abroad, and so on.

Using the preceding information as a guide, it is possible to distinguish different degrees of repression against intellectuals in socialist countries. Periods can be differentiated on the basis of two criteria: first, can intellectuals avoid repression if they comply with the authorities? Second, how severe are the repressions against intellectual activity? Using these criteria, distinctions can be made between periods during which intellectuals have avoided repression through compliance with the state and those during which the mere condition of being an intellectual insured repression. In general, it can be argued that a relationship exists between the scope of repression against the intelligentsia and the severity of such repression. Periods during which the coercive apparatus casts its net the furthest are normally those during which the intensity of repression has been the greatest.

The Cultural Revolution in China during the 1960s and early 1970s, and the Pol Pot regime in Cambodia in the mid-1970s, are examples of anti-intellectual campaigns in which repression was directed en masse at the intelligentsia. The severity of these repressions was rather great, particularly in the latter case, where even a subtle demonstration of education could result in extermination. In the USSR, Stalin's 1930s purges were characterized by a relatively comprehensive attack on the intelligentsia, although members of the party apparatus were victimized as well, with very little regard for their individual characteristics. Of course, this period also witnessed the imprisonment and elimination of innumerable people who were not members of the intelligentsia or the party apparatus.

During other periods of Soviet history, circumstances were such that only a segment of the intelligentsia was the target of repression, and the severity of repression was comparatively low. For example, in the first years after 1917, only older intellectuals associated with the tsarist regime were subjected to various restrictions, for they were considered untrustworthy and often failed to demonstrate sufficient loyalty to the Revolution. Similarly, in the years following World War II, only Jewish intellectuals faced a particularly high probability of being demoted or arrested. In like fashion, members of the intelligentsia were specifically targeted as the first victims of the Soviet occupation of the Baltic republics (as well as of the 1939 Nazi occupation of Poland). For instance, in 1940, on the eve of the election of the Lithuanian parliament, the Soviet authorities arrested 1,500 local members of the intelligentsia. Then, in June 1941, 36,000 active Lithuanians, mostly professionals, were deported from the country (Alexeieva 1984, p. 45).

By contrast, there are special periods in the histories of the Soviet Union and some other socialist countries during which the leader has been inclined to consider the intelligentsia a political ally. This is particularly common when a leader embarks upon the road to liberalization. Khrushchev was the first Soviet leader to attempt to treat the intelligentsia this way. However, he did so very inconsistently and without a clear understanding of the resulting realignment of power.

Gorbachev's regime was the first in Soviet history, as well as in the history of other socialist countries, to openly declare itself friendly toward the intellectuals, and to truly treat them as a primary ally. It allowed the intellectuals to discuss openly, for the first time in Soviet history, the deep enmity toward and discreditation of the intelligentsia by the Soviet system, dating back to the first days of the Revolution (see, for instance, Vasiliev 1989). These new attitudes toward the intelligentsia, and especially toward the intellectuals, shattered the fundamentals of the Soviet system and required its radical liberalization. By the middle of 1989, it was still unclear whether a new political system with radically new attitudes toward the intellectuals was emerging, or if the Soviet state would return to its traditional hostility and suspicion of the creative intelligentsia, thereby restoring several old elements of its political structure.

The benign attitude of any leader toward the intellectuals and the intelligentsia inevitably engenders vehement opposition from several members of the Politburo and the party apparatus, and policies regarding the intelligentsia become major issues in the struggles within the political establishment.

INTELLECTUALS AS EXPERTS

There is distance between the dominant class and the intellectuals not only in that the apparatus attracts the least qualified and educated people (even if they do have diplomas and Ph.D.'s), but also in that the elite is reluctant to incorporate true intellectuals and high-ranking professionals into the state and party apparatus. For the most part, the intelligentsia has been excluded from participation or even substantive consultation in the policy-making process.

This was the case even during the period between 1964 and 1968 when there was substantial interest in technocratic theories of development, which were based on the participation of scientific experts in decision making. During that time, a number of specialists with close ties to the Central Committee anticipated being called upon to offer their expertise in the preparation of policy. They felt that their knowledge made them substantially more valuable than the apparatchiks of the Khrushchev era, whom they replaced. Yet, by the late 1960s, it had become clear that the leadership was essentially uninterested in taking advantage of the available scientific knowledge.

Not only have Soviet intellectuals been absent from the ranks of the party and state apparatus, but their participation as experts in the decision-making process in the USSR has been very limited. During the Brezhnev era, the role of intellectuals as advisors in decisions of great importance was minimal. Decisions regarding the economic, social, and political development of the country, as well as those regarding foreign policy, were determined not by experts, but by the General Secretary, his staff, and members of the Politburo.

In order to understand the interactions between the leadership and the intellectuals, however, it is important to recognize not only the numerous cases involving dismissal of expert opinions, but the ease with which the authorities found scholars willing to endorse with "scientific arguments" any idea advanced by the ruling elite. This phenomenon rendered claims of "the scientific method" in approaching social issues utterly ridiculous.

The revelations of glasnost during the late 1980s confirm that major decisions were made without serious and thoroughly objective thought.

Prominent scholars, formally invited as advisors, simply said what was necessary to endorse whatever idea was accepted by the leadership. This was the case with the Soviet irrigation projects of the 1970s, a pet idea of Brezhnev's leadership. These projects involved the rerouting of Siberian rivers to the south and the building of numerous channels and power stations, all of which caused enormous and irreparable damage to the ecology of the area. Soviet publications of 1986–1988 reveal that the Soviet Academy of Sciences and especially the Institute of Water Problems endorsed all of these projects, despite the evidence, arguments, and doubts expressed by those who were not "official" experts (see Zalygin 1987; *Nash Sovremennik*, no. 7, 1985; no. 1, 1987; *Og.*, no. 40, 1987, pp. 24–27).

When, during glasnost, it finally became possible to illuminate the decision-making processes of the Brezhnev era, only one example could be found of any expert objecting to the intentions of the leadership: Oleg Bogomolov, director of the Institute of Socialist Countries, sent a memo to the Politburo arguing against the planned invasion in Afghanistan.

The Animosity of the Apparatchiks

Despite tremendous increases in the formal education of the apparatchiks and their intensive contacts with the intellectuals and the West, Soviet bureaucrats are, for the most part, even more hostile to the intellectual community than are the leaders who, from time to time, look for some accommodation with the cultural and scientific elite.

Neizvestnyi managed to capture this incompatibility of the apparatchiks and the intellectuals:

> Nowhere have I met such a low level of culture and professional skill as above. And when I became familiar with these people, I felt an aesthetical fright which turned into a social one. And exactly at this time I lost my last illusions, which were being engendered by contact with the technical intelligentsia. Apparatchiks perceive any actions—Plisetskaia's dances, Shostakovich's music, my sculptures—as personal insults and some inconvenience.
>
> (Neizvestnyi 1984, pp. 30–34)

Glasnost has provided Soviet intellectuals, with their dramatic and often tragic experiences, an opportunity to tell the world, firsthand, how deeply hostile and malevolent the party bureaucracy is toward real culture and its pursuits. As Vasil' Bykov put it, "Bureaucracy and culture are incompatible. Bureaucracy needs power, and culture is not wanted by it" (Bykov 1989).

Another prominent intellectual, the film director Klimov, recounted in 1988 what he was told by a high-ranking party official who demanded that he remove a scene from a film. After the official had exhausted all of his arguments, he said, "You argue to no purpose. Under Stalin emerged an all-pervasive system of power which none of the absolute monarchies had. You will never win" (Klimov 1988).

In their article, "Bureaucratism and Bureaucracy," Lev Gudkov, Iuri Levada, and coauthors wrote that the party and state apparatus ultimately intend to destroy creative activity and the positive role of the intelligentsia in society (Gudkov, Levada, Levinson, and Sedov 1988, p. 81; see also the interview of the actor Strzhel'chik in *MN*, July 3, 1988).

Vladimir Legostaiev, a party official from the Central Committee, even acknowledged the party's deep anti-intellectualism, which, according to Legostaiev, isolates the party from "the spiritual quests of society, leaving only the role of estimator or even censor of the spiritual process" (*Pravda*, May 3, 1989).

Gorbachev's regime engendered radical changes in the relationship between the party apparatus and the intellectuals. Because the General Secretary declared the intelligentsia and the intellectuals his major confederates in his struggle for perestroika, the party apparatus was forced, albeit unwillingly and often with open contempt, to change its tactics when dealing with the intellectuals. The party apparatus, however, took advantage of any opportunity to obstruct implementation of the Kremlin's policy, and to demonstrate who ultimately continued to call the shots (see *LG*, September 3, 1986; January 28, 1988; *Sovietskaia Kul'tura*, October 4, 1986).

It is clear that, despite Gorbachev's support of the intellectuals, the deep enmity of most party officials, including those promoted by Gorbachev's regime, survived and was manifest in 1987–1989. Their rancor against the intellectuals materialized each time the conservatives had the opportunity to reveal their true feelings (Nina Andreieva's article in March 1988 is only one of many examples; see *Sovietskaia Rossia*, March 13, 1988).

The Attempt to Create a Tame Intelligentsia

Having faced the hostility of almost all of the old, prerevolutionary intelligentsia, the Bolsheviks almost immediately began the task of creating an intelligentsia that would be completely devoted to the "cause," that is, completely submissive to the authorities. Three distinct periods can be identified in connection with this endeavor: the first decade after the Revolution; the late 1920s and the first half of the 1930s; and the 1970s.

Having encountered considerable hostility from the majority of the Russian intelligentsia, the Soviet political leadership decided to target a specific group within the intellectual community within which to establish a foothold: specifically, young intellectuals educated before the Revolution who had yet to attain high status. Likely candidates were found mostly among provincial intellectuals, particularly among Jews and other minorities who had suffered from discrimination in tsarist Russia. The intellectuals who joined the new authorities were primarily writers, poets, and critics; only a few were natural scientists. The success of this official strategy is confirmed by the prominent role in Soviet literature and cultural life played by those from the so-called Odessa school, as well as by authors from Kiev and the south (e.g., Bagritski, Kataiev, Babel', Petrov, Il'f, Ehrenburg, Olesha, Maiakovski, Sel'vinski, Bulgakov, and Shwartz).[4]

For almost a decade, the first segment of "true" Soviet intellectuals was apparently a willing instrument in the hands of the Soviet political elite. By the late 1920s, however, tensions between these intellectuals and Stalin's leadership began to increase. This increase occurred primarily because, while these intellectuals were largely devoted to the Revolution and its ideas, Stalin saw, among his revolutionary devotees, more and more enemies of his regime. At the same time, the revolutionary intelligentsia was becoming more and more critical of developments in the country. Some even tried to reflect their attitudes in their work, such as Mikhail Bulgakov's *Master and Marguerite* (1929/1940), and Evgeni Shwartz's *Naked King* (1934) and *Shadow* (1940).

Eventually, the alliance between the regime and the revolutionary intelligentsia deteriorated to the point of persecution of almost all of the members of the intelligentsia by the state. Of all the groups in the intelligentsia, the revolutionary intelligentsia was victimized much more than any other. Babel', Vladimir Kirshon, Vsevolod Meierkhold, Boris Pil'niak, and many others perished in the gulag.

By all accounts, the political leadership did not want to enlist people educated before the Revolution, even if they professed dedication to the new order. Rather, the new regime preferred to breed professionals in Soviet institutions, where access to higher education could be barred to children of the old classes and of the prerevolutionary intelligentsia. Since the early 1920s, the Soviet authorities had intensively trained a new Soviet intelligentsia—an intelligentsia absolutely servile to the party, brought up in complete submission to power, with a conscience free of revolutionary ideas.

By the mid-1930s, Stalin was so sure that he had an intelligentsia completely loyal to the system that he eliminated higher education admission policies that favored special groups of the population. As soon as the

---

[4] With the expansion of Russophilism in the 1960s and 1970s, the Odessa school became the major target of many representatives of "the Russian party," such as Piotr Palievski, Stanislav Kuniaev, and Oleg Mikhailov. By castigating and derogating Odessa authors, Russophiles could satisfy two of their passions: hatred of Jews and of Marxism.

mass terror ceased, however, it became obvious that the new Soviet intelligentsia, particularly the intellectuals, were in fact deeply hostile toward the Soviet political and social order. This animosity became especially obvious in light of the events in Czechoslovakia.

In response to the political resistance of the intellectuals, the Soviet leadership (led first by Khrushchev, and then followed, more radically, by Brezhnev) began its third attempt at creating its "own" intellectuals. The new policy toward intellectuals adopted by the Soviet leadership in the early 1970s included the long-term goal of creating an "ideal scholar," devoid of the faults characteristic of the present generation of scientists. This policy involved all stages of education, beginning in secondary school.

After considerable vacillation, the political elite decided to maintain a negative stance toward schools for gifted children. In the 1960s, when science held its highest social position, these schools had mushroomed throughout the country, on the initiative of leading scholars such as Mikhail Lavrentiev and Andrei Kolmogorov. Schools at Novosibirsk University and at Moscow University attained world fame. In the 1970s, however, these schools came under attack by Soviet officials (an attack that ran parallel to a general anti-intellectual political trend). The assault was coordinated by the Ministry of Education and its Academy of Pedagogical Sciences (see Koval'chuk and Naumova 1983, p. 169; Turchenko 1969, p. 109). For the most part, attempts by the Academy of Sciences to defend these schools ended in failure. Although the accusations leveled against these schools (e.g., that the schools were hotbeds of dissident ideas among future students) were transparent and not well concealed from the public, further development of these schools was stopped, and some schools were dismantled. By the mid-1980s, there were only forty mathematical classes in Moscow, meeting only about 4 percent of the demand for such classes. The school reform decree (Strizhov 1984) made no mention of special schools, nor did a book devoted to the best schools in Moscow (Babanski 1985).

The status of special schools and classes did not improve from 1985 to 1988. In line with the spirit of the times, the critique of these schools emphasized the class composition of the students (primarily the children of apparatchiks and the cultural elite), an argument not without merit. Rather than requiring objective, fair selection procedures for these schools, however, the authorities, with their anti-intellectual orientations, preferred to maintain their hostility toward these institutions (about these schools in 1985–1987, see Smilga 1987).

Successive levels in the educational system attracted even more attention from the political elite. Once again, the elite approached admission to upper schools from a political point of view. Under Brezhnev's direction, Soviet leaders initiated two key innovations regarding the enrollment of students in universities that should be considered further manifestations of the anti-intellectual stance adopted by that leadership in the 1970s: the introduction of admissions quotas directed against the intelligentsia, and the introduction of political references for applicants.

The policy adopted in the 1960s involved a quota system formally oriented toward encouraging the admission to universities of children of workers and peasants. There is no question that this Soviet "affirmative action policy" had a great deal of merit, since it protected those children who, if only examination criteria were applied, would have less chance of being admitted than would the children of the intelligentsia.[5] Unfortunately, however, the policy has been widely used by the elite as a tool of repression against the intellectuals, in particular by obstructing the admission of their children into the country's best universities. Soviet leaders assume that the children of intellectuals, by virtue of their surroundings, are infected with the bacilli of liberalism. Thus a reduction in the number of children from intellectual backgrounds, especially those from the cultural centers, is believed to hinder the dissemination of dissident ideas in the country.[6] Once again, considerations based on merit, the quality of students, and the impact of this policy on the future of science and the economy have been wholly ignored.

In implementing its anti-intellectual strategy, the Brezhnev leadership introduced a rule that required all applicants to present to university admissions committees a reference signed by the administration and Komsomol party secretary of the applicant's secondary school (or last place of work). A direct political evaluation of each applicant was mandatory, and the importance accorded these references increased with the status of the institution. The importance of the reference was minimal (if it did not contain a negative political evaluation of an individual) if a boy or girl entered a provincial, nonprestigious institute like the Agricultural Institute in Irkutsk, but it was of crucial importance if he or she applied to Moscow University or to Moscow Physical Technical Institute.

The next element of Brezhnev's policy was a dramatic intensification of political indoctrination in the upper schools. As with applicants for schol-

[5] In 1968, of all graduate students in the Academy of Science, only 25 percent were children of workers and 7 percent were children of peasants. In spite of the "affirmative action" policy, the situation has remained unchanged. Surveys of scholars conducted in the late 1970s discovered that the children of workers and peasants made up no more than 30 percent. Moreover, a considerable portion of graduate students (about 28 percent) had relatives with advanced degrees (Kugel 1983, pp. 96–98).

[6] A Soviet study has established that families of the intelligentsia have a much greater impact on their children's "choice of life goals" than do the families of workers (Pashaiev 1984, p. 78).

arly degrees, the political elite equated the quality of a student's professional training with his or her political education. Every official document issued during Brezhnev's years by official Soviet bodies regarding higher education, such as the decision of the Central Committee and the Soviet Government (1980), persistently reiterated that both requirements were of equal importance (*Kommunist* 6, 1980).

Political criteria became even more important when young people applied to graduate programs. Graduate students were naturally regarded as those who would constitute the next generation of scholars. Therefore, in the 1970s, considerable effort was made to prevent politically suspicious or even neutral students from joining graduate programs. The political nature of graduate student selection, their political training, and their inclusion in different kinds of social and ideological work increased tremendously after 1968. Again, every official document related to graduate programs demanded political vigilance from those responsible for graduate education (see Kugel 1983, pp. 96–98; *Kom.* 1, 1972; 17, 1976).[7]

Despite the filters at previous stages of the selection process, the final action—appointment as a fellow in a scientific institute or a professor in a university—was the most essential. Since the late 1960s, the political elite had essentially established a new mode of appointing scientists and of awarding degrees and titles. Never had the role of party committees and the KGB been as crucial in this last stage of the selection process as during that time period. Once again, every official public document adopted by the elite emphasized the role of the party in the selection of scholarly cadre (*Kom.* 1, 1972).

The most significant change affecting scholarly advancement was the inclusion of a large number of scientific positions in the nomenclature. Formally, this meant that even the appointment of a scholar in a secondary provincial research institute, let alone positions connected with the teaching of the youth, required the endorsement of a party committee. The higher the status of the position, the higher the level of the committee that made the endorsement (Voslenski 1980).

The 1977 constitution provided the Soviet political elite with the legal right to consider political loyalty as a necessary condition for securing intellectual work. In line with this new policy, the elite included stipulations in the new official statute that connected the awarding of degrees with political loyalty. Recipients of degrees "must demonstrate that they

---

[7] The following remarkable observation was made in a Soviet publication on the sociology of science: "Some time ago the involvement of graduate students in social activity at universities and research institutes did not attract proper attention. In recent years, active participation in social work became obligatory for every graduate student" (Kugel 1983, p. 143).

can master Marxist-Leninist theory, give positive evidence of their scientific production and social work, follow the norms of communist moral teachings and be guided in their behavior by the principles of Soviet patriotism and proletarian internationalism." Moreover, the same statute contained another clause that enabled scientific institutions to deprive individuals of their degrees if they committed any unpatriotic action or manifested disloyalty toward official ideology (*Kom.* 15, 1975). Through these actions, the Soviet political elite declared political loyalty to be at least as important as the quality of a scholar's dissertation. The elite also publicly proclaimed that any scholar would be stripped of his or her degree if the Soviet leaders found his or her behavior inconsistent with the current political and ideological line.

As will be shown later, Brezhnev's strategy, coupled with the intensive corruption of the intellectuals, was rather successful. By the mid-1980s, a considerable portion of the intellectual community consisted of bogus members whose only concern was the preservation of their status, thus rendering them faithful and loyal supporters of a regime that treated them as if they were the real creative intelligentsia.

Mikhail Zadornov, a popular satirist of glasnost, characterized the interactions between the party and the intelligentsia in the mock greetings of the residents of a city to the General Secretary: "How is everything going in our city? Those with gifts for the arts went to work in the arts, those with abilities for science, in science, and those who have inclinations for the economy went to the economy. However, those who were lazy as youngsters and who have no talents went to the komsomol and trade unions [even in Glasnost the satirist dared not identify the party, but it was more than obvious to his listeners], and they became the leaders of those who had talents, until their subordinates also lost their abilities under their direction" (*Teatr*, March 1988, p. 190).

Soviet authors of the late 1980s not only denounced Brezhnev's policies, which reduced the intellectual's autonomy, but also his justification of breeding intellectuals as a special caste necessary for the scientific and cultural progress of the country—an idea with few open advocates in a society moving toward democracy (see Sevastianov 1988).

SUMMARY

For the intellectuals, the most important political actor in socialist society is the political elite. The relationship between the intellectuals and this elite is of a deeply contradictory nature. On the one hand, the political elite supports the intellectuals as those necessary for the implementation of the elite's goals. On the other hand, the political elite sees the intellectuals as a group regularly in opposition to the current regime.

The history of the USSR, as well as that of other socialist countries, exhibits cyclical oscillations in the attitudes of the elite toward the intellectuals—from harsh repressions to treatment of intellectuals as allies in the process of modernizing society.

CHAPTER TWO

The Intellectuals' Values and Orientations: Between Hedonism and Altruism

WORKING under the assumption that intellectuals may be considered a special group within Soviet society, this chapter will attempt to describe their main values, which are primarily determined by the character of the intellectuals' professional work and their higher level of education. Of course, the description refers to genuine intellectuals, although the bogus intellectuals usually try to imitate the values of their genuine counterparts.

VALUE CONFLICTS AND HIGH FLEXIBILITY

First, it can be argued that no other group encounters value conflicts as often as do the intellectuals. In general, value conflicts increase with one's level of education, and thus reach a peak in the mentality of the intellectuals. Of course, many intellectuals are consistently committed to a distinct value system, but few are actually fully consistent in their behavior, and no single group in Soviet society expresses mutually exclusive views as frequently as does the intelligentsia.

The intellectuals' conflicts stem from the fact that education and, especially, creativity arouse both hedonistic and moral aspirations. The typical intellectual simultaneously desires power, comfort, and prestige, as well as democracy, respect for tradition, and equality, with prosperity for the masses. Individuals in other segments of Soviet society are generally much more single-minded in their life goals: they are largely oriented toward hedonistic concerns and display considerably less interest in political freedoms or the defense of other groups in society. As such, individuals outside the intelligentsia often display less hypocrisy and cynicism, for they experience fewer contradictory inclinations.

Upon close observation, the intellectuals do not appear ascetic or puritanical, or concerned only with issues of truth and the welfare of others. Like the rest of society, they too yearn for mundane pleasures like power, wealth, and prestige, as well as for the immediate gratification of their desires. Intellectuals are even more attracted to some hedonistic goals than are other groups, perhaps due to their special connections to the centers of power. These connections increase the probability that the intellectuals' desires will be fulfilled, compared to those of workers or peasants and, as we know, the intensity of desire is usually proportional to the probability of its realization.

The intellectuals' deeply conflicting system of values and desires explains why the rift between "values for me" and "values for others" is greater among intellectuals than among the rest of the population (see Shlapentokh 1980, 1984). Many intellectuals expect that "other" members of their community will be consistent in pursuing explicitly intellectual goals, particularly in terms of relations to power.[1]

The complexity of the intellectuals' mentality derives not only from conflicting values directly related to their behavior and genuine views of the world, but also from the important role of another set of values: induced, or temporary, values.

Induced values emerge as a response to current, usually temporary, changes in the social milieu. These values provide individuals with goals or moral standards that correspond to the new patterns of behavior imposed by the authorities or by public opinion. Thus, the need to adjust psychologically, as well as materially, to the strong anti-American campaign in the early 1980s forced many intellectuals to foster anti-Western values in their consciences—values that, whatever their immediate strength, were capable of disappearing almost immediately as soon as the pressure ceased. This was clearly demonstrated in the mid-1980s, when many intellectuals rather quickly changed their views on a number of issues in accordance with the new liberal spirit characteristic of the period of glasnost (compare, for example, the 1985 and 1989 works of the prominent journalist Stanislav Kondrashov).

The concrete values of an intellectual depend on various components, including his or her ethnic, social, and cultural background, his or her level of professional excellence, place of residence, personal experience, age, and other factors. Still, the most important influencing variable in the value system of the intellectual and the dynamics of that system is the society's political climate, particularly the scope of political repressions visited on the opposition. The political climate does much to account for

---

[1] Chukovskaia recounts how Akhmatova was angered that Boris Pasternak, whom she loved and respected immensely, consented to be placed, when he became seriously ill, in the Kremlin hospital. This was during the time when *Doctor Zhivago* was entering its period of harassment. Akhmatova argued that "when you write what Pasternak did, you should not claim an individual ward in a hospital of the Central Committee." Chukovskaia, who passionately loved both great poets, was irritated by this remark. She recalled that while in Tashkent during the war, Akhmatova, having herself developed typhoid, "went berserk . . . when it seemed to her that she would be sent to an ordinary hospital, and was very glad when, thanks to the efforts of friends, she was transported to the individual ward in the local 'Kremlin' hospital" (Chukovskaia 1980, p. 219).

the structure of the intellectuals' value system, specifically for the content of opinions expressed in private and, especially, in public.

Although they exhibit various combinations of values, the intellectuals may be divided into several major groups, depending on which values are central, in respect both to outward behavior and verbal activity. The main ideological trends in the intellectual community will be discussed in later chapters.

The following section describes the most important values influencing the material and spiritual behaviors of Soviet intellectuals.

Homo Sum, Humani Nil a Me Alaenum Puto [Nothing human is alien to me]

An increase in mass education in a country tends to contribute to the expansion of desires and needs in the areas of physical comfort and spiritual development. If rising real incomes are not accompanied by simultaneous development in education and culture, there is a tendency toward increases—as may be witnessed in the Soviet countryside—in socially problematic behavior such as alcoholism. During the age of aristocracies, it was common for aristocrats to combine their wealth with cultural development and artistic patronage in the creation of the refined life-styles the bourgeois sought to imitate (with little success).

Intellectuals today have replaced the old nobility in the binding of material comfort and cultural enrichment. The Soviet people, in search of exciting and interesting life-styles, do not look to the party bureaucracy, but to the cultural elite. Like the aristocrats of old, contemporary intellectuals tend to denigrate those absorbed with the bourgeois accumulation of money—but also share with their historical predecessors the tendency to become dissatisfied if they themselves do not live in material comfort.

Soviet data reveal the significant role of material incentives in the activities of scientists, although other factors such as creativity and social recognition remain more important. Some studies of Soviet scientists suggest that a proportion of them consider material incentives very important to their activity, and no less than half are dissatisfied with the material rewards of scholars (Kelle et al. 1978; Shanov and Kuznetsov 1977; Sheinin 1980).

In the last three decades, conspicuous consumption and concern for material comfort have increased significantly among Soviet intellectuals. Three factors appear to have contributed to this trend. First, contacts with the West have increased, providing a distinct standard of comparison. Second, the role of social ideals has declined markedly, and cynicism has increased in the intellectual community, especially in the 1970s. Finally, the pernicious influence of bogus intellectuals indifferent to their professional calling, who began to outnumber the true priests of creativity, has significantly influenced the escalation of wild consumerism, even among real intellectuals.

Altaiev (apparently a pseudonym), the author of a brilliant article on the Soviet intelligentsia in the post-Stalin era, has asserted that one of the cardinal differences between the post-Stalin intelligentsia and its predecessors in prerevolutionary Russia lies in the "bourgeois character" of the former. Having forgotten earlier asceticism, these intellectuals crave comfort, good apartments and clothes, and travel abroad (Altaiev 1970, p. 10).

Oleg Dmitriev, a prominent poet, paints a similar picture of Moscow writers who, during their meetings, almost completely ignore professional issues in their heated discussions, but "debate about the number of copies which a given author managed to publish, royalties, the number of travels abroad, what apartments writers have, who flirts with whom, and so on" (Dmitriev 1988). Similarly, Vladimir Drozd, a writer, in his soul-searching articles, depicted his colleagues who, at the Congress of Writers, ran during the intermissions to special shops in order to get their share of foreign goods (Drozd 1987, p. 13).

Vishnevskaia's book, *Galina* (1984), illustrates the importance of material comfort to Soviet intellectuals. Both of the main characters in the book, the prima donna ballerina of the Bolshoi Theater and her husband, the famous Mstislav Rostropovich, were greatly preoccupied with the systematic improvement of their living standards. In one scene, Galina criticizes her husband for his quest for money, suggesting that he should reduce his concert commitments and live a more calm and creative life. She apparently has no impact, for after each trip abroad, new Western goods are collected for the Moscow apartment. After one trip, their car is so overloaded with Western gadgets for the kitchen and the bathroom that it can barely be driven. However, even with this preoccupation, Rostropovich and his wife emerge as committed intellectuals, who defy several warnings and shelter Solzhenitsyn in their country home, ultimately resulting in their expulsion from the country. A number of other Soviet intellectuals, including the most prominent members of the liberal movement, were noted for their great interest in material well-being (see Orlova 1983, p. 302).[2]

Yet, from the 1940s through the 1960s, the proportion of those prepared to sacrifice material well-being for the sake of social or professional ideals was much higher within the intelligentsia than in other groups.

[2] The intellectuals' dissatisfaction with their material condition is revealed in the mass defections of musicians, dancers, and artists. These highly talented people left the country primarily for nonpolitical reasons: they could not fully exploit their creative skills, and were not rewarded to the degree they desired.

Russian history is filled with examples of intellectuals who preferred poverty to submission before autocratic rulers, including Mandel'shtam, Andrei Platonov, Anna Akhmatova, Marina Tsvetaieva, and Bulgakov. Many Soviet intellectuals who joined the democratic movement of the 1960s, such as Lev Kopelev, Alexander Galich, Vladimir Voinovich, and Georgi Vladimov, had to contend with marked material impoverishment after having previously enjoyed a high standard of material well-being.

PRESTIGE: THE MAIN HEDONISTIC VALUE

With regard to prestige, the intellectual community is extremely homogeneous: the principal concern of almost all intellectuals is for public recognition. Of course, it is possible to identify a few intellectuals who are generally insensitive to public opinion, but even in these cases it can be argued that such individuals simply prefer a different form of prestige.

The intellectuals have typically been accused by their detractors of a variety of egotistic qualities, such as vanity, conceit, and exhibitionism. There is no question that, in the Soviet Union, education and intellectual development are related to the need for public recognition. Again, as in the case of material comfort and power, education provides the preconditions for the enjoyment of prestige, a pleasure less available to those with less education.

The intellectuals can clearly compete with the old nobility in vanity, and in mutual envy. It is no surprise that the French authors of the seventeenth and eighteenth centuries known for their descriptions of the nobility's life-style (e.g., La Rochefoucault, La Bruere, and Laclos) are so popular among the Soviet intelligentsia. The memoirs of Soviet intellectuals, despite their authors' desires to enhance their own images, are replete with facts betraying great vanity (Ashkenazy 1985; Goliakhovski 1984; Solzhenitsyn 1975c; Vishnevskaia 1984).

Despite her love for Akhmatova, author Lidia Chukovskaia could not conceal from readers numerous details revealing this great woman's sensitivity to any sign of recognition, and how she studiously compared manifestations of fame accruing to her and to Pasternak (Chukovskaia 1980). Similarly, an author who knew Dmitri Shostakovich intimately and loved him dearly reluctantly recognized that the great composer "secretly and insatiably loved fame and the fuss around his name" (Glikman 1983, p. 323).

The interminable quest for prestige explains why envy is one of the strongest feelings of many intellectuals (both genuine and bogus ones). This envy often undermines the solidarity of intellectuals against their common enemies. After much life experience, and with evident sadness, Daniil Granin wrote in 1988 that many years ago, when he was just starting his career as a writer, he "believed piously in the brotherhood of talented people who are so few and who have to defend each other," an illusion he no longer harbors (Granin 1988b, p. 9).

The envy that devoured the feelings of many intellectuals and was the main source of their numerous vicious deeds has been graphically portrayed in several stories and movies made by Soviet authors since Granin's "Sobstvennoiemnenie" (1956) (see the novels of Iosif Gerasimov; and Iuri German's story "Let the Dog Bark," 1966/1988).

PROFESSIONAL PRESTIGE: CONFLICTS BETWEEN COLLEAGUES AND THE STATE

Two types of prestige are important to intellectuals: professional prestige and civic prestige. The first type refers to recognition for professional achievement, while the second denotes popular appraisal of a professional's political activity.

High professional prestige is a necessary condition for successful creative activity among nearly all intellectuals. While all types of work demand encouragement and public recognition, creative activity, because of the unpredictability of the quality of its products, demands a higher level of such encouragement and recognition. That is, because the product of creative activity is by definition nonstandard, it can be treated as either a great achievement or a complete failure. Variations in judgments of intellectual work are many times greater than those of the results of routine work.

Professional prestige is also necessary for intellectuals because it facilitates the process of creative activity in the material sense. In other words, renowned scholars and writers have many more opportunities than their lesser-known colleagues to pursue their work, obtain necessary resources, get their books published, and so on. In Soviet society, prestige is a form of capital that tends to fill the role occupied by money in other societies.

Professional prestige is accorded to intellectuals from two different sources in Soviet society: the state, and other intellectuals. While interrelated, these two sources of prestige are, in many cases, at odds with one another, with politics usually being the cause of the divergence (about the two types of professional prestige in the USSR, see Dmitri Likhachev's article in *Literaturnaia Gazeta*, December 2, 1987).

Although recognition by peers is the most authoritative, the state is often unhappy with peer evaluation due to the conflict in socialist society between "good" and "red" experts. As will be demonstrated, the authorities are very careful in their choice of whom to recognize, particularly when individuals display ambiguous, or, even worse, disloyal, political attitudes. Thus, the gap between official prestige and peer prestige can be rather large.

A survey of fifteen hundred scholars in various research institutes of the Soviet Academy of Sciences in the 1970s found that only 35 percent were satisfied with the official system of evaluating their work. When asked who could best judge their scholarly work, 48 percent indicated experts in their areas, 16 percent chose the scientific council of their institute, and only 4 percent cited the director of their institute (Kelle et al. 1978, pp. 135–137). Thus, although disparities between official and collegial assessments tend to increase during times of political reaction and decrease during periods of liberalization, a regular struggle occurs between official and unofficial prestige in the Soviet Union at all times.

Intellectuals are often divided in their appraisals of official and collegial prestige. The majority of genuine intellectuals would like both forms of recognition. When forced to choose between the two, however, intellectuals, particularly bogus ones, most often prefer the recognition of the state, which can bring titles, medals, and material privileges to a scholar or writer (see Zinoviev 1985, p. 186). The differences between the two forms of prestige have been most notable in literature and in the arts, and were at their most extreme in the 1970s. At that time, some authors, such as Georgi Markov or Anatoli Sofronov, were lavishly supported by the state, given leading positions in the cultural hierarchy, and granted numerous privileges. At the same time, other writers, such as Bulat Okudzhava, Vladimir Vysotski, and Galich, who were extremely popular in the country, were totally ignored by the establishment (unless, of course, some attention was required in order to take administrative action against them).[3]

It is during periods of thaw that the officially sanctioned ranks of intellectuals face open challenges. Due to the broader freedoms available during these periods, it becomes possible to expose the true value of writers, scholars, and others, independent of the regalia dispensed by the political leadership. This was the case in the early 1960s, when several "glorious" authors, such as Anatoli Surov and Mikhail Bubennyi, plummeted into total oblivion.

A full and genuine purge did not occur until 1986–1988, however,

---

[3] The gap between official and peer prestige depends directly on the relations between the state and the intellectual community. This gap emerged almost immediately after the Revolution. By 1928 Viktor Shklovski had already introduced the concept of the "Hamburg Test," which referred to the true assessment of each intellectual's value, as opposed to that made by the authorities. The term was derived from the custom of Hamburg wrestlers to gather occasionally to test the real strength of each athlete, since the outcome of public matches was often predetermined for mercantilistic reasons and therefore failed to reflect the real abilities of the wrestlers (see Shklovski 1928).

when it became possible to seriously evaluate the merits of intellectual products. During those years, many officially supported writers, such as Piotr Proskurin, Markov, and Mikhail Alexeiev, all but disappeared from the reading lists of the Soviet people (see Gudkov and Dubin 1988, p. 179).

Given the dominance of bogus and mediocre intellectuals in the Academy of Sciences and other organizations formally representing creative intelligentsia (e.g., the Union of Soviet Writers, the Union of Artists, etc.), collegial evaluations of intellectual performance became almost undistinguishable from governmental evaluations. This phenomenon was particularly evident during the election campaign of January–April 1989, when each organization of intellectuals elected its delegates to the new Soviet parliament. The events in the Academy of Sciences provide an excellent illustration of the situation at that time. For the most part, the Presidium of the Academy nominated administrators, rejecting the candidacies of outstanding and honest scholars respected by the intellectual community, such as Sakharov, Roal'd Sagdeiev, and others. Only the open revolt of the Academy's rank and file forced the leadership to alter its position and fill the Academy's quota of candidates with prominent and respected scientists (about these events, see *LG*, April 9, 1989; see also *Moskovskie Novosti*, February 12, 1989). During the election campaign, the leadership of the Unions of Soviet Writers and Journalists demonstrated similar hostility toward their most highly regarded colleagues.

Western Prestige As the Main Criterion

A distinctive feature of the 1970s and, to an even greater extent, the 1980s was the emergence of the West as the ultimate judge of the quality of intellectual work. The increasing supremacy of foreign appraisals over domestic assessments reflects a recognition on the part of both the intellectuals and the authorities that the current system of domestic appraisals, both official and professional, is wholly unacceptable.

The move toward favoring Western recognition originated in the 1950s when the political elite, with its deep mistrust of domestic intellectuals (especially scholars), surreptitiously began to use Western estimates of intellectual work as the most objective assessments of the value of such work. In the mid-1960s, the decisive role of Western recognition became more and more evident, and intellectuals (including those who presented themselves as Russophiles and haters of the West) began to vie for popularity abroad.

During the period of glasnost it became possible to discuss openly the role of the West as final arbiter of intellectual value. Iuri Gleba, a member of the Academy of Sciences, wrote in 1988 that "we will not raise the level of our science if we do not reject domestic estimates. . . . The most sober, even if bitter, estimates are not state prizes, not patents, but the indexes of citations and the number of publications in the best international journals" (Gleba 1988).

When Sotheby's organized its first auction of paintings in Moscow in 1988, the results—the phenomenal success of unknown and unofficial artists and the total failure of the members of the artistic establishment—were accepted by the Soviet media as a sentence with no chance of appeal (*Komsomol'skaia Pravda*, July 9, 1988).

CIVIC PRESTIGE: THE COMPLICATED RELATION WITH PROFESSIONAL STATUS

Civic prestige is a measure of the recognition of an intellectual's political boldness. By definition, civic prestige is gained through opposition to the state, and it is impossible to acquire this prestige via collaboration with the authorities. Participation in official activities, such as holding a position in an official body or traveling abroad to defend Soviet policy, cannot enhance civic prestige—indeed, it can only diminish it. In the 1970s, because of their public activities, Georgi Arbatov, director of the Institute of the USA and Canada, and Alexander Chakovski, writer and editor in chief of *Literaturnaia Gazeta*, were viewed by the public as bearers of great official prestige, but were barely considered citizens by Soviet intellectuals.

The explanation of the strictly oppositional nature of civic prestige is clear. Support of official policy demands no qualities thought to be admirable, whereas opposition to such policy requires considerable courage and honesty.

Ideally, an intellectual hopes to be recognized both as a great scholar, writer, or artist, and as a courageous individual, defying the government in defense of scientific or social ideals. Few people, however, enjoyed the prestige of the entire intellectual community and the mass intelligentsia as did Sakharov and Solzhenitsyn in the 1960s, both of whom were highly respected as professionals and as courageous individuals. In many cases, intellectuals had to choose between civic and official prestige, and decide whether to pursue one form of recognition or the other.

From 1985 through 1989, the intellectuals accorded the highest civic prestige by the intellectual community and by the intelligentsia in general were those who had participated in glasnost since its inception in 1985 and 1986. They were granted such prestige because, while aware of the high probability of a counterreaction and cruel revenge on the part of the Stalinists and chauvinists, they continued to defend democratic ideas, pressing further and further in debunking the Soviet system and its ideology (this issue will be discussed further in chapter 9).

Professional and civic prestige are related to one another in a complex fashion. In general, high professional prestige enhances civic prestige. In Soviet society, professional prestige serves as a form of protection, and intellectuals with strong professional credentials have greater latitude in the expression of political views than do lesser-known intellectuals. For example, Sakharov would have been far more restricted in his oppositional activity had he not enjoyed the enormous prestige of his fellow physicists. Similarly, the wide recognition of Solzhenitsyn's early novels granted him a measure of freedom that would have been unavailable to an unknown writer.

The case of *Metropol'*, an illegal magazine produced by a group of Moscow intellectuals in 1979, provides an interesting illustration. Among the writers involved were Andrei Voznesenski, Bella Akhmadulina, and Vasili Aksenov, as well as some unknown writers such as Nikolai Popov and Viktor Erofeiev. When the authorities began to mete out punishments to the magazine's contributors, the well-known authors received only small reprimands. Within two years, Voznesenski had completely restored his professional status, was permitted to travel abroad, and published his poems in *Pravda*; Akhmadulina even received a prestigious medal in 1984. By contrast, those contributors who had not achieved prior fame fell into seemingly permanent disgrace.

The complex nature of civic prestige was not immediately understood by the authorities. They were slow to realize that civic prestige was enhanced by professional prestige, as well as by official attacks on intellectuals. The leadership took two steps in the 1970s to diminish the civic prestige of those engaged in oppositional activity. First, professional promotion became contingent on certain political requirements (as discussed in the previous chapter). Second, the leadership began to avoid public condemnation of disloyal intellectuals, preferring more subtle attacks instead. Through these actions, the authorities reduced the relationship between professional and civic prestige, and forced many intellectuals to choose between the two. In the 1970s the atmosphere was so gloomy that a significant number of intellectuals clearly agreed to forego their civic prestige in order to preserve their official recognition.

Surveys of the readers of *Literaturnaia Gazeta*, one of the most popular journals among the Soviet intelligentsia, revealed that the most popular intellectuals were those who, in one way or another, challenged the authorities. In the 1968 survey, respondents were asked to name their favorite contributors to the journal, the authors of their favorite books of the last year, and their favorite poets and literary critics. On each list, readers supported those intellectuals with the greatest reputations for critical writing. Those with the most critical orientations were joined only by those who were considered "moderates" at the time of the survey, such as the writer Konstantin Simonov, the literary historian Irakli Andronnikov, and the surgeon Nikolai Amosov. The list of the favored authors included the writer Konstantin Paustovski, the poet and editor of *Novyi Mir* Alexander Tvardovski, the poet Evgeni Evtushenko, the columnist Leonid Likhodeiev, and the writers Solzhenitsyn and Kornei Chukovski. Not surprisingly, authors cited as least-admired were those loyal to the regime: Vsevolod Kochetov, Vadim Kozhevnikov, Semion Babaievski, Boris Polevoi, and others. Among the least-favored literary critics were also those associated with the authorities, such as Alexander Dymshits, Vladimir Ermilov, Iuri Idashkin, and Dmitri Starikov (see Shlapentokh 1969b).

The support provided by the mass intelligentsia and students inspires the intellectuals with energy, confidence, and a feeling of importance in their work.

THE YEARNING FOR POSITIONS IN THE HIERARCHY

The intellectuals' contradictory nature is clearly revealed in their attitudes toward political power, the principal factor in the Soviet system. The intellectuals' love-hate relationship with power has existed throughout history, and there is ample evidence of its existence in archaic time, such as in ancient Athens or Rome (see Vatai 1984).

When discussing the issue of power, it is necessary to distinguish "positive" and "negative" viewpoints regarding power. The former refers to attitudes that see power as a desired end, while the latter alludes to views that consider power undesirable. Among intellectuals, power is seen simultaneously as a positive source of gratification and as a negative source of pain and frustration.

Education, general higher learning, and creative skills have, in many ways, made power, like prestige (and power generally begets prestige), even more desirable among intellectuals than among other groups. As Altaiev contends, "issues related to power hold a leading place in the mentality of the intelligentsia: power has become a religion" (Altaiev 1970, p. 18; see also Dmitriev 1988). The imaginations of the intellectuals suggest possibilities for the uses of power that are unknown to other groups—groups that are more likely to see power only as a path to individual gratification.

For intellectuals who enjoy commanding people, power is attractive as a direct and immediate source of gratification (a "terminal value," in Milton Rokeach's terminology). A significant number of Soviet scholars, writers, and painters hold administrative positions with great pleasure, and use these positions to insulate themselves from their rivals.[4] Many Soviet intellectuals willingly accept positions as officials in various unions. Among the secretaries of the Writers' Union in the 1970s were such respected authors as Sergei Zalygin and Olzhas Suleimenov. Even Shostakovich was a secretary of the Composers' Union, and gave official speeches on behalf of the organization. But it is true that, for the most part, especially in the 1970s, such positions were not normally held by those with the greatest commitment to their professions and were more commonly filled by bogus intellectuals—less-skilled intellectuals hoping to achieve high status in nonprofessional ways.

The willingness to accept an administrative position clearly increases with age and with the decline of one's creative faculties, and thus research institutes are normally headed by those who have ceased their research activities (about age and creativity in the USSR, see Kozlova 1983). More often these intellectuals appear in the literature as coauthors with more active researchers, or as authors of books actually written by subordinates. In fact, the opportunity to exploit one's subordinates for this purpose is one of the advantages of holding an official position in a research institute in the USSR.

The intellectuals' yearning for power in no way weakens during periods of liberalization. In fact, it is exactly during these periods that the leadership views the creative intelligentsia as its ally, and that the intellectuals become aware of unique opportunities to obtain high positions in the official hierarchy—positions previously available only to their bogus colleagues and to hack party officials. Thus, although rather passive in times such as Brezhnev's, many genuine intellectuals go to great lengths during periods of thaw in order to secure an administrative post either in government or, at the very least, in the academic system. No matter what explanations the intellectuals use to justify their interest in power (most often such actions are said to be "for the benefit of the cause"), the scramble for managerial positions often creates conflicts among intellectuals and undermines their drive toward the modernization of society.

Having watched the activists of perestroika race for power in 1985–1989, the philosopher Valentin Tolstykh suggested that such power negatively influences the creativity of these intellectuals. With sadness, Tolstykh further noted that many artists and scholars who were "mobilized

[4] Raisa Orlova vividly described the dramatic figure of Alexander Iashin, one of the best Soviet writers of the 1960s and the author of the famous *Levers*: "Within Iashin himself were combined a striving for truth (the retribution for that striving could have been the loss of everything gained) and a fear of martyrdom, together with the desire for a normal sheltered life, a life sheltered for the sake of literature, for the creation of books. Iashin frequently repeated, 'I want to be a director.' He wanted to be in charge, no matter what. He wanted to sit on the presidium. He wanted power" (Orlova 1983, p. 287).

by perestroika" and accepted leading administrative positions in their organizations had "not passed the test of power," and had begun to treat
"ordinary intellectuals" in a manner similar to that used by their predecessors in the Brezhnev regime (*Sovietskaia Kul'tura*, May 22, 1989).

SOVIET INTELLECTUALS AND THE PARTY

Party membership in the Soviet Union, especially for the intellectuals,
usually means direct participation in the mechanisms of power and the
performance of functions related to control over others. Equally important is the fact that the threat of exclusion from the party (which in most
cases means the end of one's career) compels intellectuals—as all other
party members—to obey orders from above and even to participate in
campaigns against their colleagues.

It is interesting to note that Stalin was never overly concerned about
the rate of party membership among intellectuals. He stressed on a number of occasions that the distinction between communists and noncom-
munists in Soviet society was largely a formality, and that there was nothing "more stupid or reactionary" than a policy of promoting only those
who are members of the party, while ignoring the more talented and innovative nonmembers (Stalin 1952, p. 375). Indeed, Stalin may have had
greater respect for those scientists who were not party members: without
exception, all of the presidents of the Academy of Sciences during his rule
were nonmembers. Even such a celebrity as Trofim Lysenko was not a
party member. The post-Stalin leadership, however, apparently considered this policy to be an unaffordable luxury. In the leadership's view,
party membership was highly important for intellectuals, for it served as
a demonstration of political loyalty and readiness to follow party directives.

The attractiveness of party membership in the 1960s and 1970s was
such that the majority of outstanding intellectuals entered the party and
participated in all party activities. This was particularly true of the generation of scholars, writers, and actors that began its professional life during that period. By the early 1970s, about 60 percent of Doctors of Science and about 50 percent of Candidates of Science were members of the
party (XXIV S'ezd Kommunisticheskoi Partii, 1971; *TsSU*, 1974; see also
SK, June 8, 1985, p. 2). Similarly, more than 50 percent of writers were
party members, and, of the participants at the Russian Writers' Congress,
87 percent were party members. Party members made up one third of all
composers and filmmakers and two thirds of all journalists and members
of the Academy of Sciences (*LG*, December 18, 1985, p. 3; *Pravda*, June
29, 1989).

It should be noted that while the leadership sought to recruit influential

intellectuals into the party in the 1970s and promoted lesser-skilled scholars into official positions on the basis of party membership, membership
privileges were withheld from some intellectuals. This policy reflected a
desire to avoid a preponderance of intellectuals within the party, not only
for ideological reasons, but also because it was more difficult to run the
party when intellectuals constituted the majority in a party cell. There
were only a few cases in the 1960s when a party organization rebelled
against the leadership, and in nearly all of these, intellectuals or professionals were the key activists.[5] Likewise, it is no surprise that almost all
of the intellectuals active in perestroika—including those who eventually
became more radical even than Gorbachev, such as Iuri Afanasiev and
Gavriil Popov—were party members (Andrei Sakharov was a conspicuous exception to this rule).

THE SEARCH FOR PROTECTION

Power is attractive to intellectuals not only because of the rewards and
privileges it affords, but also because it can aid one in the attainment of
professional goals. As a precondition for the performance of their professional tasks, many intellectuals seek to obtain the support of the leadership by taking part in various political actions. Once they are protected
by a benevolent elite, such intellectuals hope to pursue their creative activities unhampered.

Some members of the intelligentsia believe that cooperation with the
authorities has no deleterious political effect on their work or on their
image in the eyes of their colleagues. Others who recognize that such collaboration may have negative consequences nonetheless pursue connections with those in power.

Several prominent figures in Soviet science have collaborated politically
with the authorities in hopes of preserving their freedom of activity. The
famous historian Evgeni Tarle, who was totally devoted to his vocation,
was delighted when, after his exile in 1931, he was called to the Kremlin.
He later wrote to a friend that he "was received with warmth and bril-
liance; everything will be done, they want me working." Later, Stalin personally (and for the most part benignly) supervised Tarle's activity, allowing the historian to publish dozens of books and receive the Stalin Prize
three times (*Sovietskaia Kul'tura*, December 5, 1989). The chemist
Nikolai Semionov, the mathematicians Leonid Kantorovich and Sergei

---

[5] Given its ambivalent feelings about the intellectuals' party membership, the leadership
has sought to maintain a stable number of intellectuals in the party, and even to decrease
their numbers during some periods. According to Ovsei Shkaratan's data on the Tartar
republic, about 15 percent of intellectuals in Kazan in 1975 were party members. Among
professionals, the figure was even slightly higher, at 20 percent (1982, p. 49).

Sobolev, and the physicist Gersh (Andrei) Budker are all additional examples of competent scholars who had no illusions about the nature of the Soviet system, but who nonetheless cooperated fully with the authorities in the 1960s and 1970s.

Of course, political compromise is far more damaging to the professional work of writers, social scientists, and film directors than to that of natural scientists (although the latter have much to lose by disobeying the authorities in the selection of graduate students and colleagues, or by refusing to withdraw their critique of scholars favored by the party, and so on). There are many writers, such as Sholokhov and Iuri Bondarev, who began their careers as promising authors but killed their talent through permanent political concessions. Still, there are a few examples of a writer's creative skills having withstood open collaboration with the state. Valentin Kataiev, one of the best Soviet writers, is one such example. For all of his productive life, Kataiev has been a party member on good terms with the leadership. During the Stalin era, his compliance with the regime was apparently incompatible with his creative capacities, and he produced countless mediocre novels, such as *The Regiment's Son* (1945) and *For Soviet Power* (1948). An exception during this period was *A Single Sail Shows White* (1936), which was quite good. Under subsequent regimes, Kataiev maintained party loyalty and served for a time as editor in chief of the official magazine *Unost'* (Youth). He also participated in campaigns against other writers, including Pasternak and Solzhenitsyn (*P.*, February 15, 1974), and in the glorification of Soviet leaders (Gladilin 1980). At the same time, in the 1960s and especially in the 1970s, he revealed his excellence as a writer in such works as *The Sacred Well* (1967).

Vasili Grossman skillfully captured this important aspect of the intellectuals' attitudes toward power. Viktor Shtum, the principal character in Grossman's book, *Life and Fate* (1980), struggles desperately against his detractors who, because of his Jewish origin, denigrate his breakthroughs in nuclear physics. Dismissed from his research institute and deprived of the opportunity to continue his work, Shtum has a chance to partially restore his position, but only if he yields to the demands of the administration and recants the "sins" he is accused of committing. He rejects this course of action. Then, in a miraculous turn of events, Shtum is personally contacted by Stalin himself, who is preoccupied with the development of nuclear weaponry. In a matter of hours, he is visited in his home by his principal opponents, who apologize for their harassment of him and invite him to return to work with remarkable new opportunities for research. Shtum is overjoyed, but is quickly contacted and asked to sign a letter addressed to Western scholars denying the existence of persecution of scientists in the country. Shtum is well aware of the nature of the persecution of scientists, but he realizes that refusing to sign the letter will jeopardize his career at a time when he has been offered the opportunity of a lifetime. The physicist, who only a few days earlier was prepared to face arrest rather than go against his conscience, reaches for a pen to sign the letter.

Given the intellectuals' traditional contempt for bourgeois values, it is remarkable that they failed to understand sooner that, under some conditions, significant amounts of money allow individuals to be independent of and indifferent to the attitudes of either the state or the capitalists, thus allowing individuals to pursue their own interests. It was not until 1988 that a Soviet author characterized the wealth of rich American intellectuals not with opprobrium, but rather as a positive factor that allows "the scholar not to bow before a politician or capitalist" (Sevastianov 1988).

The Role of Fear

For many intellectuals, amicable relations with the authorities are less a matter of protection, a high standard of living, official prestige, or a condition for normal creative work, but are more a requisite for simple physical survival. The nature of the Soviet system is such that individuals may experience swift changes of position—that is, a privileged position may either be retained or may be exchanged with that of an outcast. There is usually little middle ground. During the Stalin era, the prospect of such an exchange of positions, from that of the privileged to that of an inmate in the gulag, hovered over every apparatchik, scholar, and intellectual.

Chukovskaia and Nadezhda Mandel'shtam vividly described how the fear of Soviet power never left Akhmatova, a woman with extraordinary self-respect and pride. Akhmatova dared not write down her famous poem "Requiem" (about mass terror in Stalin's times) until 20 years later, almost a decade after Stalin's death. During the terrible times when she traveled to Moscow from Leningrad to try to rescue her son who had been arrested, her close friends refused to put her up the second time, and the poet did not blame them—she understood the meaning of fear (Chukovskaia 1980, p. 434; Il'ina 1987, p. 30; MN, no. 17, 1988, p. 7).

In summarizing her feelings over four decades, and having named a chapter in her memoirs "Fear," Mandel'shtam wrote, "Akhmatova and I once confessed to each other that the strongest feelings which we ever knew, stronger than love and jealousy, stronger than anything which is human, were fear and its derivations: the heinous awareness of shame, restrictions, and full helplessness" (Mandel'shtam 1972, p. 198).

The sentiments of Akhmatova and Mandel'shtam were echoed by Evgeni Gabrilovich, an old and experienced filmmaker. Speaking (rather philosophically) about his life across the last five decades, Gabrilovich commented: "As a close witness of those years, I can contend that the Academies of Sciences, Arts, and Marxism, in establishing the moving forces of history, have neglected a crucial, and perhaps even the most important, mainspring: fear. In order to understand so many of the puzzles, secrets, and absurdities of our complicated life, it is necessary to comprehend, most of all, the real significance of fear" (*SK*, June 17, 1989).

Memoirs discussing the 1949 anticosmopolitan campaign (which could have been published only in the period of glasnost) graphically depicted the fear that plagued the intellectuals, as well as the numerous cases of betrayal between friends and colleagues. Sergei Iutkevich, a prominent film director, recounted how his friend Mark Donskoi, the famous film personality, ardently attacked him at a public meeting devoted to the denunciation of cosmopolitans (Iutkevich 1988, p. 106). Similarly, Simonov joined in the persecution of those he had previously protected (Borshchagovski 1988, p. 161; Rudnitski 1988, p. 151).

During Stalin's time, and to a lesser extent later, any act of benevolence on the part of the authorities was perceived by many intellectuals as a sign of "salvation" from arrest or dismissal from one's job. Raizman, a prominent film director, recounts what happened when his friend Mikhail Romm, the famous Soviet film director, was awarded a medal in 1937: Romm ran upstairs shouting "I got the Order of Lenin; they will not arrest me now" (*SK*, June 4, 1988).

Two great Soviet intellectuals—the famous film director Sergei Eisenshtein, and the brilliant actor Nikolai Cherkasov—chronicled the content of their 1947 meeting with Stalin regarding their film, *Ivan the Terrible*. The text, published thirty-one years later, shows how the world-famous author of *Battleship Potemkin* asked the leader for directions regarding the length of Ivan's beard, while the actor courted approval of various scenes in the movie (*MN*, August 7, 1988).

For three decades after Stalin's death, Soviet intellectuals, especially those from older generations, were unable to shake their mortal fear of the authorities. This was especially true for those released from the gulag. Poets Nikolai Zabolotski and Anatoli Zhigulin did not risk telling even their closest friends of their horrendous experiences (about Zabolotski, see *Novoye Russkoye Slovo*, November 25, 1986).

Even more remarkable was the behavior of Sergei Korolev, the legendary pioneer of the first Soviet missile project, who spent nine years in the gulag and was released in 1947. Even after Stalin's death, when Korolev was the most prominent member of the scientific-military complex, he spoke to no one about his experiences, including his wife (Pastukhova 1987, p. 19).

When, during a meeting with intellectuals in 1957, an angry and unrestrained Khrushchev figuratively called for the deaths of those who deviated from the party line, Margarita Aliger, a famous poet, fainted, explaining later that she took the leader's words at face value.

It is remarkable that many intellectuals—including veterans of the last war who regularly faced death at the fronts—displayed no more courage than did those who had never passed serious tests in their lives. In 1987 Arbatov, the director of the Institute of the USA and Canada, who himself was the typical conformist in the 1970s, wrote (probably of himself as well as others): "I thought several times: why people who bravely fought during the war later often behaved as cowards as citizens, were afraid of bad opinions about them from 'above' more than bullets, fell into despondency only because of a superior's peremptory shout, even of frowning eyebrows, and were ready to raise hands, betraying their conscience and convictions" (Arbatov 1987, p. 4).

The political trials of intellectuals, which were ever-present in the Soviet scene between 1953 and 1982, the seizure of Grossman's book, *Life and Fate*, as well as many other events during this period, kept the fear of the Soviet state fresh in the conscience of the intellectuals.[6] Despite all of this, however, the fear gradually diminished, and more and more people (although not all) began to believe that those not engaged in direct conflict with the authorities were safe from arrest and other dire consequences.

It eventually became clear that neither a book published by a Soviet magazine nor a refusal to take part in a campaign against a political outcast or against the West would lead to arrest or even to dismissal from one's job. The displeasure of the authorities would translate primarily into the blocking of one's promotion, impediments to publication, a prohibition on traveling abroad, withdrawal of some material privileges, and so on. Yet the expectation that the intellectuals' courage would be enhanced by the disappearance of physical threats to freedom and life was only partially borne out. The fear of those in power continues to be a leading psychological feature of many Soviet intellectuals. In addition, the feeling that "they can do anything to you" has not evaporated from the mentality of the Soviet intellectuals, and the fear of material deprivation and of the loss of official prestige still persists among them.

Although in the 1970s the fear of those in power was significantly di-

---

[6] During this period, many authors, fearing confiscation of their manuscripts and possible arrest, continued to use precautions as they wrote. For example, Solzhenitsyn carefully hid everything he wrote after 1962, the year of his official recognition as a Soviet writer, and Zhigulin placed four copies of his memoirs with friends (see *MN*, August 31, 1988).

minished relative to the past, it remained sufficiently strong that many intellectuals severed their relations with friends and colleagues who became targets of official critique. Alexei German, a famous film director, described how, when his movies started to be shelved, his circle of friends became smaller and smaller, and ultimately he had no one to invite to his birthday party (see Kornilov 1988).

The lingering fear of the Soviet state is also clearly illustrated in the actions of Shostakovich, the great Soviet composer. Shostakovich had been continually harassed during the Stalin era, although he was circumspect in his actions after 1953. He participated in a number of political activities organized by the authorities, and made many public speeches praising the wisdom of the party. Various sources, including his son, Maxim Shostakovich, unanimously suggest that Shostakovich in fact deeply hated the Soviet system. According to these sources, he adjusted to it only out of the fear strongly ingrained in him since the 1930s, when he had thought himself on the verge of complete catastrophe. One source suggests that Shostakovich cried only two times in his life: when his first wife died, because of great grief, and when he joined the Communist party, because of shame (see Ashkenazy 1985; Vishnevskaia 1984; Volkov 1979; see the interview with Maxim Shostakovich, NRS, April 30, 1981).

Riazanov's famous movie, *Garage* (1980), depicts the fuss in a research institute over the construction of a garage for personal cars. One of the movie's heroes, observing the petty interests of himself and his colleagues and their fear of the superiors who could now deprive them of a material privilege, namely, a space in the garage, remarks with great sadness, "Well, in the past, we were afraid of something terrible, and this forced us to make a compromise with our conscience; but now, when nothing like this threatens us, why are we so cowardly?"

Recalling the spirited participation of hundreds of Soviet writers in the denunciation of Pasternak for *Doctor Zhivago*, Alexander Borshchagovski (who himself took part in similar acts even later, in the 1970s) asked in the article, "The Feeling of the Guilt" (1987): "How could it happen? None of us was afraid of repressions: was it the simple concern about the publication of a new book, about material well-being, that could so distort the soul?"

It is remarkable how slow intellectuals were to rid themselves of fear in the first years of Gorbachev's regime, which ordained glasnost and called upon the intelligentsia to express their most critical ideas freely.

By 1988 the fear of the state was removed only from the surface of the intellectuals' consciousness. A long letter published in *Sovietskaia Rossia* (March 13, 1988) by Nina Andreieva, a Leningrad professor, full of strong attacks against liberals, sent trembles through almost all admirers of glasnost, who were then immediately forced to reconcile the idea of their defeat without trying to protest (about the reaction of the intelligentsia to Andreieva's letter, see Strelianyi 1988a, p. 3; see also Sheinis 1989; *MN*, June 12, 1988).

Even at the height of glasnost, Soviet intellectuals (along with the rest of the population) remained unconvinced that the new liberalism was irreversible or that the old times of repressions could not come back (about the fears of intellectuals in this period, see Vasilieva 1988).

Even those with strong convictions regarding the incompatibility of despotism on the one hand and creativity in the social sciences, the humanities, literature, and ultimately also in the natural sciences on the other hand, must acknowledge that, in some cases, intellectuals can work rather productively under mild (and sometimes even harsh) despotic regimes. There are several explanations for an enlightened, "soft" dictator coexisting with creative intellectuals: the ruler's yearning for the role of Maecenas, as well as for the public prestige that intellectuals can bring his regime; the political neutrality of some intellectual works; the tendency for some of these works to be morally and politically profitable for the dominant ideology; and so on.

Several examples of peaceful coexistence between a dictator and the intelligentsia can be found throughout history, including that of the USSR. During Brezhnev's period, for example, a number of authors (such as Trifonov, Astafiev, and Rasputin) published excellent novels. Likewise, film directors (such as Riazanov, Balaian, and several others) produced numerous good movies, and a few theater directors (like Liubimov and Efros) staged brilliant spectacles. Moreover, in order to outsmart censors during periods of mild repressions, authors are often forced to improve the sophistication and refinement of their works, sometimes making them better than novels or movies produced in free societies. In addition, the public is far more involved in reading great classic works and reflecting on "eternal issues" during periods of mild repression than during times of comparative freedom. Despite these benefits, however, there is little doubt that the balance of despotism, including that of Brezhnev's time, has extremely negative effects on culture.

MESMERIZATION WITH POWER

The fear of power, and the quest for the protection afforded by power, frequently diminish the critical skills of intellectuals, who begin to find nonexistent merits in the power holders. The sophistry of these intellectuals then helps them to rationalize their groveling before power much better than ordinary people are able to. The intellectuals' idolization of power holders reaches its peak when those in power also pretend to possess an ideology attractive to intellectuals (e.g., either Marxist or nationalistic) and extend their favor to intellectuals. This happened to almost all intellectuals upon whom Stalin bestowed his benign attention.

The memoirs of Simonov, written on the eve of his death in 1979 and which were not to be published in the foreseeable future, are remarkable as an illustration of this phenomenon. Published in 1988, these memoirs demonstrate how the critical faculties of this talented writer and rather kind person were paralyzed when evaluating even the most heinous deeds of his great protector. Simonov always found some rational excuse or even endorsement for Stalin's actions—from the cruel anti-Semitic campaign of the late 1940s to the arbitrary control of literature and arts (Simonov 1988; about Simonov's memoirs, see Batkin 1989b, and Shlapentokh 1989b).

Of course, Simonov, a mediocre author, was not the only writer to produce such works. In the early 1930s, Pasternak, a genius of Russian literature, published a letter of condolence in connection with the death of Stalin's wife in which he wrote "on the eve [of Nadezhda Alliluieva's death], I had been thinking deeply and persistently about Stalin as an artist for the first time. In the morning, when I read the news [about Nadezhda's death], I was as shocked as if I myself had been present there and saw everything."

Such words about a man whose despotism and cruelty was a well-known fact by this time (and was, by all accounts, the direct cause of Nadezhda's suicide)—words which came only a year or two before Mandel'shtam's famous and unforgiving poem on Stalin—could hardly be interpreted as motivated by anything but admiration (mixed, of course, with fear) of the strong ruler (see Sarnov 1989a, p. 167).

Even more horrible was the behavior of Tvardovski, a future leader of Soviet liberal intellectuals and the editor of *Novyi Mir*. In the early 1930s, while he was studying in Moscow, his family, peasants from Smolensk, were exiled to Sibir, where they were exposed to immeasurable suffering. As described by his brother in his documentary novel published in 1988, the family placed all their hope on Alexander. They received a letter from him which said: "Dear relatives, I am not a barbarian and not a beast. I beg you to brace up, tolerate, work. The elimination of the class of kulaks does not amount to the elimination of people, especially of children." Then, after this consolation for people on the edge of death, he added, "I cannot write you more . . . and do not write me." For several years the future poet knew nothing of his family, and during this time wrote his poem praising collectivization (Tvardovski 1988).

Commenting on this novel, Iuri Burtin, who was on the editorial board of Tvardovski's *Novyi Mir* in the 1960s and who in 1985–1988 became a leading envoy of perestroika, ascribes Tvardovski's actions not to a lack of personal courage, but to the total belief of young Alexander in revolution and the Soviet order, "which could do only saintly things." Similarly, Tvardovski had a strong conviction that collectivization was indispensable for the construction of a new society, regardless of the victims involved, even if they include one's own family (*Iu.* no. 3, 1988, pp. 30–32).

Recalling her life during the Stalin era, Lidia Ginzburg, a respected Soviet literary expert, suggested (with little plausibility) that she and her friends, such as Mandel'shtam and Pasternak, had tried to overcome their "individualism," to blend in "with the people" building a new society, and to be on the side of the dominant force. She even contended that Pasternak was upset when he did not get a medal in the 1930s, because without one he felt excluded from "society" (Ginzburg 1988).

Fascination with power remains during periods of liberalization, although there is a significant reduction in the number of intellectuals for whom proximity to supreme power is the highest goal. As will be shown later, the adulation accorded Gorbachev by liberal intellectuals was due not only to his program of reforms, but also to his unprecedented inclination to extend the aura of power to genuine intellectuals and to be on good personal terms with many of them, including regular meetings and calling their homes.

In 1989 the philosopher Tolstykh, referring to the intellectuals of perestroika, wrote that in the Soviet Union "the skill to love superiors is developed and venerated as in no other country." He admonished the intellectuals to "keep their distance" from power and not to "compromise their freedom and autonomy" (*SK*, May 22, 1989).

PROFESSIONAL WORK IN THE LIVES OF INTELLECTUALS: CREATIVITY AND WORK SATISFACTION

Personal identification with one's work, particularly among professionals, is one of the most important characteristics of modern society. The willingness of individuals to change their occupation represents the opposite of this identification. People's attitudes range from complete identification with their occupations to complete indifference and readiness to change jobs. The degree of identification is determined by two factors: the external rewards for work (income, power, and prestige), and the internal rewards (diversity and opportunities for self-actualization).

Data from both the Soviet Union and the United States clearly suggest that work satisfaction increases with the complexity of the tasks involved. Since there is a high correlation between the complexity of work and the education of those who perform it, it is not surprising that there is also a high correlation between education and work satisfaction. On the basis of different studies in the Soviet Union conducted over the last three decades, it appears that the proportion of satisfied workers in different groups is roughly as follows: among manual workers, 25–50 percent satisfied; among engineers, 40–60 percent satisfied; among scholars, 50–80 percent satisfied (Aitov 1983; Iadov 1979; Iadov et al. 1967; Kelle et al. 1978; Kugel and Nikandrov 1971; Natalushko 1981; Shcherbakov 1975). Data from the United States show the same relationship: the more complicated and creative the job, the larger the proportion of those who are satisfied with it (Andrisani et al. 1977; Campbell et al. 1976; Kohn 1969).

It is impossible to provide a clear answer as to why people prefer and are more likely to identify with complex and creative work than with monotonous and routine work. Certainly various factors account for this tendency, such as the degree of self-actualization, high prestige, and high incomes associated with this work.

Close identification with one's work tends to make people concerned with their occupation's place in society. This is particularly true in Soviet society, where an individual's status is almost exclusively determined by his or her job. People in all occupations want high material rewards and prestige from their jobs, but those who identify strongly with their work also want favorable conditions in pursuing their work.[7] Of course, the intellectual community is not homogeneous in its concerns about the conditions of its work. But true intellectuals who are professionally active are particularly concerned with such conditions.

A favorable political climate is necessary for any occupation, but intellectuals are particularly strongly affected by the vagaries of the Soviet political structure. Soviet circumstances have clarified the importance of the conditions necessary for intellectual work, which are often taken for granted in the West. Soviet intellectuals, particularly social scientists and figures in literature and the arts, who suffered more under the Stalinist system than did natural scientists, were deprived across seven decades of a number of conditions, including:

1. Full freedom of discussion of issues related to the social consequences of scientific research; social scientists are even deprived of the right freely to discuss professional issues;

[7] At the same time, it would be wrong to ignore the intellectuals' material demands. Their dissatisfaction with their material rewards often stems less from the unfair remuneration of their work compared to that of others, but from the discrepency between an intellectual's standard of living and the actual professional achievements, which can lead to the prosperity of mediocre but politically loyal people and to the impoverishment of the truly creative (Zinoviev 1985).

2. Freedom to publish, make movies, and organize exhibitions without censorship;
3. Free access to information, including that from foreign countries;
4. Freedom of contact with foreign colleagues, including freedom to travel abroad;
5. The right to self-government of the profession, including the right to select heads of professional organizations;
6. Freedom to select their own colleagues and graduate students.

In general, the demands of the Soviet intellectuals in the professional domain have been of a political character. They became well known from a variety of publications of Soviet emigrants and defectors in the 1970s and early 1980s (about this, see Ashkenazy 1985; Berg 1983; Neizvestnyi 1984; Polikanov 1983; Popovski 1983; Sysoiev 1983; Vishnevskaia 1984; Zinoviev 1985).

Still, the eloquence of former Soviet intellectuals about the difficulties they faced in their professional work in the USSR notwithstanding, of much greater value are the accounts of those who continue to live in the country, and whose testimony therefore cannot be suspected of resulting from bias against the society they have left. With glasnost came a torrent of articles in the Soviet press about the professional work of Soviet intellectuals in various spheres, since the October Revolution and especially in the last two decades.

Theater and film directors were the first to describe the true political conditions of their work and the merciless grip of a bureaucracy that systematically destroyed the arts and their representatives (see, for instance, the sad narration of Andrei Smirnov, a famous film director who ultimately was forced to abandon his professional career, in *Nedelia*, no. 7, 1986, p. 17; see also the articles of famous theater directors Tovstonogov, Zakharov, Efremov, and others in *SK*, January 16, 1986; *LG*, December 25, 1985; *Ned.*, no. 3, 1985, p. 39; *P.*, September 5, 1985). Subsequently, other groups of intellectuals (e.g., writers, historians, sociologists, biologists, chemists, and others) joined film and theater people in disclosing their experiences in dealing with the bureaucracy.

In light of the information provided by glasnost regarding the lives of Soviet intellectuals, the works of the so-called revisionist school of American historians and political scientists (which tried to portray Soviet intellectuals' lives as "normal" and similar to those of intellectuals in the West) appeared especially exotic (see, for example, Lubrano and Solomon, 1980).

Despite the many disadvantages of the Soviet system, once the period of mass repression and blind terror ended, some intellectuals, especially those working in the natural sciences and the arts, found niches that allowed them to pursue their professional activities with relatively little political collaboration with the authorities. Of course, this required innumerable compromises, both great and small, and came at the price of the intellectuals' silent endorsement of all the injustices committed by the authorities against their colleagues, friends, and others.[8]

For most intellectuals, the Soviet political and, to a considerable degree, economic order engenders various obstacles to creative activity, even if the intellectuals are able to adjust to the conditions. However, there is also a sizable group of intellectuals, mostly belonging to the bogus group, who have linked their fate completely to the Soviet system and who draw all of their privileges from exactly those features of the system that outrage the rest of the intellectual community.

It is important to mention that this group of intellectuals, who are heartily devoted to the system, can be divided into several types. They include those social scientists who gain their bread from ideological work and even from purely propagandistic work; those natural scientists who prefer administrative activity to research; and those mediocre and talentless people who find themselves in the sphere of intellectual activity and for whom the possibility of compensating for their lack of professional skills through political servility is a real bonanza.

To some degree, it is possible to say that these intellectuals actually constitute a part of the dominant class and are willing to cooperate openly with the KGB. For example, the philosopher Elena Modrzhinskaia, the historians Tukan and Rzheshevski, and Timur Timofeiev, the director of the Institute of Labor Relations, all participated as experts for the KGB in the 1979 trial of Valeri Abramkin, the editor of *Poiski* (*Poiski* 3, 1981, p. 239). Similarly, Mikhail Shatrov disclosed in 1988 that Anatoli Egorov, a member of the Academy of Sciences and an expert on esthetics, had sent a letter to KGB chairman Iuri Andropov in 1981, insinuating that Shatrov's plays should not be allowed to be staged, due to their anti-Soviet nature (*NS*, no. 5, 1989, p. 157).

It is difficult to establish the size of this group, and it is evident that its growth is an excellent indicator of the decline in the nation's creative po-

---

[8] In recent years, a number of Soviet intellectuals from these spheres have published their memoirs (see, e.g., the musician Sats 1984; actors Mironova and Menaker 1984; theater director Obraztsov 1987; singers Shul'zhenko 1985 and Zykina 1985).

Some prominent natural scientists with relatively comfortable lives had their biographies written by official authors. See, for instance, the biography of the physicist Piotr Kapitsa (Naumova 1984), the memoirs about physicists Boris Konstantinov (Sumbaiev 1985), Igor Kurchatov (Grinberg and Frenkel' 1984), Igor Tamm (Moroz 1984), and Budker (Skrinski 1988), and neurologist Nikolai Grashchenkov (Vein and Vlasov 1985). Even many good Soviet writers were able, in their memoirs and articles, truthfully to describe their lives as being full of pleasant developments (see Kaverin 1985; Panova 1975). (About Chukovski and Shklovski; see Rubinstein 1983).

tential. By all accounts, just such a tendency appeared in the 1970s, when an increasing number of writers and scholars abandoned their truly creative work to join the army of quasi-intellectuals.

THE MORAL MODELS

Being well aware of their high level of education and creative capacity, intellectuals hold elitist attitudes toward others, although in most cases they try to hide them. The elitism of the intellectuals is not, however, directed so much against the masses, but rather toward the ruling class, which is quite often perceived as incompetent and selfish. In addition, by opposing themselves to the ruling class, the intellectuals see themselves as spokespersons for ordinary people. In nondemocratic societies, intellectuals are often the only force capable of becoming, for better or worse, critics of the current social and political order, sources of objective information on both internal and external developments, and defenders of oppressed and humiliated people. (About the same role of intellectuals in the United States, see Hofstadter 1963; see also Hughes 1988; about the same role of intellectuals in India see Jha 1977.)

During the Stalin era, intellectuals in Russia were practically the only vessel carrying from one generation to another the spirit of moral resistance to power, the determination to preserve moral integrity, and the devotion to truth. Of course, many people from all walks of life acted similarly. However, only intellectuals, because of their prominence in social life and their ability to convey their ideas, could make their courage and honesty a part of the cultural heritage, despite the many difficulties and dangers.

Few people maintained a sober view of the developments in Stalin's times. Akhmatova was one of them. Through this period, she and a few others retained the true feeling of the horror of the 1930s and 1940s, through her "Requiem" and other poems. As Anatoli Iakobson said in a poem devoted to Akhmatova, "In this time Russia, at God's request, grew fond of a soul which had to be hid and saved from corruption" (see Chukovskaia 1980, p. 614). In her turn, Akhmatova remembers in her diary, first published in 1987, that Mandel'shtam publicly declared from his exile in Voronezh, "I do not renounce either those who live nor those who are dead." And she added, "This should not be forgotten." She also mentioned that Mandel'shtam's depositions after his arrest were impeccable, and lamented, "How few of our contemporaries can say, alas, the same about themselves" (Akhmatova 1987, pp. 73–74).

Pasternak set another example of moral courage. He was the only writer who refused to sign a letter approving the death sentences of Soviet generals in 1937, despite numerous threats (about this episode, see Kaverin 1987, p. 113). In addition, he regularly sent parcels of food to his friends incarcerated in the gulag, a feat that was beyond imagination at that time (Voznesenski 1988c, p. 6).

Andrei Platonov also belongs in the intellectuals' pantheon of heroes. From the mid-1920s on, he wrote novel after novel, all of which were rejected by publishers as anti-Soviet. (In the age of glasnost they were published and were praised as honest masterpieces and as deeply insightful into the Soviet reality.) Despite the constant rejections, he stuck to his vocation and died in misery (about him, see Borisova 1988, p. 4).

Now, in the late 1980s, with the gradual exploration of the past, new names of intellectuals who risked their lives to preserve their integrity and high morals have come into the light. Among these are the famous sculptor Vera Mukhina (about her, see Rekemchuk's story in *SK*, August 6, 1988), Grossman (Taratuta 1987, p. 23) and a few others. Other events bear witness to the courageous deeds of some intellectuals. Veniamin Kaverin, the famous writer, can truly be proud to say that he never mentioned Stalin's name in any of his works, despite the fact that he was quite a prolific author in the 1930s and 1940s (Kaverin 1988, p. 5).

Soviet intellectuals, with the support of the mass intelligentsia, have been the leading force in opposing the Soviet political elite during the whole post-Stalin period, up to 1985. The sense of the Soviet intelligentsia's special role as defenders of human dignity and ideals was very strong in the 1960s and early 1970s. When Boris Slutski exclaimed, in a poem published after his death, that "to be the intellectual of the USSR means to choose a difficult lot," he reflected the spirit of the times, a spirit that changed significantly in the next decade (Slutski 1987, p. 78).

In order to assess the involvement of Soviet intellectuals in the political process, Liudmila Alexeieva and Valeri Chalidze carefully analyzed data regarding demonstrations and meetings of an oppositional character in the period from 1956 to 1983. Of 403 such events, 33 percent consisted entirely of educated people. If one also includes students, this figure rises to 44 percent. At the same time, the intelligentsia participated in demonstrations and meetings with a "mixed" composition, comprising 29 percent of all meetings. Thus, the intelligentsia was present at 73 percent of all oppositional actions. By contrast, only 11 percent of the activities exclusively involved workers, and the figure drops to only 7 percent for peasants.

The intelligentsia's leading role in the political opposition prior to Gorbachev's regime was also reflected in the main goals of these various protest actions. Sixty-four percent of the actions were devoted to the defense of human rights and related issues, and 29 percent of the actions were related to nationalistic issues, which are actively supported by the intelligentsia. By comparison, economic demands inspired people to risk oppositional activity in only one percent of the cases (Alexeieva and Chalidze 1985, pp. 142, 145; see also *Kontinent*, no. 40, 1984, pp. 392–393).

During the 1970s, a period of political reaction, a severe, if largely unsuccessful, campaign was launched against dissidents and the liberal movement, particularly during the latter half of the decade. During this period it was Soviet intellectuals, albeit in smaller numbers than had earlier been the case, that ensured the continuity of resistance against the leadership. Some intellectuals had joined the liberal and democratic movements in the 1960s, assuming that, under the new circumstances, they would not face serious consequences, and that, in fact, they might acquire new prestige or even promotions from political leaders who supported liberal causes. By the 1970s, however, it was clear to all that a price would be paid for dissident and liberal activity. Still, large numbers of intellectuals not only continued confronting the authorities, but also joined the democratic movement for the first time. Included in this group were such individuals as Anatoli Koriagin, Viktor Nekipelov, Tatiana Velikanova, Gleb Iakunin, and Raisa Lert.

Although the number of intellectuals who challenged existing power structures in the 1970s was not great, the "social resonance" of the intellectuals' activities was often tremendous, generating chain reactions with diverse consequences. Having examined Soviet political life in the 1970s, Gudkov, Levada, and their coauthors wrote in 1988: "It is difficult not to admire that in the hardest times, in the atmosphere of humiliation and pinches, the people of high culture decently served the ideals of truth, continued the traditions of our intelligentsia, creating rational, good, eternal things" (Gudkov et al. 1988, p. 81).

More important is what Anatoli Marchenko wrote in his last book, *Live As Everybody*, about the Soviet intelligentsia. Marchenko, a martyr of the Soviet dissident movement and worker in his professional life, said: "I am now convinced that not a small group, not single outstanding individuals, but the whole stratum makes the opposition to official ideology, the regime on the whole, and the double thinking, spread in our country. This stratum is, in my opinion, the best part of our intelligentsia" (see *NRS*, April 29, 1988).

Two methodological considerations must be weighed when assessing the figures describing the intellectuals' martyrdom. First, one must consider the proportion of intellectuals willing to take certain personal risks in the interest of the masses, as well as the proportion of other social groups who take similar risks. Soviet data suggest that intellectuals, relative to their total numbers, were the most active segment of the population in this area prior to the late 1980s.[9] Second, it is important to rec-

---

[9] In discussing the intellectual community's moral support of resistant activity, the ex-

ognize that the minority of the intellectuals who take such political risks were only able to do so because of the moral support they received from the intellectual community as a whole. The majority of intellectuals supported, either openly or secretly, the actions of individuals like Sakharov and Orlov and, depending on the circumstances, revealed this support in one way or another.

The assertion that intellectuals, even if only a few, are more likely to sacrifice their individual interests to those of society, is not meant to suggest that the moral potential of the intellectual community is fixed and

---

ample of Czechoslovak intellectuals comes to mind, since they became the principal victims of the Czech invasion and Husak's policies. Almost all the participants in the events of 1968 were prevented from continuing their professional work and were forced to accept manual work. In addition, they knew that their children would be prohibited from attending a university. For most of them, these consequences were not unexpected. They knew approximately what would occur if the Soviets decided to interfere in the liberalization process. Still, many intellectuals continued to defend their ideals even after the invasion, fully aware of the implications of their actions. Between 1970 and 1975 over five thousand intellectuals who actively voiced their own scientific or political opinions were imprisoned, receiving average sentences of three and a half years (Hruby 1980, p. 149). Even in 1977 a number of Czech intellectuals, including Milan Huble, Jan Zesar, and Zdenêk Mlynar, signed the famous Charter 77, for which they were harassed by the authorities. Having observed the crackdown on Czech intellectuals after the 1968 invasion, Louis Aragon referred to it as the "Biafra of the spirit," while another writer called it "intellectual genocide." Tens of thousands of writers, journalists, teachers, social and natural scientists were expelled from the party and lost their professional positions. Many were compelled to work as unskilled laborers, while others were not allowed to take any job at all and were threatened with starvation. Research institutes and universities were closed, and their faculties were forced to work at street cleaning, sewage disposal, and window washing (Hruby 1980).

The peaceful revolution in Prague in the fall of 1989 provided the Czech intellectuals (as well as the students) with a long-overdue reward for their decisive role in the country's twenty-two-year struggle for democracy. Vaclav Havel, a writer who spent several years in prison and who refused to emigrate from the country, became president and began guiding his country through its new era. During 1989, as the Stalinist system cracked throughout Eastern Europe, there was no other socialist country in which the intellectuals' contribution to the process of democratization was as high as that in Czechoslovakia. (Of course, the Czechoslovakian intellectuals who had been forced to collaborate with the regime since the invasion greeted the radical shift in history with mixed feelings, including fear of rebuke and even contempt from their braver colleagues.)

Polish intellectuals have also been an important force in the struggle for the democratization of society throughout the entire post-Stalin era. The working class, by contrast, has tended to arise more sporadically and for briefer periods. Polish intellectuals not only joined Solidarity but continued the resistance against Jaruselski long after the military coup of 1981, including the boycott of television, radio, and official newspapers and magazines.

Whatever one may think of the activity of U.S. intellectuals in the 1930s and 1960s, it is clear that much of this activity exposed them to risks, if on a different scale than their East European counterparts, a fact completely ignored by Paul Hollander (1981). The "Red Scare" of the early 1920s and early 1950s showed that the United States was not immune to the repression of those seeking to raise dissenting voices and engage in dissident activity.

unchangeable. In fact, this potential is altered by the influence of various circumstances and depends on the reproduction of models of moral behavior. The more intellectuals reveal themselves as committed to resistance against the authorities in defense of the people, the higher the probability that each subsequent generation of intellectuals will follow their example. Similarly, the capitulation of the intellectual community to the power of the leadership will lead to the demoralization of each subsequent group.

The demoralization of the intellectuals during Stalin's times had a tremendous effect on their behavior after 1953, leaving the seeds of fear in their souls for many decades to come and motivating many of them to commit dishonest acts even when there was no actual threat to their lives. With Khrushchev's thaw, intellectuals began restoring their moral potential, gradually increasing their moral requirements of one another. In the 1960s the Russian intelligentsia began to adopt the norms of their prerevolutionary counterparts, even if the majority still dared not challenge the authorities.

This process was broken in the 1970s, not by actual or feared repression, but by corruption. Evtushenko recalls an incident typical of this period: a dynamic young writer with a liberal reputation had just become a boss in the Writer's Union. The young writer came to Evtushenko and offered him a deal: Evtushenko would receive support if he would simply promise to vote against dissident writers at the request of the authorities—authorities who, in the words of the ambitious young man, "knew better than we who is guilty and who not" (Evtushenko 1988).

The demoralization of this period was so profound that even in 1985 and 1986 many intellectuals lacked the courage to join the General Secretary in his crusade for the liberalization of society. (About the low morale of Soviet intellectuals in the 1960s and 1970s, see Levada and Sheinis 1988a, p. 9.)

INTELLECTUALS AS THE MOUTHPIECE OF THE PEOPLE AND OF THE MASS MEDIA

The political role of the intellectuals as spokespersons of the masses is proportional to the degree of freedom in the country. A more restricted media and fewer opportunities for unofficial associations and gatherings increase the importance of intellectual activism, since the masses have fewer opportunities to speak publicly for themselves. For this reason, it may be argued that intellectuals in societies where the press is more open are less likely to view themselves as the voices of the people. Thus, in nondemocratic countries, intellectuals tend to function as substitutes for an open press. Of course, they can function as the public's one objective source of information only under a moderately repressive regime. During the Stalin era, intellectuals either maintained total silence or participated in official ideological and propagandistic work. By contrast, the intellectuals' role as an information source for the public was probably most important in the Khrushchev and Brezhnev eras. During these periods, people culled pieces of information about the state of society and the popular mood not from mass media but from poems, novels, plays, movies, those rare sociological publications that contained objective data, and from the speeches of intellectuals at various gatherings. As soon as restrictions over the mass media are relaxed, the intellectuals' role as providers of information for people immediately declines.

Developments in 1985–1988 clearly confirm this thesis. With Gorbachev's glasnost, the Soviet mass media achieved a degree of freedom unparalleled in Soviet history. Professional journalists became leaders in critical activities, surpassing other categories of intellectuals who had been the leaders of such activities in the 1960s (e.g., writers, poets, film directors, scholars, and especially sociologists).

Another development, however, was even more important. Again, for the first time in Soviet history, ordinary people secured both the right and the opportunity to express their true feelings and opinions in the mass media. Letters to the editor, as well as articles written by ordinary people, emerged as the most challenging and exciting parts of Soviet periodicals, competing in their influence on public opinion with publications from the most prominent intellectuals.

The atmosphere of glasnost encouraged a number of self-made philosophers, economists, and historians, who, with the originality of their approaches to social issues, easily competed with professionals. One of these was biologist Sergei Andreiev, who published an essay on Soviet bureaucracy (Andreiev 1988; see also Andreiev's article in *Neva*, no. 1, 1989). Another was Nikolai Travkin, a builder who rose to prominence as a leading liberal politician in 1990 (*AF*, March 2, 1990).

The decline in the political role of the intellectuals as an oppositional force in the latter 1980s is also related to the outburst of the youth movement. In the 1960s, the Soviet youth, unlike their peers in the West and even in socialist countries such as Poland or Yugoslavia, were almost totally passive and made no attempt to assist their professors in liberal activity, not to mention assisting the dissidents. By contrast, from 1986 to 1989, Soviet young people became the most dynamic political force in the country, creating thousands of so-called informal associations in support of various unorthodox political ideas, often leaving the most energetic of intellectuals in the dust.

CONCLUSION

No other group in Soviet society experiences value conflicts as profound as those of the genuine intellectuals. Their higher level of education and creative activity further their yearnings for material comfort, prestige, and power. At the same time, however, they are more absorbed than are other people with their professional lives and with their desire to defend the masses, even at the risk of being persecuted by the authorities. Conflicts between the values espoused by Soviet intellectuals underlie their contradictory behavior and explain their vacillation between courageously challenging the state and capitulating before it.

CHAPTER THREE

The Intellectuals' Subculture: A Quest

THE EXISTENCE of the intellectuals as a distinct social group is manifest most clearly in their life-style. At the same time, however, the intellectuals' life-style is not entirely distinct and separate from that of other groups in the Soviet population; there are particularly strong commonalities between the creative intelligentsia and the mass intelligentsia. The differences in life-style between, say, a prominent novelist and an unknown engineer may be minimal and may reflect only differences in income and access to deficit goods and services. For the most part, the subcultures of the intellectuals and the mass intelligentsia are similar, and the differences are more quantitative than qualitative.

Because of the myriad restrictions facing Soviet intellectuals and professionals in their working lives, creative leisure-time activities are a primary interest for many of them. Vladimir Iadov's study of Leningrad engineers found that 62 percent were oriented toward intellectual and creative pursuits in their free time, and a substantial percentage indicated that leisure time was the most valued part of their day (Iadov 1979, p. 60). As restrictions at work became more numerous and cumbersome during the political reaction of the 1970s, the role of creative activity during leisure time assumed greater importance.

Intellectuals are not exempt from the influence of mass culture and, in this respect, they share some commonalities with the masses, including workers. Data from the USSR suggest that the role of newspapers and radio in the lives of the Soviet people is not related to social status and educational attainment. In terms of newspaper reading and radio listening, only those with the very lowest levels of education differ markedly from the rest of the population (Shlapentokh 1975, p. 28).

Many products of Soviet mass culture attract the interest of broad segments of the population, either by including something for each distinct group or by focusing on a topic of wide appeal. An early 1970s television series, "The Seventeen Moments of Spring" (after Iulian Semenov's script), attracted a wide audience. To hold the intelligentsia's interest it featured weakly disguised parallels between the Nazi and Stalinist political machines, and for the masses, the series provided an exciting espionage story, with a Soviet "James Bond" infiltrating Hitler's centers of power. The bardic poet Vysotski succeeded in attracting a following from all segments of society with his artistic statements on hypocrisy, dishonesty, and arbitrariness in Soviet society.

Yet, despite interclass similarities and the rapid growth of education among the working class and peasants, the gap between the life-style of the intellectuals and that of the rest of society remains great. The principal differences separating the two are found in "spiritual life," interests in the humanities, and the use of leisure time. Although obvious differences exist in material living standards and interpersonal and intrafamilial relations, these distinctions are less clear than are those in the area of leisure activity. In addition, the growth of glasnost in 1985–1988 had a noticeable impact on the intellectual subculture, making it even more distinct from Soviet mass culture in many ways.

The specific culture of the intellectuals helps one understand both the intelligentsia's enthusiastic support of Gorbachev's innovations in 1985–1988 and the workers' ambivalent attitudes toward the same changes. Glasnost clearly addresses the intellectuals' deep interests in culture, products of high quality, objectivity, and free discussion. By contrast, those with less education are more interested in radical progress in material life, something Gorbachev's regime has failed to achieve. A worker from Kiev summarized the resulting sentiments, saying "And what does perestroika mean? The intelligentsia obtained the right to prattle to their hearts' content. However, in the life of our enterprise nothing has changed" (*Sovietskaia Kul'tura*, June 7, 1988).

THE SPIRITUAL INTERESTS OF INTELLECTUALS: HIGH APPRECIATION OF ORIGINALITY AND COMPLEXITY

Several factors contribute to the distinctiveness of the intellectual subculture. Intellectuals are attracted to a segment of the "cultural products" market which, to varying degrees, overlaps that of "mass culture" but is also more oriented toward "high culture." It is safe to assume that intellectuals, whatever their profession, are interested in the humanities, particularly classic literature, history, philosophy, and the arts (i.e., classical music, painting, and sculpture).

Soviet intellectuals are virtually obsessed with originality and innovation in literature and the arts—far more so than are other social groups. In most cases, the intellectuals' assessment of the value of any product of human activity depends on its novelty and uniqueness. This criterion of originality occupies a primary role in the professional activity of genuine Soviet intellectuals, and extends to their evaluations of all spheres of social life.

The element of originality in a literary work is so important to Soviet intellectuals that a unique approach may itself be sufficient to attract a wide audience. Thus, modernistic art in the USSR, while generating hostility among the bureaucracy and the masses, sparks great interest among the creative intelligentsia. It was scholars who sheltered abstract paintings in the 1960s and the 1970s when they were considered illicit by the authorities, and the intellectuals have been consistent supporters of the bardic poets, experimental theater, and other innovative areas in cultural life. The masses, on the other hand, have tended to be united with the political elite in their opposition to radical developments in the literary or art world.

In addition to originality, intellectuals are also attracted by complexity. They are drawn to complicated works that stimulate and challenge the mind, and they maintain that only intricate and puzzling works of literature or art yield satisfaction. Thus, film directors such as Federico Fellini or Michel A. Antonioni from the West and Andrei Tarkovski from the Soviet Union became extremely popular among the intellectuals, while attracting no following among the masses.

Studies of newspaper readers in the late 1960s examined how films of varying sophistication and complexity attracted different audiences. Readers were asked to rank films with obscure and challenging messages as well as films with less sophisticated messages. *Trud* readers, the majority of whom had not completed their secondary education, ranked the "complex" films in eighth place out of twelve. *Izvestia* readers, half of whom had completed their higher education, ranked these films in third place (Shlapentokh 1969a, p. 61).

The same pattern is found in reference to the "difficult" poets, such as Mandel'shtam, Akhmatova, Pasternak, and Tsvetaieva, who attract a wide following among intellectuals but are viewed with indifference by the masses. When these poets were rediscovered in the late 1960s, after years of oblivion, they were among *Literaturnaia Gazeta* readers' twenty most popular poetic writers but were largely ignored by readers of *Trud*. Similarly, classical music, and especially modern classical music, has few admirers among the less educated and attracts its audiences from among intellectuals.

Coding and Decoding Works of Literature or Art

Part of the Soviet intellectuals' attraction to complexity in culture stems from the relationship between complexity and the use of culture to convey political and social messages. Works that challenge the political ideology must do so in subtle and intricate ways. Because of the barriers to creative expression inherent in censorship, writers and film directors are compelled to "code" their work with various allusions, associations, and hints. Thus any high-quality literary or artistic work is to some degree allegorical and requires special "decoding" efforts.

For example, in 1960 Voznesenski was able to publish a poem dedicated to the recently deceased Pasternak only by pretending that it was devoted to Lev Tolstoy, a trick understood at the time only by the Moscow literary circle. It was explained to the general public almost three decades later, in Voznesenski's article in the period of glasnost (Voznesenski 1988a). A number of Soviet writers and film directors have gained notoriety for their ability to encode in their works various messages addressed to educated audiences. Fazil Iskander was the most popular author of the 1960s and 1970s to use parables and allegories (Iskander 1983, 1988). Authors of historical novels, such as Iuri Vl. Davydov (1970) and Iuri Trifonov (1973), also used their works as vehicles for conveying secret encoded messages about Soviet society.

The tendency of Soviet authors to send coded messages to the intelligentsia led to the emergence of a new genre in the 1960s: science fiction loaded from beginning to end with parallels between Soviet society and societies functioning on remote planets. The recognized champions of this genre were Arkadi and Boris Strugatskie, two brothers whose novels, such as *It Is Difficult to Be God* (1964) and *Snail on the Slope* (1966–1968), were considered brave, albeit hidden, broadsides against the regime.

Film director Tarkovski was particularly skilled at such encoding, and his films, such as *Andrei Rubliev*, *Mirror*, and *Soliaris*, aroused considerable debate as viewers sought to interpret the hidden messages. (In 1975 Batkin spent two hours at a special seminar analyzing *Mirror* and explaining all its metaphors. He published this analysis in 1988; see *Iskusstvo Kino*, November 1988.) Other directors have produced films that yielded highly disparate interpretations. Gleb Panfilov's *I Ask the Floor*, which concerned the life of a female mayor in a Soviet city, was such a film. Some viewers saw the work as a trivial apology for Soviet officials, while others viewed it as a scathing attack on them.

Soviet theater directors and playwrights also preferred productions filled with subtle allusions and symbolism to those that were forthright. The Theater on Taganka, directed by Iuri Liubimov in the 1960s and 1970s, became particularly well known for the metaphoric nature of its productions. Following Liubimov's lead, other theaters in Moscow and Leningrad presented subtle allegorical works to attract audiences of intellectuals.

Plays based on historical subjects were regularly used to deliver hidden messages, as were modern reinterpretations of old classics. The Theater Sovremennik (The Contemporary) in Moscow achieved great success in the 1960s with its historical trilogy on the history of Russian revolutionaries: the Decembrists, the Populists, and the Bolsheviks. Each segment contained numerous allusions to the present and inspired active debate among the intelligentsia. During the same period, the Vakhtangov Theater staged Leonid Zorin's *Dion*, about a poet in the Roman empire, with various parallels to modern society. Classical works from such figures as Anton Chekhov, Mikhail Saltykqv-Shchedrin, Nikolai Gogol, and Alexander Ostrovski, after being given a modern interpretation, were also used (especially by the Theater Sovremennik) to stimulate thought on contemporary issues.

Because of the tendency toward embedding secret messages, many literary and artistic works have become virtually inaccessible to those lacking either the intellectual sophistication or the knowledge of history and politics necessary to decode them. In fact, as a result of censorship, a special symbolic language has emerged within the intellectual community, knowledge of which is needed to understand much of contemporary Soviet culture. It has become nearly impossible for those outside the Soviet intellectual scene to understand films like Tarkovski's *Mirror*, or novels like Trifonov's *The Old Man*. The coding and decoding of artistic works has become an important element of intellectual activity in the USSR and is a common topic for conversation at social gatherings.

Opposition toward Anything Officially Approved

Along with their special interest in originality and complexity, the intellectuals, much more than any other group, value critical attitudes toward reality. Critically oriented books, movies, and articles in newspapers are highly appreciated by those who see in critique the most important faculty of reason. Intellectuals were the first to hail the initial critical publications of the late 1950s and were the first to greet glasnost, primarily because it provided an outlet for the critical spirit of the people. As one author of glasnost put it, "Only critical thought is able to create real spiritual values" (*Pravda*, March 18, 1988, p. 271).

Comparisons of the readers of *Literaturnaia Gazeta* and *Trud* in the 1960s clearly illustrate this point. As has been noted, the readers of the former magazine were predominantly members of the intelligentsia, while the readership of the latter was largely made up of workers. In studies carried out in the 1960s, *Literaturnaia Gazeta* readers indicated their preferences for Simonov, Bulgakov, Solzhenitsyn, and Ehrenburg, the last three of whom were considered antagonistic to the official ideology. *Trud* readers preferred such authors as Polevoi, Mikhail Shemiakin, and Kozhevnikov, all of whom were considered loyal supporters of the Soviet system. The only figure to appear on both lists was Simonov, who, although considered liberal, was also close to the political establishment.

The most disliked authors among *Literaturnaia Gazeta* readers were individuals known to be conservative, if not Stalinist. They included Kochetov, Kozhevnikov, Babaievski, and others. Of the fourteen writers on the least favored list of *Literaturnaia Gazeta* readers, only one had a liberal reputation.

For most intellectuals, opposition to official culture also means closeness to the West; for others, opposition means the expression of nationalistic or religious themes. Interest in Western culture or in old traditions spurned by the state is revealed in many of the pursuits of the Soviet intelligentsia, including their book and film choices, their search for Western or prerevolutionary artifacts, their desire for travel to the West, and the high value they have accorded Western or old Slavic music.

It is noteworthy that the fashionable "forbidden fruits" have changed significantly throughout the course of Soviet history. While most intellectuals of the 1960s covertly read "leftist," pro-West literature, the intellectuals of the 1970s primarily read the "right," nationalist, and religious works that circulated in the underground literature. The gap between the intellectuals' and the officials' appraisals of works in literature and the arts is, of course, always changing. This gap reaches its nadir during periods of liberalization. For example, in 1962–1963 Solzhenitsyn was not only idolized by the intellectuals but was hailed by Khrushchev, and he was only one step away from receiving the highly prestigious Lenin Prize. The gap between the two types of appraisals diminished still further under Gorbachev's glasnost, when the supreme leader extended his public sympathies, or at least his respect (albeit with some reservations), to many intellectuals held in high esteem by the intelligentsia, such as Sakharov, Tatiana Zaslavskaia, Chingiz Aitmatov, and several others. Even more important during periods of liberalization has been the addition of the works of liberal authors to lists of officially supported works.

HIGH INTEREST IN FICTION AND POETRY

A characteristic feature of Soviet intellectuals is the importance of literature in their lives. The intellectuals, and the more highly educated in general, spend much more time reading fiction than do the rest of the population. Data from the early 1970s illustrate this pattern. Survey respondents were asked what types of reading they had done the day prior to the interviewers' visit. Across all categories of reading materials, including newspapers, magazines, and books, respondents with higher levels of education indicated that they were more likely to have read something in each category (Shlapentokh 1975, p. 28). Data from other studies confirm these findings (see Chubar'ian 1979; Shkaratan 1982; Solov'ieva 1978).

Still, it is less the frequency of reading that distinguishes the highly educated from those with less education than it is the nature of that which is read. Those with higher levels of education spend considerably more time reading professional literature and popular scientific literature than do the less educated. In a study conducted in Estonia, professionals spent ten times as much time reading professional literature and five times as much time on popular scientific literature than did unskilled workers. In addition, professionals spent more than twice as much time reading autobiographies (Khansen 1977, p. 71).

The more educated segments of society also displayed greater interest in poetry than did those with less education. About one fourth of professionals, but less than one tenth of unskilled workers, indicated an interest in poetry (Khansen 1977, p. 78).

The highly educated are also more demanding in their selection of literary works. The readers of *Literaturnaia Gazeta* and *Trud* differed strongly in the number of literary works indicated as dear to them. Of the twenty-five hundred respondents, *Trud* readers named almost one thousand works as being their favorites, while an equal number of *Literaturnaia Gazeta* readers named only one hundred. These figures suggest that *Literaturnaia Gazeta* readers were more selective than were *Trud* readers, who were more likely to say that the last book they read was among their favorites (Gol'denberg 1969, p. 115).

Differences in literary tastes are also revealed in data regarding attitudes of readers toward various periodicals. *Trud* readers were more likely to subscribe to popular magazines such as *Rabotnitsa* (Woman Worker) and *Zdorovie* (Health) whose articles are less challenging and are oriented toward less educated readers. *Literaturnaia Gazeta* readers were more likely to be attracted to literary magazines with sophisticated prose, poetry, and critical articles, such as *Novyi Mir* and *Internatsional'naia Literatura* (Shlapentokh 1969b).

As is evident, literature is a very important part of Soviet intellectual life. The discovery of a new book (or movie) of high quality is sufficient reason for a special telephone call or a meeting with a friend, and a new book is often the major topic of discussion at the intellectuals' social gatherings. And the mentality of Soviet intellectuals and of other educated people is replete with literary heroes, associations, and worlds created by writers from all periods, particularly from the Russian classics. It is often difficult to understand the parlance of a Soviet intellectual without knowing his or her stock of literary impressions and associations.

THEATER: THE PEAK OF INTEREST IN THE 1960s

As with any other cultural product, when addressing the attitudes of Soviet intellectuals toward the theater it is necessary to distinguish between attitudes at different levels of abstraction—for example, attitudes toward theater in general, toward the Soviet theater in particular, and toward the specific theater accessible to the intellectuals.

In general, the importance accorded the theater by the Soviet population increases with the level of education, although age is probably even more important an influence in the determination of theater attendance. For example, a study of residents of Kurgan, a city in western Siberia, found that 70 percent of those with an elementary education and 13 percent of those with a secondary education regarded the theater as an unimportant part of their lives. Among those with a higher level of education, the figure was only 8 percent (Volkov 1975; see also Sedletski 1976; Shkaratan 1982, p. 51).

With its greater interest in the theater, the intelligentsia is much more demanding of the productions it attends than is the rest of the population. When productions become hackneyed and bleak, the intelligentsia ignore the theater, as was the case with many Soviet provincial theaters in the 1970s (see Zudilova 1975, p. 167). By contrast, when the intelligentsia, and particularly the intellectuals, are able to influence theatrical producers and receive productions addressed specifically to them, as was the case immediately before and after the Revolution, the theater becomes a very important part of their lives, much more so than in the lives of the rest of the population.

This pattern was clearly revealed in the 1960s, when it became possible to create theaters oriented almost exclusively toward the intellectual community, such as Theater Sovremennik (The Contemporary), directed by Oleg Efremov, Teatr na Taganke (The Theater on Taganka), under the direction of Liubimov, and Leninski Komsomol Theater, directed by Anatoli Efros and later by Mark Zakharov (see Gershkovich 1984; Gorbanevskaia 1985; Smekhov 1988). Like the periodicals *Novyi Mir* and *Literaturnaia Gazeta*, these theaters were the strongholds of the intellectuals in the 1960s, and to some degree in the 1970s. Attendance there became a symbol of belonging to the intellectual community. Soon, as attendance became associated with prestige, many people began to go as a sign of conspicuous consumption and were more concerned with being seen there than with the productions themselves. Despite this trend, however, these theaters demonstrated that they had distinct audiences which consisted, above all, of intellectuals.[1]

---

[1] Since the intellectual subculture is often viewed as a model by other segments of society, including the apparatchiks, both theaters became status symbols for Soviet officials. Despite the strongly liberal overtones of the productions, which the apparatchiks criticized, the apparatchiks still exploited their privileged positions and their access to tickets for each performance. In addition, they used the tickets to reward others (e.g., hairdressers, physicians, or the teachers of their children) for various services. In the mid-1970s, the director of So-

In 1985–1988, the theater's role as the mouthpiece of the intelligentsia was significantly less than had been the case in the 1960s. In 1988, however, theater in Moscow was still far more important in the lives of the intelligentsia than in New York, or even in London or Paris (see the interview with Liubimov after his trip to Moscow in 1988, *Novoye Russkoye Slovo*, July 5, 1988). In 1988 it was Ermolov's Theater, with Valeri Fokin as director, and the Leninski Komsomol' Theater, with Zakharov, which were the major carriers of liberalism in the Moscow theater. At the center of the ideological debates at this time were Shatrov's political plays, most of which featured Lenin as the main hero (Shatrov 1988).

Even more significant in the cultural life of the country than the official theaters were the numerous "informal" drama schools that mushroomed in Moscow (in 1988 were two hundred schools; the most popular among them were directed by Mark Rosovski, Oleg Tabakov, and Alexei Levinski) as well as in many provincial cities (*Literaturnaia Gazeta*, August 24, 1988).

The influence of education and occupation is even stronger with respect to attitudes toward painting and music than toward the theater. Interest in painting is almost completely restricted to intellectuals. Soviet data suggest that the educational levels of those attending exhibitions is very high, as is the case among those who attend classical music concerts.

Do You Speak English?

Knowledge of foreign languages—particularly English—is essentially a monopoly of two groups in the population, intellectuals and apparatchiks (primarily those who must interact with foreign countries on an official basis). Of course, knowledge of a foreign language is a prestigious asset for all groups in the population, and it is the dream of most parents to send their children to schools where languages are major subjects of study. Intellectuals and bureaucrats, however, tend to be more oriented toward this goal than are other groups. Of course, these groups—especially the apparatchiks—also have more opportunities to pursue the study of languages.

Knowledge of foreign languages helps intellectuals maintain contact with the West and thereby neutralizes some of the effects of mass media. It is not surprising that, during the Stalin era, those who showed great

---

vremennik told me that as many as 40 percent of the tickets had gone directly to the booking offices of the Central Committee, the Council of Ministers, and the KGB. As a result, he complained, much of the audience consisted of people far different than those the theater sought to attract. In an attempt to counteract the invasion of apparatchiks and their aides, the theater gave tickets to intellectuals "under the counter," before they were confiscated for the use of officials.

interest in foreign languages were looked upon suspiciously. Moreover, knowledge of a foreign language allows a person to read materials which, had they been translated for samizdat, would be a greater crime. It is one thing to read George Orwell's *1984* in English and another to read a samizdat translation of the book. In view of the nearly permanent flow of literature from abroad, foreign languages made it possible in the 1960s and 1970s to keep abreast of cultural developments in the West. In addition, foreign languages helped to circumvent some of the jamming of foreign radio broadcasts in Russian by permitting access to untranslated radio, and they aided communication with foreigners.[2]

HOUR-LONG CONVERSATIONS

Verbal communication plays a critical role in the intellectual subculture. In this respect, the Soviet intellectuals and intelligentsia, like their counterparts in most of Eastern Europe, differ from their counterparts in Western Europe and the United States. Russian tradition, to some degree, accounts for the tendency of the Soviet people to spend hours talking, often long into the night. This image was skillfully portrayed in Alexander Herzen's memoir, wherein he depicted the young Russian Hegelians of the 1830s and 1840s who would forget all about their everyday concerns and allow days and weeks to pass as they discussed the subtleties of German philosophy. Western visitors who find themselves in a Moscow kitchen or a gathering of intellectuals observe the tendency of the Soviet people to become absorbed in discussion (Lee 1984; Shipler 1983; Smith 1976).

While the role of tradition is important in this regard, the significance of conversation in Soviet intellectual life is predominantly due to repressions on the part of the political regime. Indeed, this factor was clearly important to the intellectuals who faced the repression of the tsar before the Revolution. It is under such repressive circumstances that one is likely to find figures such as Timofei Granovski, who was a prominent historian

---

[2] A characteristic episode from Soviet history illustrates the influence of foreign languages on Soviet cultural life. During the 1950s, the process of de-Stalinization was occurring much more rapidly in Poland than in the USSR. In an effort to reduce the gap between Polish and Western culture, Polish publishing houses and periodicals began to publish the works of authors who had previously been unknown east of the Elbe, such as Albert Camus, William Faulkner, Ernest Hemingway, Franz Kafka, and Jean-Paul Sartre. At the same time, the Polish press became substantially more diverse and colorful than its Soviet counterpart, featuring far broader and more objective coverage of the West. Given this situation, Soviet intellectuals began to study Polish so as to be equipped to read the books and news still prohibited in the USSR. Knowledge of Polish became a key indicator of interest in Western culture and information. Thousands of intellectuals quickly became subscribers to such Polish periodicals as *Polityka* and *Przekrój*.

in the mid-nineteenth century but published virtually nothing in his life-time.

Verbal communication is most important in political systems that are only moderately repressive; when repression is complete, as was the case under Stalin, the distinction between the written and spoken word vanishes. The occupants of the gulag who were imprisoned for expressing dissatisfaction with the regime were for the most part verbal, not written, critics. By contrast, in societies where the level of repression is very low, the means of communication does not matter a great deal: one can write as easily as one can speak.[3]

Intense verbal communication plays a significant role in the lives of all people in Soviet society. Among intellectuals, however, it is a particularly important value which, if it conflicts with other values, is likely to win out. Soviet intellectuals have created a virtual cult of conversation and derive great pleasure from it. Only in conversation can they reveal their true opinions and feelings. It is in the significance accorded conversation that the radical distinction between the public and private spheres is revealed, a topic which will be examined in detail in subsequent chapters.

In his novel *Intermission* (1986), Iulius Edlis describes the life of the Moscow intelligentsia through the person of his hero, Gleb Ruzhin, who spends all of his creative energy in conversation. In this way, Edlis's hero preserves for the future this extremely important element of the intellectual subculture in post-Stalinist Russia.

The importance placed by the Soviet people, especially the intelligentsia, on friendship stems largely from the role of verbal communication in their lives. The pleasure of a conversation depends on the degree of trust between the participants, and in a society where informers are assumed to be everywhere, only a friend is a dependable confidant (see Shlapentokh 1984).

The significant role of verbal communication in the intellectual subculture also accounts for the special importance of seminars and conferences in the lives of the highly educated. Once again, however, the importance of seminars and conferences fluctuates with the political atmosphere in the country, reaching maximal importance in periods when publications are still strongly censored but when the authorities do not harass people for oppositional comments in oral communication. During the liberal period of the 1960s, when conditions permitted greater freedom of publication, seminars and conferences lost some of their significance. During

---

[3] It is amusing to read, in a book devoted to the Soviet scholar Mikhail Bakhtin, that "to compensate for the scarcity of paper, which made publication difficult, intellectuals conducted much of their business in speech, a means of communication loved by Russians" (Clark and Holquist 1984).

other periods, seminars and conferences are major centers for the communication and dissemination of ideas not allowed in print.

It is therefore understandable that Soviet seminars and conferences (particularly in the 1960s, when conditions were more favorable) are much more exciting than those found in the West, especially in the United States. The atmosphere at sociology conferences tends to be highly stimulating and controversial, particularly because there are always some scholars, usually those who are younger, willing to challenge established orthodox figures with bold questions. The excitement of such interchanges and of the oral discourse in general is such that many discussions are more memorable to scholars, and even more valuable, than much that is printed in books and articles.

The case of Levada illustrates this well. Having been officially persecuted in the 1970s for his book *Lectures in Sociology* (1969), Levada was practically cut off from public activity. Yet his prestige in the intellectual community has not diminished, and on occasion he has been permitted to conduct seminars, which have immediately become major cultural events in Moscow. Although restricted in print, Levada continues to exert great influence over his colleagues.

CHANGES IN THE PERIOD OF GLASNOST

In the second half of the 1980s, liberalization significantly changed many aspects of the intellectuals' cultural life. The decoding of literary works as a special exercise almost disappeared from the intellectual life of the country. The most popular works of this period, such as Anatoli Rybakov's *Children of Arbat* or Dudintsev's *People in White Robes*, contained nothing between the lines, and, instead of resorting to associations, bluntly revealed their hostile attitudes toward Stalin and his times. Similarly, satire and anecdotes, the beloved stuff of the intelligentsia, were also victims of the first years of glasnost. Only when Gorbachev's policies started to skid and the role of mythology began to increase once again did mass media and official speech satirists like Mikhail Zhvanetski and Genadi Khazanov start to restore their popularity, which had been immense in the 1970s and early 1980s.

Liberalization also engendered declining interest in the West, its culture, and its information. Of course, the intellectuals and the intelligentsia as a whole continued to voraciously read foreign novels, which could now be found not only in the magazine *International'naia Literatura* (International Literature), but also in other "thick" literary periodicals. During this period, these periodicals published several previously prohibited works, including Orwell's *1984* and even *Animal Farm*. Still, gone was the previous fascination with foreign literature and the frenetic interest in foreign radio stations, newspapers, and weeklies. Giddy publications in the Soviet press, with their astounding revelations about Soviet life, seriously eroded interest in the West, which had previously been considered the single arena of "the real life."

Glasnost influenced Soviet verbal culture on several levels. First, intellectuals were finally able to publish ideas they had previously dared discuss only with close friends. In addition, the strong intensification of genuine political life greatly increased the number of subjects for discussion, which only served to strengthen interpersonal communications. Finally, with the drastic decline of fear, the number of people with whom any individual could discuss political matters increased significantly. Thus the scope of the Soviet intelligentsia's verbal activity certainly increased during this period.

CONCLUSION

The cultural life of the Soviet intelligentsia is radically different than that of the masses, a relatively unknown phenomenon in the United States. No group in the USSR is as absorbed with literature and the arts, appreciates originality and objectivity in cultural products, or is as interested in Western culture as is the intelligentsia. Because of this deeply rooted yearning for high culture, the Soviet intelligentsia and especially the intellectuals always greet the liberalization of Soviet-type societies with great enthusiasm.

CHAPTER FOUR

Soviet Intellectuals: Oppositional Views and Inconsistent Political Behavior

SINCE the mid-1950s, the Soviet intellectuals, whose political views clearly oppose official ideology and official domestic policy, have engaged in political activity directed against the Soviet political elite and the order that elite represents.

IDEAL AND MATERIAL FORMS OF INTELLECTUAL OPPOSITION

The oppositional activity of Soviet intellectuals is manifested in two interrelated forms: ideal (verbal) and material. Since the true intellectuals' main weapons are their intellect, creative capacities, and erudition, their primary threat to the system is through ideal, or verbal, activity: speeches, articles, movies, and verbal communications with colleagues, students, and the general public. However, since the socialist state regularly obstructs the intellectuals' oppositional cultural activity, they are forced to engage in material activities, which drastically increases the political significance of their behavior.

By engaging in material activities—such as those related to samizdat (not only writing for this "publishing house," but also participating in the duplication and dissemination of samizdat works), illicit meetings, or demonstrations—the intellectuals are able to declare their views on political issues, views they cannot disseminate through the official mass media. In this way, the intellectuals can begin to deprive the all-mighty Soviet state of its monopoly on information and on political activity in general.

With the creation of samizdat in the 1960s, as well as through educational and scientific seminars prohibited by the authorities, the intellectuals created a "second culture," which to some degree parallels the "second economy" created by people far from the intellectual stratum. Both the second culture and the second economy serve to undermine the state's monopoly in several vital spheres.

THE SOVIET PENAL CODE: CHANGING PUNISHMENT FOR POLITICAL DEEDS

The intellectuals' oppositional activities range from feeble gestures that are sometimes imperceptible to outsiders, to direct confrontation with the coercive Soviet apparatus. In the end, the measure of both an oppositional act and the degree of courage displayed by an intellectual is the level of retribution engendered by the act.

Of course, there is no automatic correlation between political crime and punishment in Soviet society. On one hand, prior to 1989 the Soviet penal code operated with a concept of "anti-Soviet propaganda" so broad that it encompassed virtually any act. Thus the political leadership, while formally observing all laws, could send an intellectual (or any other citizen) to prison or exile for the slightest political offense. On the other hand, the scope of political repression (the main element of the Soviet regime) is determined by the specific leadership at any given time, which in turn is influenced by many factors, both domestic and international. Because of these competing influences, the actual chastisement for any particular concrete political deviation is, in many cases, simply a matter of probability. People who regularly perform the same transgression receive different penalties, a circumstance that has a tremendous impact on the political behavior of intellectuals.

When pondering an intended political action (the publication of a critical article, a brave speech at a party meeting, the signing of a protest letter, or participation in an illicit gathering), Soviet intellectuals usually try to assess the possible consequences for self, friends, and family. Miscalculating the reaction of the authorities is a typical feature of Soviet life. Intellectuals most often make such mistakes at political junctures, when the political elite changes its policy toward the intellectuals. This happened at the end of the 1960s when many intellectuals joined the protest letter campaign, assuming that the Kremlin would treat this political action no more severely than it had in the past.

From 1985 to 1989, the intellectuals (as well as other Soviet people) faced a new problem—that of evaluating not only Gorbachev's regime and its chances for survival, but their own risk in supporting the regime as well, keeping in mind any possible retribution if the conservatives eventually gained the upper hand.

THE TEST OF OFFICIAL PATIENCE: THE MAIN CRITERIA

The intensity of an intellectual's opposition to the political elite is determined by a number of factors, four of which are most important: (1) the organizational background of the political act; (2) the degree of official control over the domain in which the oppositional activity takes place; (3) the involvement of the West; and (4) the object of the critique and the sphere of the oppositional activity.

The confrontational potential of any action and the contribution of each factor to this potential depend upon the specific political situation, since, as noted above, the rank of any given act on the "Soviet–anti-Soviet" scale changes drastically over time. A behavior denounced yesterday as "anti-Soviet" will be treated as "normal-Soviet" tomorrow, and vice versa (Voinovich's book, *The Anti-Soviet Soviet Union*, 1985, was devoted to, among other things, the fluidity of the criteria for what is considered "Soviet," "non-Soviet," and "anti-Soviet").

With the deepening of glasnost from 1986 to 1989, the Soviet people read on an almost daily basis newspaper articles that removed the label of "anti-Soviet" from various deeds. Still, despite fluctuations in the classification of political acts performed by intellectuals, the post-Stalin Soviet political elite has been essentially consistent in its separation of loyal and disloyal political behavior.

The Organizational Background of the Political Act

Prior to 1985, the Soviet political system was absolutely incompatible with the existence of organizations not completely under its control. Thus the degree of an intellectual's anti-Soviet behavior depended primarily on the organizational background of that behavior. Two dimensions are important here: (a) whether the intellectual acted as a single individual rather than as a member of some weak or strong organization; and (b) whether the intellectual performed the political act within the framework of the Soviet establishment rather than on his or her own initiative or through an organization created outside the Soviet system.

Despite having proclaimed collectivism a major Soviet value, the political system considers any collective action directed against superiors an aggravating factor, even if the goal of the protest is ideologically irreproachable. Because of this, almost all of the intellectuals' actions in the initial stages of the liberal movement were individualistic. When intellectuals began to create organizations in the 1960s and 1970s, however, the Soviet leadership chose to ignore international reaction (this was during the peak of detente) and moved toward total persecution of intellectuals engaged in oppositional organizational activities.

The Degree of Official Control over the Domain in Which the Oppositional Activity Takes Place

Just as the Soviet leadership in the 1960s and the 1970s was more tolerant toward individual than collective critique, it also distinguished between actions of individual intellectuals, depending on the backdrop of these actions. It was one thing for an intellectual to use an officially sponsored meeting for a critical speech or publish a courageous article in an official magazine (in these cases, the intellectual's "crime" is shared by the officials who allowed the action), but it was another thing completely if the critique was presented outside official institutions, for instance, sending a novel to samizdat or abroad.

The case of "weak" organizations needs to be discussed separately. Along with individual activity, or participation in well-defined organizations such as the Moscow Helsinki Group in 1970, there are relatively stable interactions between intellectuals that occur without leadership, formal members, or clear goals. Along with samizdat, the bard movement of the 1960s, which I will discuss later, was one example of this type of weak organization. Despite the absence of formal organizational features, these movements stimulated intensive interactions among hundreds, perhaps thousands, of people who managed to coordinate their efforts without the benefit of a central structure.

In the officials' view, however, there was a radical difference between the bard movement and the samizdat movement. The former was born and developed within officially endorsed institutions—clubs, cafés, libraries, and so on—whereas the latter emerged independent of official bodies and, from the very beginning, was not legitimized with official slogans as was the bard movement. As a result, intellectuals participating in the bard movement, even as organizers, incurred much less risk than those involved in copying and disseminating samizdat literature.

The Involvement of the West

The third factor influencing the seriousness of oppositional activity is related to contact with the West. Since the contraposition of the Soviet system to that of the West has been an essential feature of Soviet ideology and Soviet political order, any critical act of a Soviet intellectual that involved the West was regarded as much more dangerous than a purely domestic action. The intellectuals' enlisting of the West in critical activity increased gradually, if not linearly, from the late 1950s on, beginning with the Valeri Tarsis and Pasternak affairs (both men sent manuscripts to the West for publication) and eventually culminating in the 1970s in the creation of a committee to monitor the Soviet government's compliance with international agreements.

The Object of the Critique and the Sphere of the Oppositional Activity

The fourth criterion used by Soviet authorities to evaluate an action's seriousness, as well as any subsequent punishment to be meted out, is the target of an intellectual's critique. It has always been relatively excusable for an intellectual to criticize some individual flaws in Soviet life, or even some officials. This sort of critique has to be allowed (or even encouraged) by the political elite, a circumstance that usually takes place in the first years of a new regime.

Although the risk of retaliation increases when a critique is aimed at the Soviet economic system, or even worse, the social system, the most dangerous target of critique is the Soviet political order and its political institutions, such as the Politburo and its leader, the KGB, the courts, or the police. It comes as no surprise that, in the 1960s and 1970s, few intellectuals dared challenge these institutions, given the history of such challenges. In the first decade of the liberal movement, the liberal opposition shied away from these targets as much as possible.

Of course, oppositional activity reaches its peak when intellectuals not only criticize political institutions, but challenge them through their material actions as well. Such actions might include public meetings and demonstrations denouncing the KGB, the courts, and the Soviet political order in general. It was not until 1989, four years into Gorbachev's regime, that it became possible to mildly criticize the Politburo, the General Secretary, and the KGB.

LEVELS OF OPPOSITIONAL ACTIVITY: FROM LEGAL TO ILLEGAL CONFRONTATION

If we combine all four of the above criteria, it becomes possible to identify four levels of oppositional political activity that differ from one another in their intensity.

The first level, which might be labeled "mild legal critique," is comprised primarily of individual critiques of flaws in Soviet life, or even in some systemic features of Soviet society, carried out from within normal Soviet institutions (such as officially sponsored meetings, official magazines, or books published by Soviet publishing houses).

The second level, "semilegal activity" bordering on activity that could be strongly reprimanded by the state, is comprised of the activities of intellectuals in weak organizations that are under loose official control.

The third level, "mild illegal activities" outside official control, includes the participation of intellectuals in weak organizations that are completely outside official control, as well as direct individual challenges to the KGB, publication abroad, and individual contact with the West or with Western correspondents in the USSR.

The fourth level, "strong illegal activity," includes the activities of dissident organizations, as well as collective contacts with the West.

To some degree, these four levels of oppositional activities parallel stages in the development of the liberal movement when it took its first steps in the 1960s. The next chapter will discuss this development, using various concrete examples.

Throughout most of Soviet history, oppositional activity has been made up of a liberal, and in some cases (i.e., in the national republics) nationalistic, critique of the Soviet political and economic system. Only from 1986 to 1989 did opposition from the right become an important political phenomenon. Of course, the dominant regime was not equally hostile toward opposition from the left and the right, from liberals and conservatives, from Westernizers and Russophiles. In each case, the latter could always count on the understanding and compassion of those who controlled the state machine, while the former met only ire and cruelty. Still, despite the radical differences between the two types of opposition, the intellectuals share many common features as they act against the current leadership.

Conformity in Public Deeds, Opposition in Private Views

Most Soviet intellectuals and members of the intelligentsia are much more critical of the Soviet system than are the rest of the population, and a considerable number of them are strongly hostile to it. In the post-Stalin era, only a minority of educated people have accepted the Soviet political and social order without reservation and are sincerely devoted to it.

Surveys conducted in the 1960s that examined the attitudes of the most active and educated part of the Soviet population (the readers of *Pravda*, *Trud*, *Izvestia*, and *Literaturnaia Gazeta*) clearly demonstrated that, along with the intellectuals, even the mass intelligentsia on the whole was critical of the current regime. In assessing these data, it is necessary to note that, as various studies suggested, the Soviet people of the 1960s were far from being frank with interviewers and often concealed views critical of the system (see Shlapentokh 1973, 1987).

A late 1960s survey of *Literaturnaia Gazeta* readers is particularly important here. *Literaturnaia Gazeta* had, and continues to have, the most educated audience of all Soviet periodicals. In order to measure the political attitudes of readers, the following indicators were examined:

1. The readers' interest in articles about "problems of socialist democracy." In the 1960s, such an interest implied support for the liberalization of Soviet society.
2. Attitudes toward the magazines *Novyi Mir*, which, at the time, was the most authoritative voice of the liberal intelligentsia and of authors who would later become dissidents or emigrants, and *Iunost'* (Youth), the latter of which was also popular among liberals in the 1960s.
3. Attitudes toward writers critical of the system.
4. Interest in Russian literary classics either frowned upon (such as works by Dostoevsky) or even prohibited (such as works by Bunin).

Based on these indicators, members of the intellectual community were found to be consistently more critical of the regime than were any other group of readers. For example, only 2 percent of readers with an elementary education and 6 percent with a secondary education indicated they were dissatisfied with articles on the development of democracy in the Soviet Union. Among readers with scholarly degrees, the proportion was 22 percent. Only 7 percent of those with an elementary education and 9 percent of secondary school graduates were regular readers of *Novyi Mir*, while 32 percent of people with higher education and 45 percent of those with degrees indicated regular readership. Among members of the last two groups, only 6 and 5 percent, respectively, reported reading the very conservative *Oktiabr'*. *Literaturnaia Gazeta*'s highly educated audience also manifested a strong interest in Soviet writers critical of the regime. Almost all of the authors hailed by the respondents were critical toward the regime. Sixty-nine percent of the authors positively endorsed by the respondents published their works first in *Novyi Mir*.

It was remarkable that Solzhenitsyn, by 1967 already under harassment and a symbol of resistance to the system, was among the four most popular authors, especially among the intellectuals. In face-to-face interviews, almost 25 percent of the respondents directly expressed their respect for Solzhenitsyn. The popularity accorded Evtushenko, also the epitome of nonconformity, had carried strong political overtones—almost 50 percent of the respondents named him as best poet.

The readers' reactions to the question regarding the Russian classics also revealed oppositional attitudes to be positively related to education. Following Tolstoy and Chekhov, readers favored Ivan Bunin, the emigrant writer whose works the leadership had reluctantly permitted to be published in the 1960s. At the same time, the majority of writers who were supported by the authorities because they were regarded as critical of the prerevolutionary regime (such as Herzen, Goncharov, and Gorky) were much less favored (Shlapentokh 1969a, 1969b).

During the 1960s, it was possible to measure the Soviet peoples' attitudes toward the mass media fairly directly. Since in the 1960s the mass media was wholly identified with the regime, critical attitudes toward newspapers and television provided valid indicators of the peoples' stance toward the current order in general. According to data from various surveys, one third of all respondents with a higher education expressed negative attitudes toward various aspects of the central Soviet newspapers (Shlapentokh 1969a, 1969b, p. 75).

Twenty-two years later, Levada and his colleagues from the Center for Public Opinion Studies in Moscow carried out another survey of *Literaturnaia Gazeta* readers. Unfortunately, unlike the 1967 survey, the one in 1989 was not based on a random sample of readers but on a questionnaire printed in the newspaper and returned by the respondents (*Litera-turnaia Gazeta*, March 29, 1989). Despite this defect, however, the data from the survey accurately reflect the views of the Soviet intelligentsia (who make up 75 percent of the magazine's readership). These data are corroborated by those from several other surveys conducted in the country in 1987–1989, including that by Boris Grushin, which was carried out at about the same time as Levada's. Grushin and Levada used the same questionnaire, but Grushin examined a national random sample using face-to-face interviews to collect the data. With the freedom accorded by glasnost, Levada and Grushin were able to accomplish what I could not in the 1960s—that is, pose direct political questions to the Soviet people.

It is remarkable that 200,000 *Literaturnaia Gazeta* readers returned Levada's questionnaire. That figure translates into an almost 5 percent response rate, an unbelievably high percentage for a survey based on a printed questionnaire and an eloquent indicator of the political activity of the intelligentsia during a time when *Literaturnaia Gazeta* and several other periodicals were lashing out against the official ideology.

In response to the question, "What are the causes of the current diffi-culties," the respondents (who were free to endorse as many alternatives as they wished) cast most of their votes for "the arbitrariness of bureau-cracy" (63 percent), followed by "corruption, alcoholism, speculation, and pilfering" (61 percent), "technical backwardness" (56 percent), "egalitarianism and the suppression of initiative" (48 percent), and "mis-takes in the governing of the country" (42 percent). Only thirty-five re-spondents pointed toward "the decline of socialist ideals" as the cause for the country's ills.

Taken together, these figures suggest that the intelligentsia criticized the Soviet system from a primarily liberal perspective, a thesis strongly sup-ported by other data from the same survey. When asked about possible solutions to the country's crises, the highest number of respondents rec-ommended giving "peasants the right to possess land and equipment" (66 percent). Further endorsements included suggestions to "drastically cur-tail army and military expenditures" (55 percent), "give all power to local government" (34 percent), "reduce assistance to other countries" (33 per-cent), "improve planning" (33 percent), and "invite foreign capital into the country" (32 percent). It is noteworthy that 17 percent of the respon-dents named Sakharov "the hero of the year," placing him second only (but significantly) to Gorbachev (68 percent), while only 1.5 percent of the people in Grushin's national survey named Sakharov.

Equally significant are data regarding the popularity of liberal authors and emigrant writers among active readers (again, primarily those with a higher education). A survey conducted by the Institute of Books in 1988 found that 60 to 80 percent of the respondents read the works of Iskander and Okudzhava, the prominent liberals, as well as those of Solzhenitsyn, Galich, and Iosif Brodsky (*Moskovskie Novosti*, April 9, 1988). Another survey from the same Institute found that all of the twelve most popular essayists in 1988 were liberals (*MN*, March 23, 1989). The popularity of liberal authors among current Soviet readers was also confirmed in a study by the Lenin Library (*Izvestia*, January 31, 1989).

An even more eloquent indicator of the oppositional mood of the Soviet intelligentsia is the data collected during the first session of the Congress of People's Deputies in May and June 1989. This session was an immense step forward in the democratization of Soviet society, and delegates were free to speak out on almost any issue and even to criticize the General Secretary. Yet a considerable proportion of the Soviet population was dissatisfied with the views of the conservative majority in the Congress (a majority evidently controlled by the party apparatus), with the procedures of the debates, and with Gorbachev as the Congress's chairman (see the analysis of the Congress in Kliamkin, *MN*, July 2, 1989). According to Public Opinion Center data from a national random sample survey, 42 percent of the respondents with a higher education expressed negative opinions regarding the Congress, while only 18 percent of the respondents with lower levels of education voiced similar sentiments (*Argumenty i Fakty*, July 7, 1989).

The foregoing data confirm that the oppositional mood of the Soviet intelligentsia and of intellectuals in post-Stalin Russia is beyond doubt. Even those whom the Soviet leadership managed to corrupt and force into almost complete cooperation and who do their best to adjust psychologically to their everyday lives carry a deeply hidden hatred of their masters, which they reveal at the first opportunity.

Even in the stormy 1960s, however, only a minority of intellectuals took part in activity openly oppositional to the Soviet political elite or expressed their views through their behavior. The majority of the intellectuals who regarded themselves as critics, or even enemies, of the Soviet system or the regime at the time found ways to preserve their views while avoiding confrontation with the authorities. Two important features of Soviet society helped them to do this: (1) the gross distinction between private and public life in Soviet society, and (2) the mythology that allows Soviet people to pursue behavior in direct contradiction to their professed values. The discussion of these features will begin with the public life/ private life distinction.

But first we must note that both features of Soviet society help not only to vindicate intellectuals from public behavior inconsistent with their personal views, but they also allow intellectuals to preserve these views (and not simply adjust them to current official ideology and policy) during periods when they lack the mettle to defend their ideas publicly. They can wait for the times when it becomes possible for their views to be heard.

The private sphere of Soviet life is particularly important in preserving one's oppositional views. It is in this sphere where the discontent of the intellectuals brews, where the Sakharovs and Solzhenitsyns get their primary civic education, and where Gorbachev's glasnost was prepared. Public and private life can be distinguished in several ways, but perhaps the most important criterion separating these spheres is an outsider's access to information about an individual's deeds and thoughts, a criterion that is especially important for intellectuals. In fact, to a substantial degree, private life can exist virtually only within primary groups (mainly family and friends), since only these groups, with their clear boundaries, allow members to identify outsiders with whom the flow of information must be controlled. Preventing the spread of potentially dangerous information diminishes the risk of state or public intervention in the lives of group members and reduces the likelihood of official harassment.

The distinction between private and public life is significant in Western society as well, including in the United States (see Bellah et al. 1985; Benn and Gaus 1983; Moore 1984; Sennett 1977). However, the gap between the two spheres is much greater in Soviet-type societies, where the primary group and the private sector perform many functions to help people to survive and satisfy their various needs—functions that are for the most part in conflict with the system. For the intellectuals, private life first and foremost provides a forum for the free exchange of ideas and genuine feelings—an arena for venting real love and hatred and unleashing suppressed sentiments. (About private life in the USSR, see Shlapentokh 1989a.) In addition, private communications among intellectuals provide information that is otherwise unavailable and therefore play such an important role in their lives. Private networks in the intellectual community also facilitate the exchange of illegal literature, tapes, and videocassettes and assist in the organization of various semilegal and illegal private political meetings.

Still, despite the importance of preserving the integrity of private life, and of maintaining an atmosphere able to support the germ of resistance during periods of political reaction, it is the public activity of intellectuals that is of utmost importance. Each intellectual has a distinct profile reflecting his or her public and private behavior. The gap between these two spheres, as well as the character of political behavior in each, is an accurate indicator of relations between the intellectuals and political power at any given time. In addition, this gap is related to the degree of confrontation or cooperation between intellectuals and the authorities.

Political Activity: Only with Friends and Relatives

During the Stalin era, the level of repression was such that not only was unofficial public political activity impossible, but even private communications on important social and political issues were rare. In the 1930s and 1940s, even close friends often avoided discussing issues divergent from official policy.

After 1953, private communication gradually became more open. As it became clear that the mass repressions of the 1930s were over, intellectuals and other segments of the populations began to talk more freely. Following the Twentieth Party Congress in 1956, conversations between individuals opened further. Of course, even at this point, few people would openly discuss the atrocities of the Stalin era as being a natural outgrowth of the Soviet system, and conversations generally followed the officially sanctioned interpretation of the period. Even in 1962 Akhmatova refused to discuss the names of those who had provided her with underground information and angrily rebuked others who violated this rule (Chukovskaia 1980, pp. 412–413).

As each year passed without bringing increased repression, Soviet intellectuals became less restrained in their interpersonal contacts. By the early 1960s, after a decade free of Stalinist repression, the situation had changed markedly and discussions of political matters came to occupy a central place in conversations between intellectuals. The developments of this period—such as samizdat, foreign radio, tourism abroad, the "camp theme" in literature, and articles in leading magazines—all provided countless topics of discussion for gatherings at work and at home. To some degree, the level of activity suggested that people were trying to make up for the decades lost to hypocrisy and timidity under Stalin.

Salons emerged in a number of locations, providing forums for intellectuals to meet and discuss political and cultural issues. Besides Academic Town (see chapter 1), salons operated in other academic centers, at Pushchino and Chernogolovka, and in Moscow and Leningrad (for a description of these gatherings see Zinoviev 1976).

The political significance of the salons was great. They contributed to the development of political sophistication among intellectuals and facilitated the shedding of many of the political ideas inculcated as a natural part of life in the USSR. The social significance of the salons was equally important, for they encouraged people to be honest in public and to openly defend their liberal ideas. In fact, the prestige accruing to salon participants within the intellectual community rivaled that offered by official titles and ranks. It is not surprising then, as would become known later, that nearly all of these salons, particularly those in Novosibirsk, were under KGB surveillance and were frowned upon by the authorities.

Private political and cultural activity clearly reached its peak in the 1960s. In Leningrad, however, private cultural gatherings again became popular toward the end of the 1970s (Kolker 1985, p. 110).

The 1985 victory of party liberals, headed by Gorbachev, visibly influenced the character of private life in the USSR. With the most daring liberal ideas receiving official approval, private homes became centers for discussions of conservative and nationalistic programs, which could be only partially defended publicly. Vladimir Drozd, a prominent Ukranian author, wrote in 1987 of the enemies of perestroika: "They gather in the evenings, sit into the dead of night, usually in the kitchen, and fervently smoke and berate everything new which has come into our life" (Drozd 1987, p. 13).

Thus, while the main dissident figures at private gatherings in the 1960s and 1970s were those who cautiously professed democratic ideals, the dissidents of the late 1980s were conservatives and nationalists praising Stalin and preaching rabid xenophobia and anti-Semitism.

TYPES OF POLITICAL BEHAVIOR: FROM OPEN CONFRONTATION TO UNFLINCHING LOYALTY

Under "normal conditions," the gap between the private and public behavior of intellectuals in socialist society is quite large. This distance decreases only during periods of liberalization.

Various combinations of critical behavior in public and private life create different types of political behavior among intellectuals. It is possible to understand these variations theoretically by placing them on a scale of political behavior consisting of six zones.

1. Open Opposition

At one end of this scale is a "zone of open (illegal) opposition," which includes the third and fourth levels of oppositional behavior described above (mild illegal activities outside official control, and strong illegal activity). Depending on the particular historical circumstances, "open opposition" in a socialist society may include direct unauthorized contact with international public opinion, the production of unauthorized books or journals, participation in demonstrations against official policies, or the publication of prohibited material abroad. Of course, individuals who engage in such public displays of opposition will also be expected to voice their opinions on a full scale in the private realm.

In fact, all known dissidents of the 1970s, such as Sakharov, Orlov,

Vladimov, or Kopelev, were, until their exile or arrest, people who made practically no distinction between private and public spheres. Moreover, the entire human rights movement, as initiated by Alexander Esenin-Vol'pin, rejected traditional revolutionary ideas, which regarded conspiracy and secrecy as the only way to combat despotism. The human rights movement explicitly encouraged the intellectuals and the entire intelligentsia to erase the borders between public and private life and to behave in both arenas according to Soviet laws, which formally allow all political freedoms.

This point of view was clearly formulated by Larisa Bogoraz, who, in her letter to Brezhnev, declared that the repressions of writers for their professional works were "acts of arbitrariness and violence," and that she would defend this view in private conversations as well as in any open public discussion (see Kaminskaia 1984, p. 151).

2. Legal Opposition

The next point on the scale is the "zone of legal opposition," which is comprised of the first and the second levels of oppositional behavior (mild legal critique, and semi-legal behavior). As mentioned earlier, the boundary between "open (illegal) opposition" and "legal opposition" may shift, depending on the circumstances.

In the 1960s the most significant forms of legal opposition included the publication of materials with critical tendencies, dissenting speeches at meetings, seminars, conferences, and other public or nonpublic gatherings, and the signing of protest letters addressed to official bodies. During this period, the probability of official sanctions for such activities was low, and in fact, in some circumstances, it was possible to find support among high officials for such actions and actually be rewarded in some way for participation in these actions.

Legal opposition to official ideology is usually combined with some action that demonstrates apparent loyalty to the regime. This tactic is especially characteristic of periods of "thaw," when a new leadership cautiously begins to lessen political control over the intellectuals and allows them to express some of their ideas and feelings, on the condition that, at the same time, they express their devotion.

Following Stalin's death, a number of obviously oppositional intellectuals adopted such tactics. For instance, Olga Bergolts, a prominent poet, published a mélange of "patriotic poems" of rather low quality, as well as deep lyrical pieces that were clearly at odds with the spirit of official ideology (*Novyi Mir*, no. 8, 1956). Similar tactics were chosen by Ehrenburg, Kaverin, Emmanuil Kazakevich, Semion Kirsanov, Tvardovski, and other intellectuals, who, at the first opportunity, moved toward critique of the regime and its ideology.

As would be expected, those who participated in legal forms of opposition were also privately consistently critical of the leadership, a fact of great political significance given that views expressed in private also impact on public developments. Private critical activities, beyond the mere voicing of opinions, also included reading samizdat, organizing or attending a salon where political issues were regularly discussed, or creating private seminars devoted to sensitive issues.

The real opinions of intellectuals as expressed in their private communications were described by Chukovskaia in her *Notes on Anna Akhmatova* (1976, 1980). Between 1938 and 1962 Chukovskaia, the daughter of a famous Russian poet and literary critic and herself a well-known writer and one of the bravest Soviet intellectuals, maintained a diary devoted mostly to her contacts with Akhmatova, "the goddess of Russian poetry." From the two volumes of *Notes*, one gets a feeling for the intensely private lives of intellectuals in Leningrad and Moscow, lives separated from official life by a thick wall. Only KGB stooges could bridge both worlds.

In 1986–1988 the majority of the legal critique of the system came from conservatives and nationalists. A number of committed enemies of Gorbachev's programs, such as Proskurin and Anatoli Ivanov, presented themselves as supporters of perestroika, only so they could publicly voice ideas diametrically opposed to the spirit of this program, just as liberals such as Fiodor Burlatski and Len Karpinski had done in the 1960s.

3. Private Critique

The third point on the scale of political behavior is the "zone of private critique," involving patterns of behavior that combine politically loyal public activities with private critical sentiments. Thus individuals whose behavior places them in this zone must lead double lives: in public they are loyal servants of the regime, but at home they attack the regime and display undeniable scorn toward it.

The behavior of the famous writer Vera Panova was typical of this pattern. As recounted by Kiril Koscinski, a Leningrad writer who knew Panova quite well, she was "privately often straightforward and sharp" in her evaluation of the authorities. Nevertheless, although she expressed to Koscinski her sympathy for his brave social behavior, she was apparently driven by fear and voted in 1960 for his exclusion from the Writers' Union. Two years later, she did the same with Pasternak, whose poetry she adored (*Strana i Mir*, no. 6, 1985, p. 91).

In the 1970s Soviet intellectuals again returned to their kitchens to discuss political issues. Confessing how he had skirted any action in support of Sakharov, Brodsky, or Galich during these times, Alexander Ivanov, a famous writer, asked himself in 1987, "Where had I been then, what was I doing?" and answered, "I held snooks [Soviet gestures of insult] in both pockets, orated in the kitchen, was very sincere with the closest friends, but even with them only in a low voice" (Al. Ivanov 1987).

4. Indifference

The fourth area on the scale is the "zone of indifference," wherein patterns of behavior display complete conformity to official expectations in both the public and the private realm. Such behavior, however, is largely automatic. Individuals displaying indifferent behavior are personally committed neither to nor against the regime, and generally avoid discussions of sensitive issues, as much for lack of interest as for a desire to avoid trouble.

In the 1950s, and even in the 1960s, during the period of general agitation, dozens of outstanding Soviet scholars manifested no serious interest in the political life of the country. Despite numerous disclosures in the late 1980s about life in the 1960s, we know almost nothing of the political activities of such people as the physicists Landau or Gersh Budker.

5. Public Support of the Regime

The next point on the scale is the "zone of public support," comprised of patterns of behavior involving active cooperation with the authorities. Such behavior includes participating in party activities at the workplace, conforming professional work to the current ideological standards, moderately supporting the actions of authorities against colleagues, signing statements in the media in support of official decisions, and even fulfilling special assignments from the KGB or party officials.

In their private lives, individuals who engage in such behavior are much more restrained than are "legal opponents." When communicating with close friends or relatives, however (especially after a few glasses of vodka or cognac), they may divulge their true, private feelings toward the regime, and even recant their behavior, particularly that involving the betrayal of a colleague. Alexander Zinoviev (1976) vividly described this soul-searching process at Moscow drinking parties.

The period of glasnost has been the only period in Soviet history (with the exception of that during the war with Hitler) when the majority of true intellectuals were not ashamed to express their loyalty to the regime and its leader. For this reason, the years between 1985 and 1988 were, for many intellectuals, the happiest years of their lives.

6. Consistent Loyalty

The final point on the scale is the "zone of consistent loyalty," which involves activities in support of the regime in both public and private life. Unlike persons whose behavior places them in the fifth zone, consistent loyalists not only accomplish all their political and ideological assignments with zeal, they even display their own initiative in this realm. Given their political commitment, they usually go beyond even the expectations of their superiors. These individuals display no remorse for their actions, and there is seemingly nothing that will dissuade them from their support of the regime.

This devotion to the regime, however, should not lead to the assumption that all such intellectuals truly adhere to the official ideology. They may have personal differences, even major ones, with the regime. But they differ from those in the "zone of public support" because they carry their public commitment directly into their private lives, which influences their behavior with families and friends. Only in their most private moments alone with themselves will such individuals be critical of the system. Each regime relies on this group of intellectuals, especially those who are bogus intellectuals, to provide service and to praise new slogans. While early Soviet history boasts of considerable numbers of such individuals, notably fewer existed in the 1960s and 1970s. In times of official ideology's decaying impact, most intellectuals find little to adhere to, and respond with either cynicism or pessimism.

The situation is different during periods when the regime becomes dynamic and tries to radically change the system and its dominant ideology. During these times, the number of intellectuals who identify themselves with the regime increases tremendously. Such was the case in the aftermath of the October Revolution, during Khrushchev's period, and especially in Gorbachev's time.

Given that individuals' political actions are the metric for their placement on this scale, and that people may change their actions, it is possible for people to move from one point on the scale to another under different political circumstances. As indicated above, the boundaries between the zones may also shift under changing conditions. Within any given period of political stability, however, this scale serves to separate members of the intellectual community into six groups: open opponents, legal opponents, private critics, passive intellectuals, and consistent public supporters. (For another typology that partially overlaps with these, see Churchward 1973, pp. 136–139.)

Very few intellectuals belong to the same group for all of their political lives. The majority move from one type of political behavior to another, depending on the political climate, which is the main variable determining the behavior of the intellectuals. For this reason, the biographies of many intellectuals are full of what seem to be mutually exclusive patterns of behavior. Even Pasternak and Mandel'shtam published very official poems, and Tvardovski was among those who praised collectivization.

Justification of Conformity: The Mythology of the Intellectuals

As mentioned earlier, even in the 1960s only a minority of the intelligentsia dared openly confront the regime and, in the following decade, their numbers became even smaller. Very few intellectuals continued to express their views openly in the 1970s, and an even smaller proportion continued to participate in actual oppositional activity.

How is it possible for individuals to hold views hostile to the regime while publicly presenting themselves as loyal and, in some circumstances, even assisting the authorities in the harassment of colleagues? Even those who are politically active in the private sphere must explain to themselves and others why their public actions fail to adhere to what they preach in conversations with friends and relatives. Moreover, even those who go beyond making oppositional speeches or private communications and take part in some private political actions have to explain why they do not do even more.

This discrepancy between opinions and behavior, which is rather typical of intellectuals in nondemocratic societies, is sometimes difficult for Westerners to understand. Individuals in the West are accustomed to a conformism involving compliance with the dominant values and are rather unfamiliar with situations where compliance in behavior is coupled with noncompliance in viewpoints, at least to the degree this situation can be found in the USSR (Kiesler and Kiesler 1969; Shlapentokh 1982).

The conflict between behavior and opinions is the most important psychological feature of Soviet-type societies, for people at virtually every level of society find difficulty in harmonizing their ideas and their conduct. This conflict is particularly acute among the intelligentsia and especially among the intellectuals, however, because this group holds the most antagonistic views toward the Soviet system, while also finding it necessary to cooperate with the bureaucracy and publicly take positions in accordance with the official ideology. Ultimately, the conflict between the attitudes and behavior of intellectuals stems from a more basic conflict between certain internalized values that directly influence their behavior. As indicated previously, none of the other social groups in Soviet society are exposed to such a clash between values as are the intellectuals.

In most cases, hedonistic values, coupled with the fear of repression, triumph over values that compel intellectuals to confront the authorities. The period of political reaction that began in the late 1960s confirmed that only a few intellectuals could resolve their conflict in favor of the values of democracy, religion, and resistance. Yet even in that period of despondency and regular betrayal of political ideals in everyday behavior, the majority of the intellectuals avoided falling into an abyss of complete cynicism. They sought to preserve their self-image as far as possible, which required them to support, at least at a verbal level, some moral values.

As is currently true of most of the Soviet population, the intellectuals of the 1960s and 1970s found the solution to their conflicts in the development of a special "mythological" level of consciousness. That is, it can be argued that the Soviet mentality, in a manner characteristic of people in repressive societies, can be described by a two-level model. The first level, which is the pragmatic level, consists of the internalized values that shape actual behavior. The second level, which is the mythological level, is involved in the maintenance of one's self-image and of relationships with the social environment, particularly with the power of the authorities. In contrast to the pragmatic level, the values and beliefs that constitute the mythological level are not deeply internalized and may change rapidly as external conditions are altered and require new values. (On the two-level model, see Shlapentokh 1986; see also an article by the Soviet sociologist Popova [1984], who independently developed a similar approach; about the mythology of Soviet intellectuals, see Altaiev 1970, pp. 22–23; Pomerants 1981; Shragin, 1977.)

At the same time, values which for the most part have operated only on the mythological level and which in no way interfere with material behavior can, in time, become quite deeply internalized, actually becoming a part of the pragmatic level. Thus almost all of the myths used by Soviet intellectuals with clearly critical views to justify their passive behavior (e.g., oppositional activity only in the private sphere, or not even there) gradually turn in the minds of many of them into more or less strong convictions, which are practically impossible to distinguish from simple rationalizations. Because of this, when outsiders discuss myths that an intellectual appears to exploit only as cover for his or her craven behavior, the intellectual often considers this a slanderous attack, contending that the "myth" reflects his or her genuine views, which then determine his or her behavior.

First, it is necessary to distinguish between two kinds of myths used by the intellectuals to justify their conformity—"current" myths employed to vindicate current deeds, and "retrospective" myths to acquit the actions of the past. As such, in keeping with the current vs. retrospective distinction, I will first discuss the myths used by the intellectuals of the

1970s and early 1980s to justify their surrender to Brezhnev's regime, and then I will move to the mythology employed for the vindication of their behavior in the past.

Current Mythology

"I Am a Patriot"

Official patriotism, or devotion to the Soviet Union and the current regime, has been among the few official values to be internalized by many Soviet intellectuals and, in some cases, to determine their behavior. The stability of this value for intellectuals is not to be exaggerated. Allegiance to this value, which often means compliance with orders from the authorities, has always been strongly rewarded. During the darkest years of Stalin's reign, however, it was obvious to even the most ardent patriots from among the true intellectuals that official patriotism, when in conflict with other values, such as international peace, creativity, or access to information, endangered the highest interest of the country and ultimately other interpretations of patriotism. Therefore, any readiness to embrace well-rewarded official patriotism and the most blatant official propaganda (for instance, about the origin of the cold war) always casts doubt on the motives of those intellectuals indifferent to the flaws of the regime and, particularly, to the persecution of their colleagues.

Patriotism was the major justification for most of the meanness and insensitivity to the suffering of others during Stalin's times. For example, Simonov, who was generally an intelligent, talented, and kind person, presented in his very sincere memoirs an articulate example of the active use of patriotism to vindicate his participation in the anticosmopolitan campaign and his many other cruel deeds (Simonov 1988).

For many prominent scholars, official patriotism (often coupled with the status of classified scholar) continued to play a major role in justifying their passivity during the democratic movement of the 1960s. The potency of the myth of patriotism employed against any form of oppositional activity during this period helps one understand the significance of Sakharov's challenge to the political and scientific establishments of the time.

With the gradual decline of official ideology and the development of the democratic movement, the role of official patriotism as a justification for political passivity eventually lost its importance, and by the late 1970s it was used by only a few intellectuals with liberal tendencies. With the rise of Russophile ideology, however, patriotism, both official and unofficial, became a leading value in the major ideological battles of the 1970s and 1980s.

"Any Politics Is Dirty"

The antipolitics myth, employed widely by the demoralized intellectuals of the Brezhnev era, argued that, as long as state and political power existed, it would be impossible to create a truly humane society. Intellectuals who subscribed to this myth did not see great differences between the Soviet and Western political systems. While pointing to the shortcomings of the Soviet system, they also sought to expose the weaknesses of Western democracies, particularly the disproportionate influence of the economic elite on elections, the mass media, and other vital areas of social life.

The central, unifying work of literature for this group of intellectuals was Fiodor Dostoevsky's *The Possessed*, a late-nineteenth century critique of the Russian revolutionaries, with their yearning for political power and their cruelty toward those who disobeyed them. In the early years of Soviet history, this book enraged many revolutionaries, including Lenin and Maxim Gorky, and was condemned as a libelous attack on Russia's revolutionary movement. In subsequent years the book attracted the attention of many Soviet intellectuals, and Dostoevsky was seen to have uncovered how political power, even in the hands of idealists, can become a weapon for the fulfillment of narrow, elitist goals (Pliushch 1979, p. 379).

In the 1970s, *The Possessed* was used by some intellectuals to attack the oppositional activities of their colleagues, especially those of dissidents. They argued that such individuals would only repeat the same process of consolidating total power under the cover of idealistic slogans. Paradoxically, the antipolitical intellectuals would than find themselves serving the same interests as the authorities they apparently mistrust. Though they criticize oppositional activity for different reasons, these individuals pursue goals similar to those of the authorities.

Politics were ignored in the memoirs of various prominent Soviet intellectuals who either collaborated with the authorities or were neutral on political matters (see the memoirs of Dolmatovski 1988; Efros 1985; Kataiev 1981; and Obraztsov 1987).

"Only Moral Self-Improvement Is Important"

While some intellectuals insist that, given the nature of political power, there is no point in sacrificing individual wants and needs for the sake of political confrontation and oppositional activity, others advocate a similar position through appeals to "human nature." Those ascribing to moral and religious myths hold that only individual moral development can create a happier society, while attempts to alter the political system will leave the individual unimproved. Religious morality is generally taken to be the key to social progress.

Igor Shafarevich, one of the human-rights movement's most active participants in the early 1970s, became, by the late 1970s, the most eloquent spokesman for the moral and religious view. In an interview with a foreign correspondent in 1978, he declared that "What we need—it is the maximum spiritual changes with minimal external changes. We need to return to God and our people, the feelings of national goals, and the feeling of responsibility before history and to the future of our people" (*Khronika Tekushchikh Sobyti*, no. 44, 1978, p. 39). In emphasizing religion over politics, these intellectuals appear directly to continue the work of the contributors to *Milestones*, the collection of essays produced by disappointed intellectuals in the aftermath of the defeat of the 1905 Revolution. Nikolai Berdiaev, the editor of this collection, had reproached the Russian intelligentsia for its atheism, rationalism, and unhealthy interest in social justice and the distribution of wealth (Berdiaev 1909, pp. 1–22). Another contributor, Sergei Bulgakov, accused the intelligentsia of, among other things, indifference to "absolute norms and values, which . . . can be brought only by religion" (p. 50). He offered Christianity as the only valid alternative to the secular heroism of the revolutionaries, which focused on grand achievements in society but remained morally sterile at best. Mikhail Gershenzon, a third contributor, criticized the intelligentsia for its preoccupation with "social problems" and "politics," as well as its neglect of "mental health" and of concern for the perfection of the individual conscience (pp. 70–96).

"Dissidents Are Inferior"

Myths that denounce politics naturally engender myths about the inferiority of dissidents. Along with justifying their own behavior, the conformist majority in the intellectual community also formulated arguments to denigrate those who remained faithful to principles that had been supported almost unanimously in the 1960s. Thus the demoralized intellectual community eagerly searched for information with which to vilify the dissidents, deprive them of their aura of sanctity, and reveal them to be as weak, vain, and concerned with comfort, power, prestige, and sexual pleasure as was the rest of the intellectual community.

For example, a book prepared by the KGB and attributed to Solzhenitsyn's first wife and containing a number of moral insinuations against her former husband was actively coveted by Soviet intellectuals (Reshetovskaia 1977).[1] Many intellectuals of this period also gloated over the

[1] In an interview with *Moskovskie Novosti* almost ten years after the publication of her

rumors that Sakharov was a spineless puppet in the hands of his unceremonious and cruel Jewish wife Elena Bonner (see Iakovlev 1988, which contains aspersions against Sakharov and his wife; see also Bonner 1986).

And, of course, news of the "breaking" in prison of two prominent actors from the Moscow dissident movement—Piotr Iakir and Viktor Krasin (who yielded to their prosecutors and came to an agreement with Andropov himself, naming all the participants in the dissident movement)—was received by many intellectuals not so much with sadness as with ill-concealed satisfaction. The event was seen as another argument vindicating these intellectuals' retreat from any form of oppositional activity (about Iakir and Krasin's case, see Krasin 1983).

Finally, many people during this period tended to believe that dissidents were abnormal people whose confinement in psychiatric hospitals was quite justified. For example, Mikhail Kheifets describes a meeting with Professor Averbakh, the leading psychiatrist in Leningrad, who, in a private conversation with Leningrad writers, attempted to convince them, presumably sincerely, that General Piotr Grigorenko was really mentally ill (Kheifets 1978, pp. 64–65).

"High Professional Performance Above All"

Another argument employed by Soviet intellectuals in the post-Stalin era to justify avoidance of direct political activity is that of professionalism. This view holds that professional activity must be all-encompassing, and that any diversion or distraction should be avoided. As previously discussed, the prestige of professional work in the Soviet intellectual community is very high when conpared to the period before the Revolution. (As Izgoiev, another *Milestones* contributor, argued, "The average member of the mass intelligentsia mostly does not like his profession but does not know it"; see Berdiaev 1909, p. 122.)

In the 1960s–1980s, an important part of the cult of professionalism in the USSR was the belief that achievements in professional activity could greatly improve the conditions of Soviet society, and could bring progress to all spheres of life, including the political system. This image of the scholar dedicated to his or her profession and to society is found in many works of liberal writers and film directors (see Daniil Granin's novels, *I Am Going to Meet the Storm*, 1962, and *Prospectors*, 1954). The cult of professionalism was also employed by intellectuals to avoid the

---

book, Reshetovskaia insisted that her manuscript had been very heavily edited and that many chapters charitable toward Solzhenitsyn had been dropped. She did, however, acknowledge that the KGB had deftly exploited her despair after her divorce and her resentment against her former husband, for whom she had secretly typed *The Gulag Archipelago* (*Moskovskie Novosti*, August 20, 1989).

dissident movement of the 1960s, and even more so later. Sakharov addressed this issue directly in his famous open letter on "The Responsibility of Scholars," when he appealed to academics to participate actively in political life, particularly in the defense of their colleagues, and not to reduce their lives to the fulfillment of their "professional duty" (see Babenyshev 1981, p. 40).

As Alexeieva noted, the cult of professionalism was especially strongly exploited by the liberal intelligentsia in Leningrad, which was very much afraid that "the slightest discontent of their superiors, and all the more the KGB, can lead to the complete loss of their social status." Therefore, those in Leningrad were particularly active in the elaboration of this concept, according to which "professional activity is not only a means for getting means of sustenance, but is the meaning of life and its justification: I preserve and develop Russian culture—this vindicates any sacrifices" (Alexeieva 1984, p. 330).

The same argument was widely used by scholars who wanted to avoid lending support to dissidents, and even by those who took part in their persecution (Amalrik 1982, p. 54). Leonid Pliushch recounts how two prominent Kiev scholars—Viktor Glushkov and Nikolai Amosov (the latter became very active as a champion of perestroika)—as well as a number of lesser-known scientists, tried to cover their collaboration with the authorities in the persecution of liberals and in supporting the Czechoslovakian invasion by referring to "the interests of the institute, and science." Glushkov, for instance, even asked one of the dissidents he had fired from the Institute of Cybernetics not to disseminate the content of his speech about this invasion because he had said what he had only out of concern for scientific progress (Pliushch 1979, pp. 247–248). Even such a great man as Shostakovich widely used this argument to vindicate his amazingly conformist behavior in the 1960s and 1970s (see Neizvestnyi 1984, p. 17). Similar professional arguments were employed by Sakharov's colleagues, both at the Physical Institute in Moscow and at the research institutes in Gorky, to justify their passivity toward his exile to Gorky. A leading Gorky scholar begged Mikhail Levin, an old friend of Sakharov's who came to a conference in Gorky, not to visit the exiled scholar, "because otherwise 'they' will not allow any more scientific gatherings in our city" (*Iz.*, January 26, 1990).

"Don't Tease the Bosses"

A considerable number of intellectuals actively used as justification of their conformist behavior the idea that each nonconformist act provokes the leadership, which eagerly awaits any excuse to crack down on the intelligentsia.

The feeling that the KGB was behind any seemingly noncontrolled action was widespread in the Soviet Union in the 1970s and beyond. Prior to 1985 the Soviet people believed in an almighty political police that used various tricks to trap those who silently disliked the system. This conviction was so strong that some of the most suspicious intellectuals saw the Twentieth Party Congress simply as a gimmick for the discovery of the system's hidden enemies. Other intellectuals in the same category suggested that the emigration of the 1970s was launched as provocation for fomenting anti-Semitism in the USSR. These feelings were brilliantly described by Zinoviev in *Homo Sovieticus* (1982). This paranoia was fueled by mutual suspicion that any intellectual who behaved out of line was simply performing a task for the KGB. The more challenging his or her speeches and conversations, the greater the grounds for believing in his or her sinister role (Amalrik 1982, pp. 82–83; Pliushch 1979, pp. 278–280).

Certainly, it is difficult to separate genuine belief in the omnipresence of the KGB from the exploitation of this belief in justifying one's own craven behavior. In any case, it is known, for instance, that the respected writer Panova regarded the publication of *Doctor Zhivago* abroad as a major provocation against the Soviet intelligentsia (about this, see Amalrik 1982, p. 83).

Retrospective Mythology

In the preceding section I considered the mythology used by intellectuals to vindicate their current political behavior and their conformism toward the Soviet authorities. When old repressive regimes are replaced, however, liberal intellectuals begin to examine their behavior retrospectively, in the context of a new political situation. Although the retrospective and current mythologies share some common features, they differ significantly from each other in several ways. Specifically, the retrospective myths contain more elements of regret, embarrassment, and recanting.

In 1988–1989 Soviet intellectuals started intensive examinations of their past political behavior. Their scrutiny of the past immediately intertwined with the ideological struggle between the main factions of the intellectual community—liberals (or Westernizers) and Russophiles. The struggle between these two factions in the late 1980s mirrored that of the 1960s, although in the later battle the recriminations were related not to reporting to the political police but rather to cringing before the authorities, participating in infamous campaigns against colleagues and telling glaring lies.

The Arguments of the Liberals

Among other things, liberals reminded conservatives, for instance, how they persecuted Pasternak in 1958–1960 and Tvardovski in 1969–1970.

Pasternak's case, which in 1986–1987 was mentioned only indirectly and without "naming names," finally received considerable publicity in 1989. In discussing the meeting of Soviet writers who condemned Pasternak and decided to exclude him from the Writers' Union, liberals cited all of those who took the floor to castigate the great poet. Evtushenko and Voznesenski were especially active in the restoration of the events surrounding Pasternak in those tragic years (*MN*, June 5, 1988).

The case of Tvardovski, another liberal martyr, was also at the center of public confrontations in 1988. The polemics were primarily concerned with the notorious letter in *Ogoniok* (no. 30, 1969) against the editor in chief of *Novyi Mir*. The letter was signed by eleven writers, including Mikhail Alexeiev, Proskurin, Nikolai Shundik, Anatoli Ivanov, and other conservative activists (about this letter, see Burtin, *Oktiabr'*, no. 6, 1987; see also Burtin 1988; Il'ina, *Og.*, no. 2, 1988; Lobanov, *Nash Sovremennik*, no. 4, 1988; Oskotski, *Knizhnoie Obozrenie*, January 29, 1986).

Still, because of Gorbachev's disapproval, liberals could publicly attack only a few people for their past deeds. Among these were Tikhon Khrennikov, the official leader of Soviet music since 1948 (see *MN*, no. 48, 1987; no. 6, 1988; *Sovietskaia Kul'tura*, May 12, 1988, and June 16, 1988), Mikhail Rutkevich, the former director of the Institute of Sociological Research (see *SK*, December 19, 1987), and Piotr Fedoseiev, vice president of the Academy of Sciences (see Vodolazov 1988).

The Arguments of the Russophiles

Russophiles, in their turn, reminded many liberals about how they obediently served the Stalin and Brezhnev regimes. Apollon Kuz'min maligned the past of Iuri Afanasiev, who was the head of a division in the Komsomol Institution in the 1970s (*NS*, no. 3, 1988, p. 154), and Kozhinov and Viktor Chalmaiev attacked the late Trifonov, recalling that this leading liberal writer of the 1960s and 1970s was the author of the novels *Students* (1950; awarded the Stalin Prize in 1951), which hailed the anticosmopolitan campaign, and *The Old Man*, which denounced it (Kozhinov 1987, p. 172; Lobanov 1988, p. 156). Similarly, Alexander Kazintsev reminded the admirers of *Children of Arbat* that its author, Rybakov, had been a loyal author in Stalin's time and had won the Stalin Prize (*NS*, November 1988, p. 165), and Bondarenko exhorted liberals to recall that Vitali Korotich had vehemently praised Brezhnev's works (*Literaturnaia Rossia*, October 28, 1988, p. 28).

While trading mutual vituperations, intellectuals could not avoid recanting their own conformity and spineless behavior in the past.

The Recanting

With glasnost, Soviet intellectuals almost immediately faced a problem with strong roots in Russian culture, that of religious values and recanting from them. It was hardly accidental that the first strong anti-Stalinist movie was entitled "Repentance" (1986).

It was revealed that Alexander Fadeiev, a leader in Soviet literature during the Stalin era, committed suicide in 1956, almost immediately after the Twentieth Party Congress, at which he recanted his participation in Stalin's regime and in the death of many writers. Information regarding Fadeiev's death had been concealed for thirty years and was revealed only in 1987; the content of Fadeiev's last letter is still kept secret (see Ivan Zhukov's article, "The Death of the Hero," Og., nos. 30 and 31, 1987).

In 1987 and 1988 the process of settling past scores began in earnest. Several patterns of justification for past behavior soon arose. In 1987 Likhachev encouraged the entire Soviet people, particularly the intellectuals, to recant their past and their active or passive participation in the functioning of an immoral and corrupt society (Likhachev 1987). However, only a few intellectuals truly followed Likhachev's appeal and repented for their earlier deeds and beliefs. One of these was Boris Efimov, who, in his article "I regret . . . ," confessed that even though his famous brother, Mikhail Kol'tsov, was sent to the gulag and killed, he himself had remained a devotee of Stalin and participated in ignoble political campaigns in the 1930s and 1940s (Efimov 1988, p. 3). After Sakharov's death, Iuli Khariton, a leading Soviet expert on nuclear weaponry, very reluctantly, and under journalistic pressure, squeezed out a few words to recant signing the 1973 open letter against his old friend and colleague. He added, however, that "he disagreed with Sakharov on the nature of socialism and capitalism" and that he "had not anticipated the consequences of this letter for Sakharov." In addition, he found nothing wrong with having failed to demand that the authorities return Sakharov from his Gorky exile or with having failed to correspond with Sakharov during the Gorky period (Dos'ie, no. 1, 1990, p. 19). In fact, of the forty Academy of Science members who signed the infamous letter against Sakharov, only the physicist Sergei Vonsovski ever recanted fully and uncompromisingly (Iz., January 26, 1990). Likewise, Iuri Zamoshkin was among the rare liberals who recognized publicly "the one-sidedness" of his earlier scholarly publications, particularly those related to American individualism (Voprosy Filosofii, no. 6, 1989, pp. 3–16).

The majority of intellectuals, however, despite their guilt about their past behavior, either kept silent (as was particularly true for the major activists of perestroika) or excused their actions via the myths discussed earlier. Some intellectuals, such as Bondarev, bluntly rejected the idea of recanting as "rubbish" and "silly" (1988b, pp. 343–344).

"Like All Others, I Had to Obey Power"

Some intellectuals, such as Sergei Mikhalkov and Vladimir Soloukhin, participated in nasty political actions under both Stalin and Brezhnev. These intellectuals (especially Soloukhin) were strongly attacked by liberals, who, recalling numerous cases of contemptible behavior in the past, rejected any attempt at normalizing conformism, cowardice, and immorality (see the articles of Evtushenko and Grigori Pozhenian about Soloukhin's past in *LG*, October 13, 1988). Instead of recanting or denying their guilt, however, Mikhalkov and Soloukhin rejected the incrimination as historically unfounded, ascribing it either to their convictions during that period or to the political powers they had to obey and the repressions they had feared. In addition, these intellectuals named many other people who, by their silence, endorsed the same odious campaigns. (See the interview with Mikhalkov, *Og.*, no. 12, 1988; see also that with Soloukhin in *LG*, October 13, 1988.)

Intellectuals who wished to avoid being branded servants of the regime were able to preserve at least a part of their reputation through actions or statements that suggested they continued to advocate the ideals they had championed in the past.

"I Was a True Believer"

Many intellectuals (mostly those thirty to fifty years of age) excuse their past behavior by presenting themselves as true believers in official propaganda. These intellectuals argue that they tried to do their best in their creative work for the sake of the Revolution and the country, including participating in Stalinist or Brezhnevist ideological campaigns. Ehrenburg, the first to use this excuse, contended in his memoirs (published in 1987) that despite his skepticism, he "succumbed to the common adoration of Stalin" (Ehrenburg 1987, p. 23).

In 1987 the famous film maker Iosif Kheifets contended that he was proud of the movies he made in Stalin's time, such as *A Member of the Government* and *A Deputy of the Baltic Navy* (the typical product of rude propagandists) (Kheifets, 1987).

Alexander Shtein, a prominent playwright, referred to "the music of the Revolution" and "the revolutionary conviction" of his generation to avoid condemnation of his activities. Although he did condemn his own film *The Court of Honor,* one of the worst of the Stalinist films, he claimed that he and his colleagues were able to find explanations for the mass repressions (Shtein 1987; 1988, p. 178–179). Shtein's sentiments were seconded by the famous actress Tamara Makarova, who said that, despite the repression of members of her family, "there was full trust . . . in the party and her tasks," and that she was proud of the "heroic movies" of the times (*SK,* July 30, 1987).

Some conservative intellectuals (e.g., Nikolai Shundik) have tried to apply this formula of "the true believer" to the Brezhnev era, insisting that the attacks against *Novyi Mir* in the 1960s were necessary (see *SK,* May 28, 1988).

The Philosophy of "Small Things"

Several intellectuals of the older generation, such as the well-known script writer Gabrilovich, have claimed that they "understood and saw everything" and that they did the best they could under the terrible conditions. They recognized that they were successful authors, and "they got (from the state) everything that they could" and complained that their abilities were "underutilized" (Gabrilovich 1987).

Other people have tried to refurbish their past and find actions to help present themselves in a tolerable light (see Arbatov, the director of The Institute of the USA and Canada, 1988; see also *SK,* July 28, 1987; *LG,* October 28, 1987). Several liberals have engaged in long debates about who was more or less courageous or craven during various episodes in the past. Burlatski, for instance, in an interview with *Argumenty i Fakty,* presented himself as a hero for having published (along with Karpinski) an article in *Komsomol'skaia Pravda* in 1967 decrying censorship in theaters. However, Boris Pankin, the editor of the newspaper at that time, has recalled that Burlatski tried to influence *Pravda*'s editorial board (where he worked) to shift the responsibility for the article onto his coauthor (*Argumenty i Fakty,* January 19, 1990; see also how rosily Pankin described his activities as *Komsomol'skaia Pravda*'s editor in the 1960s, Pankin 1988).

Fear As a Justification for Conformity

Of all the arguments, the claim that fear justified their actions was the most sincere and contained the least amount of rationalization. It is probably best to consider this more a confession than a myth.

In the 1970s and the early 1980s, confessions of one's own timid and even pusillanimous behavior were made only in private, since admissions of this sort were considered directly libelous toward the political elite.

Soviet intellectuals were constrained to publish only in the West those works that disclosed the role of fear in their own lives and in the lives of their friends and colleagues (see Aksenov 1982; Chukovskaia 1981; Pliushch 1979; Roziner 1981; Vishnevskaia 1984; Zinoviev 1976).

Then, with the gradual liberalization, Soviet intellectuals began speaking more freely about fear as a major explanatory factor in the behavior and the mentality of intellectuals in the Stalin and Brezhnev eras (Arbatov 1987; Borshchagovski 1987, 1988; Iutkevich 1988; Kornilov 1988; Pastukhova 1987; Rudnitski 1988).

The Imitation of Oppositional Activity: A New Invention of the Intellectuals

Another approach involved periodically engaging in actions that generated (or appeared to generate) the hostility of the authorities. During the 1970s, the poet Evtushenko was considered a champion of this technique. He intermixed a number of critical writings with a variety of other actions that demonstrated his loyalty to the regime. The same path was taken by a number of other intellectuals of the time, such as Ivan Drach and Korotich.

Yet another strategy involved occasionally assisting individuals engaged in liberal or even dissident activity. Simonov was known for such actions. Similarly, Alexei Surkov, a poet and an important official figure, protected Akhmatova and helped her to publish her poems (Chukovskaia 1980, p. 230).

A third approach can be seen in the efforts of intellectuals to deal with subjects in their books, articles, or films that satisfy both liberal public opinion and the authorities. I.N. Davydov, the prominent sociologist, provides a useful example. As one of the Moscow intellectuals who participated in the protest letter campaigns of the 1960s, Davydov later recanted his position and sought to regain the trust of the authorities without simultaneously losing the respect of the intellectual community. One effort to achieve this dual goal was his denunciation of the leftist movement in the West in the 1960s. On one hand, the leadership supported his criticism of the movement, which had deprived the elite of their monopoly over the critique of capitalism. On the other hand, the liberal intellectuals also appreciated his critique because, as indicated previously, the left in the West was seen as a threat to the advantages of Western civilization (see Davydov 1975, 1977, 1978, 1982; see also Davydov and Rodnianskaia 1979).

The peace movement was also used by many intellectuals to try to justify their narrow cooperation with the authorities in political matters. The strategy in this case was simple: because it is impossible to deny that the preservation of peace is desirable for all, it is not only excusable but laudatory that one work for the prevention of a nuclear holocaust, even if in some cases the Soviet leadership has contributed to the problem. Ehrenburg was perhaps the first Soviet intellectual to travel the world advocating peace, praising Soviet foreign policy, and supporting official Soviet actions in the international arena, while simultaneously presenting himself as a liberal defender of human rights (of course, after 1953, Ehrenburg became a consistent opponent of the regime). Among Ehrenburg's heirs in this activity are such literary figures as Evtushenko and Drach, as well as the scholars Sagdeiev and Evgeni Velikhov.

CONCLUSION

The majority of the intellectuals and the mass intelligentsia hold views highly critical of Soviet-type systems. In socialist societies, however, most intellectuals express their views privately, and only a small number are able to publicly defend their views or even be involved in "material" forms of oppositional activity. The ratio between public and private forms of political activity is the most sensitive indicator of the intellectuals' involvement in the political process. Those who abstain from public opposition employ a special mythology to help them justify their conformity. This mythology can be used to vindicate one's compliance in either present or past situations.

CHAPTER FIVE

The 1960s: The Heroic Age of Soviet Intellectuals

THE POST-1953 history of Soviet intellectuals can be divided into three periods that correspond very roughly with the Khrushchev, Brezhnev, and Gorbachev regimes. The first period extended from the mid-1950s up to 1968, the second period began in 1968 and continued through Brezhnev's death in 1982, and the third period began in 1985 and is still in force at this writing.

It is generally recognized among students of Soviet society that a new regime is established in the country with each new leader, and that these regimes differ from one another in many fundamental respects. This is also true with respect to the relationship between the political elite and the intellectual community. The attitudes of Khrushchev, Brezhnev, and Gorbachev toward intellectuals differed in important ways. In this chapter and the following one, I will discuss the activities of the intellectuals during the late 1950s and the 1960s, the period roughly corresponding with Khrushchev's regime.

KHRUSHCHEV'S AMBIVALENCE TOWARD INTELLECTUALS

The factor which, more than any other, shapes the political elite's policy toward the intellectuals is the elite's attitude toward changes in the society they control. As the political leader, Khrushchev supported the modernization of Soviet society. His political rivals, however, such as Viacheslav Molotov, Lazar Kaganovich, and Georgi Malenkov, although in agreement with him on the necessity of eliminating mass terror, opposed Khrushchev's attempts to significantly alter Soviet economic and political life. Having chosen the course of modernization and having neutralized his opponents, Khrushchev had no alternative but to cooperate to a certain degree with the intellectual community.

Khrushchev needed moral support for his anti-Stalinist policies, which had placed him in conflict with the party apparatus and the KGB. Apart from the intellectual community and that portion of the party apparatus which resented Stalin's 1930s purges no other social forces were able to lend strong and vocal support to Khrushchev. Although many of Khrushchev's innovations were favored by workers and peasants, these groups were extremely limited in their ability to voice approval because there were no free elections or opinion polls. In addition, these groups were rarely very appreciative of the de-Stalinization of political life. In many cases, they were also dissatisfied with the economic policies of Khrushchev's leadership, particularly those regarding private plots, interference in agriculture, and food shortages (the last of which were perceived as less tolerable than they had been under Iosif Stalin, despite their objective improvement). The masses, who were accustomed to Stalin's imperial behavior, were often reluctant to pay homage to Khrushchev, whose behavior was more human and emotional.

Because of these factors, Khrushchev required the cooperation of the intellectual community for his numerous modernization projects in various areas of Soviet life. His behavior toward the intellectuals, however, was all but consistent. In fact, considering Khrushchev's uncouth and even vulgar behavior when he met with various intellectuals in 1957, 1962, and 1963 (for a brilliant and shrewd description of Khrushchev's meetings with intellectuals, see Tendriakov 1988), his support of Lysenko, and the ease with which his aides pitted him against abstract painters as well as writers such as Dudintsev, Grossman, and Pasternak, it is possible to describe Khrushchev as an enemy of the intelligentsia (Burlatski 1988a, p. 435). As is clear in his memoirs, however, Khrushchev sought the collaboration of prominent figures in science and culture (Adzhubei 1988; Khrushchev 1970).

Khrushchev's bid for the intellectuals' cooperation was manifest in diverse ways. It can even be argued that the thrust of his entire liberalization effort was addressed to the intellectual community and the mass intelligentsia. For example, he reduced the intensity of censorship and permitted the publication of numerous innovative literary and scientific works, an unimaginable development only a few years earlier.

With the exception of genetics, the natural sciences were exempt from the "class approach," and physicists, chemists, and mathematicians grew confident that their professional affairs would remain exempt from party interference. Even social scientists were favored by Khrushchev's regime—economists were allowed to develop econometric approaches and to revise, albeit subtly, the fundamentals of official economic theory. Moreover, empirical sociology was allowed to reemerge, and philosophers were granted latitude to address issues in logic and the philosophy of nature. Intellectuals were also allowed to maintain contacts with their foreign colleagues, albeit to a limited degree. Although modest, these concessions were viewed as radical breakthroughs at the time.

Still, even while freeing the intellectuals from Stalin's shackles, Khrushchev failed to understand their real aspirations and their readiness to use this atmosphere to take the offensive themselves. Khrushchev was apparently convinced that he could manipulate the intellectual community at will and that it would respond to his desires. Only at the end of his leadership did he begin to grasp that the Soviet intellectuals represented an independent social force whose interests were opposed to those of the political elite.

I will try to describe the behavior of the intellectuals in the post-Stalin period using the constructs advanced in previous chapters: the types of oppositional behavior and the typology of intellectuals according to their political positions. At any stage after 1953, almost all types of behavior and political positions coexisted, but it is still possible to point out the dominant types for each period.

THE FIRST TYPE: MILD LEGAL CRITIQUE

Mild legal critique was largely predominant in the first decade after 1953. Its primary medium, which was most prevalent during the first stage of the liberal movement, was literature. The importance of literary magazines in the public life of the country reflected the prominent role of critical literature.

Another significant feature in the movement was the involvement of liberal party intellectuals, as well as that of scholars, in legal critical activity.

Critical Legal Articles, Novels, and Movies

Prior to the dramatic events of the Twentieth Party Congress, the intellectuals limited their oppositional behavior to relatively mild forms, predominantly expressed in literature containing critical hints and allusions and at some official gatherings. Ehrenburg's novel, *Thaw* (1954), provided a label for the period between March 1953 and March 1956. Along with this book, Ehrenburg's own memoirs, *People, Years, Life* (1961–1966), Panova's novel, *Season of the Year* (1953), and Leonid Zorin's play, *Guests* (1954), attracted considerable public attention (as well as official hostility) with their unusually objective portrayals of life in the Soviet Union. In addition, two previously unknown authors, Vladimir Pomerantsev and Fiodor Abramov, emerged as heroes of the period for their two articles (1953 and 1954, respectively), which were highly critical by the standards of the time. Also important were Kirsanov, Aliger, Kaverin, and Valentin Ovechkin, who forcefully argued for the importance of aesthetic value in literary work.

The Twentieth Party Congress revealed that Khrushchev had taken another step—this one quite radical—away from Stalin. In addition, due to the nature of the internal political struggle at the time, the liberalization of political life in the country had become an important weapon for Khrushchev in his bid to become the uncontested leader of the USSR. Once again, writers, using their new opportunities, began to escalate the oppositional movement in the country.

The next period began with the 1956 publication of a remarkably brave novel in *Novyi Mir*, Dudintsev's *Not by Bread Alone*, which was enthusiastically received by the intelligentsia. The author boldly described the Soviet bureaucracy and its indifference to the interests of the nation and provoked numerous discussions, some of them public. One such discussion in the Writer's Club became widely known as one speaker, the prominent writer Paustovski, used the book as a basis for arguing that Soviet society consisted of a privileged and an unprivileged class. Paustovski's speech, in which he broadly applied his impressions from a tourist voyage on a ship with high Soviet officials, became one of the first samizdat materials disseminated among intellectuals (about Dudinstev's novel see Swirski 1979).

A number of other notable figures among Soviet writers appeared in 1956, including Iashin, whose story, *Levers* (1956), remains one of the best descriptions of "double-think" among Soviet citizens, and whose later work, *Vologda Wedding* (1962), was a shocking picture of poverty in a Soviet village. Granin's *One's Own Opinion* (1956) innovatively portrayed opportunism among the Soviet people, while Kirsanov's poem, "Seven Days of the Week," attacked the dehumanized bureaucracy, and Evtushenko's poem, "Zima Station" (1956), assailed the hypocrisy of Soviet society.

In addition, editors of the *Literaturnaia Moskva* collection (1956), such as Kazakevich, Aliger, Alexander Bek, and Kaverin, deserve much recognition. This collection not only included Iashin's *Levers*, but also a number of other stories from liberal authors, including Iuri Nagibin's *Light in the Window*, which attacked the corruption of Soviet officials, Akim Iakov's, poem "Galich," which alluded to the sad experience of a small ancient Russian city, and Alexander Kron's caustic article. Because of their work as editors, these writers became the principal targets of renewed attacks by the authorities.

Of no less importance than the role of literature was the role of plays in Moscow theaters. Some of them, authored by Soviets as well as by prerevolutionary writers, such as Tvardovski's *Tiorkin in the New World*, Alexander Sukhovo-Kobylin's *The Death of Tarelkin*, Ostrovski's *A Lucrative Position*, Zorin's *Dion*, and Shwarts's *Dracon* and *Naked the Naked King*, made very important contributions to the relaxed mood.

The spirit of liberalism was also revealed in the movies of the time. Film directors began to produce movies that reflected, albeit timidly, real issues of Soviet life and contained allusions to Stalin's past and its current remnants. One of these movies (of which there were few), *Rumiantsev's Case* (1956), depicted a villainous police prosecutor wanting to jail an honest driver. *Rumiantsev's Case* aroused excitement because, for the first time, a prosecutor, albeit from the ranks of the police and not the KGB, was presented as a vile person. Even the most refined intellectuals, such as Akhmatova, were involved in discussions of this movie (Chukovskaia 1980, pp. 146–147). This film was followed by other movies such as *Man Was Born, Cranes Are Flying, Nine Days of One Year, Ordinary Fascism, I am 20 Years Old,* and *Carnival Night,* all of which overflowed with various allusions and barbs against official ideology (Mar'iamov 1985).

The next few years were fairly discouraging for Soviet writers, because Khrushchev, fearful of losing control over ideological developments following the Twentieth Party Congress, began to tighten the screws. Still, despite the retreat of some writers, such as Aliger, who recanted their "mistakes" of 1956, the process of political resistance among the intellectual community continued to grow, and new breakthroughs were made by single individuals whose actions drastically changed the political atmosphere.

Critical Memos to the Leadership

In Stalin's time, an unsolicited memo addressed only to him, with even the slightest critique of his decisions in any sphere, could very likely send its author to the gulag. Following his death, intellectuals gradually and cautiously began to exploit memos as vehicles in which to express their dissatisfaction with concrete and scientifically oriented elements of Soviet life. Usually these memos contained declarations of absolute loyalty to the leadership, Soviet ideology, and the Soviet system, as well as statements explaining the author's initiative as a manifestation of his or her desire to strengthen the state, socialism, and the world communist movement. Even with these precautions, however, many intellectuals declined to sign such memos, and those who did sign regarded themselves as heroes. These memos were looked upon with suspicion by the authorities because they carried indirect critiques of the system and because they were considered a first step to more dangerous activity. For these reasons, all of the unsolicited memos were kept secret, and most of them remained unpublished until thirty years later, in the period of glasnost.

One of the earliest memos was devoted to the defense of genetics and a critique of Lysenko's dominance in biology. The memo was prepared in 1955 and signed by almost three hundred scholars. This memo infuriated Khrushchev, who ignored all of the scientists' arguments (*Pravda,* January 13 and 27, 1989).

Breakthroughs in Publication

Many political developments, both inside and outside the intellectual community, were related to the publication of new critical literary works. As each new work appeared, it became the center of political turbulence for a longer period of time.

Usually these developments followed a certain pattern: rumors about the appearance of a critical new novel or poem would spread rapidly the day an issue of a magazine came out (most literary works in the Soviet Union are first published in magazines). The novel or poem would then become the object of intense curiosity, and copies of the magazine carrying it would be quickly snatched up in Moscow, Leningrad, Novosibirsk, and other cultural centers in the country. Magazine subscribers were often forced to make up waiting lists for friends wanting to borrow the new issue.

Readers would immediately begin debating the content of the new piece, the intentions of its author, the circumstances under which it appeared, the political meaning of the work, and the consequences facing the author and the editors of the magazine in which it was published. These topics would become the main subject of conversation on the telephone (usually in Aesopian language, since lines were assumed to be tapped), in offices, and at all private meetings and parties. Though the artistic qualities of the work would not be ignored, the political issues it raised, either directly or, more commonly, indirectly, drew the lion's share of the readers' attention. This general pattern was observed following the appearance of such works as Dudintsev's *Not By Bread Alone*, Iashin's *Levers*, Granin's *Own Opinion*, and the collection, *Tarusski Notes* (1961), which was edited by Paustovski with the active participation of Roman Levita. The latter volume showcased the works of authors who had no chance of being published elsewhere, such as Okudzhava, Zabolotski, Boris Balter, Naum Korzhavin, Frida Vigdorova, Vladimir Kornilov, Vladimir Maximov, Iuri Kazakov, and Trifonov, as well as the late Tsvetaieva's poems.

In some cases, of course, developments deviated from this pattern. This was true with the publication of Bulgakov's *The Master and Marguerite* (1967), simply because the author was no longer alive, and the publication of his work could not trigger the same chain of events as could the work of a living writer. Nonetheless, the novel's appearance was an important political event, for Bulgakov's satirical work brilliantly described life in Moscow in the 1930s under Stalinist terror.

Brave authors were often taken to task by the authorities. Scathing reviews of a novel or poem would appear in various periodicals, and other writers would be "invited" to join official campaigns against the author of some scandalous work. The pressure on writers produced many conflicts among those requested to denounce a literary work, particularly between those who would comply with and those who would defy such requests. Quarrels among writers became known to the entire intellectual community. Many intellectuals enthusiastically supported writers who not only defied the authorities by not participating in a campaign, but actually defended other authors in public. Consequently, official hostility spread beyond the author of a work to those who supported him or her in public.

The turmoil surrounding a piece naturally increased its popularity, independent of its artistic or even political merits. Intellectuals, who occupied the forefront of the literary readership and were invariably the first to devour controversial works, were soon joined by the mass intelligentsia and readers from other segments of society. Long lines of people waiting for a particular magazine issue would form in every library in the country, even in the most remote cities and villages. At this stage, foreign radio stations would also begin to discuss the developments surrounding the appearance of a critical work. Articles on the same topic would be published abroad. Western reaction created a new stimulus both for discussion and for measures taken against those involved.[1]

Although usually much more conservative than the capital, the provinces managed, during the 1960s, to attract the attention of the Soviet intellectual community. For example, two issues of the Siberian magazine *Baikal* published several very politically caustic chapters from Arkadi Belinkov's book on Iuri Olesha (nos. 1 and 2, 1976; the whole book was published only abroad). The same magazine published the Strugatskie brothers' science-fiction novel, *A Snail on the Slope* (1966–1968), full of allusions to Soviet reality. A number of brave novels, poems, and articles were also published in the Voronezh magazine, *Prostor*, in *Literaturnaia Georgia*, and in some other magazines.

[1] The Brezhnev regime was fully aware of the political implications of these literary works. Thus in the 1970s the leadership began to severely restrict the critique of works considered dangerous. This was the case with Trifonov's final novels, which contained anti-Soviet attitudes whose intensity surpassed that of many works published earlier. Rather than attack these works, however, the official press ignored them, although there were rumors that the last two novels, *Home on the Embankment* and *The Old Man*, were removed from army libraries. The practice of ignoring literature was also applied to many of the novels written by authors of "rural prose," even those directed clearly against the regime, such as Rasputin's *Farewell with Matera*. The use of this tactic meant that the Brezhnev leadership managed to avoid the emergence of a new group of writers and artists who, like their immediate predecessors, would build their fame on the political scandals created by their works.

The "Camp Theme" in Soviet Literature and the Legitimation of the Soviet System

One of the most important developments of the early 1960s, especially after the Twenty-second Party Congress and the publication of Solzhenitsyn's *One Day in the Life of Ivan Denisovich*, was the appearance of the so-called camp theme in licit literature and mass media. The camp theme penetrated poetry as well as prose and became especially strong among poets, such as Zhigulin and Zabolotski, who returned from the gulag.

This gulag literature had an enormous impact on Soviet society and, in fact, altered the ideological climate in the country. With each new work, it became increasingly evident that Stalin's terror had possessed deep roots and could not simply be dismissed as the result of a maniacal leader. This literature stripped the veneer of legitimacy from the Soviet system, and as each new literary work on the camps appeared, it became more obvious that the leadership of the country during the Stalin era consisted of criminals, cynics, and cowards. It is not surprising that one of Brezhnev's first actions following the ousting of Khrushchev in 1964 was to halt the publication of this type of literature. In fact, even the mention of those victimized under Stalin was prohibited.

Poetry As a Political Force

In the late 1950s poetry suddenly became one of the most important vehicles of expression for the oppositional mood in the country. In the beginning, poets challenged the regime with lyric poems focusing on individual feelings, an approach at odds with the official ideological emphasis on collectivism. Olga Bergolts was the first poet of the old generation to publicly defend "self-expression," first at the Second Congress of Soviet Writers in 1954, later in 1956, and in several articles (Chukovskaia 1980, p. 167).

Still, the appearance of poetry as a political force was primarily the achievement of young poets like Evtushenko, Slutski, Voznesenski, and Korzhavin. Starting first with lyric themes, these poets moved on to deal with civic issues and soon became the most popular mouthpieces of the intelligentsia and the youth.

In the 1960s poetry readings were political events. These readings attracted thousands of people, who reacted emotionally and boisterously to any poem with even the slightest hint of criticism of official ideology or policy. Evtushenko and Voznesenski were especially popular for such readings. Thousands would pack into Moscow Stadium, where each year many poets read their work on the Day of Poetry. Again, audiences were quite receptive to any politically colored works, and those who read them were hailed by the crowds.

It is noteworthy that poetry's role in the second thaw—in 1985–1987—was insignificant. The leading poets of the 1960s, such as Voznesenski and Evtushenko, were active as essayists and journalists, but not as authors of new poems.

Evtushenko directed the section in *Ogoniok* (1987–1989) devoted to Russian poetry of the twentieth century, and he published the works of numerous poets who had been persecuted by the authorities in the past. In the 1960s this section of poetry would have been a permanent sensation and a great political event. In the latter 1980s, however, it drew only moderate attention from the public. The public reacted similarly when prohibited poems by Slutski, Iaroslav Smeliakov, Semion Lipkin, Evgeni Rein, and others were published in 1987–1989.

Literary Discussions and Memorial Evenings

Literary discussions were among the significant developments in the country's political life between 1956 and 1968. Under Stalin, all exchanges of viewpoints on literary works were highly restricted and controlled by party officials responsible for cultural life. Authors who became targets of official criticism had no choice but to recant and repent.

Dudintsev's *Not by Bread Alone* marked a new era in this sphere. The book aroused such interest that a series of spontaneous and weakly controlled discussions spread across the country in 1956. The most active debates took place in Moscow and Leningrad. I have already noted the discussion at the Central Club of Writers in Moscow; other discussions occurred at Leningrad University, Moscow University, and other institutions in these cities (see Gidoni 1980, pp. 59–61; Pimenov 1979, 1980; Vail 1980).

Thereafter, literary discussions became an important part of Soviet cultural and political life. These discussions attracted large audiences and rarely neglected criticism of the state of affairs in the country, particularly in the political realm. Besides Solzhenitsyn's writings, the work of authors such as Aksenov, Anatoli Gladilin, Okudzhava, Balter, Evtushenko, and Voznesenski aroused considerable passion and stimulated politically colored speeches. Even more people were attracted to the literary meetings devoted to writers and poets who had perished or been exiled in the past.

One literary event, which took place in 1968 in the Central Club of Writers in Moscow and was devoted to Platonov, was particularly clamorous (I was present at the meeting). The key moment of this evening was a talk by Iuri Kariakin, a prominent literary critic and supporter of Solzhenitsyn's work, who employed the opportunity for a scathing attack on

Stalin and his contemporary admirers. The talk was eagerly accepted by the audience, but it resulted in Kariakin being strongly reprimanded and nearly expelled from the party. The evening devoted to Maria Tsvetaieva in 1967, with speeches by Ehrenburg, Pavel Antokol'ski, Evgeni Vinokurov, David Samoilov, and others, was also a memorable event.

In the early 1960s the official meetings of Moscow writers occasionally became political events as well. During one of these meetings in 1962, leading hack writers of the time, such as Nikolai Gribachev, Kochetov, and Anatoli Sofronov, were not elected to the board of the Moscow branch of the Union of Writers.

Satirical Activity

As strange as it may seem to a foreign reader, the dilettante satirical activities of the intellectuals in their offices began to take on very significant political overtones in the 1960s. Gradually, with the retreat of fear, intellectuals started to use official entertainment parties, which were arranged in connection with significant official dates, as important outlets for their oppositional spirit. Comic verses, humorous speeches, and facetious sketches indirectly derogated the official ideology, superiors of various ranks, obsolete traditions, and so on.

A few places in Moscow, such as the Club of Writers (where Zinovi Papernyi ran a satirical group called Galley Readings of Proofs), the Club of Actors, and the Library of Social Literature of the Academy of Sciences, became famous for their caustic, witty, and friendly evenings. The witticisms, puns, epigrams, and repartee were repeated in many offices, institutes, and private gatherings on subsequent days, and appeared among intellectuals in the other provinces within a few weeks. (About such evenings in the library of social literature, see Pomerants 1985a.)

Along with these satirical burlesques, wall newspapers were also turned into weapons. Having once been tedious, presumptuous, and generally ignored, wall papers suddenly became extremely popular in some Moscow institutes in the 1960s. One of the most famous was edited by a group of scholars headed by Alexander Zinoviev at the Institute of Philosophy. The satirical hero of this paper—the philosopher Poluportiantsev (Semifootcloth—a hint to his claim to represent "the toilers")—a stupid, almost illiterate dogmatist, became widely known in the Moscow intellectual circle and even outside it.

The role of satire increased substantially in the 1970s, when satirical writers and actors were practically the only people able to reveal the people's true attitudes toward their lives. The fame of such authors and actors as Arkadi Raikin, and later Zhvanetski and Khazanov, grew in the late 1970s and early 1980s.

Novyi Mir: The First Organ of the Intellectuals

In the early 1960s Khrushchev began escalating the level of his denunciations of Stalin as part of his ideological policy. This circumstance was exploited by Tvardovski, the editor of *Novyi Mir*, who began to publish a variety of novels and articles that critically and objectively described life in the Stalin era as well as the current situation. The most notable of these publications was Solzhenitsyn's *One Day in the Life of Ivan Denisovich* (1962), which was soon followed by a number of other stories from the same author. The appearance of *Ivan Denisovich* was an event of extraordinary importance. For the first time in Soviet history, readers were exposed to literature on a highly controversial issue without ideological distortion. Solzhenitsyn's novel forced all of Soviet society to employ new criteria in the evaluation of public acts, from political speeches to poetry.

Besides Solzhenitsyn's work, *Novyi Mir* printed a number of other significant works that advanced democratic ideas in one way or another. Among the most important were Iuri Bondarev's *Silence* (1962), the continuation of Ehrenburg's memoir, *People, Years, Life* (1964), Zalygin's *On the Irtysh River* (1964), Boris Mozhaiev's *From the Life of Fiodor Kuz'kin* (1966), and Iuri Dombrovski's *Custodian of Antics* (1966).

As mentioned earlier, *Novyi Mir* enjoyed enormous popularity during the 1960s among the intelligentsia, particularly among intellectuals. After the purge of *Novyi Mir*'s editorial board in the early 1970s, the magazine ceased to voice democratic views. The intelligentsia and the intellectuals immediately reacted to the new developments in the magazine, and the proportion of *Literaturnaia Gazeta* readers who followed *Novyi Mir* dropped to 5 percent. At the same time, the proportion who regularly read *Oktiabr'* remained stable (Fomicheva 1978).

During the 1960s conferences of *Novyi Mir* readers organized by its editorial board always attracted large crowds. One such conference took place in Novosibirsk (August 1965), and an exciting atmosphere filled the hall where Tvardovski and his staff met with the magazine's followers, I among them. Some of the presentations, particularly that by Iosif Gol'denberg, the sociologist and philologist, were especially impassioned. A number of speakers described how they eagerly awaited each new issue, how they feared that each issue would be the last, and how they attempted to guess why a particular issue had been delayed in publication. The talks were received with strong approval, although Tvardovski kept his distance to avoid undermining the tenuous status of the magazine.

A number of other periodicals enjoyed wide popularity among intellectuals during the 1960s. These included *Iunost'* (Youth), *Znanie i Sila* (Knowledge and Force), *Nauka i Zhizn'* (Science and Life), *Internatsional'naia Literatura* (International Literature), and, of course, *Literatur-*

naia Gazeta (Literary Gazette). Never before could the intelligentsia claim so many periodicals that reflected, to varying degrees, their own perspectives.

Exhibitions As Arenas of Political Struggle

In the 1960s exhibitions of paintings acquired strong political overtones. Along with writers who had perished in Stalin's times, painters who shared the same fate or who had simply been ignored previously (such as Kuz'ma Petrov-Vodkin, Pavel Filonov, Vladimir Tatlin, and Robert Falk) became magnets for the Soviet intelligentsia. Exhibitions of foreign painters such as Pablo Picasso and Jan Mari Leger were also considered political events.

In this regard, the history of the art museum in Academic Town in Novosibirsk is very typical. It was created by an art enthusiast, Mikhail Makarenko, with the active support of the leading members of the Siberian section of the Academy of Sciences, the president of which, Mikhail Lavrentiev, was known for his interest in modern paintings. The museum managed to organize exhibitions of several artists that had been prohibited in the past. Some prominent artists, such as Marc Chagall, promised their help. When the political reaction started in Academic Town in 1968, however, the museum, despite scholars' attempts to resist the pressure of the regional party committee and probably the KGB, was closed (Makarenko 1974, pp. 79–99). The real political battles of course raged not at the exhibitions of old, even avant-garde, artists, but at those of living artists who refused to follow the requirements of socialist realism. The first such exhibition took place in Moscow in 1962 and became famous for a verbal dual between Khrushchev and the sculptor Neizvestnyi.

At an exhibition five years later, "unofficial painters" (nonmembers of the Artists Union) were, for the first time, able legally to show their works. Unfortunately, this exhibition, organized by Alexander Glezer, a public director of the club Friendship in Moscow, lasted only two hours before being closed by the authorities. This reprisal, however, failed to dampen the painters' determination to exhibit their works. They began to invite people, including foreigners, to private exhibitions. These events turned their studios into political clubs in which, along with the arts, all issues that aroused people were discussed (Neizvestnyi 1984).

In addition, the painters nurtured the idea of organizing public exhibitions and eventually set one up on the outskirts of Moscow, on Profsouznaia Street, in 1974. The exhibition was broken up by police with the use of bulldozers and has therefore always been known as "the bulldozer exhibition." This act became a major political scandal, arousing the anger and scorn of world public opinion, so the authorities allowed the artists to set up a "second show" of paintings, on a legal basis, in Izmailov Park (Glezer 1981, 1984; *Sovietskaia Kul'tura*, November 14, 1987). Since then, exhibitions by abstract painters and other nonconformist artists have, from time to time, been officially allowed. This is a rare example of a process by which initially illegal actions lead to their subsequent legalization by the authorities (see Alexeieva 1984, pp. 307–309; *Vol'noie Slovo*, no. 20, 1975, pp. 67–71).

In the giddy days of glasnost, unlike in the 1960s, paintings played an insignificant role. Because the Soviet political establishment had become accustomed to vanguard and abstract paintings, vanguard exhibitions of young artists in Moscow (1986–1988) generated only moderate interest among officials and drew only modest public attention.

The legalization of abstract painting culminated with the official support of private businesses and with the emergence of "informal organizations" tolerated by the authorities. Abstract artists were not only the first to create their own organizations (such as Hermitage in Moscow), but were also among the early enthusiasts of the new economic course and of the opening of the USSR to the West. These changes permitted intensive contacts with art dealers and radically improved the artists' material status.

The most politically visible and popular artists during the period of glasnost were those who employed the nonrealistic technique in paintings with strong political messages, primarily anti-Stalinist messages. On the other side were painters such as Il'ia Glazunov, whose exhibitions openly praising prerevolutionary Russia and the Orthodox church became rallying points for the Russophiles. Russophiles (including some from the highest echelons of power, including Raisa Gorbachev) vehemently defended Il'ia Glazunov against art critics who pointed out low artistic values (see Osipov 1978; see also *Strana i Mir*, April 4, 1987, pp. 74, 79–83).

Party Intellectuals for Reforms

Another significant development of the 1960s was the emergence of a group of party intellectuals who advanced liberal ideas and hung their own career hopes on the victory of liberal tendencies within the leadership. This group consisted of two kinds of intellectuals. One group, the minority, was made up of apparatchiks within the bureaucracy, while the second was comprised of intellectuals who maintained close ties to the party apparatus. The closeness of the second group to the authorities was visible in a number of ways, including frequent visits to the party headquarters, especially Central Committee headquarters, participation in the preparation of party documents (speeches and reports of the leadership, decisions of the party and the government, and so on), playing leading roles in various political conferences, official trips abroad, and publication in the two most important party periodicals, *Pravda* and *Kommunist*.

Among members of the first group, the liberal apparatchiks, it is important to note the role of Alexei Rumiantsev. Rumiantsev held a number of important positions during this period, including editor in chief of the international party magazine, *Problems of Peace and Democracy*, editor in chief of *Pravda*, vice president of the Academy of Sciences, and, most significantly, member of the Central Committee. He was effectively the leader of the liberal wing within the party, which also included Georgi Shakhnazarov, Vadim Zagladin, Iuri Krasin, and Arbatov, all senior workers of the Central Committee, as well as Burlatski and Karpinski, who served on *Pravda*'s editorial board.

Among the prominent members of the second group were Iuri Zamoshkin, Nikolai Inozemtsev, Stanislav Menshikov, Bonifatsi Kedrov, Ivan Frolov, and Gennadi Osipov. All these individuals were scholars protected by Alexei Rumiantsev.

During the 1960s party intellectuals were influenced by two very different reference groups: the party apparatus as such and the liberal intellectuals already involved in direct confrontation with the authorities. Also during the 1960s, party intellectuals were consistent with and supportive of Alexander Dubcek's policies in the Czechoslovak party apparatus, and they monitored the developments in Prague quite closely. Probably no group wished Dubchek more success than did this group of intellectuals. Until the late 1960s this group was quite socially active, largely in publications and in efforts to promote other liberals in different areas of social life. Alexei Rumiantsev had a staff of ghost writers, including such brilliant intellectuals as Leonid Batkin, Levita, Mikhail Gefter, Mikhail Loiberg, and Kariakin, who annually produced dozens of articles and books advancing the liberal approach to political, economic, and cultural problems.

Most liberal party intellectuals have what might be called a "liberal subconscious." That is, all other things being equal, they will adopt a liberal stance. If, however, they perceive even the slightest conservative signal from those in power, they will quickly adopt a more conservative stance (see, for example, the behavior of Arbatov and Frolov, who joined the liberals during the first thaw, collaborated closely with the political elite in the 1970s, and again joined the liberals in the latter 1980s).

Scientific Conferences and Symposia

During the 1960s various gatherings of scholars often acquired political significance. Given the atmosphere of liberalization and the impression that the country was beginning to progress, many scientific conferences, regardless of their designated subjects, became arenas for the discussion of political issues. If a conference was devoted to, say, chemistry or physics, then discussions of social and political matters were conducted outside official meetings, in hallways or hotel rooms. In conferences devoted to the social sciences, sharp discussions developed during the official sessions. These dialogues often continued after the sessions and on into the night. There were always young people in attendance who would bravely raise difficult questions that would prevent other participants from skirting acute social and political issues.

A number of gatherings of economists, especially those in Academic Town, were also distinguished by bold speeches at sessions. Economists such as Albert Vainstein, Alexander Lurie, Viktor Bogachev, Raimond Karagedov, Aron Katsenelinboigen, and Igor Birman were renowned for their confrontations with official economic analyses.

Along with conferences, other types of meetings played important roles in the political activity of scientists. These included the "schools," one- or two-week seminars where leading scholars lectured on recent developments in their fields. These schools attracted many talented young scientists, including graduate students. One of the best-known schools was organized by Iulo Vooglaid, a prominent Estonian sociologist and founder of Soviet sociology (Vooglaid 1967, 1968, 1969). Schools convened by economists, such as those in Bakuriani in 1966 and in Terskol' in 1969, were also places where liberal ideas were developed and where people could find like-minded colleagues.

The sociology seminars and conferences were particularly notable. Since its resurrection in the late 1950s, sociology has been considered a symbol of modernization and democracy in the USSR. Only mathematical economics could compete with sociology for prestige among intellectuals and professionals. The attractiveness of sociology was enhanced because for two decades it continued to be a stepchild of the authorities and was permanently and tightly controlled by party officials. Thus, until the early 1970s, good professional sociologists were identified by the public, if not as dissident, at least as liberal opponents of the regime and its ideology. As a result, sociology gatherings of any sort had an oppositional tone of hidden confrontation with the authorities. The conference in Sukhumi in 1967 clearly manifested the liberal and democratic orientation of most sociologists. (On the conference, see Levada and Urlanis 1968.) A number of other sociology conferences held in the country in the 1960s can also be regarded as political events, such as those in Leningrad in 1965, in Novosibirsk in 1966, and in Ulan-Ude in 1967.

Of equal importance were the sociology seminars, regular meetings of sociologists which thrived in the country in the 1960s. One particular meeting of the seminar regularly led by Levada in Moscow became extremely popular due to a speech by Grigori Pomerants in 1965 on the cult of Stalin (Pomerants 1985a, p. 98). Levada later headed two well-known seminars, one at the Institute of Concrete Social Research (1967–1972), and the other at the Central Economic and Mathematical Institute (1975–1977). Most seminars were dismantled at the request of the authorities.

Along with sociological seminars and conferences, those devoted to cybernetics also became arenas for social criticism. These meetings acquired this oppositional character because cybernetics had, only a few years earlier, been labeled a bourgeois science. Because of this, participants in cybernetics meetings considered themselves almost legal oppositionists. Moreover, cybernetics at that time claimed to be a general science capable of fertilizing all other sciences and guaranteeing their rapid progress. This arrogance gave speakers the "right" to involve themselves in discussions of affairs in all domains of social life. (About one such cybernetics conference in the 1960s, see Berg 1983, pp. 148–152.)

The Debunking of Official Myths

The intellectuals' various forms of legal political activity were concentrated on two primary goals: the debunking of official ideology and the defense of culture against the political elite. In the 1960s, because of the thaw, it became possible for the first time for intellectuals to launch a serious attack against the main ideological dogmas, a job completed twenty years later with glasnost.

The intellectuals' critiques of the official ideology fell into two main categories. In the first category were actions that opposed certain basic tenets of the official ideology; in the second were activities that supported values and ideas opposed to the official perspective on the world. In the first area, intellectual activities of the 1960s sought to demonstrate the inconsistencies between officially pronounced values and their actual realization in practice. Such central values included the idea of the leadership role of the working class, the notion of socialist democracy, the welfare of the people as the chief concern of the political elite, and socialist internationalism. Similarly, intellectuals sought to illustrate how certain key official values were, in practice, detrimental to the needs of the population. Principal targets here included the values of the central planning system and the monopoly of state ownership of the means of production.

In the second area, intellectual activity challenged official ideology through support of certain humanistic and individualistic values denigrated by official propaganda. Intellectuals supported values typically associated with the West that were at odds with the official ideology, including the values of parliamentary democracy, political and intellectual pluralism, and individual privacy. This support included intellectual advocacy of certain traditional values, such as religiosity and cultural/ethnic nationalism. Finally, intellectuals sought to demonstrate that, in contrast to official pronouncements, the majority of the population did not observe the official values, even if they claimed to support them.

Although intellectuals aggressively opposed the official value system, they worked even harder to undermine the imagery created by the dominant ideology. One of the basic ways in which ideologies provide legitimacy to ruling groups, in addition to propagating certain values, is through the demonstration that existing reality is in accord with these basic values; that is, ideologies seek to show that the fundamental values are being realized, or at least approached, in practice. Thus, in order to be effective, ideologies must compel individuals to perceive reality in ways consistent with these values. In this context, a large part of the intellectual activity of the 1960s involved exposing certain distortions of reality promulgated by the ideological apparatus. During the brief period of liberalization, a considerable proportion of intellectual activity was devoted to "reconstructing" the public's perception of reality.

During the 1960s writers were a leading force in the exposure of official Soviet myths. With considerable skill and deftness, they attacked the notion of the superior standard of living in the USSR. Abramov, Vasili Shukshin, Viktor Astafiev, and other representatives of the school of "rural prose" unveiled life in the countryside, while urban life was the focus of such writers as Nikolai Voronov and Vitali Semin. The notion that Soviet youth were consistently devoted to the realization of official policy was critiqued in the work of writers associated with the magazine *Iunost'* (Youth), such as Aksenov, Gladilin, Balter, and Okudzhava. The myth of the Soviet people's commitment to official morality was undermined by such novelists as Valentin Rasputin, Shukshin, Trifonov, Voinovich, and Vladimov. The idea of "socialist democracy" was criticized in the works of Ehrenburg, Dudintsev, Iashin, Paustovski, and Korzhavin. The ideology of ethnic harmony, and especially the myth of the absence of anti-Semitism, was examined in the writings of Evtushenko and Anatoli Kuznetsov. Soloukhin and writers in the "rural prose" tradition attacked the notion that the Soviet people were essentially indifferent to religion.

Filmmakers were also involved in the exposure of official mythology. Films like *Chairman* (1964) revealed the realities of rural life, while *Your Contemporary* (1968) unmasked the activities and hypocrisy of Soviet officials.

With the resurgence of sociology in the USSR in the late 1950s, sociologists also participated in the debunking of the official image of reality. The work of sociologists was particularly important because, unlike the contributions of writers and filmmakers, their arguments could not be attributed to artistic imagination. Sociologists rooted their critiques in empirical evidence gathered through modern research techniques, which gained legitimacy through the official lauding of "science."

Sociologists, such as Vladimir Shubkin (1970) and Iuri Arutiunian (1968, 1971), launched their offensive against the notions of the homogeneity of Soviet society and the leading role of the working class, while Vladimir Iadov (1967), Viktor Perevedentsev (1975), and Zaslavskaia (1970) critiqued the idea that the Soviet work force was motivated largely by ideological commitment. Mass media sociologists, such as Grushin (1968), Vooglaid (1967, 1968, 1969), and I (1969a, 1969b), sought to undermine the myth of the efficiency of the official ideology and the media. Anatoli Kharchev (1964), Igor Kon (1967), and Sergei Golod (1977) produced evidence contradicting the ideological postulates regarding the strength of the Soviet family and the people's lack of interest in sexuality. Shubkin (1970) and Vadim Ol'shanski (1966) revealed the weakness of the myths regarding the harmony of Soviet collectives.

Intellectual activity was also directed toward providing a more realistic picture of life in the West. The articles of Viktor Nekrasov (*Novyi Mir*, no. 4, 1965) and others who traveled to the West made a great impression on Soviet readers.

Another target of intellectual activity in the 1960s was the official image of the past. Solzhenitsyn and other writers provided a new picture of life in the gulag during the 1930s and 1940s, and their revelations further undermined the credibility of the official ideology concerning the present as well as the past. Novelists, including Zalygin, Vasili Belov, and Mozhaiev, made the first attempts to reinterpret the history of collectivization, while Pavel Nilin and Boris Kardin cast doubts on the official images of the Civil War in their writings, just as Grigori Chukhrai did in his film, *The Forty-First* (1956). Intense reconsideration of the past, however, did not begin until 1986.

The Promotion of High Culture

Along with ideology, culture in the narrow sense (literature and the arts) was another object of the intellectuals' legal critical activity. At first glance, it would seem that the role of intellectuals as superior judges and custodians of culture should be objected to neither by the elite nor by other groups in society, if only because the intellectuals are creators of cultural values. Even in this sphere, however, the intellectuals' claim on the spiritual leadership of society was met with fierce resistance by the rulers. As mentioned earlier, the elite attacked the intellectuals in this sphere in several ways. The elite tried to discredit the intellectuals, calling them highbrow adherents of an elitist culture, incomprehensible to ordinary people, which served only the narrow circles of a few connoisseurs. The stronger the elite, the more actively it bolstered popular and mass culture.[2] Stalin, Hitler, and Mao were all consistent enemies of vanguard art and of any other art not accessible to the unsophisticated. The same line, albeit in more refined form, has been pursued by Stalin's successors.

The inclination of the elite toward mass and popular culture can be attributed to two circumstances. First, the elite has always tried to isolate the intellectuals from other strata of the population. Either overtly or covertly, the elite systematically pits ordinary people against the "eggheads." The discrediting and derogation of the intellectuals' latest cultural achievements is often employed in campaigns aimed at defaming the intellectual community. (About the attitudes of intellectuals toward mass culture, see Shils 1972.) Second, the elite consists primarily of people with very mediocre education and cultural tastes. In this sense, rulers and apparatchiks are really much closer to ordinary people than to intellectuals. Their tastes are very similar to those of the majority of whom they rule.

Because of the elite's permanent opposition to the development of high culture, intellectuals are almost unremittingly engaged in the defense of new cultural achievements. In the 1960s the defense of cultural values against the regime was one of the most important goals of Soviet intellectuals, who defended, at one time or another, many seemingly different values: cultural modernism, cultural heritage, and Western culture.

Since the political elite obstructed the development of new trends in Soviet culture as much as possible, intellectuals spent a great deal of effort helping innovators in literature and the arts. For example, the intellectuals' support for Voznesenski's modernist poetry was of crucial importance for the survival of this poet, who was subjected at the beginning of his literary career to scathing official critique.

Intellectuals supported new tendencies in music with equal vehemence. Not only Shostakovich and Alexander Prokofiev, but also lesser-known composers such as Alfred Shnitke enjoyed the support of the intellectual community.

Intellectuals enthusiastically greeted the avant-garde theaters in Moscow, such as Sovremennik and, especially, Iuri Liubimov's theater, On Taganka, as well as many semiofficial theaters.

While backing new trends in culture, intellectuals also tried to curtail the decline in the quality of works in official literature and the arts, using

---

[2] In the entire history of the Soviet state, it is virtually impossible to find an excellent literary work that gained the approval of the authorities, except during the Revolution and the first years after it, and during the war against Germany in 1941–1945. During both periods, the distance between quality and the dominant ideology was minimal, and some officially praised works were truly good, such as the poems of Maiakovski or the war novels of Nekrasov and Kazakevich.

any opportunity to castigate those authors who tried to make up for lack of talent and diligence with noisy demonstrations of political loyalty. In the late 1950s intellectuals managed to scuttle the career of the mean and ungifted playwright Anatoli Surov, and they significantly damaged the reputations of such hack writers as Sofronov, Gribachev, Kochetov, and others.

Intellectuals, of course, were the most consistent advocates of abstract paintings and supported nonconformist artists in many ways, including buying their works.[3]

Soviet intellectuals devoted equal attention to the defense of their cultural heritage. Their efforts were directed toward supporting figures of literature and the arts who were persecuted by Stalin or who emigrated after the Revolution, and Russian cultural achievements that the authorities spurned as incompatible with official ideology. They fought tenaciously for the literary rehabilitation of such writers as Akhmatova, Mandel'shtam, Tsvetaieva, and Babel' and such painters as Petrov-Vodkin, Falk, Filonov, and Mikhail Larionov, as well as for the restoration of the status in Soviet culture of such emigrants as Bunin, Sergei Rakhmaninov, Fiodor Shaliapin, Chagall, Kazimir Malevich, and others. In addition, the intellectuals, Westernizers and Russophiles alike, fought for the preservation of cultural monuments from the past, including churches and other buildings related to religion. They also promoted respect for all cultural traditions based on religion.

In the 1960s, the intellectuals were also successful in propagating the achievements of foreign culture. The elite tends to be hostile toward Western culture, and if it had its way, the degree of cultural isolationism in the world would be very high. It was the intellectuals who, surmounting the resistance of the elite, fought for cultural exchange with foreign countries and defended the importance of incorporating the best achievements of alien culture into Soviet culture. Since 1953 intellectuals have been exploiting any possibility to familiarize the Soviet people with Western literature and the arts. It was through the efforts of Ehrenburg that Western painters—from impressionists to abstractionists—entered Soviet cultural life. (See Ehrenburg's publications on Western culture, for instance, his *Chekhov, Stendhal, and Other Essays*, 1962.) Soviet intellectuals were also eager to destroy the wall separating the Soviet people from modern Western literature. Using various devices and tricks, they gradually introduced William Faulkner, Franz Kafka, Albert Camus, Ernest Heming-

---

[3] Among others, two leading members of the Soviet Academy of Science, Lavrentiev and Sergei Lebedev, were known in the 1960s as Maecenas of Soviet abstract paintings. Lebedev, in particular, bought many of the paintings of Vladimir Muraviev, a talented nonconformist painter.

way, Erich Maria Remarque, Heinrich Boll, and many others into the Soviet cultural milieu.

With the same verve, the intellectuals tried to break through the roadblocks barring penetration of new Western music—classical as well as popular—into the country. Shostakovich, in particular, was one of those who put his authority behind such music.

Intellectuals returned to the crusade for high culture after 1985, with new opportunities offered by glasnost. Through glasnost, intellectuals, particularly liberals, introduced the public to authors who had been previously prohibited for political reasons. These authors included the poets Nikolai Gumilev and Vladislav Khodasevich, the writer Vladimir Nabokov, and the theater personality Mikhail Chekhov.

THE SECOND TYPE: SEMILEGAL ACTIVITY

The most important element of the second type of oppositional behavior was the intellectuals' use of legal Soviet organizations to further the interests of the liberal movement. Perhaps the most prominent case was the bard movement, which engaged thousands of people in liberal activity. In addition to this movement, intellectuals managed to create centers of liberal activity in various scientific institutions, a new phenomenon in post-Stalin Soviet history.

Another element of semi-legal activity involved intellectuals directly challenging the political leadership, the KGB, and the Soviet political order in general, even if only through legal means. They demanded punishment for squealers who had helped send their colleagues to the gulag, and they refused to admit any political "guilt," regardless of the price. Moreover, they began to openly support their friends and colleagues accused of political crimes, even if this support was through legal channels. Taking advantage of all legal means, intellectuals used opportunities afforded by party meetings as well as exhibitions to confront the Soviet political leadership, occasionally even face to face. Semi-legal activity thus played a leading, though not exclusive, role in the mid-1960s, as well as during other periods.

The Bard Movement

Soviet intellectuals must thank technological progress for their next political achievement. In the early 1960s a completely new cultural phenomenon emerged in the country: the appearance of the bards, who performed their own musical compositions. This was perhaps the first spontaneous movement in Soviet history to encompass hundreds of thousands of people, predominantly the intelligentsia and students.

As tape recorders became widely available, the songs of the bards were made available throughout the country, out of the control of the authorities. Moreover, the bards performed publicly in various institutions in Moscow, Leningrad, Novosibirsk, and elsewhere. Foremost among them was Okudzhava, followed by Galich, Vysotski, Viktor Kim, Iuri Visborn, and many others of varying quality.

The first bardic songs were purely lyrical, but under the circumstances, even this approach directly defied the official ideology and its emphasis on social issues couched in communist terminology. Even these first songs contained many political allusions and, through the 1960s, political themes gradually gained prominence in bardic compositions. At this point, the movement found the poet Galich, a specialist on such themes.

Vysotski, the third of the great bards, took a middle line between Okudzhava and Galich, expressing himself in songs that honestly and frankly described the thoughts and feelings of ordinary Soviet people. He found support not only among the mass intelligentsia, but among workers and even among apparatchiks, which constituted a major victory for him. As a true poet of all the people, Vysotski became a powerful medium by which the intellectuals could influence the masses. In terms of depth of impact, no one surpassed him. The principal themes of Vysotski's songs, such as the hypocrisy of everyday life, the absurdity of propaganda, the manipulation of ordinary people by the authorities, the aggressiveness of the people and their hostility toward their superiors, dealt significant blows to official ideology and its characterization of ordinary people.

In the 1970s, while the popularity of other prominent bards was waning (due to repression, particularly for Galich, who was forced to emigrate in 1973), Vysotski's fame grew steadily. He died an idol in 1980, probably unique in the country but still ignored by the state. His funeral became a major political demonstration, frowned upon by the authorities, with many thousands participating. With glasnost, the state joined Vysotski's cult; it allowed the abundant publication of his collected poems as well as the distribution of his recordings.

Listening to the songs of the bards became an important reason for social gatherings, and the themes of these songs often transformed such gatherings into arenas for political discussions. Interest in bardic compositions became a nearly infallible indicator of liberal orientations, and in this way the songs also served to bring together those with common political views.

The bard movement reached its peak in 1968 when Under Integral, the famous club in Academic Town in Novosibirsk, organized the first all-Union festival of bardic songs. This action heralded the advent of a new stage, one on which the bard movement could become more organized. The festival became an unprecedented political activity, conspicuously directed against official ideology. For nearly an entire week in March, the residents of Academic Town (including me) were absorbed in the performances of the composer-singers. The principal figure of the festival was, of course, Galich. For the first and last time as a bard, he played to an enormous audience. All of his performances displayed the character of a political challenge to the regime, and in many cases, people listened while standing and accompanied his performances with thundering applause. The festival provided the pretext for the regional party committee to interfere in the life of Academic Town. Local newspapers published articles denouncing the festival and the atmosphere in the town, and the regional party secretary organized a series of meetings at factories at which workers prepared to organize a march into Academic Town to protest the activities there.

The authorities had long frowned upon the bard movement and had attempted whenever possible to hinder its development. They seized the opportunity to shut down the club, Under Integral, and prohibited all contacts between various units in Soviet cities that dealt with the songs. By the end of the 1960s, the bard movement had been destroyed as a political force. The bards survived the political reaction of the 1970s, however, and even remained active in the mid-1980s, at least in Moscow, with their Club of Dilettante Songs. Moreover, in 1987–1989, the bard movement and its leaders were canonized and highly praised by the official mass media (see *Sovietskaia Kul'tura*, August 19, 1989).

Centers of the Democratic Movement

The bard movement prompted leading scholars in many of the research institutes of the Academy of Sciences to become Maecenas of unofficial art and literature in the country. As never before, scholars invited poets, writers, painters, and sociologists to their workplaces, often without the permission of party committees. This not only satisfied the scholars' need for new impressions and information, but also publicly demonstrated their support of those in the disfavor of the regime and in opposition to it. Several institutes in Moscow, headed by such scholars as Mikhail Leontovich, Kapitsa, and Boris Astaurov, were among those to support opposition intellectuals.[4] Solzhenitsyn's first public meeting with his readers occurred in the Institute of Nuclear Energy in Moscow in 1966.

[4] Kapitsa allowed Liubimov, the director of the famous Theater on Taganka, to use his *veche*, a special telephone line that served only officials of the highest ranks and allowed him directly to contact officials of the highest rank, bypassing secretaries. As Liubimov recounts, this service helped him immensely in his tortuous political intrigues, and allowed him to save his productions and even the theater itself on several occasions (Gorbanevskaia 1985, p. 440).

Still, during the 1960s the real sanctuary of oppositional intellectuals was Academic Town in Novosibirsk, which became a mecca for all prominent Soviet and foreign intellectuals. They were attracted by a spirit of intellectual freedom absent elsewhere—a spirit resulting from the unique status of the Siberian Section of the Academy of Sciences, which was less closely controlled by local party committees than were other institutions at the time. Thus the scientific center in Novosibirsk became the place where new trends in the Soviet social sciences, such as mathematical economics and sociology, enjoyed their greatest support.

Academic Town scholars manifested their political activity in a variety of ways. The club Under Integral (along with other clubs such as Grenada [poetry] and Sygma [movies]) played an important role. Its founders, Anatoli Burshtein and Grigori Iablonski, transformed the club into a venue for the most interesting discussions, and it was considered a great honor to be invited to the club and participate in them. The club always seemed to attract a full house, and discussions there almost invariably acquired political overtones.

There were also a number of apartment-salons where people regularly gathered to exchange views on various topics, nearly always with political implications (for instance, there were those headed by Raisa Berg, Igor Poletaiev, and others; I was also among this group).

Novosibirsk University, located in Academic Town, also added to the unique climate. One of the major goals achieved during the development of Academic Town was the unification of teaching and research, an approach contrary to the normal separation of the two throughout the rest of the country, where faculty were generally restricted to teaching activities, and research was carried out by other specialists. Thus professors at Novosibirsk University were radically different, because nearly all were also active researchers.

With the large number of researchers on the faculty at Novosibirsk University, its character was quite different from that of other institutions. Relationships between students and professors were generally closer and less authoritarian than was the case elsewhere, which resulted in a more politically active student body than existed at other schools in the USSR. For example, a number of students, under the guidance of academician Alexander Alexandrov, the secretary of the party organization for the university at the time, conducted a mock trial of anti-Semites in the country.

In addition, the new institutes created in the 1960s as a result of pressure from liberal intellectuals, such as the Central Economic and Mathematical Institute and the Institute of Concrete Social Research, were also notable for their liberal leanings. Both of these research institutes, segments of the Academy of Sciences, represented previously prohibited disciplines; thus they emerged as units opposed to an official ideology that had stifled developments in these fields for a long period. This was especially true with respect to the Institute of Concrete Social Research. Its first director, Alexei Rumiantsev, a leader of party liberals, gathered many liberal intellectuals into the institute, including some who had been reprimanded for ideological deviations or for participation in dissident actions, such as signing protest letters. In the late 1960s the Institute of Concrete Social Research was the most liberal institution in the country and a constant target of conservatives.

The Central Economic and Mathematical Institute was second only to the Sociology Institute in its liberal reputation. Its director, Nikolai Fedorenko, a consistent opponent of ideological economists, sought to fill his staff with unorthodox economists and researchers such as Katsenelinboigen, Viktor Volkonski, and Stanislav Shatalin (Katsenelinboigen 1980).

The Condemnation of Intellectuals—Squealers

Following the public disclosure of Stalin's terror, and the return of some intellectuals who had survived arrest and the gulag (e.g., Belinkov, Oksman, Shalamov), it became possible to reveal the names of those writers and scholars whose reports to the political police had sent many of their colleagues to prison and to their deaths. Absolutely forbidden before 1956, such action became more and more common in intellectual circles in the wake of the Twentieth Party Congress. This was especially true in Moscow, where the liberal intelligentsia was much bolder than in the provinces. Between 1956 and 1960, demands to identify those who had been stooges, either openly or secretly, became more and more vociferous. Paustovski was among those demanding sanctions against the squealers, who, from the 1930s to the 1950s, included Nikolai Lesiuchevski, Veniamin Dymshits, Lev Nikulin, Lev Uspenski, Samarin, and others. (About the developments that followed the revelation of names in Moscow of writers thought to have perished in the gulag, and Paustovski's allegations against those who betrayed them, see Trifonov's novel, *Time and Place*, 1982; see also Belinkov 1976; Chukovskaia 1980, pp. 223, 559, 604.) This movement demanding punishment of informers and slanderers was stopped almost at its inception, however. The political leadership, even under Khrushchev, wanted to avoid a "squaring of accounts" and a serious investigation of the events in the period of "The Great Terror" (Medvedev 1989b, p. 13).

Party Meetings

Prior to 1956, party meetings at all levels were completely ritualistic, and the political elite and the highest echelons of the party hierarchy paid little attention to them. Following the Twentieth Party Congress, however, this situation changed drastically, when a number of party meetings occurred throughout the country in which party members took the floor to denounce official policies of the past. In most cases, it was intellectuals who used the podium for these attacks on the regime. Two of these meetings were particularly noteworthy.

The first took place almost immediately after the Twentieth Party Congress, when the party organization at the Physical Institute of the Academy of Sciences in Moscow discussed Khrushchev's secret report on the cult of personality. For the first time in party history, a majority of organization members adopted a resolution indicating "no confidence" in the Politburo—a body thought to consist of people responsible for Stalin's atrocities. By a special resolution of the Central Committee, however, the party organization was dismantled.

The second of the two noteworthy meetings, the 1961 district party conference in Moscow, was the setting for the speech of General Grigorenko, a professor of military science. This speech was a major political event and resulted in the general's transfer to the Far East, which ultimately pushed him into the ranks of the most active of Soviet dissidents (Grigorenko 1982, pp. 237–261).

Public Debate with the Leader

The near-deification of the Soviet leader was one of the most important political processes in the USSR before 1985. Public criticism of any of the leader's statements was normally regarded as virtually a criminal offense.

If a citizen is honored with a personal meeting with a Soviet leader, he or she is expected to demonstrate complete devotion and full agreement with anything the leader says. Those who dared disagree with Stalin even in mild ways, in discussions related to their responsibilities, were treated by the public as virtual heroes, as was Marshal Georgi Zhukov. Stalin's successors have deviated little in this respect. None have revealed any willingness to tolerate open arguments, even in meetings with only a few others present.

Neizvestnyi, then a little-known sculptor, was the first Soviet intellectual to disagree publicly and clearly with Khrushchev, at the leader's visit to an exhibition of abstract paintings in 1962. Evtushenko bravely came out in defense of Neizvestnyi, reproaching Khrushchev for his attitudes, and Ehrenburg defended all abstract painting against Khrushchev's attacks. Khrushchev was also criticized by Ovechkin at a public meeting in 1962.

Defense of One's Own Convictions

The idea of defending oneself publicly, even against the most absurd accusations of the authorities, was alien to even the most courageous intellectuals during the Stalin era, as well as in the first years following Stalin's death. When, in 1954, Akhmatova, one of Russia's foremost poets, was publicly asked by foreigners what she thought about her denigration by the notorious Andrei Zhdanov, she answered that "she found both documents—Zhdanov's speech and the party decision—correct" (Chukovskaia 1980, p. 49). Aliger, a well-known Soviet poet, repented many times for her liberal errors, even after 1956 (see for instance, *Literaturnaia Gazeta*, October 8, 1957; see also Babenysheva 1981, p. 277), as did Evtushenko, Voznesenski, and Aksenov in 1963. Even Pasternak did not dare to challenge his detractors in 1958.

In the 1960s the reactions of Soviet intellectuals toward their denunciation by the authorities began to change. Alexander Nekrich was one of the first to follow a new pattern of behavior. His book, *Forty-First*, which described the Soviet Union's lack of preparedness for the war with Hitler and Stalin's responsibility for many mistakes, was published in 1963. It was acclaimed by the public as an honest book, although Stalin's blunders were already well known in the USSR after Khrushchev's secret speech at the Twentieth Party Congress. With the transition of power from Khrushchev to a new regime that clearly wanted to restore Stalin's authority, however, Nekrich and his book were discredited by the entire new ideological machine, though he was initially supported by the scholarly community. (Even during the officially sponsored debate in the Institute of Marxism-Leninism, a citadel of Soviet ideology, twenty of the twenty-three participants had backed the book.) For more than one and a half years, officials sought to compel Nekrich to repudiate his own book, but they were unsuccessful. An old party member and veteran of the last war, Nekrich was ultimately excluded from the party and forced to leave the country. (About this case, see the interview with Nekrich twenty-five years later in *Moskovskie Novosti*, October, 22, 1989.)

Another who staunchly defended his personal views was Levada, the famous sociologist whose book, *Lectures on Sociology* (1969), was strongly criticized by party officials. (About Levada, see Shlapentokh 1987.)

The political trials of the late 1960s were, in a sense, also a triumph for the intellectuals. Defendants at these trials were very different from those tried during the 1930s. Under Stalin, all defendants sought to present themselves as admirers of the leader and faithful communists who had been mistakenly accused. But defendants in the 1960s and later approached the matter very differently. The majority of those on trial boldly defended their views and actions and adopted stances far from the conformism of earlier defendants. Among them were Andrei Amalrik, Andrei Siniavski, Iuri Daniel, Vladimir Bukovski, Brodsky, and Alexander Ginzburg. (See "My Last Word: Speeches of Defendants at the Trials in 1966–1974," VS, nos. 14–15, 1974; Kaminskaia 1984, pp. 164–166.) Moreover, with the help of samizdat, the details of these trials became available to the public, which learned for the first time that their compatriots were willing to risk their freedom for their firm convictions. The notion that the public defense of one's views was worth the subsequent sanctions was new to those who, since the 1920s, had lived with the feeling that any resistance to the state would be worthless. This represented, then, another episode in the moral development of the Soviet intelligentsia.

The Defense of Friends and Colleagues

Just as Soviet intellectuals moved very slowly toward defending their own views publicly, they moved equally slowly toward achieving the resolve required to defend publicly those whom they loved and respected and whose attitudes they shared.

They were convinced that, under mortal threat, it was natural for them to make speeches that teemed with invectives supplied by the authorities against a current ideological culprit. As late as 1958 a number of decent writers, including Panova, Inber, Shklovski, Sel'vinski, and Slutski, participated in the campaign against Pasternak (see Chukovskaia 1980, p. 348).

As they were partially released from such all-encompassing fear, however, many intellectuals rapidly began not only to refuse to contribute to the persecution of a culpable fellow intellectual, but they began publicly and more frequently to take his or her side. Even in the Pasternak case, such intellectuals as Viacheslav Ivanov, Chukovskaia, and Valentin Asmus unequivocally lent support to the persecuted poet. The campaign in defense of the poet Brodsky, put on trial in 1964–1965 for "social parasitism," was probably the first sign of the changing behavior of Soviet intellectuals. Led by the writer and journalist Vigdorova, many writers and other intellectuals raised their voices to demand the acquittal of the talented young poet.

The civic courage of the Soviet intellectuals, especially writers, peaked in the mid-1960s, when several of them came to the defense of Siniavski and Daniel, and later of Solzhenitsyn.

When, at the end of the 1960s, political reaction began to rage, the number of intellectuals willing to defend those under fire began to decline again (although the number of "abstainers" still remained much greater than two decades earlier). In addition, the number of intellectuals willing to aid the authorities in destroying the careers and freedom of colleagues began to increase.[5] By the 1970s intellectuals once again had the same fear of the authorities they had had in the past (a development to which I will return later).

THE THIRD TYPE: ILLEGAL ACTIVITY IN SOVIET INSTITUTIONS

The most important elements of the third basic type of oppositional behavior involved the emergence of movements completely outside official control. For the first time, these movements, including protest letters and samizdat, challenged the state's monopoly over information. In both cases, intellectuals spontaneously created weak organizations that embraced the cream of the intellectual community.

Other examples of illegal activity in Soviet institutions included publications abroad, the refusal of some Soviet lawyers to follow standard instructions during political trials, and the mass contacts of intellectuals with foreign correspondents. This type of behavior was prominent in the late 1960s.

Samizdat

The protest letter campaign of the mid-1960s occurred simultaneously with the burgeoning of samizdat. The dissemination of unofficial literature actually began before 1964, probably in the mid- to late 1950s. One of the first pieces of samizdat, the summary of Paustovski's speech on *Not by Bread Alone*, was circulated in Moscow in 1956. Subsequent samizdat documents, such as General Alexander Todorski's letter to the film director Mikhail Romm, on Stalin's purge of the Red Army, and Fiodor Raskol'nikov's "Open Letter to Stalin," became popular not only in Moscow, but in other cultural centers as well. Another early piece of samizdat was Vigdorova's description of Brodsky's trial in Leningrad in 1964 (see Pliushch 1979, p. 50; Orlova 1982).

The real upsurge of samizdat began in the mid-1960s and was directly stimulated by Solzhenitsyn's unpublished works. *Cancer Ward* and *The First Circle* were among the first major pieces of samizdat to circulate. Other important works, such as Ginzburg's *Into the Whirlwind*, Pasternak's *Doctor Zhivago*, some stories by Varlam Shalamov, and the testi-

---

[5] Agness Barto, at the request of the Soviet authorities, conducted a review of the works of Siniavski and Daniel, which was used in the trial against them (see Chukovskaia 1979, p. 106).

mony of Anatoli Marchenko, also became highly popular works of samizdat. In the 1970s the most popular works were Solzhenitsyn's *The Gulag Archipelago*, and Nadezhda Mandel'shtam's *Memoirs*, along with the novels of Voinovich, Vladimov, Kornilov, and others.

The production of samizdat can be regarded as another step in the creation of an independent social institution designed to satisfy the cultural and political interests of the intelligentsia —interests ignored by those in power. A number of enthusiasts assumed the lion's share of the risk by typing and disseminating the literature themselves (the mathematician Iulius Telesin deserves special notice), and they were soon joined by others who contributed to the cause.

In fact, samizdat was so numerous in the early 1960s (according to some sources, more than three hundred authors gave their works to samizdat; Alexeieva 1984, p. 243; see also Reddaway 1972) that many among the intelligentsia read almost nothing but unofficial literature. The most courageous of them collected this output and built their own samizdat libraries, although many of them were later arrested and sentenced to significant jail terms (e.g., the Riga mathematician Lev Ladyzhenski). During the search of Pimenov's apartment, KGB agents found 250 samizdat publications in his library (*VS*, no. 8, 1973, p. 7).

Over time, nonfiction samizdat materials came to include a variety of historical investigations of secret official documents, transcripts of political trials, memoirs, and collections of political materials (such as Iakubovich's letter to the General Attorney about the show trial of Mensheviks in 1932). Samizdat also included translations of the works of censored foreign authors, such as Orwell's *1984*, Milovan Djilas's *New Class*, Arthur Koestler's *Darkness at Noon*, and Hemingway's *For Whom the Bell Tolls*. Materials related to political trials, such as those prepared by Iuri Galanskov and Ginzburg, particularly aroused the ire of the authorities, and the editors of such collections were sentenced to long jail terms. In the 1970s nonfiction materials dominated samizdat works. Examples are Roi Medvedev's historical works, Valentin Turchin's "Inertia of Fear," and the essays of Pomerants, Boris Shragin, and others.

Some of the most important samizdat contributions, the underground periodicals, are worthy of special attention. The authorities were particularly hostile toward these forms of samizdat because they were aware that part of Lenin's success in his struggle against tsarism could be attributed to the organizational role of such Bolshevik newspapers as *Iskra* and *Pravda*.

The first underground journal, *Syntaxis*, was founded by Alexander Ginzburg in 1959–1960. A number of subsequent periodicals, such as *Veche* (Council), *Zemlia* (Land), *Evrei v SSSR* (Jews in the USSR), *Poiski* (Search), *Nadezhda* (Hope), *Maria*, *Seiatel* (Sower), and many others with various ideological and political orientations, emerged but disappeared due to reprisals by the political police.

Of all samizdat periodicals, the most important was the *Chronicle of Current Events*, which continues to be produced after more than fifteen years (see Litvinov 1976). This journal has been the focus of the authorities' attention because of its immense popularity both inside and outside the country. In addition, it has generated a network of correspondence around the country, by all accounts reaching high into the hierarchy and even into the KGB itself, thus eliciting increased KGB animosity. The KGB was partially successful in its struggles against this periodical when leading figures among its editors, such as Piotr Iakir, Liudmila Alexeieva, and Tatiana Velikanova, were arrested, jailed, or expelled from the country.

The real recognition of samizdat came years later, in the late 1980s. The authors, disseminators, and readers of samizdat who had been persecuted by the authorities (many of them continued to be harshly persecuted until 1986) could hardly believe that an article entitled "Samizdat" could appear in a leading Soviet newspaper and could praise this enterprise (*Komsomol'skaia Pravda*, February 9, 1989), or that a television network would invite a samizdat activist such as the historian Arseni Roginski to its most popular program, "Vzliad" (Glance), even presenting him as a hero and an expert.

In addition, glasnost permitted the publication of practically all samizdat works. For almost three years in a row, Soviet literary magazines have maintained a high level of popularity, due in large part to the samizdat of the 1960s. The memoirs of Eugenia Ginzburg, Nadezhda Mandel'shtam, and Gnedin, as well as the novels of Sergei Platonov, Bulgakov, Pasternak, Dombrovski, Voinovich, Andrei Bitov, and Iskander, attracted immense audiences and contributed considerably to the prosperity of various literary magazines in the late 1980s.

Samizdat, which seemed to disappear from the public arena in the early years of glasnost, reappeared in 1987–1988, primarily because of the development of civil society and the stormy rise of informal organizations. When samizdat reappeared, its focus was on numerous periodicals, which were the organs of the new informal organizations. A typical example of this type of magazine was *Otkrytaia Zona* (Open Zone, the term used by gulag inmates for society outside of their own "closed zone"). It was published using computers (a major innovation since the 1960s, when the use of typewriters allowed the production of only four copies) by the Moscow club, Democratic Perestroika, headed by Oleg Rumiantsev. By early 1989 the club had published nine issues of the magazine. Dozens of other samizdat magazines were published in 1988–1989 in the Baltic republics, as well as in many other regions of the country.

For the most part, samizdat was sponsored by the informal organizations that mushroomed throughout the country in 1987–1989. According to Sergei Grigoriantz, the editor of the influential samizdat magazine *Glasnost*, there were 300 "big" samizdat periodicals in 1989 (Sirotkin 1990). Other sources have offered other figures: a special article on contemporary samizdat in an official Soviet magazine (what an eloquent sign of glasnost!) compiled a list of 150 Samzidat periodicals (*Sovietskaia Bibliografia*, no. 2, 1989), while an author in *Literaturnaia Gazeta* referred to 520 Samizdat periodicals in the Russian language alone (*LG*, January 10, 1990).

Protest Letters

The Brezhnev regime's political orientation became clear almost immediately after its seizure of power. Brezhnev's 1965 speech on Victory Day, with its laudatory references to Stalin, as well as the measures taken against both the "camp theme" in literature and discussion of the horrors of the Stalin era were evidence of the new directions the leadership would take.[6]

The intellectuals began their counteroffensive in 1965. It was triggered by Larisa Bogoraz, the wife of Daniel, who was arrested with Siniavski for his publications abroad. Bogoraz sent the first open letter to the General Attorney, in which she boldly accused the prosecution of using illegal methods to convict her husband.

In contrast to 1956 and 1962, when the intellectuals escalated their political activity with the permission and even encouragement of the leadership, the new steps taken in 1965 were initiated by intellectuals alone and in direct opposition to the leadership. In this phase, scholars (especially those from the natural sciences) took the leading role, and an unprecedented campaign was launched against the restoration of the cult of Stalin and the policies of the Stalin era (Cohen 1982, pp. 177–182).

The principal means of protest at this time was the use of letters signed by hundreds of people and sent to the Soviet leadership. The letter protesting the rehabilitation of Stalin, signed by twenty-five leading intellectuals (Artsimovich, Kapitsa, Sakharov, Tamm, Nekrasov, Paustovski, Chukovski, and others), was the first major action of this type. This letter,

---

[6] In fact, the first protest letter was sent to Khrushchev in the aftermath of his visit to the exhibition of abstract painting in November 1962. The letter, which demanded that Khrushchev not resort to old methods of repression against painters, was signed by the writers Simonov, Ehrenburg, Chukovski, and Kaverin, the physicist Igor Tamm, the chemist Nikolai Semionov, the sculptors Sergei Konenkov and Vladimir Favorski, the composer Shostakovich, and the film director Romm. Even Alexei Surkov, the former head of the Writers' Union, signed it (see Johnson 1973, pp. 9–10).

which was widely disseminated in Moscow and then in other cities in the second half of 1964, initiated a new phase in the liberal movement. Many other letters followed this first one, and many became familiar to the Western press.

One letter, protesting the internment of Alexander Esenin-Vol'pin in a psychiatric hospital, was signed by nearly one hundred Moscow mathematicians. Another, protesting the emergence of neo-Stalinism, was signed by over sixty Moscow writers. A letter in support of Solzhenitsyn was endorsed by a variety of prominent writers, including Antokol'ski, Viktor Konetski, and Viktor Sosnora. Other important letters included one in opposition to the political trials, which was signed by three dozen scholars in Academic Town, and the one from seventeen Ukrainian writers, all party members, also protesting these trials.

By the early 1970s, 181 letters had been sent to the Soviet government and other official bodies, another 35 to newspapers, 45 to individuals or groups in various professions, and 9 to "world public opinion." According to Amalrik's calculations, about one thousand people signed such protest letters, with scholars and literary figures constituting about two thirds of the signatories. Representatives of the mass intelligentsia made up another 13 percent, and students about 5 percent (Amalrik 1978, p. 26). Those who signed these letters faced a variety of political repercussions. About 15 percent were fired from their jobs within one month of signing a letter. A number of other signatories were expelled from the party, removed from their teaching duties in universities, and in some cases, even evicted from their homes (see also Berg 1983, pp. 262–280).

Intellectuals who signed protest letters were restricted from publishing their work or from traveling abroad. In many cases, signatories were kept in official disgrace for as long as ten years. Those endorsing letters were also denounced at meetings held for just this purpose, although officials were able to compel very few people to publicly condemn those who signed letters. The majority simply remained silent, and a few even sought to defend those who were targets of official denunciation.

The events surrounding the signing of protest letters produced a number of ethical problems that were quite new to the intellectuals of the 1960s. Up to this point the behavior of the Soviet people, including intellectuals, was shaped by the ethics of the 1930s, which had developed at a time when anyone could be arrested and imprisoned at any moment. Under such conditions, virtually any means of protecting oneself, short of reporting on others or, especially, slandering innocent people, were considered justifiable. The ethics of this period did not require that a person come to the defense of those being persecuted by the authorities. Still, those who continued to pursue friendly relations with "enemies of the people" or even with their children were viewed as heroic individuals.

Pasternak, for example, maintained communication with a number of people who were being held in jail.

The developments surrounding the protest letters revealed that a new political situation had emerged in the country, along with a reinterpretation of the "ethics of survival." People began to evaluate their own political behavior and that of others in new ways. These new moral standards were considerably more demanding than the old ones, for they required greater political activism, largely because the sanctions against opposition activity had been substantially reduced. The new political morality was revealed even as protest letters circulated and people were asked by their friends to add their names to the lists. Many people, of course, were highly reluctant to endorse such letters, and this often produced serious division between friends and acquaintances.

The next phase in the moral dilemma emerged when those who had endorsed letters became objects of official inquiry and denunciation. Those who attended party meetings often did not know how they should behave. As a result, there were periods when interpersonal relations became extremely tense and many friendships were destroyed forever, such as the period between March and April of 1968 in Academic Town.

Like samizdat and several other forms of oppositional activity, the protest-letters movement, after twenty years, finally received open public recognition, and the authors of these letters were hailed as heroes (see Levada and Sheinis 1988b; *LG*, November 16, 1988).

Open Letters

One of the most important political developments was the transformation of protest letters usually addressed to various official Soviet bodies—the General Secretary, the chairman of the government, the Presidium of the Supreme Council, the editorial boards of leading newspapers—into open letters. The latter differed from earlier protest letters in that they were explicitly addressed to *urbi et orbi*, that is, to everybody, to Soviet and international public opinion. Earlier letters had become public only when someone, without the consent and sometimes against the will of other signatories, submitted a letter to foreign correspondents. (About this complicated issue, see Berg 1983.) Thus, this development represented yet another breakthrough in the destruction of the information monopoly of the Soviet state.

Changing the Behavior of Attorneys

The democratic movement of the 1960s also exerted an important influence on the actions of attorneys representing political defendants. Previously, attorneys in political trials had played essentially ritualistic roles that had little to do with actually representing the rights and interests of the defendants. Consequently, few defendants paid much attention to the personality of the specific attorneys appointed by the courts.

In the 1960s, however, a new breed of attorneys emerged who, when defending political dissidents, took their duties seriously. Some Moscow attorneys, such as Sofia Kalistratova, Dina Kaminskaia, and Boris Zolotukhin, were brought in to represent certain political defendants and frequently came into direct confrontation with the entire Soviet judicial system. In the late 1980s these lawyers were hailed as heroes (Bukovski 1978; Kalistratova 1989; Kaminskaia 1984).

Publications Abroad

The publication of Pasternak's *Doctor Zhivago* in the West in 1957 triggered numerous significant political events. Unfortunately, some Soviet writers demonstrated little courage regarding Pasternak's case, as a number of prominent figures participated in the denunciation of the poet they loved and respected (see Ivinskaia 1978). Many writers (e.g., Aliger, Nikolai Chukovski) considered the foreign publication of Soviet writers an immoral action (Chukovskaia 1980, p. 581).

At the time, it seemed that the entire Pasternak incident, which ended with his death, was a defeat for the intellectuals. Yet this was not the case. In demonstrating the possibility of publishing works abroad which had been prohibited inside the country, Pasternak had ushered in a new era in Soviet political life. With the actions of Pasternak, as well as those of Valeri Tarsis, who published two novels (among them, *Ward 7*) in England in 1962, Soviet intellectuals acquired a powerful weapon in their struggle against the regime. Those who followed Pasternak and Tarsis in openly publishing in the West included Chukovskaia, Solzhenitsyn, Voinovich, Vladimov, Bitov, Sosnora, Pomerants, and others. Whatever future measures the authorities might take, they are unable to deprive the intellectuals of this weapon.

In the period of glasnost, all of the authors who secretly smuggled their works to the West, including those who, like Siniavski and Daniel, published their works under pen names, were not only totally "rehabilitated" but were even praised for their courage (see, for instance, *Moskovskie Novosti*, September 11, 1988).

Contacts with the West

The wall between foreigners and Soviet citizens has stood firmly throughout most of Soviet history, and, like publication abroad, contact with foreigners had, prior to 1986–1987, been viewed by the Soviet authorities as virtually illegal, even if it involved only a brief chat with a stranger. Still, there has been a notable increase in contact between the USSR and the West since 1953, and access to Western culture and mass media has been much easier than was true under Stalin. The World Youth Festival in Moscow in 1957 was significant in that it allowed Muscovites to see and even speak with foreigners for the first time in decades. The American Exhibition the following year was also important in this regard, as was the first Moscow International Film Festival in 1959. Yet, in spite of these events, the Soviet people remained relatively well protected from Western "infection" until the early 1960s.

Intellectuals such as Pavel Litvinov and Amalrik were the first to scale the wall separating the Soviet people from the world. They did so openly and on their own initiative, thereby destroying the political elite's strict control over contact with the West. As Amalrik put it, they had "thrown out a challenge not only to the KGB, but also to one of the most important unwritten laws of Soviet society: a kind of agreement between cat and mouse to the effect that the mouse will not squeak if the cat starts to eat him" (Amalrik 1982, p. 23). Moreover, intellectuals established their own channels of communication with the West, which played an important role in the political developments of the country. Consequently, it is no surprise that, in the 1970s and early 1980s, the authorities considered the reduction of free contact with the West a critical element in their offensive against the intellectual community.

Funerals

Throughout the 1960s and the early 1980s, the funerals of prominent intellectuals often became political events. The funerals were conducted in a tense atmosphere, replete with official agents. Many who attended had clearly come to demonstrate their allegiance to the ideas of humanism and democracy, which were associated in various ways with these writers.

Pasternak's funeral in 1960 was the first in a sequence of such events. Pasternak died in official disgrace, having been excluded from the Writers' Union and denounced in the press. Although the authorities carefully sought to bury the writer in a private and uneventful way, they were unsuccessful. A number of people came to pay their respects, including Kornilov, Asmus, Paustovski, Kaverin, Iashin, Liubimov, Kazakov, Lev Kopelev, Vigdorova, and Viasheslav Ivanov, and the famous Soviet pianists Maria Iudina and Richter played Bach and Mozart before the funeral. Despite the efforts of the authorities, the meeting over the tomb went far beyond mere formalities, with some attendants hinting in their speeches that the poet had been harassed to death by the regime (Chukovskaia 1980, p. 328; Ivinskaia 1978).

The funeral of Valeri Pavlinchuk, a physicist from Obninsk, a scientific center in the Kaluga region, also became a political event. Pavlinchuk had been an active member of the democratic movement and those who attended his passing, because of the presence of Litvinov and Bogaraz among the mourners, were labeled sympathizers of dissidents. Some of them, such as Levita, were expelled from the party and fired from their positions.

Other funerals carried similar connotations. The ceremony for Alexei Kosterin, the writer and dissident, was practically an open political demonstration, with over three hundred mourners, of whom General Grigorenko played the leading role (Grigorenko 1982). The same can be said about the funeral of Tvardovski in 1971 (Medvedev 1973, pp. 185–193).

THE FOURTH TYPE: STRONG ILLEGAL ACTIVITY

The fourth type of political behavior—organized "material" actions that directly challenge the Soviet political order and its main bodies, including the KGB—played a leading role in the late 1960s. This type of behavior assumes the emergence of political leaders among the intellectuals. The political opposition of intellectuals did not reach its peak, however, until the middle of the next decade when, despite the political reaction, intellectuals created various committees openly opposed to the state.

The Challenge to the KGB

The Soviet people entered the post-Stalin period with a boundless fear of the political police and with the firm conviction that the KGB knew everything about them and was capable of sending them to a concentration camp at its whim. For its part, the KGB sustained this dread, although in Khrushchev's times it tried to dispel this fear somewhat, and in Brezhnev's times it attempted to embellish the image of the "chekist" (a member of the political police during the civil war).

The intellectuals were the first to do an unbelievable thing: they began to defy the KGB not only when they were summoned to KGB headquarters or at an interrogation when they were arrested, but in their open speeches, open letters, and publications as well. Solzhenitsyn was one of the first to openly accuse the KGB of violating the law. Sakharov repeated these accusations a few years later. They were joined by Voinovich, who described at length how the KGB tried to frighten him into abandoning his dissident activity, all the way up to poisoning him (Voinovich 1985). Vladimov went even further and wrote a novel about a KGB team watching the life of a dissident writer (Vladimov 1983). Many others challenged the KGB in samizdat publications (see, for instance, Podrabinek's "State Terrorism," in *Poiski*, no. 2, 1980, pp. 201–203; Pliushch 1979, p. 451).

Still, the most passionate and courageous defiance of the KGB was that of the Ukrainian poet Vasil' Stus, who, in his open letter, "I Accuse," labeled the KGB a "criminal police organization, openly inimical to the people." His letter was all the more remarkable in that he wrote it while imprisoned in the gulag, completely at the mercy of his jailers, who later pushed him (either directly or indirectly—it is unclear) to his death (*VS*, no. 2, 1976, pp. 38–44).

Attendance at Political Trials

As part of the Soviet system of coercion, the courts were considered seemingly impervious to the criticism of ordinary people. Any attempt to obstruct the processes of Soviet courts was deemed virtually impossible and fraught with serious consequences, nearly akin to a paramilitary assault on a police station.

Toward the end of the 1960s, however, Soviet intellectuals began to overcome this barrier and appeared at the Soviet courts to demonstrate their opposition to the procedures used by the judicial system to illustrate the antisocial character of the defendants. As early as the trial of Revol't Pimenov and Boris Vail, which occurred in 1957, the majority of witnesses openly sided with the defendants. Many friends of the defendants came to the building where the trial was taking place and expressed their sympathy for them (Pimenov 1973, pp. 42–45). The trial of Ginzburg, Galanskov, Alexei Dobrovol'ski, and Vera Lashkova was also noteworthy in this regard. Some two hundred people spent the entire four days of the trial near the courtroom, for they were barred from the hearing itself. Some even came into direct physical confrontation with KGB agents (see Amalrik 1982; Grigorenko 1982; Vladimov 1980).

Since that point, virtually every political trial in the country has occasioned some oppositional activity by dissidents or sympathizers demonstrating their support of the accused and their condemnation of the Soviet judicial system. Sakharov and Grigorenko were particularly diligent in these demonstrations, seeking to appear at any political trial in the country and often making dangerous trips from Moscow to other cities where dissidents were being tried.

Material Help to Political Prisoners

In its effort to monopolize all means of influencing human behavior, the Soviet state tried until 1987–1988 to completely control each citizen's standard of living, including attempts to restrict all unofficial channels used to obtain material goods, since these channels reduce one's dependence on the authorities.

The Soviet state was particularly uncompromising in its drive for absolute control over all facets of the lives of those considered political criminals. For this reason, the intellectuals' provision of material assistance to political prisoners, as well as to members of their families, was a political event of great importance, representing yet another fissure in the monopoly of the state.

The first such parcels and letters were sent to political prisoners in the spring of 1966. After 1968 this assistance was regular and well organized. Money for food and clothing was collected through networks of friends and acquaintances, which included many hundreds of the intelligentsia. The next step in this sphere of activity was Solzhenitsyn's creation in 1976 of the Russian fund for assistance to political prisoners (Alexeieva 1984, pp. 262–264).

Political Gatherings and Demonstrations

In addition to activities at political trials, oppositional activity among intellectuals sometimes included participation in public gatherings and demonstrations clearly directed against the leadership. This activity, however, was limited to a relatively small number of participants.

The first unsanctioned public gatherings took place in Moscow in the late 1950s, when young people collected to read poetry near the monument for Vladimir Maiakovski. Even then the authorities frowned on such gatherings, for in these gatherings was seen the germ of more troublesome political actions (see Bukovski 1979; Pimenov 1979–1980; Vail 1980).

The next phase of public gatherings included those that developed around the monument in Pushkin Square in Moscow in 1965. These events were organized to occur on December 5, the anniversary of the day in 1936 on which the Soviet constitution, detailing a variety of human rights, was adopted (Bukovski 1979). The gatherings in Pushkin Square were in support of an argument advanced by Esenin-Vol'pin that eventually became widespread in the democratic movement of the 1970s—that there was no need to introduce new laws to protect the rights of Soviet citizens, for these laws were already on the books. Instead, what was necessary was to observe the laws that already existed. As in most of these situations, it was the intellectuals who gathered in Pushkin Square in 1965, and they assembled each subsequent year, up through the late 1970s.

Equally important was the January 1967 demonstration in opposition to the trial of the dissidents Galanskov, Ginzburg, Dobrovol'ski, and Lashkova. To illustrate their disapproval of this trial, students at Novosibirsk University used the cover of night to paint a series of slogans on public buildings. For a few hours the following morning, residents of Academic Town were able to contemplate the painted words condemning the Soviet judicial system and likening it to that of Nazi Germany.

The political activity of the 1960s peaked when seven individuals, including the poets Natalia Gorbanevskaia and Vadim Delone, the linguist Bogoraz, and the mathematician Litvinov, demonstrated against the Soviet invasion of Czechoslovakia in August 1968. A number of other intellectuals reacted publicly to this event. Evtushenko, for example, wrote a poem about Russian tanks in the streets of Prague. Boris Orlov, the *Izvestia* correspondent in Czechoslovakia, refused to dispatch deceptive articles to the newspaper and was summarily dismissed (about this case, see *LG*, December 13, 1989). Still, no one defied the invasion as strongly as did the seven dissidents who unfurled a banner for a few seconds before being subdued by the KGB. All were sentenced to jail terms and passed a number of years in exile. Ultimately some would go abroad.

Solzhenitsyn's Historical Contribution

The case of Solzhenitsyn is an important chapter in the intellectual movement of the 1960s. His contribution to the political opposition cannot, however, be reduced simply to his writings, despite their significance. Solzhenitsyn, in fact, declared a personal war against the Soviet system.

Solzenhitsyn's novels left no doubt as to his attitudes toward the Soviet system. The works of the former gulag inmate unambiguously conveyed his rejection of the system as a whole. Unlike other critical writers, he could not be interpreted as being moved by a concern for the progress of socialism. In his view, one could have no illusions as to the possibility of a humane socialism.

Solzhenitsyn boldly and uncompromisingly challenged the KGB publicly, including its head, Iuri Andropov. On one occasion in 1966 he publicly attacked the KGB during his speech at Lazarev's Oriental Institute at the height of the KGB campaign against him. In 1971 he came out boldly in defense of his friend, Alexander Gorlov, who had been caught in Solzhenitsyn's country house by KGB agents and beaten after he obstructed their search of the grounds. Solzhenitsyn prepared an open letter to Andropov in connection with the incident, demanding that those responsible for the attack on Gorlov be punished (see Gorlov 1977; *VS*, no. 21, 1972, pp. 11–13; see also Scammell 1984, pp. 526, 530–531, 561–562, 590–591).

In 1967 Solzhenitsyn wrote a letter to the Congress of Soviet Writers arguing for the elimination of the official practice of censorship. He was clearly aware that the congress could not approve such a proposal. His intent was to stir up a political scandal, to embarrass the conformist writers, and to create tension between the intellectual community and the political elite. To some degree, he achieved his goals. About one hundred writers supported this letter (Solzhenitsyn 1975c, p. 181).

Solzhenitsyn's rebellious behavior sparked numerous other political events. By the late 1960s and early 1970s, when Solzhenitsyn was regularly harassed by the KGB, a number of prominent intellectuals came to his defense, such as Mstislav Rostropovich and Chukovskaia. Over time, the conflict between Solzhenitsyn and the authorities became even more intense. But by then it was not the political elite who aggravated the conflict, but the author himself. He took the political offensive, continuing to publish his works in the West and maintaining regular contact with foreign correspondents, in blatant defiance of the warnings of the authorities.

The publication of *The Gulag Archipelago* (1973–1975b) represented the culmination of his struggle with the Soviet system. This work dealt the system a blow of remarkable proportions, the historical consequences of which perhaps even surpassed those of Khrushchev's secret speech at the Twentieth Party Congress in 1956. *The Gulag* illustrated how the system created by the Bolsheviks had, from the beginning, been poisoned by the use of the cruelest methods of preserving their dominance. He further demonstrated that each period of Soviet history had victimized a specific stratum of the population. In his next work, *Lenin in Zurich* (1976), Solzhenitsyn came out openly against the founder of the Soviet state and again demonstrated his incompatibility with the system.

Sakharov's Moral Challenge to the System

Sakharov's decision to participate in the democratic movement was also one of the most important political events of the period. Sakharov was an outstanding scientist who proclaimed himself a champion of democracy in the USSR and came to accept the struggle for social progress as his major life goal. Before Sakharov, most natural scientists had participated only in isolated actions against the regime, such as signing protest letters, and none considered political activity their central concern. By contrast, Sakharov adopted political opposition as a permanent part of his life and became a leader of the democratic movement.

Sakharov's transition from a member of the privileged Soviet establishment to the ranks of political opposition was an unprecedented shock for the Soviet bureaucracy and for the society as a whole. Before Sakharov, no dissident had been part of the favored segment of society. For example, one would expect Solzhenitsyn to be hostile toward the system, having been its prisoner and victim in the gulag. Others, such as Siniavski or Daniel, were little-known writers whose status in Soviet society had been modest. But Sakharov had been virtually at the pinnacle of the Soviet hierarchy. Decorated three times with the highest Soviet honor, the title of Hero of Socialist Labor, and a highly regarded member of the Academy of Sciences, he had virtually everything a Soviet citizen could want. Neither he nor his relatives had been offended by the regime in any way and, as an ethnic Russian, he was exposed to no national discrimination.

Thus Sakharov's challenge to the system was unprecedented in Soviet history. Never had one so privileged risked everything to side with the subordinate class in the USSR. In fact, Sakharov's actions cast doubt on the moral foundations of the system, even for those completely loyal to it. His statements that the USSR did not meet the demands of a normal civilized society greatly influenced the Soviet people, who were educated to have considerable respect for science and scientists.

One of Sakharov's merits was that he not only shook the legitimacy of the Soviet system, but he developed a program for social and political reform for the country (Sakharov 1968). Unlike Solzhenitsyn, he offered a policy that was quite realistic and took the characteristics of the system into full consideration. For this reason, the authorities were far more concerned with Sakharov than with Solzhenitsyn. Solzhenitsyn's vision of a future Russia, based on an autocratic, religious state, cut off from the national republics and concentrated on the development of the northeastern region, was so divorced from possibility as to be substantially less threatening than Sakharov's program.

Sakharov continued his political activity literally up until his dying day. He died on December 14, 1989, only a few hours after he last challenged the Soviet leader at the second session of the Congress of People's Deputies. In this last public appearance, Sakharov defended the multiparty system and was treated rudely by Gorbachev, who, only two months later, accepted the idea of a multiparty system as unavoidable. Sakharov's funeral drew many thousands of people who paid a tribute he never received when he was alive.

Vasili Grossman—A Model of Intellectual Heroism

The 1960s produced a figure who was, in some ways, more tragic than any of the decade's other heroes. Until the mid-1950s, Vasili Grossman was a well-known and relatively successful official writer (despite having been victimized by the anti-Semitic campaign carried out in the last months of Stalin's life). During the war, however, Grossman started to revise his orthodox views, and after 1953 began to write as a new man.

Of course, official ideology remained all-pervasive during the first post-Stalin decade: the bravest intellectuals pledged their support (both publicly and privately) for Marxism and human socialism, hailed Lenin as Russia's great benefactor, and knowingly overlooked numerous heinous episodes from Soviet history. Solzhenitsyn was still only considering *The Gulag Archipelago*, and it would be several years until Sakharov would start his political activity (which, by then, would be well fitted in socialist ideology).

Yet, in the 1950s, Grossman, forecasting the genuine liberalization of the human mind, was already writing his two great books, *Life and Fate* and *Forever Flowing*—books that analyzed the Soviet system, Lenin's activity, and Soviet history, and that, when published in the USSR in 1988–1989, aroused stupefication, admiration, and hatred.

When the manuscript of *Life and Fate* was seized by the KGB in 1961, Mikhail Suslov, the country's ideological dictator, promised that it would remain unpublished for three hundred years. Although the confiscation of the manuscript (and of what the KGB believed were all of the copies) failed to prevent its eventual publication, it definitely contributed to Grossman's premature death only a few years later (1964). Grossman died not knowing that he had penned a book that would be compared (not three centuries, but two decades later) with Tolstoy's *War and Peace*, that he would be one of the first to dare to speak of Lenin and the Russian traditions of serfdom as a truly free man, and that his name would, in the late 1980s, be one of those most often mentioned in the Soviet press.

General Grigorenko: The Intellectual from the Army

General Grigorenko's contribution to the democratic movement was most important because he came from the army, one of the least progressive segments of Soviet society. A confirmed communist and ardent supporter of the Soviet system, Grigorenko moved steadily into confrontation with official Soviet policy following the Twentieth Party Congress. He began his political activity with a remarkably bold speech at a party conference and moved into other realms, such as publicly defending the Crimean Tartars who were struggling for the right to return to their ancestral home.

As a department chair in one of the most prestigious military academies, Grigorenko was less a representative of the army than of the military intelligentsia. That is, he was a part of a segment of the military that has grown in response to scientific and technological advances in warfare and includes many individuals from civilian professions, such as physicists, engineers, chemists, and mathematicians. The loyalty of the military intelligentsia to the regime is, of course, vitally important to the leadership, for the military intelligentsia directly controls the weaponry so central to the Soviet military. Their advanced levels of education are of even greater significance, for they have considerable influence over other groups in the officer corps. The case of Grigorenko is unique among the military intelligentsia. Nonetheless, the leadership can take little consolation in this, since, in Soviet-type societies, for each act of public defiance there are many other people who would take similar actions should the appropriate circumstances present themselves.

CONCLUSION

The 1960s were the most heroic period in the postrevolutionary history of the Soviet intellectuals. It was the only period when intellectuals, at significant risk to their welfare and future, openly challenged the authorities. None of the activists of glasnost demonstrated the kind of courage required by those who defied the system twenty years earlier.

In the 1960s the intellectuals managed to break the state's monopoly in many fields—contacts with the West, the dissemination of information and works in literature and the arts, and the organization of meetings and demonstrations. For the first time in Soviet history (and so far, the last time), the intellectuals (and not the leader, as was the case in Gorbachev's period) set their own agenda for political action, thereby laying the first bricks of Soviet civil society and creating the conditions necessary for a lunge toward liberal society. Moreover, the intellectuals advanced from their ranks leaders who became moral authorities for the nation and who successfully competed with the official ideology in their influence over the masses.

CHAPTER SIX

Liberal Socialism: The Main Ideological Trend of the 1960s

SOVIET INTELLECTUALS, as well as the mass intelligentsia, entered the 1950s both physically and intellectually terrorized. With few exceptions, most notably among those intellectuals brought up before the Revolution, the intellectuals shared the official vision of Stalin's Russia: even if the intellectuals could not approve of the developments of the 1930s, they considered them inevitable parts of a history determined by objective laws demanding great sacrifices for the creation of a new society (see Grigorenko 1982; Kol'man 1982; Orlova 1983; Simonov 1988; Ulanovskie 1982).

The magic of "historical necessity," discovered by Marxism, was successfully inculcated into the minds of even the most sophisticated intellectuals, not only in the USSR but even in postwar Poland and Czechoslovakia, countries with strong intellectual traditions and close cultural connections with the West. This indoctrination occurred despite the already available, albeit limited, information on the events in Russia following 1917 (see, for instance, Hruby 1980; Milosz 1953).

After 1953, with the disappearance of mass terror and the gradual release from all-encompassing fear, Soviet intellectuals began the process of reconsidering their world views, particularly of life in their own country. In analyzing this process one must once again remember that, given their ironclad dependence on the Soviet state, most intellectuals try, especially at the beginning of each reassessment, to preserve their ties to the official ideology and the party apparatus.

In examining ideological trends among the Soviet intellectuals, I will deal primarily with those ideas which, although discussed at private meetings, were published in one way or another, either by Soviet editors or in samizdat. The ideas that remained within private circles will, as a rule, be ignored here, even if their originality or importance for the future were great.[1]

The three trends to be discussed—neo-Leninism, technocratism, and

---

[1] Several authors have discussed the ideological trends that have emerged in the USSR since 1953, and a number of different classifications of these trends have been developed (Amalrik 1982; Biddulph 1972; Feuer 1969; Ianov 1978 and 1988; Shtromas 1981; Tokes 1975).

liberal socialism—shared three very important features: they could all be considered "universal," "Westernized," and "scientific." That is, they assumed the existence of general laws of social development for mankind, they saw the West as a model in one respect or another, and they looked to science for the solution to many problems. These features were rejected by Russophilism, which entered the Soviet political scene as a visible ideological force in the late 1960s and became the leading ideology of the following decade. (Russophilism will be discussed in chapters 7 and 8.)

A considerable number of intellectuals, as well as members of the mass intelligentsia, reject all of the ideologies just described. These intellectuals have lost their belief in any ideology that assumes solidarity or even the slightest degree of submission of individual interests to common goals. Many look for spiritual salvation either in mystic cults or in the pursuit of egotistical pleasures of all sorts, while showing contempt for all types of moral exhortation, whatever the origin. I will return to this issue in chapter 7.

NEO-LENINISM: THE YEARNING FOR IDEOLOGICAL CONTINUITY

In the years immediately following Stalin's death, intellectuals were able to analyze Soviet society only from within the framework of a Marxist-Leninist world view. During this period, the leading ideas to reach public awareness about Soviet society's future development were those based on the restoration of the Leninist principles of social and political life. Proponents of these ideas, dominant among active intellectuals until the mid-1960s, dreamed of the genuine restoration of "the Leninist norm of party and social life." In fact, there were no formal differences between neo-Leninist and official ideologies. The former simply demanded that official slogans be implemented into life. The generic features of this ideology included praise of the October Revolution, as well as support for both the one-party political system and for internal party democracy.

The neo-Leninist view of Soviet society, as it emerged after 1953, recognized the political monopoly of the party and its centralized control over society, as well as its rejection of "political pluralism." The neo-Leninist view demanded a return to the political climate of Lenin's times and stressed guarantees against the repression of the Stalin era. In addition, neo-Leninism stressed respect for party cadres and party intellectuals, the restoration of internal party democracy (including the right to create oppositional political factions), creative attitudes toward Marxist theory and ideology, the elimination of anti-Semitism from official policy, the free flow of information, and the development of critical activity among all people for the benefit of socialist construction.

While recognizing the October Revolution as a desirable, or at least unavoidable, event, the neo-Leninists differed among themselves in their evaluations of Soviet history and their definitions of the current Soviet system. Most rejected the entire period after Lenin's death, while some accepted industrialization and even collectivization but condemned what had happened since 1934 (the beginning of the Great Terror). Although the majority of neo-Leninists considered the current Soviet society to be socialist, albeit with many imperfections, other neo-Leninists labeled the Soviet system "state capitalism." In substance, the neo-Leninist model was primarily addressed to "genuine" communists and those truly devoted to the ideas of Marxism (see Zimin 1981).

From 1953 to 1963, public criticism could be voiced only by those with loyal political credentials, and for this reason only an ideology very close to the official one could be used as the basis for critical activity. This explains why neo-Leninism was the only nonofficial ideology in this period to have active advocates. Its most authoritative and active mouthpiece was A. Rumiantsev, a high party dignitary, who represented party liberals until his dismissal in 1972. He preached neo-Leninist ideology in numerous articles and books (for instance, see Rumiantsev 1965, 1970).

Novyi Mir, the intelligentsia's main instrument of communication in the 1960s, advocated primarily neo-Leninist ideology during this period; in only a few cases did it go further, moving toward liberal, pluralistic socialism or liberal Russophilism. According to Tvardovski, the editor in chief, and his lieutenants, such as Alexander Dementiev and Vladimir Lakshin, the October Revolution was a great and positive event, but Stalin made it impossible for the Soviet people to enjoy its fruits (see Dementiev 1969; Lakshin 1977, 1980; Tvardovski 1974, 1985).

Besides Rumiantsev and Tvardovski, neo-Leninist ideology inspired a number of prominent intellectuals such as Lev Kopelev (1978), Karpinski (1972), Grigorenko (1982), and many others.[2] These intellectuals adhered to the legal forms of neo-Leninism, which did not directly challenge the party leadership. Alongside this legal neo-Leninism existed an illegal form, which demanded action against the dominant political elite, who were seen as betraying the ideals of the October Revolution.

---

[2] The so-called old Bolsheviks, including those who returned from the gulag, constituted a special group. Only a few of them, like Maria and Nadezhda Ulanovskie (1982), Evgeni Gnedin (1982), and apparently Ginzburg (1979) broke with the ideology that had inflamed them in their youth. The majority continued to regard themselves as true communists, faithful to the ideals of the Revolution. Of course, they disapproved of Stalin's atrocities, especially those committed against communists, but they find no grounds for revising their worldview. Mira Blinkova (1983) described a typical representative of this group, the historian Viktor Dalin. In the 1960s Dalin, who had spent many years in the gulag, still considered the day when he listened to Lenin at the Congress of Komsomol the happiest day of his life. Dalin ended a speech at a jubilee in his honor with an appeal to the audience to join him in singing "The Internationale," which stupefied liberal historians.

Most of illegal neo-Leninism's advocates were young students who, even before 1953, had begun to create their own groups based primarily on the careful reading of Lenin's works (Lenin's *State and Revolution* was especially popular in these circles), which, in the eyes of these young people, demonstrated the incompatibility of the current system with Lenin's ideas. One example of such a group was the Communist Party of the Youth (or KPM in its Russian abbreviation). This group, created by fifty-three teenagers in Voronezh in 1948, is but one of several groups to emerge in the 1950s and 1960s (Zhigulin 1988).

Neo-Leninist circles emerged in Moscow University (Krasnopevtsev's circle), in colleges in Leningrad, Gorky, Kasan', and elsewhere (Kopelev 1978, p. 42; Pimenov 1979–1980; *Vol'noie Slovo*, no. 2, 1972, pp. 105–108). As Boris Vail and other former inmates of the camps have pointed out, the gulags of the post-Stalin era were filled with committed young followers of Leninism. They have described curious scenes in which prisoners requested copies of Marx's *Das Kapital* or Lenin's works, and other similar works for study, works the KGB officers had never read (Gidoni 1980, pp. 164–165; Vail 1980). As Mikhail Kheifets (1978) suggests, because the popularity of neo-Leninist and Marxist ideologies was waning and fewer true believers existed, their supporters vanished from the camps by the 1970s (p. 125; see also Pliushch 1979, p. 297).

As mentioned earlier, neo-Leninism was popular among Soviet intellectuals chiefly from 1953 to 1963, after which it began to retreat under the pressure of liberal socialism. Of course, neo-Leninism, as a concept that rejects a multiparty system, still exists on the Soviet political scene (Alexeieva 1984, p. 355).

During the first years of Gorbachev's regime, despite the new freedom of expression, the neo-Leninists (or Soviet "new left," as they began to call themselves) were almost invisible. Nearly all of the critics of the old system were Westernizers or Russophiles who spurned the neo-Leninists for different reasons. As inflation and social differentiation increased, however, and the standard of living of many groups declined, the new left became more vocal, particularly among the youth, although it made little significant encroachment into the intellectual community. (About the new left see Kagarlitski 1988; O. Rumiantsev 1989.)

Early in the period of glasnost, Lenin's name and his works continued to be widely used by liberals, especially those close to the party. In this way they substantiated their political and economic concepts, most of which, however, had very little in common with Leninist views, particularly those concerned with democracy. The most ardent among those who exploited Lenin for their own liberal purposes made sharp distinctions between the disappointed, pessimistic, and ailing Lenin after the civil war and the self-assertive and nondemocratic Lenin of earlier periods. A similar distinction was made by the intellectuals in the 1960s regarding Marx, when radical distinctions were made between the young and the old Marx, in favor of the former (see, for instance, Migranian 1988, p. 100). Still, it was possible to find true Leninists, almost indistinguishable from liberal Stalinists, who suggested that the early 1920s could serve as a model for present-day Soviet society.

Soviet Technocracy: Unrestrained Belief in the Power of Science

In the mid-1960s, neo-Leninist ideology was gradually replaced in the minds of active intellectuals by three new schools of thought: technocratism, liberal socialism, and Russophilism. All three schools initially grew out of official ideology and accepted or rejected various elements of it.

Technocratism was closest to neo-Leninism and the official ideology in that it retained the same strongly elitist approach to the governing of society. Its proponents simply adopted the official postulate of Marxism as a science, and argued that professional experts should make all important decisions according to the most recent scientific achievements. The core of the technocratic view held that, above all, Soviet society required rapid progress in the sciences and that such progress could aid the resolution of nearly all problems confronting society. Its advocates were inspired by the progress of cybernetics and applied mathematics, and they stressed the widespread use of computers and quantitative methods in all spheres of economic, social, and political life. The 1960s were characterized by a near-blind faith in scientism and the unlimited possibilities of scientific progress (see Shreider 1969).

The impact of scientism was very strong in the first political writings of Sakharov, who normally represented other intellectual trends in the country. He even started his first manifesto by voicing praise for "the scientific method of directing policy, the economy, arts, education, and military affairs" and he regretted that "the scientific approach has still not become reality" (Sakharov 1970, p. 25). The Sakharov of the 1980s would never again refer to "the scientific method" as the main authority.

During this period, mathematical economics began to develop in the country. Many intellectuals, such as Fedorenko, Moiseiev, Abel' Aganbegian, Kantorovich, Katsenelinboigen, Glushkov, Igor Birman, Viktor Belkin, and others, began to use computers and mathematics in economic management and pushed for the computerization of planning and the broad use of mathematical methods. Optimal programming was promoted as having the ability to radically improve the state of the economy and create a basis for a leap forward (see Katsenelinboigen 1980).

In many cases, advocates of technocracy and liberal socialism united to confront conservative ideologists and officials. Liberals consistently supported cybernetics and computers as important vehicles for progress, while proponents of technocracy backed most liberal ideas relating to various spheres of life. Still, these two groups had very different relationships with the authorities. While liberals remained in regular opposition to the official ideology and were generally the foundation from which dissidents sprang, advocates of technocracy maintained contact with the leadership and were often anxious to reach the higher echelons of power in the party apparatus. These two groups differed above all in their assessment of what was most important for the progress of Soviet society. For liberals, democracy was the necessary ingredient; for technocrats, science.

Technocratic ideas were practically swept away in the 1970s, and by 1985–1988 there were almost no technocrats among Soviet intellectuals. Authors like Moiseiev, who continued to defend technocratic ideas as well as planning and programming based on science, were seen as mavericks and anachronisms in the atmosphere of the late 1980s (Moiseiev 1988).

The evolution of the views espoused by Aganbegian reflects the changes in society in general. Aganbegian, who was regarded as Gorbachev's major economic advisor in the first days of his regime, had, from the late 1950s until the middle of the 1980s, preached the use of mathematical planning methods as the major solution to the economic problems of the country. As an ardent advocate of mathematical economics he was awarded various degrees, plus membership in the Academy of Sciences. In the mid-1960s he became director of the Institute of Economics and Industrial Production in Novosibirsk, and in the early 1980s he was appointed chairman of the economic section of the Academy of Sciences. After 1985, however, he was almost totally oblivious to his old religion, and, in numerous articles and speeches during the Gorbachev era, almost never mentioned optimal programming or other gimmicks of mathematical economics as being relevant to the future of the Soviet economy. (Compare Aganbegian and Belkin 1961; Aganbegian and Kazakevich 1969; Aganbegian et al. 1972; and Aganbegian et al. 1974 with Aganbegian 1987, 1988a, 1988b, and 1989.)

THE MOVE TOWARD LIBERAL SOCIALISM

The ideological evolution of the Soviet intellectuals proceeded very rapidly after 1953, as if they wanted to overcome in a few years the consequences of two decades of spiritual stagnation. By the beginning of the 1960s, many intellectuals had already begun to move away from neo-Leninism.

The growing influence of liberal socialism occurred alongside a gradual decline in the prestige of Lenin and the rapprochement of Lenin and Stalin in the minds of intellectuals and the mass intelligentsia (Solzhenitsyn 1976; Zimin 1981, pp. 144–146).[3] Both leaders came to be seen as responsible for the horrors of the past forty years, and Stalin was no longer considered the sole source of such developments. The October Revolution was deemed a negative event that aborted the democratic developments started by the February Revolution.

Having released themselves from the magnetism of Lenin and the October Revolution, and with the first torrents of information on life in the West and the new data on Stalin's times, many intellectuals began moving toward a more skeptical attitude regarding the supposed superiority of the Soviet system over modern capitalism. Of course, not all of these intellectuals dared, even in the 1960s, to formulate their attitudes toward the two systems in an unequivocal way.

In analyzing the historical experience of their country following the Revolution, the intellectuals made what was for them a sensational discovery that confirmed what they had only suspected before: that it was not economic relations which determined the nature of Soviet society, but its political structure. That is, political power was, in fact, the major determinant of Soviet history, and probably of the history of many other societies as well.

Of course, political power was not neglected in Marxist writings. Lenin himself demonstrated a preoccupation with power. He perceived almost all developments primarily through the prism of the struggle for power. Stalin also clearly understood the role of power, even in his speeches and publications. Despite all of this, however, official ideology had managed to persuade the majority of the intellectuals of the validity of a central Marxist thesis: that of the basis and the superstructure, which implies the leading role of the economic structure in social life.

Only in the mid-1960s did the intellectuals come to understand the key role of political power in Soviet-type society. From this period on, Soviet intellectuals became almost obsessed with the theme of political power. They realized that Soviet society was fundamentally political, and that the solution to any serious social or economic problem depended on changes in the Soviet political structure.[4]

---

[3] The avalanche of anecdotes on Lenin in 1970, the year in which the Soviet authorities celebrated the hundredth anniversary of his birth, was a final milestone in the private debunking of the first Soviet leader.

[4] The end of the 1950s brought a growth in interest in literature about societies with strong political power and their leaders. Despotic Russian tsars like Ivan the Terrible, Peter the Great, and Nikolas I were the subjects of special curiosity, as were the details of Stalin's life. (It is interesting that hatred of Stalin was combined with an insatiable quest for infor-

156 . Chapter Six

The idea of the primacy of political power in Soviet life, and therefore also of the party apparatus and the KGB, gained almost absolute consensus among intellectuals. Even at this time, however, the liberal intellectuals were divided into two groups, the "liberal socialists" and the "democrats."

The members of the first group continued to believe, despite the new circumstances and the new information that had become available, that socialism was the real goal of mankind and must replace capitalism throughout the world, and in the different constituent features of socialism (human freedom, integration, creativity, and so on). For these intellectuals, Soviet society could not claim to be socialist. These intellectuals devoured with special interest all materials containing Marxist analyses of Soviet society. Djilas's *The New Class* was their bible. They were also particularly drawn to the writings of old Russian social democrats, who became Lenin's opponents after October 1917. During this period, Roi Medvedev was certainly the most eloquent spokesman for this group (Medvedev 1975; see also Abovin-Egides 1984, p. 224; Liubarski 1984, p. 69; Turchin 1978).[5]

The intellectuals in the second group, unlike those in the first, held that the Soviet Union operated under a truly socialist system. They insisted that the Soviet system, despite its cruelties, was real socialism. For these intellectuals, the February Revolution in 1917 was the most promising event in recent Russian history because it could have paved the way to the "normal" capitalist development of Russia.

Up to this point in the 1960s, the "democrats" considered the installation of capitalism and bourgeois democracy to be absolutely utopian. They were therefore united with the liberal socialists in the conviction that the essential economic features of the Soviet system—state ownership of the major means of production and consequently the political monopoly of the party—were irreversible.

---

mation about him, a fact that irked many people.) Because of obvious parallels with Soviet society, Soviet intellectuals were fascinated with the history of the Roman empire, with its powerful caesars (Suetonus's *The Life of Twelve Caesars* and Plutarch's *Comparative Biographies* were among the most coveted books), and by the Oriental despotic societies and the so-called Oriental mode of production, which also pointed to the decisive role of political power.

[5] Many authors regard Medvedev as a mouthpiece of neo-Leninism. There is no doubt that, in many of his writings, Medvedev presents himself as an orthodox Marxist and Leninist. At many times, however, he has clearly declared himself an advocate of political pluralism, not only within the Communist party, but in society in general. He has underscored the necessity for political opposition in the USSR (see, for instance, Medvedev 1975)—a fundamental fact that places him much closer to liberal socialism than to traditional Marxism. (The contradictions in Medvedev's works were aptly used by Shafarevich in his scathing attacks against Marxism and socialism; see Shafarevich 1978.)

As Soviet intellectuals reflected on this question, it became clear that, regardless of one's attitude toward the Bolshevik Revolution, assumptions regarding the irreversibility of Soviet socialism were traceable to the problem of restoring private ownership of the means of production long after a socialist revolution had transformed the economy and built thousands of new enterprises, conglomerates, and scientific institutions. While socialism can be created "artificially," it was felt this was not possible with capitalism. In the opinion of many intellectuals, the emergence of capitalism required a deeply ingrained respect for private property—a condition, Soviet intellectuals felt, that could not be redeveloped. Thus the only choice was to move toward some new type of social system. In the 1960s the liberals, with their strong belief in the might of the Soviet state, clearly lacked the imagination to envision a time when the General Secretary would become the champion of privatization and call for the dismantling of collective farms and the transformation of state enterprises into private cooperatives.

With the recognition that Russia could not find its way back to capitalism (a realization that engendered a wide variety of reactions) and that its people would have to live from "birth to death in a socialist society," to use Zinoviev's phrase, intellectuals (including "democrats") began to debate the most desirable future for their country. Soon, many became advocates of liberal society, through which social production would be combined with political pluralism (some, like Medvedev, used the term "real socialist democracy"; Medvedev 1975, pp. 30–47). The Czech phrase, "socialism with a human face," best exemplified this social and political outlook (see also Zinoviev 1985, p. 187).[6] With liberal socialism in mind, however, the debate turned to a more basic topic: Was it possible to establish liberal socialism in general, and under Soviet conditions in particular?

The debates surrounding these issues raged fiercely throughout the intellectual community during the 1960s. Could authoritarian-type socialist societies be transformed? Could the Soviets produce a new form of socialism radically different from that associated with Stalin or Lenin—a socialism capable of incorporating political pluralism, a system fundamentally different from neo-Leninist ideology, with its focus on the crucial role of the Communist party? Did socialist societies have the flexibility necessary to develop new structures? The intellectual community was divided between the optimists, primarily liberal socialists, who believed

---

[6] As Viktor Sokirko aptly observed, liberal socialists could also be called "constitutional socialists," an allusion to affinity with the prerevolutionary "constitutional monarchists" and to the ultimate loyalty of actual intellectuals and their precursors to power (*Poiski*, no. 2, 1980, p. 18).

in the possibility of substantive change, and the pessimists, mostly "democrats," who argued that the Soviet system precluded any serious reform.

During the 1960s the optimists dominated Soviet public life. Rejecting views denying the possibility of change, these intellectuals cited one of the obvious fallacies of Marxism: while Marx had brilliantly described nineteenth-century capitalism, he had erred in predicting capitalism's inevitable collapse. Capitalist societies proved to be substantially more flexible than had been anticipated by Marx, or even by non-Marxists like Jean Sismondi or Thomas Malthus.

Liberal socialists of the 1960s held that socialism, like capitalism, was characterized in its early stages by rigidity, oppression, and antagonistic contradictions, but that it could move into another phase. This new phase of socialism was characterized by a new momentum, profiting from such advantages as the planned economy, scientific and rational principles of government, collectivism, and equality.

Unlike neo-Leninist ideology, the ideas of liberal socialism, such as its emphasis on political pluralism and its negative assessment of Lenin and the October Revolution, could not be propagated in licit literature. Having won, by the end of the 1960s, the minds of the majority of the intellectuals, liberal socialism was elaborated and defended, but mostly in private communications and in samizdat.

Sakharov became the main exponent of liberal socialism in the USSR. His first samizdat publication, "A Reflection on Progress, Peaceful Coexistence, and Intellectual Freedom," was a manifesto of liberal socialism (Sakharov 1968). Sakharov's writings of the late 1960s and early 1970s were filled with Marxist terminology and Sakharov's declaration of his allegiance to such concepts as "the vitality of the socialist course," "Leninist principles," "the working class as a major force (along with the 'progressive intelligentsia') in social progress," "the leading role of the Communist party," "Marxist-Leninist socialist direction," "the attractiveness of Communist ideology," and "international monopolist capital" (Sakharov 1970, pp. 51, 64, 73, 79, 161, 170, 181). Many of his later written materials—the memo to Leonid Brezhnev (1970), the interview with Swedish radio and television (1973), the article on Solzhenitsyn's "Letter to the Leaders" (1974), his Nobel lecture (1975), the article "About the Country and the World" (1975), the article "The Alarming Times" (1980), and several others—described in detail the concept of liberal socialism as it was perceived at the time.

As mentioned earlier, *Novyi Mir*, headed by Tvardovski, was the primary champion of neo-Leninist ideology in the 1960s. After 1962, however, many of its materials shifted toward a pluralistic concept of society and away from the glorification of the October Revolution and Lenin.

THE IMAGE OF LIBERAL SOCIALISM

Given the preeminence of political power in Soviet-type society, the intellectuals envisioned liberal socialism as a social system with a political order significantly different than that of the current structure. This new political order would require an increase in the role of the individual in all spheres of life. Thus, at the center of the liberals' dreams in the 1960s was the "personalization" of Soviet society and the restoration of the individual's sovereignty against the omnipotence of the collective and the society.[7]

For the intellectuals of the 1960s, liberal socialism had to guarantee, above all, the functioning of genuine public opinion. The intellectuals argued that although the Soviet people were prohibited from electing leaders and shaping policy, they should have the right to express their views on various subjects, at least those unrelated to the legitimacy of the socialist order. In this regard, the role of the mass media also held the primary attention of the Soviet intellectuals. They dreamed of the abolition of censorship and of newspapers and magazines free to criticize all officials (with the exception of members of the Politburo) and able to generate and disseminate new social ideas. In particular, the intellectuals believed that conducting polls would significantly enhance the quality of the Soviet mass media's contact with the public (see Grushin 1968; Levada 1968; Shlapentokh 1969a). The liberal image of socialist society excluded, of course, political trials, the persecution of people for their views, and, most of all, political prisoners.

As mentioned in the previous chapter, Soviet intellectuals also considered it necessary to modernize the official ideology and purge it of a number of obsolete dogmas, such as the leading role of the working class and the importance of the "class approach" to all social issues. The liberal model included broadening the individual freedoms of Soviet citizens beyond the freedom of speech. The intellectuals of the 1960s did not really anticipate achieving the full range of rights available to people in the

---

[7] The extolling of the individual and of his or her needs, reason, and capacity to choose sensible options without directives from above became a new fixture in various Soviet publications. Even the mere inclusion of the terms "the individual," "the personality," or "the human being" was exciting for Soviet authors, as was all existentialist terminology dealing with freedom of choice, life goals, and so on. The mere title of Kon's book, *Sociology of Personality* (1967), aroused great excitement among the intelligentsia. One of the chapters of my book, *Sociology for All*, was entitled "The Choice of the Individual" (it dealt with such issues as choosing the size of one's family, occupations, mass media, place of residence, and so on). Again, the title was itself highly hailed by readers as another manifestation of the "personalization" of the approach to Soviet issues. Adam Schaff's book in Polish, *Marxism and Personality* (1962/1970), was avidly read by those who were able to do so.

West. They did, however, expect that it would be possible for individuals to live anywhere they chose in the country and to remove restrictions on people moving to the major cities; that visits abroad could be more accessible; that individuals could have greater access to information on Western society; that the history of the Soviet Union could be approached more realistically; and that art and literature prohibited in the past could be made available.

The liberal program of the 1960s spoke of the democratization of Soviet society only sketchily and with some hesitation—almost no one seriously believed that it could be accomplished. This was true not only for legal publications, movies, and plays, which did not even hint or allude to an interest in democratic elections or a multiparty system, but for samizdat as well.

Samizdat was almost completely silent on the issue of democratization. Pavel Litvinov, an outstanding dissident, rejected a suggestion to name the movement to which he belonged "democratic," because "the Soviet people support the Soviet regime," and because the movement in no way wanted to play the role of a political party (Litvinov 1976, pp. 78–79). Orlov, also a believer in harmony in the relations between totalitarian power and the majority of the people, suggested that the main task of the progressive forces in Soviet society was only to "change the moral climate in the country," and he completely ignored political reforms (Orlov 1976, pp. 294–298). Turchin went so far as to declare himself an enemy of the struggle for a multiparty system in the USSR, since this system by itself does not guarantee political freedom, which should be at the center of the liberal movement (Turchin 1978, p. 212–213).

The theme of the genuine democratization of the Soviet political order in the foreseeable future was absent in the writings of other authoritative liberals in the 1960s and 1970s as well (see Gefter 1979). Moreover, many liberals in the 1960s and the 1970s referred to their activity as "the democratic movement," although they practically ignored all issues related to the participation of the masses in government (see, for instance, Abovin-Egides and Podrabinek 1980). It is only natural, then, that the political organization the liberal intelligentsia began to create in the late 1960s—the human rights committee (I will discuss the details later)—practically ignored all issues related to the governing of the country, such as elections and the multiparty system (see, for instance, Chalidze's "Important Aspects of Human Rights in the Soviet Union," in Carey 1972, pp. 19–49).

Sakharov was probably the only intellectual during this period to advocate using "democratization" the same way it would be used twenty years later during the period of glasnost. He even used this term in his first manifesto (1968) and later mentioned, albeit with some reservation, the importance of the multiparty system and the necessity of true elections (Sakharov 1970, pp. 79, 82). The role of democratization significantly increased in Sakharov's 1970 manifesto, "Letter to Brezhnev" (Sakharov 1974). In this document, democratization was mostly related to access to information and freedom of creativity, and was treated essentially as a mode of interaction between the party and the intelligentsia. The samizdat document raised the question of "the gradual introduction into practice of the nomination of several candidates for each position and elections for party and government organs at all levels, including direct elections" (Sakharov 1974, p. 128). In subsequent samizdat publications, Sakharov, preoccupied with the defense of dissidents from the burgeoning persecution, dropped the issue (exceptions included the interview with Olle Stenholm in 1973 and the samizdat article "About the Country and the World," 1975) and concentrated almost exclusively on human rights and the isolationism of Soviet society (see Sakharov 1974, 1978; Babenyshev et al. 1981).[8] He did not return to the democratization of the Soviet political system until 1986 when Gorbachev brought him back to Moscow.

The concept of liberal socialism as it was perceived in the 1960s assumed the elimination of any form of national discrimination. For this reason, liberal intellectuals closely resembled the nationalist intelligentsia in various Soviet republics, particularly the Ukraine. Ivan Dziuba, a Ukrainian literary critic, represented a national intelligentsia that saw in the democratic development of the Soviet Union the best hope for national autonomy (Alexeieva 1984).

The most important element of liberal socialism was related to economic reform. The liberal viewpoint argued for reducing the party's control over economic decision making and for adopting more lenient attitudes toward private initiative in agriculture and service. Legal liberal theoreticians of economic reform, such as Evgeni Liberman (1971), Lisichkin (1976), and Nikolai Petrakov (1971), sought to demonstrate that central planning bodies should be limited in influence and that consumers should determine the distribution of production, that prices needed to be flexible and responsive to supply and demand, that factories should have greater autonomy, that material incentives should be more effective, and that enterprise managers should be able to take risks related to technological innovation.

Due to the chronic backwardness of Soviet agriculture, this realm of the economy also attracted the attention of the Soviet intellectuals in the

---

[8] During his exile in Gorky, Sakharov was quite a pessimist, saying in 1982 that he "did not have any hope for democratic changes in the near future," although he added that "the mole of history digs invisibly and we know that historical changes often occur suddenly" (*Vnutrennie Protivorechia*, no. 5, 1982, p. 9).

1950s and the 1960s. Several rural economists, headed by Vladimir Venzher, insisted on freeing collective farms from the control of the party apparatus and allowing them to run their own production activities (Venzher 1966).

It is remarkable that the brave and breathtaking economic ideas of the liberals in the 1960s, including those in samizdat, looked very guarded in the latter 1980s. None of the liberals, even samizdat authors such as Viktor Burzhuademov (who used the pen name of Sokirko [1981]), raised crucial questions of economic restructuring such as the property issue or the necessity of privatization in the economy.

Sakharov was probably again the first to include "the partial denationalization of all types of economic and social activities" in the program of reforms in 1975 (see Babenyshev et al. 1981, p. 24).

ATTITUDES TOWARD "UNIVERSAL VALUES"

Since the early years of Soviet history, the official ideology has proclaimed its opposition to universal (or in the Soviet lexicon, "all-mankind") values, favoring its own specific Soviet values, based on Marxism and the class approach. By universal values, Soviet ideology normally refers to humanistic values, such as altruism, kindness, friendship, and respect for tradition.

In the 1920s a number of Soviet intellectuals, primarily those in literature and the arts and those of the younger generation, advocated a new vision of the world that challenged the culture and values of the past, as well as those of the West (e.g., Bagritski, Kataiev, Maiakovski, Babel', and others). Of course, such advocacy was not universal, and even some young intellectuals—such as Zamiatin, Shwarts, and Bulgakov—sought to defend universal values and reject the class approach.

Following Stalin's death, the intellectuals began a general offensive against the class approach and in support of universal values. Perhaps more than in any other activity, intellectuals were united in this movement, regardless of their ideological propensities. In addition, the intellectuals were able to take advantage of the political elite's growing desire to achieve respectability on both the domestic and international fronts. In fact, the intellectuals' campaign for universal values and against the class approach to morality was an attempt to prevent the Soviet population from gradually sliding into a moral vacuum. The major message that the intellectuals, particularly the writers, wanted to get across to the Soviet people was that without respect for universal, and to some degree Christian, values, they were doomed to moral degradation. Given the insignificant influence of the church on the Soviet people, the intellectuals essentially became the single group striving to raise the moral standards of behavior in the country.

Since 1953 Soviet literature has been active in the struggle to advance universal values. Two basic themes can be identified in this regard. The first was related to the defense of universal civic values, such as openness, political freedom, and equality. The second stressed more humanistic universal values such as love, friendship, honesty, and devotion to parents and family. These themes have gained momentum in different periods, depending on a number of circumstances, particularly the political climate. In the late 1950s and early 1960s both themes were promoted equally, when measured by the popularity of writers representing them. In the mid- to late 1960s civic values took a leading role; in the 1970s, with the intellectuals' increasing political apathy and the rise of the Russophile movement, humanistic values prevailed. In the second half of the 1980s, both sets of values were again praised by intellectuals. The liberals of the 1960s would surely have been stunned to learn that, twenty years later, a General Secretary would substantially outrun them in the commendation of universal values and would staunchly demand the sacrifice of the class approach in their favor.

With the blessing of the party leader, the intellectuals of the late 1980s began to reinstall one universal value after another. Granin, for instance, championed the restoration of charity and charitable institutions as an official value (Granin 1987). He was enthusiastically followed by many other intellectuals who began to openly praise "absolute values," an ostensible challenge to Marxist ethical relativism (Aitmatov 1987; Gulyga 1987).

In the 1960s, however, without even indirect support from the leadership, the rehabilitation of universal values was much more difficult than during the Gorbachev era. The humanistic orientation of the Soviet intelligentsia led to the rediscovery of writers from the 1920s and 1930s whose works had been prohibited until the 1960s. Bulgakov and Andrei Platonov became especially prominent during the 1960s. Bulgakov's *The Master and Marguerite* embodied the intelligentsia's belief in the existence of stable and invariant principles in the face of a rapidly changing modern society.

The intelligentsia's longing for humanistic universal values is revealed in the notable popularity of poetry at the time. The role of individual experience and the emphasis on the human personality found in the works of the lyric poets led to the great notoriety of several poets whose works were prohibited under Stalin. Poets such as Sergei Esenin, Mandel'shtam, Pasternak, Tsvetaieva, and Akhmatova were extremely popular in the 1960s. Even more popular were contemporary poets who united civic and humanistic values in their work. It was this emphasis on universal values, rather than artistic merit (which was often rather modest) which explains the popularity of such poets as Evtushenko and Voznesenski.

The Soviet intellectuals' support for universal values also accounts for the rise of bardic poetry in the 1960s. Once again there were two clear tendencies in support of civic and humanistic values. Poets in the first group included Galich and Vysotski; in the second group, the most prominent was Okudzava. As in general literature, civic values were particularly stressed in the 1960s, while humanitarian values were emphasized in the 1970s.

The restoration of universal values was also associated with the rise of "rural prose," the writers of which displayed Russophile tendencies. Those associated with this movement include Shukshin, Abramov, Evgeni Nosov, Rasputin, and Astafiev. Their criticism of official ideology, often subtle and laced with nationalistic and antimodern overtones, made considerable progress toward the restoration of universal values.

The intelligentsia's strong interest in classical Russian literature is important here as well. The 1967 survey of *Literaturnaia Gazeta* readers found that the intelligentsia was becoming attracted to those older Russian writers who addressed the more eternal problems of human life and universal values such as Tolstoy, Chekhov, Fiodor Dostoevsky, Alexander Kuprin, Bunin.

Preferences regarding foreign authors also indicated support for those addressing universal values. Most popular were those writers focusing on issues of humanity and individualism, such as Ernest Hemingway, Erich Maria Remarque, Heinrich Boll, Graham Greene, and J. D. Salinger.

The advancement of universal values proceeded with much less vigor in the social sciences than in literature and the arts. Nonetheless, Soviet philosophers and sociologists made significant steps in this direction. For example, we can compare two publications, one from Vladimir Tugarinov (1960) and one from Oleg Drobnitski (1977). Tugarinov was a typical champion of official ideology. Striving to keep abreast of the times, in 1970 he published the first book in the USSR to have the word "value" appear without quotation marks. In his book, Tugarinov rejected all notions about universal values, finding them inadmissible in Soviet philosophy. In contrast, Drobnitski's book, published posthumously in 1977, rather than rejecting ethical absolutes sought to combine absolute universal values with the moral relativism of Soviet Marxism. In the process, Drobnitski legitimized universal values in Soviet philosophy.

THE POLITICAL STRATEGIES OF SOVIET INTELLECTUALS

How did the liberal Soviet intellectuals of the 1960s envisage implementing their dream of liberal socialism? In answering this question, it is necessary to examine their perceptions of the Soviet political scene and its main actors. They acknowledged five main participants in Soviet political life: the political elite; the party apparatus; the intelligentsia (the most creative part of which consisted of the intellectuals themselves); the masses; and the West. The party apparatus, especially at the local level, was dismissed by intellectuals as an active force. (Later, in the second half of the 1970s and especially during glasnost, the Soviet intellectuals began to reconsider their views on the social role of the party apparatus, and they began to regard the apparatus as much more capable of obstructing serious change than had been supposed in the 1960s.)

Intellectuals also ascribed little importance to the political activities of the masses. Although they hunted for any details regarding the workers' riots in Novocherkask and Karaganda in the early 1960s, the intellectuals did not regard the workers (not to mention the peasants) as active actors capable of forcing the leadership to make modifications in the system. Moreover, they actually resisted the active participation of the masses in the opposition movements, because they feared the outbreak of violence and were, in general, dedicated foes of revolution.

Beginning in the mid-1950s, the liberal intellectuals operated with two political strategies, both of which targeted the political elite and regarded the intelligentsia and the West as the major pressure groups. In essence, their political strategies in this period stemmed from their belief that the modernization of Soviet society and its liberal modification were in the best interests of the political elite. This idea stemmed from a feeling on the part of the intellectuals that Soviet society was behind the West economically and for this reason was fraught with various dangers that would force Soviet leaders to look for innovations in the Soviet system. The behavior of the first leaders after Stalin—Malenkov and Khrushchev—supported such a view.

The hopes of the Soviet intellectuals for a leader who would choose the road of sweeping reforms were also linked to the logic of internal political struggle in the Kremlin, which, it was believed, would compel one of the rivals to stake out a position in favor of liberalization. Of course, the transformation of Khrushchev into a denunciator of Stalin in the process of his struggle against the Stalinists provided support for this theory. The stories of Alexander Shelepin's flirtation with the intellectuals in the late 1960s, when he had not yet lost hope in the struggle with Brezhnev, only nourished such ideas.

The intelligentsia, particularly its creative part (i.e., the intellectuals), was regarded by the liberal intellectuals as the major progressive force in socialist society. Science's expanding role in modern society and the necessity of modernizing ideology and culture seemed to them to guarantee that the political elite would be very receptive to the position of the Soviet intelligentsia. Grigori Pomerants, one of the most prominent leaders of the liberal intelligentsia, praised this "new God-bearing stratum" as "the most progressive social group," and proclaimed them "unable to ignore political events which arouse moral feelings" and champions of "a modern form of righteousness" (see Medvedev 1975, p. 402). These themes appeared again in several publications during glasnost.

The liberal intellectuals considered the West to be another positive actor in internal Soviet developments, although the fear of being labeled agents of foreign "special services" led liberal intellectuals to develop this idea gradually. The potential positive role of the West was not fully recognized until the 1970s, with the creation of the Helsinki group. Since 1953 (and even before), however, liberal intellectuals had been aware, even if they had not wanted to admit it to themselves, that pressure from the West was one of their best chances, and sometimes their only chance, to extricate concessions from the political elite.

Liberal intellectuals saw the West's potential primarily in the desire of Soviet leaders to ease tensions in international relations and to obtain credit and technology from Western countries. Soviet influence on international public opinion, as well as control over foreign Communist parties, were also among the factors on which liberals counted, especially in the 1960s. And last but not least, every Soviet leader has been extremely mindful of his image in the West. The intellectuals considered the leader's desire to look good to be serious leverage in their political activities. All of these ideas seem to receive their ultimate confirmation in the actions of the Gorbachev regime.

Liberal intellectuals, well aware of the complex character of Western society, saw their eventual allies in the following actors on the Western political scene: the mass media; governments; political figures; intellectuals; leftist political parties (including Communist parties); and religious organizations. For the intellectuals, the roles played by each of these actors in the internal political development of the USSR has changed over the last two decades (for instance, Western governments have been called upon for help only since the late 1970s). Over the entire period since 1953, however, the Western mass media and their correspondents in Moscow have been regarded as the liberal intellectuals' main allies.

The two strategies developed by liberal intellectuals for targeting the political elite can be labeled "closed" (or "educational") and "open" (or "pluralistic"). Although both have coexisted since 1953, the first was dominant in Khrushchev's time and the second during the Brezhnev regime. The "closed" strategy advanced as its main champions liberal intellectuals with access to the Central Committee, such as Ehrenburg, and liberal intellectual party members such as A. Rumiantsev. The "open" strategy demanded other figures, such as Solzhenitsyn and Sakharov.

The belief that serious progress could be made if Stalin's heirs realized both the real situation in society as well as the ways to improve it seemed reasonable enough, particularly because, in the first years after 1953, Soviet leaders had also manifested a desire to establish contacts with the intellectual community. The creation of a special institution of consultants at the Central Committee was a practical step in this direction, since the main duty of the consultants was to provide their bosses with a broad vision of any issue and to enroll scholars in the elaboration of memos. In light of such a view of the Soviet political leadership, the intellectuals at first saw as their main role the enlightenment of the leaders and the people around them. They paid a great deal of attention to contacts with the leaders' aides (see Burlatski 1988c; Neizvestnyi 1984). As one author aptly observed, unlike their ancestors—the Russian prerevolutionary intelligentsia that saw as its vocation the education of the masses—the Soviet intellectuals of the 1960s regarded as their mission the coaching of Soviet leaders (Altaiev 1970, pp. 25–26). The idea of enlightening the leaders was dominant until the mid-1960s. Then, with the move toward re-Stalinization and with the hostility toward liberal intellectuals exhibited by Brezhnev's team, the intellectuals' perceptions regarding their political role were significantly altered.

The goal of the second, or "open," strategy was to deprive the political elite, even if only partially, of its monopoly on the mass media, public gatherings, contacts with the West, and other spheres of social life. The aim was to force the political elite to yield to pressure from the intelligentsia, with the latter being supported by the West.

The "closed" concept of political behavior in the early 1960s assumed almost secret contacts between the political elite and its liberal educators (intellectuals themselves, as Zinoviev colorfully depicted in *The Yawning Heights*, enjoyed cloaking their trips to the Central Committee and to meetings with party dignitaries in a shroud of mystery). In contrast, the new "open" strategy of the late 1960s demanded quite the opposite: it required publicity for the intellectuals' actions, and as much of it as possible. The intellectuals considered the wide dissimination of their thoughts and activities to be their main weapon in the struggle against the elite, which they now sought to educate not in the offices of the "Big House" (the intellectuals' nickname for the Central Committee building), but on the streets, in the courts, and especially through the Western mass media.

It is noteworthy that with Gorbachev's ascension to power in 1985 and with his courtship of the intelligentsia, the liberal intellectuals returned decisively to the first, or "closed," strategy. In 1985–1988 the intellectuals concentrated all their efforts on supporting and educating the new leader and abandoned their efforts at pressuring him. Afanasiev's *There Is No Alternative* (1988a), a collection of liberal writings, is an excellent

168 · Chapter Six

example of this shift. Even the most radical authors of the book, such as Batkin, neither suggest nor allude to the necessity of forcing the political leadership, through some public actions, to follow the course regarded by the intellectuals as reasonable. In 1989, however, some intellectuals once again started to move toward the second, or "open," strategy.

THE PERCEPTION OF THE MASSES AS A POLITICAL ACTOR

From the very beginning of the liberal movement, Soviet intellectuals have been skeptical about the role of the masses in the Soviet political process, and have manifested only modest interest in the masses' quality of life.[9] Soviet history, with its countless examples of the masses' inability to resist the political elite's manipulations, suggested to the intellectual community of the 1950s and 1960s that "the people" could not be relied upon as a force in the intellectuals' efforts to improve life in the country. Moreover, the Soviet intellectuals of the 1960s, not without the influence of the political elite, believed that involving the masses in active political struggle could engender only violence, anarchy, and disorder. Alexander Pushkin's famous epigraph to one of his novels—"Let God not allow us to see the Russian riot, meaningless and cruel"—was repeated over and over again in Moscow and Novosibirsk salons and to some extent symbolized the intellectuals' attitudes toward the people as a political actor (in 1988, the same sentence by Pushkin was cited approvingly by Eidel'-man, a leading liberal). One samizdat author recalled the words of an old Russian liberal who, in 1909, in the aftermath of the revolution quenched by tsarism, wrote that "we have to be grateful to this power for their defense of us with bayonets and whips from the blind wrath of the people" (*Poiski*, nos. 5–8, 1983, p. 191).

Despite regarding themselves as the single group capable of defending the interests of the workers and peasants, the liberal intellectuals of the post-Stalin period adopted skeptical and even somewhat contemptuous attitudes toward the masses (see, for instance, Berg 1984). This stance was radically different from that of their ancestors, the prerevolutionary Russian intelligentsia, who had rather worshipped the ordinary people

[9] It was not until the late 1970s that the intellectuals became increasingly interested in the standard of living of the masses and that the Helsinki Soviet Committee could assert that "it is the first Soviet human rights association that addressed both social and economic issues" (Chalidze 1982, p. 124).

Samizdat, which had been almost completely indifferent to the material life of the people and to economics in general in the 1960s, could boast of several serious publications by the end of the 1970s. Among the most significant of these were essays by Lev Timofeiev, especially his "Technology of the Black Market and the Peasant Art of Starvation" (1982), and by Sokirko (1983a, 1983b).

and felt guilty before them. (About the attitudes of the old Russian intelligentsia toward the people, see Berdiaev et al.'s *Milestones*, 1909.)

The Russophile intellectuals who became active in the late 1960s held slightly different attitudes toward the masses. They shared with liberals a deep disrespect for the new generations of peasants and workers, whom they viewed as infected and spoiled by urban civilization in its Soviet version. Indeed, writers such as Rasputin, Astafiev, Abramov, and especially Shukshin outdid one another in deriding Soviet-made toilers. At the same time, the Russophile authors held the Soviet intelligentsia and city dwellers in general in even greater disrespect, and they continued to look for oases of high morals among ordinary people, especially old peasants. Of the characters in the writings of these authors, it is Daria, the old woman in Rasputin's *Farewell with Matera* (1980), the older people in Abramov's stories about life in northern Russian villages (Abramov 1973, 1982), Ivan Afrikanovich in Belov's *Usual Business* (1971), Viktor Likhonosov's old couple in *Farewell with Briansk's People* (1985), and the Siberian hunter Akim in Astafiev's *Tsar-Fish* (1984b) who are practically the sole bearers of moral values in their milieu.

Even Russophiles, however, do not believe the masses to be capable of positive political activity. As Vladimir Osipov wrote in his magazine, *Veche*: "It seems to me that we should not count on 'the pressure from below.' Our people are not 'political.' They either endure a long time, or burst into rebellion, . . . meaningless and cruel" (*VS*, nos. 17–18, 1975, p. 12).

This mistrust of the masses as an active force on the Soviet political scene increased between 1956 and 1968. Initially, the intellectual community viewed the political passivity of the masses as resulting from a shortage of information and from their memory of the repression of the Stalin era. Thus many intellectuals were convinced that greater access to information, such as that from foreign radio, would lead to changes in the people's political orientations. Moreover, Soviet researchers, as well as officials, who noticed the seeming unwillingness of survey respondents to express negative attitudes toward various features of Soviet society, attributed this to widespread insincerity and to fear of revealing their true attitudes.

For example, a 1966 study sought to determine how many Soviet newspaper readers disagreed with the positions taken by *Izvestia* journalists on a variety of issues. Interestingly, while the journalists themselves anticipated that about one third of readers would disagree with their views, the survey of the readership found only 9 percent of readers indicating dissension from the opinions in the paper (Shlapentokh 1982, p. 413). While the researchers initially attributed these figures to the insincerity of the respondents, further analysis led them to conclude that this explanation was insufficient, and that large numbers of the Soviet people actually supported official policies. Such information only bolstered the intellectuals' mistrust of the masses. In this context, they were forced to conclude that, if progressive change were to occur in the Soviet Union, it could stem only from struggles between the intellectual community and the political elite.

ATTITUDES TOWARD REVOLUTION

The negative, antipopulist attitudes of the intellectuals toward the masses also implied the rejection of revolution as a means for social transformation.

By the end of the 1960s, the rejection of revolution became part of the intellectuals' general negative orientation toward the existing system and especially toward the price paid by the Soviet people for the achievement of socialism in the USSR (about this, see Gnedin 1982; see also Solzhenitsyn 1981a). This price included millions of victims throughout the various stages of Soviet history—the civil war, the famine of the 1920s, the collectivization, the destruction of the prerevolutionary intelligentsia, the purges of the 1930s, the genocide of various peoples during the war, and the persecution of intellectuals during the 1940s and 1950s.

As far as possible, the intellectuals, no matter how deep their hatred of the Soviet system and whether liberal or otherwise (neo-Leninists and Russophiles), sought to demonstrate in their work their aversion to revolution of any kind (Solzhenitsyn's "Letter to the Leaders" is a good example). Novels, stories, films (for instance, Chukhrai's *Forty-One*), and plays (such as the trilogy in the Theater Sovremennik [The Contemporary]—*Decembrists, Populists, and Bolsheviks*; and Trifonov's *Old Man*) with even mild antirevolutionary themes were enthusiastically received by the public. The antirevolutionary stance of the Soviet intellectuals forced them immediately to condemn the Chinese Cultural Revolution—a radically different stance than that of the majority of American liberal intellectuals.[10]

[10] In a content analysis of books about China reviewed in *The New York Times Book Review* over the ten years from 1970 to 1979, thirty-four of eighty-five books related directly to the Cultural Revolution. Critical comments on events during this terrible period in Chinese history were found in only 13 percent of these books. Many American and Western authors accepted at face value almost all of the Chinese propaganda of the time. They believed that the goal of the Cultural Revolution was the creation of a new culture and a new science based on truly democratic principles, with the active participation of the masses in research and education. They even thought that sending intellectuals to concentration camps, then referred to as "May 7 Schools," was a good way to combine manual and intellectual activities (see Gasster 1972; Milton and Milton 1973; Pischel 1977; Schram 1969; Selden 1979; Simone 1968). From its very inception, Soviet authors, on the other hand,

Paradoxically, the condemnation of revolution during the 1960s benefited the dominant elite. The leadership was well aware that, despite the revolutionary origins of the Soviet system, it could not place undue emphasis on the theme of revolution for fear it might be turned against them. Stalin was the first to strike this chord by prohibiting studies of populist and terrorist activity against the tsarist government. By the 1960s this policy had attained its broadest, if unpublicized, scope. Interestingly, even Lenin's statements on the use of terror had been silenced by the official ideology. Meanwhile, many Soviet people sought to locate materials that would in some way discredit the Russian Revolution, as well as the revolutions in other countries, such as France.

CONCLUSION

By the end of the 1960s the intellectual community was relatively united in its support of liberal ideas, primarily in the form of "socialism with a human face," which assumed significant liberal reforms without a serious democratic transformation. The liberal socialists of the 1960s proposed the opening of Soviet society, a more significant role for public opinion, and the modernization of official ideology. The intellectuals also supported the decentralization of management, encouragement for private labor activity, and improvement of material incentives for efficient work.

In the early 1960s liberal intellectuals laid their hopes for the implementation of their ideas on the supreme leader who, having been enlightened by them, was expected to understand that his interests as well as those of the entire system demanded the liberalization of Soviet society. Later, many intellectuals became more inclined to pressure the leadership with intensive oppositional activity and the creation of civil society.

---

reacted to the Cultural Revolution with sincere disgust and horror (see, for instance, Burlatski 1979).

CHAPTER SEVEN

Intellectuals in the Time of Political Reaction

THE BRIEF FLIRTATION WITH INTELLECTUALS

Especially since Khrushchev's ouster in 1964, the Soviet leadership has recognized that science, literature, and the arts pose a serious potential threat to its legitimacy. This was driven home during the first five years of the Brezhnev era, as the intellectual community continually demonstrated its willingness to advance democratic notions and engage in oppositional activity.

Despite these alarming signals, the Brezhnev regime moved quite cautiously during its early years. Even while continuing to harass those who publicly came out against the regime (e.g., the trial of Andrei Siniavski and Iuri Daniel), Brezhnev engaged in a brief flirtation with the intellectual community. Never in Soviet history had the officially recognized role of the intellectuals been so great as in 1964–1967. Party policy was reflected in Alexei Rumiantsev's article, "The Intelligentsia and the People," published in *Pravda*, February 21, 1965 (although the author went further than Brezhnev's leadership would have preferred; see Rumiantsev's recollection about this article twenty-five years later in *Pravda*, January 1, 1990).

The leadership, recognizing its tenuous and insecure position following Khrushchev's expulsion, sought to present itself as a true supporter and admirer of honest scholarship, to contrast with the wavering of the preceding leader. Several branches of science profited during these early years, including sociology, mathematical economics, and genetics. This period was also notable for the increasing role of professional competence, rather than strict political loyalty, in the selection of individuals for scientific work.

During this period, the lives of literary figures tended to be more dramatic than those of other intellectuals, as the trial of Siniavski and Daniel suggests. But it was also during this time that *Novyi Mir* became increasingly popular and that several progressive writers gained popularity.

THE PRAGUE SPRING: A FATEFUL EVENT FOR SOVIET INTELLECTUALS

It is likely that the crackdown on Soviet intellectuals had been planned well in advance and was being formulated in tandem with the coup against Khrushchev. The apparent delay in the crackdown may be traced to the Brezhnev regime's need to consolidate itself fully, as well as to disagreement within the Politburo concerning appropriate actions to be taken against the intellectual community.

Whatever one may speculate regarding the events of the mid-1960s, the developments in Czechoslovakia were undoubtedly taken as a final warning of the implications of allowing the intellectuals too much influence. One of the most striking features of the events in Prague was the active role of writers, scholars, journalists, and other members of the intelligentsia. In addition, the relative passivity of the working class during these events undoubtedly increased the leadership's perception that the principal threat to its power lay within the intellectual community. For confirmation of this perception, the leadership had only to recall the role of intellectuals in other Eastern European "disturbances," such as the Petofi circle in Hungary during the 1956 rebellion and the student demonstrations in Poland in 1968.

Following the invasion of Czechoslovakia, the fate of the Soviet intellectuals was sealed. The Soviet leadership was convinced of the danger of its "technocratic" policy toward intellectuals, which valued their technical competence over their political orientations. It became clear that, in assessing the appointment or promotion of intellectuals, political criteria should again become paramount and that a Stalinist approach, albeit in milder form, should be redeveloped. Through this approach, the Brezhnev regime could follow the pattern of Stalin's anticosmopolitan campaign of the early 1950s, when professional skills were sacrificed for the sake of political servility.

GLORIFYING THE WORKING CLASS AND DENIGRATING INTELLECTUALS

As the seriousness of the events in Czechoslovakia—and the intelligentsia's involvement in these events—became evident, the Soviet leadership responded by initiating an ideological campaign against the Soviet intellectuals. The campaign was designed to diminish the intelligentsia's role in socialist society. Of course, such a campaign had to be carried out with care because of the central importance of science and scientific development to the official Soviet ideology. Thus the goal of reducing the intelligentsia's importance was sought through a sudden glorification of the working class.

Prior to the emergence of this ideological campaign, Soviet sociologists had collected a variety of data illustrating the popular perception of the status of the working class. It had been found that the prestige of working-class occupations was quite low among Soviet youth, and that only a small proportion of young people expressed a desire to enter such occupations and enlist in the "leading class" of Soviet society. In this context, the efforts of the leadership to reactivate the cult of the working class resulted less in elevating the position of workers than in downgrading the image of the intelligentsia. Ultimately, the intent was to enhance the leadership's legitimacy by undermining its most vocal critics and praising the class the leadership claimed to represent. The decision to emphasize the importance of the working class in the official ideology was also shaped by certain practical considerations: while the leadership could not claim to speak on behalf of the intelligentsia (which had its own voices in Solzhenitsyn and Sakharov), it could pretend to represent the interests of the workers. Aside from occasional disruptions, like those in Novocherkask and Karaganda, the working class was traditionally silent and had no effective voice.

The existence of hostile sentiments among Soviet workers toward the intelligentsia was revealed in a survey of *Pravda* readers (Shlapentokh 1968). The survey ended with the open-ended query, "Do you have any additional remarks or comments?" About one third of the respondents replied to this question, and of those a significant proportion used the opportunity to express their animosity toward both intellectuals and bureaucrats.

Efforts to generate hostility among workers against the more privileged intellectuals and students are, of course, not uncommon in socialist (or other repressive) societies, as leaders often attempt to undercut the emergence of alternative elites. The Chinese Cultural Revolution stands as one of the most prominent examples, particularly in the recruitment of the working class to participate in the leveling of privileges and influence. Yet conditions in the USSR in 1968 required a somewhat different approach, because worker animosity toward the intelligentsia was coupled with perhaps even greater hostility toward the party apparatus, and many workers viewed the two groups simply as segments of the same ruling elite.

The campaign to glorify the Soviet working class thus did not reach the height or the scope of the Chinese Cultural Revolution, although it was still quite strong and had significant implications.[1] The ideological campaign began, as is typical in the USSR, with the appearance of many ar-

[1] One example of the direct confrontation between workers and intellectuals occurred in 1968, when the newspaper *Sovietskaia Rossia* (Soviet Russia) published some articles allegedly written by a worker and directed against Tvardovski, the editor in chief of *Novyi Mir*. These letters aroused great anger among the intellectuals. Tvardovski was skeptical that the letters were authentic and accused the newspaper of faking the signature. (About this episode, see Chukovskaia 1976; Solzhenitsyn 1975c.) Around the same time, the secretary of the Novosibirsk party organization, Fiodor Goriachev, warned the intellectuals of Academic Town that the workers were willing to enlighten them with lessons in patriotism and political fealty.

ticles and books on the leading role of the working class in socialist society, especially in the Soviet Union.[2] The campaign began in May 1968 when two party officials, Richard Kosolapov and P. Simush, wrote in *Pravda* that the Soviet intelligentsia was in need of the "guiding and educative influence" of the working class and, of course, of the "party of the working class" (May 25, 1968). From this point on, the campaign gained momentum and Brezhnev himself began to take an active part in lauding the working class, offering a portrait of the "advanced" worker, who was clearly superior to any representative of the intelligentsia (Brezhnev 1972, pp. 483–484).

Throughout the next decade, subsequent publications on the working class followed this pattern. In their book, *Scientific Revolution, the Working Class, and the Intelligentsia* (1973), Leonid Bliakhman and Shkaratan described these two segments of Soviet society. With reference to the working class, the book enumerated several virtues, such as their freedom from servility, their longing for the best in culture, and their desire for further development. The intelligentsia, however, apparently had no laudable qualities worth mentioning, and the authors limited themselves to a simple definition of the intelligentsia as those engaged in highly qualified mental labor (pp. 160–161).[3]

The conservative journal *Oktiabr'* also participated in the anti-intellectual crusade under the direction of Kochetov. In 1969, the journal published Kochetov's inflammatory, neo-Stalinist novel, *What Do You Want?* Other novels even more hostile toward the intelligentsia, including Ivan Shevtsov's *Plant Louse* and his *In the Name of Father and Son*, both

[2] It is curious that in one of his texts related to World War II Stalin suddenly declared that the Soviet intelligentsia played a "leading helping role" with respect to workers and peasants (Stalin 1945). This statement deviated completely from any of his other actions, and the reason for it remains a puzzle. In the 1970s, when the restoration of the Stalinist cult was partly combined with an anti-intellectual campaign, Stalin's dictum was often facetiously revived by me. The official ideologues could not believe that their beloved leader had been so inclined toward the intellectuals, even if unintentionally.

[3] Almost twenty years later, in 1990, Shkaratan could be found (with a new coauthor) among the ranks of those condemning the Soviet system—not only decrying it as a version of the despotic "Asian mode of production" (an idea that had been expressed privately in the 1960s), not only denying that Soviet society should be credited for any achievement during its seven decades of existence, and not only denouncing the working class (especially unskilled workers) for their support of "statism" (an incredible shift from the homage paid to this class in 1973), but rejecting the entire concept of socialism as "a dream, slipping from the hands like a bluebird" (Radaiev and Shkaratan 1990). Do these new opinions represent the evolution of Shkaratan's views on socialism, the disclosure of ideas secretly nourished for many years, or simply his permanent conformity? No one can answer these questions about Ovsei Shkaratan, or about any of the other intellectuals who energetically supported Brezhnev's ideology, only to later become the biting Zoiluses of socialism and Communism.

of which enraged the intellectual community, also appeared during this time (Shevtsov 1988).

The Russophile movement performed a special role in the denigration of the intelligentsia. In line with Russophile tradition, intellectuals were characterized as being opposed to the working class not only on the basis of antisocialist and anti-Soviet ideas, but also on the assumption of the intellectuals' hostility toward Russian culture and traditions. Authors like Mikhail Lobanov (1968) and Viktor Chalmaiev (1968) compared the intellectuals to the uneducated masses of Russians, who were held up as the bearers of true Russian values and the creators of true Russian culture. This conflict was replayed twenty years later, as Russophiles and Stalinists renewed their campaign against the intellectuals, accusing the latter of being the bearers of corruption and Westernization.

The cult of the working class was particularly strong during the early 1970s, a result of the influence of party extremists during this period. The glorification of the working class later subsided, emphasis on social homogeneity increased, and it became possible once again to discuss the intelligentsia in more positive terms. Nonetheless, the central thesis of the leading role of the working class remained intact until 1987. Gorbachev reiterated this idea in 1986, in his report to the Twenty-seventh Party Congress (Gorbachev 1986, p. 6). Moreover, with the exacerbation of the political struggle in 1988 and 1989, especially in connection with the spring 1989 election, party apparatchiks who failed to garner the support of the masses revived the use of "the workers card" against the intelligentsia in attempting to justify their defeat. Party bureaucrats again accused the intellectuals of having antisocialist and anti-Soviet tendencies and of harboring animosity toward workers, and again suggested that it was necessary to raise the role of the working class and to increase the number of workers in the Soviet parliament. In some cases, these bureaucrats repeated verbatim the slogans of Brezhnev's 1968 regime (see the material on the meeting of the Central Committee, *Pravda*, April 27, 1989).

Party apparatchiks' attempts to incite workers against the intelligentsia, especially against intellectuals living in the capital, such as Sakharov or Afanasiev, increased substantially during the session of the Congress of People's Deputies (May–June 1989; about the incitement of the masses against the intelligentsia in Gorbachev's period, see Vasil' Bykov's article in *Pravda*, November 24, 1989; see also *Nedelia*, November 19, 1989).

THE "CHINESE CARD"

Liberal intellectuals who chose not to break with the regime often attempted to alter the leadership's position toward the intellectual community. These intellectuals linked their hopes to the Sino-Soviet conflict and the stark anti-intellectual posture of Mao's leadership, especially during the Cultural Revolution. It was hoped that the split between Moscow and Peking would cause the Soviet leaders to adopt a position opposite to that of Mao, that is, a more conciliatory stance toward the intellectual community. Some analysts suggested that the leadership, fearing the spread of egalitarian and antibureaucratic sentiments among the Soviet masses, would be compelled to alter their position vis-à-vis the intelligentsia.

Soviet intellectuals were nearly convinced that confrontation with China would push the leadership into an alliance with the West, ultimately leading to a renewal of the liberalization process halted in the late 1960s. Burlatski was among those who criticized Maoism in an attempt to curb the anti-intellectual drift of the Soviet establishment. During the 1970s he published dozens of articles and books that harshly denounced the Cultural Revolution and Maoism in general (see Burlatski 1970, 1979). Rumiantsev, Burlatski's chief, also participated in the anti-Maoist campaigns for the same reason (Rumiantsev 1969).

It is noteworthy that the "Chinese threat" played a prominent role in Solzhenitsyn's "Letter to the Soviet Leaders" (1981), which argued that the Soviet leadership should devote all its energies to halting the spread of Maoism.

In the end, however, the strategy of the intellectuals was ill-fated. The leadership succeeded in improving relations with the West and even signed the Helsinki Accord without weakening its anti-intellectual policies. The leadership rejected the efforts of liberal intellectuals to launch a massive ideological campaign against China comparable to that directed against the West, undoubtedly because such a campaign would have provided a prominent place for pro-Western intellectuals. In order to avoid encouraging the political activity of intellectuals, the leadership thought it best to reject their offers.

Brezhnev's Anti-Intellectualism

In the early 1970s Brezhnev's leadership adopted another approach toward the intellectuals. This approach was drastically different than Khrushchev's handling of the creative intelligentsia, and, unlike Stalin's policy, it focused to a much higher degree on the coalescence of intellectuals with the Soviet system. In contrast to their predecessors, especially Khrushchev's group, the Brezhnev team capably elaborated a long-term policy aimed at the complete elimination of any serious political dissent in the intellectual community.

The new program of dealing with intellectuals was comprised of several items. The most important were: (1) the legalization at the Twenty-first Party Congress and in the new constitution (1977) of direct party control over intellectuals (previously, even under Stalin, the system pretended not to interfere with the work of the intellectuals) and open recognition that clear political loyalty to the leadership was a condition for access to intellectual activity (this had never been stated explicitly, and never had such demands been included in official documents); (2) the introduction of political criteria for selection of potential intellectuals, beginning in high school (never before had the political loyalty of children been checked so openly); (3) the inclusion of leading intellectuals in the party (Stalin was rather indifferent to the party membership of scholars); (4) the involvement of intellectuals in direct cooperation with the KGB (done before, but seemingly to a much lesser degree); and (5) the active involvement of leading intellectuals in ideological work (again, never before done at such a scope).

The political leadership presented the new policy as a compromise offer to the creative intelligentsia. While asking the intelligentsia to become politically docile, the elite in return accepted a number of obligations toward those who would agree to be consistently politically loyal to the current leadership. First, the leadership promised systematic promotion and a successful career to those who accepted its offer, regardless of their professional excellence. Second, the elite promised safety and stability to loyal intellectual servants, again regardless of professional achievements or failures. Certainly, there would be no repetition of Stalin's times, when even the most ardent devotee could be dismissed and sent to the gulag simply at the whim of the dictator or his myrmidons. In addition, the elite actually vowed to make a distinction between the public and private lives of intellectuals, allowing them not to be afraid because of critical comments made in private communications. Third, the elite pledged that all privileges (not only material, but also those related to professional activity such as resources and the ability to publish), especially the right to go abroad, would go first to loyal intellectuals.

Silence As a Weapon

The new policy toward the intelligentsia involved shifting the emphasis from direct political pressure on intellectuals to a more subtle process of controlling the selection of cadres for scientific, cultural, and artistic institutions. This approach thus sought to avoid the scandals associated with intellectual oppositional activity, and the resulting official harassment, by regulating the process by which scholars were placed into influential positions. Should a disruptive intellectual manage to achieve such an important position and use it to engage in opposition activities, the leadership would more commonly deal with the problem through silence.

After Khrushchev's ouster, social criticism disappeared almost completely from the Soviet media, public conferences, and meetings. In fact, the period following Brezhnev's ascendance was characterized by a smaller volume of critical activity than at any other point in Soviet history. This development was recognized by the public, since surveys of readers of *Pravda*, *Izvestia*, and *Trud* suggested that only one third of the respondents were satisfied with the critical role of newspapers at the time (Shlapentokh 1969a, 1969b). The general level of criticism dropped dramatically during this period, and high officials as well as liberals and radicals were exempt from public attack. Only in extreme cases, usually for international reasons, did the leadership allow public criticism of its opponents (the brief period in the early 1970s being an exception). Ignoring attacks on the system proved to be effective in avoiding publicity.

Another approach to this problem also emerged. On some occasions, oppositional tendencies in works were ignored and efforts were made to present the authors as actually loyal or only neutral toward the regime.

The use of silence against those with undesirable views generally produced the expected results and was influential in preventing a new generation of outspoken intellectuals from building their notoriety through oppositional activity. During glasnost, Soviet intellectuals assessed the damage done to Soviet culture and science during Brezhnev's rule and bemoaned "the loss of several generations" of creative people (Agisheva 1987).

SELF-INDOCTRINATION OF HIGHBROWS

The pressure on intellectuals and graduate students to participate actively in ideological work drastically increased in the 1970s. Often, those who were pushed to participate in such activities ultimately came to accept the legitimacy of their actions in order to reconcile their internal conflicts over such matters. In the process, they also convinced others of the sincerity of their involvement. Among those in the intellectual community, however, there was little acceptance of such participation. Scholars who engaged in ideological campaigns against their colleagues normally destroyed their reputations among their associates, as well as among their family and friends. Coupled with the ensuing loss of self-respect, such denigration only served to make these participants more receptive to new demands from the leadership.

Publicly alienating scholars from the intellectual community was an important part of this process. Rudolf Ianovski, head of the Department of Science of the Central Committee, wrote that such leading scholars as

Sergei Vavilov, Kurchatov, Sergei Korolev, Alexander Alexandrov, Mstislav Keldysh, Nikolai Dubinin, and a number of others had become preoccupied with the ideological education of academics (1979a, pp. 107–116; 1979b, p. 82; see also Degtiarova 1985, pp. 56–79; Stepanian 1983, pp. 301–330). The party committee secretary of a chemistry institute of the Academy of Sciences, B. Sergenev, wrote in *Kommunist* that one leading researcher in his institute, a member of the academy, headed a seminar devoted to the study of the classics of Marxism-Leninism, and another led a seminar on the relationship between modern science and dialectical materialism (*Kom.*, no. 6, 1972). Given the scholarly community's contempt for dialectical materialism, which was imposed by Soviet ideologists on scientists and had only negative effects on Soviet science (a view not likely shared by Loren Graham, who wrote about "the originality of Soviet dialectical materialism," and "the Soviet achievements in philosophy of nature," [1987, p. 431]), the participation of leading Soviet scholars in these philosophical seminars was as shameful as participating in debates about the literary merits of Brezhnev's works.

The book *Ideological and Political Education of the Technical Intelligentsia* (1982a) was typical of the ideological education of the times. Among its editors were such prominent scholars as the chemist Nikolai Emmanuel, the biochemist Alexander Baiev, and the physicist Iuri Osip'ian, all full members of the Academy of Sciences (see Ianovski 1982a). Emmanuel devoted his article in this book to "Socialist Emulation for the Rise of Efficiency of Scientific Research." The physicist Viktor Tal'rose, a member-correspondent of the Academy of Sciences, called upon scholars to study Marxist ideology, suggesting that "the patriarchs of our Soviet science, including great chemists, physicists, biologists, and mathematicians, were distinguished not only by high political culture and active interests in the domestic and international policy of our state, but also took part in the implementation of this policy" (see Ianovski 1982a, p. 137). V. Kudriavtsev, a department head in the Institute of Physical Chemistry of the Academy of Sciences, was preoccupied in his article with "the lack of political knowledge and ideological skills among some scholars who go to the West, which makes it difficult for them to defend socialist ideals in the conversations and discussions over there" (p. 101).

THE INTELLECTUALS' RESPONSE TO THE OFFER: CAPITULATION

Liberal intellectuals reacted in different ways to the harsh repressions directed against the liberal movement. Four options faced them:

1. Complete surrender to the authorities and acceptance of their offer, i.e., becoming public supporters of the regime.

2. Embracing of Russophile ideology, which was in most cases sufficient to guarantee security while allowing some sort of opposition to the regime, which was important for self-respect and for the ability to claim that the abandonment of liberalism was not dictated by selfish motives.
3. A retreat to complete passivity, with a refusal to profess personal views, even within one's circle of friends, coupled with the use of the whole range of myths described earlier to justify such behavior.
4. The continuation of open opposition dictated by a liberal position.

The political elite, of course, preferred the first option. They were flexible enough, however, also to encourage those intellectuals who moved from liberal ideology to Russophilism. The authorities looked askance at intellectuals who decided to become passive observers of political developments without lending public support to the official policy, and they became enraged with those who continued to maintain their liberal views and oppose the regime.

The 1970s were full of gloomy data on the movement of brilliant intellectuals toward open collaboration with the regime they once despised (combined with a periodic flirtation with "progressive" ideas) and on the emergence of a new breed of intellectuals who probably had no compunctions about their servile behavior. Every group of Soviet intellectuals has managed to create its own paragons of the betrayal of their ideals and of their past.[4]

Many Soviet writers revealed their groveling before the elite mainly through their harassment of braver colleagues. In 1958 participation in Pasternak's persecution could still be more or less excused—the Stalinist period was too close. However, the same acts in the late 1960s and in the 1970s were beyond any form of justification. Nonetheless, the most prominent Soviet intellectuals participated in various conferences against Sakharov, Solzhenitsyn, and other dissidents and signed numerous articles to the same effect in newspapers. These intellectuals included Shostakovich, Aitmatov, Zalygin, Bykov, and others (*P.*, July 29, 1973; August 29, 1973; September 3, 1973; September 5, 1973). Similarly, a number of prominent humanists with solid liberal reputations (many of them future activists of perestroika) took part in various activities against Chukovskaia, Kornilov, Vladimir Voinovich, and the journal *Metropol*. Among the denouncers were Rybakov, Aitmatov, Grigori Baklanov, Za-

---

[4] In a typical example, Burlatski, Evgeni Ambartsumov, Pletnev, and Iuri Krasin, leading liberals of the 1960s (the first two also prominent figures of glasnost), published in *Kommunist* a review of a book about the Soviet Union by French communists. They not only chided the French authors for defending liberal ideas they themselves had supported in the 1960s, but they went on to do something even worse: they tried to downplay the Stalinist horror of the 1930s purges as unimportant and even excusable, considering the capitalist environment of the period (*Kommunist*, no. 12, 1978).

lygin, Borshchagovski, Bykov, Georgi Tovstonogov, and others. Among writers, others who can claim the role of deserter from the liberal movement include more future stars of perestroika, such as Korotich, Drach, Granin, and Rasul Gamzatov.[5]

At a meeting of Moscow writers, Sergei Narovchatov, a well-known poet and the editor of *Novyi Mir*, thanked Brezhnev for the honor of being able to publish his memoirs, praised by the poet in superlative terms (and in an agitated tone) as a model of imitation (about this episode, see Chernichenko 1988). He was joined in his apology of Brezhnev's masterpiece by the famous poet Eduardas Mezhelaitis and by Iuri Ovchinnikov, the vice president of the Academy of Sciences (see *Moskovskie Novosti*, May 7, 1988).

In the 1970s and 1980s, even outstanding Soviet intellectuals seemed anxious to participate in the most ludicrous ideological campaigns, such as the glorification of the Stakhanov movement, an object of ridicule in the intellectual community over many decades. Meanwhile, such prominent liberals as Olzhas Suleimenov, Iulia Drunina, and others discussed this fake activity very seriously (*Literaturnaia Gazeta*, October 2, 1985). Also deserving of special attention are the Soviet intellectuals who, in the 1970s and 1980s, took part in innumerable campaigns in support of Soviet foreign policy, accusing the United States and its government of sole responsibility for international tension. In addition, a number of intellectuals participated in the anti-Zionist campaign, which in the USSR is identified with anti-Semitism. Among this group were S. Zivs, Tsezar Solodar, Tovstonogov, and others (see *LG*, October 17, 1984; February 12, 1986). Natural scientists competed successfully with humanists in collaborating with the authorities.

In the latter 1970s even the most prominent Soviet scholars who, only a few years previously, had demonstrated their civic courage, relinquished any attempts to help colleagues who were being persecuted by the authorities. In his letter to foreign colleagues, Sakharov (1982) wrote with great bitterness about his former friends and very close associates in nuclear research such as Iakov Zeldovich, Khariton, Kapitsa, and Boris

---

[5] Compared to the 1960s, the atmosphere of demoralization allowed people to square accounts with personal enemies and more successful rivals. Vishnevskaia recounts a very remarkable story. In order to prevent her and Mstislav Rostropovich from making a recording of *Tosca*—a big event in Soviet musical life—five Bol'shoi Theater soloists (Milashkina, Atlantov, and others) rushed to Piotr Demichev, Minister of Culture, to declare that individuals who supported an anti-Soviet writer such as Solzhenitsyn could not be permitted to immortalize themselves on Soviet recordings. In their outward ideological zeal, they outdid the Soviet apparatchik who was forced to cancel the recording (Vishnevskaia 1984, pp. 452–453).

Kadomtsev. The last three did not even reply to his letters (see also Marchenko's "Open Letter to Academician Kapitsa P.L.," 1981).

In light of these people's behavior, the refusal of the president of the Soviet Academy of Sciences, Alexandrov, and his vice president, Evgeni Velikhov, to enter into any contact with Sakharov was not very surprising, although it was distressing (Sakharov 1981, 1982). It is noteworthy that in November 1988, Velikhov, a leading figure of perestroika, accompanied Sakharov on his first trip to the United States, as if nothing had happened between these two physicists fifteen years ago. Moreover, Nobel Prize winner Nikolai Semionov, and Khariton, who was awarded the title of Hero of Socialist Labor three times, along with a number of other academicians (thirty-nine in all), signed a nasty letter against Sakharov published in Soviet newspapers in 1973 (a letter with the same content was signed by twenty-eight members of the Soviet Academy of Medicine; see *P.*, January 24, 25, 26, February 12, 15, 1974).

During a meeting of the Academy of Sciences at the celebration of the sixtieth anniversary of the October Revolution, Sakharov attempted to submit his written request on political issues to the presidium of the meeting. As soon as he got up and began to move in the direction of the podium, he was immediately surrounded by plainclothesmen who practically immobilized him. Not a single member of the academy made any move to help Sakharov, or even express their sympathy to him (Chukovskaia 1979, pp. 146–147).

It is difficult to assess the number of young scholars, writers, actors, filmmakers, and other intellectuals who decided to be faithful servants of the regime while still in their last years of high school.

Of course, the Brezhnev period was the happiest time for all of the mediocre and talentless individuals who performed the roles of writers, scholars, and painters. As in any other period, the elite could immediately find people who were prepared to come out as devoted servants to fulfill any assignment of the masters. This period was the golden age for such writers as Kozhevnikov, Markov, Gribachev, and Sofronov, such sociologists as Irina Changli and Rutkevich, such philosophers as Fiodor Konstantinov and Tsolak Stepanian, and so on.

At the same time, some of the most prominent intellectuals, former heroes of liberalization, actively vied for the favors offered by the authorities, such as travel abroad, new apartments, promotions, the publication of their works, and so on. Moreover, in their feverish frenzy, they apparently forgot the temporary character of any regime and joyfully accepted invitations to revel with the meanest and most corrupt people in the government such as Igor Shchelokov, the son of the Minister of Internal Affairs. Arkadi Vaksberg described the life of this gentleman: "Many celebrities—poets and musicians, painters and journalists—considered it an honor to be invited by the son of the minister. They enjoyed comfort, understanding perfectly to whom they were indebted for it. . . . Some of them now sign enthusiastic texts in favor of changes" (Vaksberg 1988b).

The demoralization and mediocratization of the Soviet intellectuals did have one positive outcome, however: it produced a great writer. Zinoviev's *The Yawning Heights* (1976), which, of course, could be published only in the West, is a brilliant monument to the decadence of Soviet intellectual life. However, the author intentionally had this decadence described by morally degraded intellectuals who, as heroes of his book, bore names such as "Slanderer," "Thinker," "Sociologist," "Neurasthenic," "Gossiper," "Schizophrenic," "Deviationist." These "heroes" were particularly outraged by the fact that people much less talented than they had surpassed them in serving the regime. The book revolves around demoralized intellectuals confronted with mediocrity; the statement that our period is the "epoch of mass production of mediocrity" is typical of those made by the heroes of the book, whose strange names also reflect the debasement of Soviet intellectuals.

Overall, the Soviet intellectual community of the 1970s viewed itself pessimistically. The sad experiences of the period with the "betrayal of the clerks" painfully shocked the Soviet intelligentsia. Their faith in the strong links between education and nobility was greatly shaken.

In 1974, in the collection *From Under the Rubble*, Solzhenitsyn, reflecting the general disappointment with the intellectuals, attacked them as a group, including not only the creative and mass intelligentsia, but the prerevolutionary intellectuals as well. All of his sympathy was with the authors of *Milestones* (Berdiaev 1909), whom he considered prophets and who, after the defeat of the first Russian Revolution (1905–1907), blamed the Russian intelligentsia and its revolutionary behavior. Moreover, Solzhenitsyn was sure that the current Soviet intelligentsia was much worse than their prerevolutionary counterparts: much more craven, egotistical, indifferent to the truth, and cynical. Even those traits of the prerevolutionary intelligentsia treated by the authors of *Milestones* as flaws—heroic ecstasy, the feelings of martyrdom and of a near yearning for death, the dream of being a savior of mankind or at least of the Russian people, exaltation at being intoxicated with struggles—were seen as alien to the current Soviet intellectual (Solzhenitsyn 1974). In the late 1970s, Igor' Shafarevich joined Solzhenitsyn in his vituperations against the intelligentsia, and, referring to Ogustin Cochin, a French historian, contemptuously referred to members of this stratum as "small people" who have tried many times throughout history to impose their will on the entire nation (Shafarevich 1989). Other samizdat, as well as legal, authors also participated in the denunciation of the intelligentsia (see Altaiev's article in *Vol'noie Slovo*, no. 7, 1972, pp. 39–40; see also Astafiev's 1986b; Belov's *All Ahead*, 1986; Shubkin 1978).

Attacks on the intellectuals came not only from the Russophiles, but even from the liberals. This criticism stemmed from frustration with the collapse of the liberal movement, a development that liberals blamed on the reticence and egotism of the intellectuals as well as on the reaction of the leadership. For example, the novelist Trifonov began the 1960s with a variety of novels that praised contemporary intellectuals and their pre-revolutionary counterparts. By the mid-1970s, however, under the influence of the new political atmosphere, Trifonov became more critical of those whom he earlier had cited with favor (see Trifonov 1983a, b, 1984).

Female writers were probably the most eloquent about the intelligentsia during the "period of stagnation." Liudmila Petrushevskaia published *In Own Circle*, a devastating description of the life-styles of Moscow intellectuals as they abandoned one moral norm after another (Petrushevskaia 1988). Tatiana Tolstaia wrote about similar subjects (Tolstaia 1988), as did some male authors, such as Iulius Edlis in *Intermission* (1986), and, to a lesser degree, writers with Russophile tendencies, such as Belov (1986).

Edvard Radzinski was another author who managed to reconstruct the atmosphere of "the period of stagnation." His play, *Sport Games of 1981*, aroused the anger of spectators who did not want to recognize themselves among its heroes. Along with these literary works, many authors published articles commenting on the past and denouncing the demoralization and cowardice of the intelligentsia in general and of themselves. Later, at the height of perestroika, Levada and Viktor Sheinis looked back on the 1960s and 1970s and examined the failure of the first attempt at reforming Soviet society—a failure they blamed, in part, on the Soviet intelligentsia, which "already had in their blood the custom to obey the first shout, even if it was not so frightening as in the past" (*MN*, May 1, 1988).

THE RISE OF RUSSOPHILISM

In the 1960s the majority of the intellectuals and the mass intelligentsia demonstrated their allegiance to liberal ideals and the Western model of life, albeit with some reservations. It is characteristic that Solzhenitsyn did not deviate from this mainstream in his major works of this period (see, for instance, *Cancer Ward*, *The First Circle*, and of course, *The Gulag Archipelago*). Yet, even in these works and, to a greater extent, in some of his short stories (such as "Matrenin' Yard" and especially in "Fragments," which were circulated through samizdat), he revealed his Russophile feelings. In total, however, he was perceived by the intelligentsia as a prominent representative of the democratic trend. During this period, Kochetov, Markov, and Leonid Sobolev were his enemies, just as they were enemies of "pure" liberals (see Solzhenitsyn 1975c). The situation began to change radically in the late 1960s, and by the mid-1970s Russophilism had become the dominant oppositional trend within the intellectual community, engulfing those who had fought actively for the democratization of society only a few years earlier. (Compare, for example, Iuri Davydov's *Labor and Freedom*, 1963, and his *Ethics of Love and Metaphysics of Arbitrariness*, 1982.)

Having started as a legal movement within the intellectual community, Russophilism soon became a part of the underground opposition as well. The Russophiles' most important dissident organization was the All Russian Social and Christian Alliance (VSKhSON) in Leningrad, with twenty-eight members and thirty candidates on the eve of its destruction by the authorities in 1961.

There was a rather strong interaction between the legal and illegal spheres. Solzhenitsyn, for instance, became a prophet for the legal Russophiles, even though they could not mention his name in their articles, and he would not praise them in the West for fear of hurting their cause. The long history of Russophilism's division into legal and dissident wings has been analyzed by Alexander Ianov (1978 and 1988).

Why did a considerable proportion of the Soviet intellectuals move to embrace an ideology they themselves despised so vigorously only a few years earlier? The shift toward Russophilism from liberalism was, of course, multiply determined. Most individual intellectuals had several reasons for changing their attitudes, and there are no reliable means to determine what reasons counted more than others.

The liberation of human spirits from the hibernation imposed by Stalin stimulated not only liberal ideas but also Russophile feelings with anti-Soviet overtones. Yet immediately after Stalin's death, with memories of his crude Russian chauvinism and his anticosmopolitan campaign fresh in mind, it was difficult to proclaim oneself an advocate of Russian chauvinism, just as it was impossible for Russian intellectuals to support anti-Semitism before the Revolution. With one decade having passed, however, and the frenzy of Stalin's chauvinism forgotten, it became possible to vent the Russophile ideas that many intellectuals still harbored but had kept hidden.

Several other factors also contributed to the spread of Russophile ideas among intellectuals. In the 1960s and 1970s, various flaws in Western life became known to the Soviet people as they began to travel to the West, read Western books with strong criticisms of Western society (for instance, the books of Truman Capote, Gore Vidal, Edgar Doctorow, and Kurt Vonnegut, which the state willingly translated and disseminated), and see Western movies with the same tendencies (such as Stanley Kramer's movies).

Disillusionment with the West also strengthened antisocialist tendencies among Soviet intellectuals, since socialism and Marxism were regarded as Western products. Rejection of socialism and disbelief in the future of communism pushed many intellectuals to embrace Russophilism as a serious alternative to the West as well as to the current Soviet system. Solzhenitsyn was the most eloquent representative of these intellectuals.

It was not only these "cognitive" developments that led intellectuals into the camp of the Russophiles, but also radical changes in the political life of the late 1960s. Two factors must be noted in this regard—the defeat of the liberal movement, and the new policy of the political elite toward Russophilism. With Soviet tanks in Prague, political pessimism began to overwhelm the Soviet liberals. Hopes for a gradual transformation of the Soviet Union into a democratic and pluralistic society were dashed. At the same time, many intellectuals began to look for an ideology that could reconcile them with political reality, with their helplessness toward the political elite, and with their frustration at the complete passivity of the Russians toward the dominant social and political order. The Russophile ideology, with its belief in the specific development of Russian history and in the superiority of Russia, her culture, and her morals over those of the West, offered the defeated liberals a serious spiritual alternative.

Two other circumstances made Russophilism attractive to many honest and bold intellectuals. Due to Russophilism's anti-Soviet overtones, intellectuals who joined the ranks of the Russophiles could avoid regarding themselves as opportunists who had changed their convictions in order to accommodate those in power.

Russophilism's attractiveness was also strongly enhanced by another development. By all accounts, the Soviet political elite decided in the late 1960s that the struggle against liberal ideology (which it considered its main foe) could be much more successful if some doses of anti-Sovietism in Russophilism were not only tolerated, but if active members of the movement who came on as strong critics of the Soviet system and ideology were actually supported in various ways by the state. The official support of Russophilism, which became obvious in the late 1960s, turned out to be probably the most important factor in enrolling many Soviet intellectuals into the movement.

It is impossible to consider it fortuitous that a significant upsurge of Russophilism in the Soviet Union began exactly in 1968, when the Soviet rulers decided to embark on a frontal attack against the liberal intellectuals. In 1968, and no earlier, the first articles with a clear allegiance to

Russophilism appeared in *Molodaia Gvardia* (The Young Guard), the organ of the Young Communist League, as well as in other periodicals (Chalmaiev 1968; Lobanov 1968).

After 1968 Russophiles received unprecedented leeway in their activities, and it is possible that the leadership even encouraged them to step up their role in Soviet spiritual life. The dismissal of Alexander Iakovlev, the acting head of the Central Committee's propaganda department (and Gorbachev's future ideologue), for his anti-Russophile article in *Literaturnaia Gazeta* in 1972 was a clear signal regarding the leadership's position on the conflict between Russophiles and "pure" Marxists. Russophiles were also attacked, again without success, by Dementiev in *Novyi Mir* (1969); this also resulted in his dismissal. (About this, see also Ianov 1978, pp. 49–52, 57–60.)

Along with *Molodaia Gvardia*, other magazines, such as *Nash Sovremennik* (Our Contemporary), *Ogoniok* (Light), *Moskva* (Moscow), *Neva*, *Don*, and *Volga*, started to publish articles, novels, and poems with obvious Russophile tendencies. These magazines were joined by publishing houses such as Molodaia Gvardia and Sovietskaia Rossia (Soviet Russia), which began to produce books with the same orientation.

A number of writers and painters with open Russophile views, which were often combined with praise for the prerevolutionary monarchy and church, such as the writer Valentin Pikul' and his numerous historical novels, and the painter Il'ia Glazunov, both of whom idealized Russian life before 1917, obviously enjoyed support at the highest levels of the hierarchy (see, for instance, Pikul' 1985a, 1985b).

Russophiles turned the All-Russian Society for the Protection of Monuments into their base and into a forum for the propagation of their views. They also easily dominated some conferences, such as the one in 1978 devoted to modern dramaturgy, and another in celebration of the Kulikov field battle. (The 1980 commemoration of this battle was a real apotheosis of Russophilism in the official press and public gatherings; *Posev*, no. 4, 1981; *Poiski*, no. 2, 1980, pp. 65–89.)[6] During the 1970s

---

[6] The conference on modern dramaturgy, entitled "Classics and Us," held in the Central Club of Writers on December 21, 1978, was one of the most aggressive actions of the Russophile extremists during the Brezhnev period. Piotr Palievski and Stanislav Kuniaev used the conference for the denigration of individuals in literature and the arts who were, either in fact or in their imagination, Jews, including Eduard Bagritski, Vsevolod Meierkhold, and others. It was characteristic that in taking this action, both speakers, along with like-minded participants (i.e., Kozhinov, Kuprianov), presented themselves not only as defenders of Russian classics against avant-gardists who would distort them, but as critics of the period that immediately followed the Revolution and civil war: the 1920s, with its emphasis on class struggle, internationalism, and world revolution. At the same time, none of the liberals who spoke at this conference (Efros, Evtushenko, Bitov, Borshchagovski) dared seriously chal-

and 1980s, they managed to promote a number of philosophers, linguists, and journalists (Kozhinov 1978, 1980; Kuz'min 1985a, 1985b; Palievski 1978) who, consistently exploiting all the contradictions in Marxism and in official ideology, were able to expound their vision of the world in numerous publications.

In the mid-1970s, Russophiles began their offensive in the movies. They created numerous films idealizing old Russia and its nobles (for instance, Andrei Mikhalkov-Konchalovski's *The Noble's Nest*, after Turgenev 1969), or the countryside and peasants (for instance, Iosif Kheifets's *Married for the First Time*, 1980, and Igor Talankin's *Stars Fall*, 1982). Another important theme was the pitting of Russian values against those of the West (Nikita Mikhalkov's *A Few Days from Oblomov's Life*, 1980).

Russophiles were also active in samizdat. Some of the earliest Russophile credos appeared in "The Word of the Nation" (see *Archiv Samizdata*, no. 590, no. 8), and in numerous articles written by Gennadi Shimanov, who also started to publish the samizdat magazine *Mnogaia Leta* (Many Years to Live) (see also Alexeieva 1984, pp. 397–398; Ianov 1978). Following this, Russophiles initiated a number of underground magazines, such as *Veche*, *Zemlia*, and *Chasy* (Clock). (About *Veche*, see Ianov 1988, pp. 168–200; about the Russophile samizdat in Leningrad in the 1970s, see Kolker 1985.)

While generally very favorable toward Russophilism and typically taking the side of the Russophiles in their sharp conflicts with the Marxists, Brezhnev's leadership also repressed those "legal" Russophiles who took too aggressive an approach against Marxist elements in the official ideology. Thus, in the early 1970s, the authorities reshuffled the editorial board of the Russophile magazine *Molodaia Gvardia* and dismissed Iuri Melentiev, who was director of a publishing house that echoed his sentiments (see Ianov 1978, pp. 52–57). Moreover, in the early 1970s the Soviet leadership took harsh measures against those Russophiles who intensified their hostility toward the current system and refused to be influenced by the authorities. Osipov and Igor Ogurtsov were two of the overly independent Russophiles who were sentenced to prison and exile (see Osipov 1978). The protection of the Russophiles in general, however, continued through January 1982, when Mikhail Suslov's death, combined with Brezhnev's near incapacitation, changed the constellation of forces in the Kremlin.

The rapid escalation of Andropov's authority proved, rather unexpectedly, to be a negative factor for the Russophiles, particularly after the

lenge the Russophiles, and in fact tried to accommodate them whenever possible (*Poiski*, no. 2, 1980, pp. 65–113).

chairman of the KGB became the General Secretary. His appointment was followed almost immediately by a series of anti-Russophile articles in *Pravda* and other newspapers (see *P.*, January 4, 1983; see also Rostislav Petropavlovski's article criticizing Iuri Davydov's Russophile book, *Kom.*, May 1983).

Andropov's death allowed the Russophiles to breathe again, and, with no foreknowledge of glasnost, they resumed their ideological campaign, feeling sure that, as had been the case for the last two decades, the Kremlin was more or less on their side (see, for instance, Kuniaev's article in *Nash Sovremennik*, February 1985).

Heroes of the Dark Ages

The political reaction in the 1970s demoralized a considerable part of the Soviet intellectual community, forcing many to leave the movement and even to collaborate with the authorities in suppressing the liberal activities of their colleagues and friends. Even so, the 1970s was a decade when the democratic movement took some new steps forward.

First, significant numbers of leading liberals took no actions that could be interpreted as a retreat from their old convictions. Writers such as Trifonov, Vladimir Tendriakov, Andrei Bitov, Kornilov, Iskander, Sosnora, and Vysotski, philosopher Pomerants, sociologist Levada, and others published almost nothing at odds with the views they had expressed in the previous decade. The nature of their public activities did not change, nor did they participate in any governmental actions. In addition, some of them (for instance, Lipkin, Lisnianskaia, Pomerants, Iskander, and Sosnora) continued to publish abroad. Not until 1987–1988, some twenty years later, were some of these authors (Iskander, Lipkin, Bitov, and others) able to witness the publication of their novels and stories in their own country.

Nonconformist artists, also very active in this period, organized a number of illegal exhibitions, including the famous Bulldozer Exhibition in Moscow (mentioned earlier) and the Leningrad exhibition near the Petropavlovsk fortress.

A significant event in this period was the attempt to publish the magazine *Metropol* without censorship. Along with famous writers such as Aksenov and Akhmadulina, a number of new personalities turned up as participants in the preparation of this illicit edition, such as the writer Evgeni Popov, the historian Batkin, and the philosopher Viktor Trostnikov (see Aksenov 1982, 1985).

A few years earlier, in 1974, Leningrad intellectuals had attempted to publish the collected works of the poet Iosif Brodsky, who had by that time asked to emigrate. The most active participants in this enterprise—

the historian Mikhail Kheifets and the writer Maramzin—were arrested. This did not, however, stop other Leningrad representatives of the so-called second culture from trying to publish, also unsuccessfully, two collections of poems: *Lepty* (Mites) and *Mera Vremeni* (Measure of Time). They did succeed in putting into circulation three samizdat magazines devoted to literature and the arts.

Despite the repression, the main periodical of the democratic movement, the *Chronicle of Current Events*, continued to be published, albeit with interruptions. Several other samizdat periodicals began to circulate during this period: *Pamiat'* (Memory), a collection of articles on historical issues which had been silenced by official propaganda; the magazine *Poiski* (Search), edited by Valeri Abramkin, Piotr Abovin-Egides, and Raisa Lert, among others; and other publications.

Additional developments included the authorities' failure to prevent the political demonstrations of December 5, 1976 (the date on which the old Soviet constitution was adopted), which were used by the liberal movement to manifest their demands. On this day, people gathered to protest around the monuments to Pushkin in Moscow, Leningrad, and Odessa.

Of greatest significance was the new wave of protest letters in 1977–1978. Unlike the participants in similar campaigns in the 1960s, those who signed these letters knew quite well what would eventually come of their actions. Nevertheless, among the signatories were not only seasoned human rights activists, but also many who had not previously participated in open opposition activities (Alexeieva 1984, p. 320).[7]

Even more notable is that a significant number of intellectuals, as well as people from other walks of life, joined the dissident movement just at the height of the political reaction. Thus the peak of Sakharov's activity falls in the 1970s, as do those of the physicists Orlov and Valeri Chalidze, writers Kopelev and Voinovich, mathematicians Andrei Tverdokhlebov, Iuri Shikhanovich, and Tatiana Velikanova, computer scientists Anatoli Shcharanski and Alexander Lavut, biologists Sergei Kovalev and Viktor Nekipelov, historians Arseni Roginski and Gefter, economist Sokirko, and psychiatrist Anatoli Koriagin. (About the dissident movement of the 1970s, see *VS.*, no. 21, 1971; no. 27, 1972, 1977; no. 38, 1980; Alexeieva 1984; Chalidze 1974, 1982; Meerson-Aksenov and Shragin 1977.)

During this period, which ended in 1987 for the inmates of Soviet camps, distinguished people perished in prisons and camps, including the

[7] The 1979 letter in defense of Velikanova, who had been arrested by the authorities, was signed by 363 Soviet intellectuals and professionals, as well as by people from other strata of the population (*VS*, no. 38, 1980, pp. 46–56).

chemist Iuri Kuk, the poet Vasili Stus, the teacher Vasili Tikhi, and the worker and writer Anatoli Marchenko.

A NEW ERA IN THE LIBERAL MOVEMENT: THE FIRST POLITICAL ORGANIZATIONS

The tenacity of the democratic movement notwithstanding, the most important development in the 1970s was the emergence of numerous political associations that challenged the state. Such organizations had a particular impact since the elite has always regarded independent organizational activity as the most dangerous type of threat to the Soviet system.

In 1970 Chalidze, along with two other physicists, Sakharov and Tverdokhlebov, created the Human Rights Committee. It was the first independent Soviet association to be recognized by an international organization: the International League of Human Rights. The Human Rights Committee conducted the first Soviet press conference, an unbelievable event in the USSR. Four years later, this association was joined by another: the Soviet section of Amnesty International, headed by Turchin.

The creation in 1976 of the Moscow Helsinki Group, whose purpose was to monitor Soviet compliance with this famous agreement, was a new step forward in the confrontation with Soviet power because intellectuals were now intruding into the most sensitive area of politics: international relations. As with the earlier organizations, physicists (Orlov and Sakharov) were again the founders of the Helsinki group. In addition, nine other prominent opposition figures signed the constitutive document (mathematicians Alexeieva and Shcharanski, Grigorenko, and Elena Bonner, among others).

The example set by Moscow intellectuals was followed by Ukrainians, Lithuanians, Georgians, and Armenians. Moreover, the Moscow Helsinki Group spurred the nascence of special-interest political associations, such as the Committee to Study the Abuse of Psychiatry and possibly the Christian Committee for the Defense of the Rights of Believers.

During the latter 1970s the Moscow Helsinki Group, with its regular press conferences, was the center of oppositional activity in the country. People from various corners of the USSR went to Moscow to win the support of this group in their struggles with local authorities. The Helsinki Group became the main target of official persecution, which eventually led to the arrest or exile of almost all its members (Alexeieva 1984, pp. 309–324).

None of the brave "dissidents" (as the human right advocates were called at the time) could have imagined that, two decades later, the official Soviet press would commend them not only individually, including through the publication of their memoirs and those of such indomitable adversaries of the Soviet system as Anatoli Marchenko or Vladimir Bukovski (about this event, see *MN*, February 25, 1990), but also as members of an extremely positive movement that acted as the sole oppositional force to "the regime of stagnation" (see, for instance, Leonid Batkin's article, "Dissident," in *Znanie i Sila*, November 1989, pp. 45–47).

EMIGRATION AT THE CENTER OF DEBATE

The Jewish emigration exerted enormous influence on Soviet intellectuals of Jewish origin—and on Soviet intellectuals as a whole—and strongly exacerbated the conflict between liberals and Russophiles. The readiness of many Jewish intellectuals to leave the country, thereby abandoning their struggle against "the system," provided Russophiles, particularly those with strong anti-Semitic tendencies, with the argument that only ethnic Russians were real patriots who took care of Russia and her culture. The emigration confused liberal Russophiles, active foes of anti-Semitism, and even committed Westernizers, who regarded their Jewish friends who were leaving the country as deserters.

Many Russophiles not only rejected the idea of treating the right to emigrate as an important political issue, but strongly condemned practically everyone who left. On the other hand, the most extreme Russophiles greeted emigration as a way of "cleansing" the motherland of "kikes." Conflict over the political role of emigration was one of the major points of dissension between the two great leaders of the opposition movement, Sakharov and Solzhenitsyn. Whereas the former made the cause of emigration the focus of his activity, the latter accused him of being diverted from much more important issues (Sakharov 1978; Solzhenitsyn 1975c). A number of other Russophiles (for instance, Shafarevich) came out against overemphasizing the role of emigration in Soviet life (see *VS*, no. 20, 1975, pp. 80–87).

While supporting emigration in principle, many liberals sharply regretted the departures of their friends and companions-in-battle, who, in leaving, left exposed those pieces of the battle lines they had defended. Lamentations and angry denunciations over this issue could be found even in the legal literature of the 1970s, such as Trifonov's last stories (1982), some of Okudzhava's songs (see Okudzhava 1984), Gleb Gorbovski's poems (1985), and, indirectly, in movies (for instance, *Mimino* or *White Snow of Russia*) and plays (e.g., *Sholom Alekheim Street 40*, Stavitski 1986).

It is noteworthy that in 1987–1988, when it became possible to speak of emigration relatively freely, liberal intellectuals began to explain and even justify the emigration of their colleagues and friends, regarding the emigration of some of them as an act of resistance and courage (see Gozman and A. Etkind's article, "Why We Do Not Go," in *Vek XXi Mir*, September 1988, pp. 32–38).

Although emigration invigorated anti-Soviet propaganda in the West and very significantly increased the amount of information on Soviet life available to Western governments and public opinion, emigration in the 1970s also served many of the goals of the Soviet leadership (of course, the general political balance of emigration for the Soviet system and the alignment of forces in the Soviet establishment for and against emigration are other questions). Emigration, voluntary and involuntary, allowed the authorities to rid themselves of many politically active intellectuals, whether Jewish or not, such as writers Aksenov, Korzhavin, Vladimir Maximov, Kopelev, Voinovich, Vladimov, Turchin, and others.

The authorities also used emigration to foment jingoist patriotism, characterizing emigrants (as well as, albeit to a lesser degree, those who married foreigners) as traitors, in contrast to true Russian patriots who would never quit their motherland, no matter what hardships they had to endure. Emigration was used for "educational" purposes at numerous meetings, at which people were summoned to condemn a colleague who had applied for an exit visa. These meetings very efficiently demoralized those liberal intellectuals forced to take the floor in the excommunication of their friends (cf. the "naming names" technique used by the McCarthy committee in the United States in the 1950s). This procedure was especially demoralizing for Jewish intellectuals. (About these meetings in scientific institutes, see Shlapentokh 1984, pp. 232–236; Simis 1982, pp. 7–22.)

Emigration also gave the sycophants among mediocre intellectuals an opportunity to regain some measure of self-respect. Now their attacks against their more successful colleagues could appear to be dictated not by envy, but rather by pure patriotic feelings. This aroused the ire of Russophiles such as Osipov (Osipov 1978).

When Soviet intellectuals left Sheremetievo, the international airport in Moscow, in the 1970s, they were usually escorted by a few dozen of their friends, none of whom believed that the famous figures would ever see their country and their friends again. The atmosphere in the airport during these departures was reminiscent of that at a funeral. Neither those who left nor those who came to see them off ever dreamed that, after fifteen years, many of the emigrants would not only receive permission to visit their homeland, but would see their novels published in Soviet magazines and their interviews published in the Soviet press and even aired on television. In the 1970s it was universally believed that Brezhenev's regime would be a "thousand-years Reich."

THE YEARNING FOR RELIGION AND CHURCH

The Upsurge of Interest in Religion

As mentioned earlier, the political reaction and growing social pessimism of the 1970s triggered the retreat of Soviet intellectuals from liberalism. These developments also account for the sharp upsurge in interest in religion, and the increasing numbers of people considering themselves religious. The ascent of religion among intellectuals and the mass intelligentsia followed essentially the same process as that inspired by the defeat of the Russian Revolution in 1905–1907, which was reflected very well in *Milestones* (Berdiaev 1909). In the 1970s, as in similar periods in other societies, religion seemed almost the sole alternative to social progress and regained its influence through the people's attempts to reconcile themselves with the world when social progress proved illusory. The paradoxical incompatibility and mutual supplementarity of Marx and Christ were exhibited to their fullest extent in Soviet life in the 1970s and 1980s.

The religious groundswell began among humanists—writers, painters, and philosophers—and then spread to natural scientists. Young intellectuals were particularly receptive to the religious message. Older people could not easily renounce their atheism because that would have been tentamount to admitting they had unduly lived their whole lives without faith—a difficult thing to accept.

It is noteworthy that religion played only a relatively weak role in the lives of Soviet intellectuals in the 1960s, at the height of the liberal movement. Even in samizdat, religious themes were not often elaborated. In Solzhenitsyn's major publications, both in licit magazines and in samizdat (for instance, *Cancer Ward* and *The First Circle*), religion was treated as a minor issue. The focus on religion in VSKhON's (the All Russian Social Christian Alliance, an underground organization in Leningrad) activity in the early 1960s was received with astonishment by those acquainted with this movement. Even in the 1960s, however, religion was a bone of contention between the political powers and the intelligentsia, and the movement of the latter toward recognizing the important and positive role of religion in social and individual life was quite clear. The spread of religion among educated Soviet citizens occurred, as mentioned before, at various levels, ranging from a superficial flirtation with religious terminology to complete abdication from "normal Soviet life" and full absorption with the religious spirit.

The Interest in Religious Literature

For those seeking a rapprochement with religion, the first stage was often an interest in literature with positive attitudes toward religion, followed by interest in purely religious books (primarily the Bible). This type of literature became increasingly popular among educated people at the end of the 1960s. Even during the 1960s, the Bible was already one of the most coveted books for the educated Soviet individual. The price of a Bible on the black market—a very sensitive indicator of people's interest—reached 100 rubles (two thirds of the average monthly salary at that time) during the 1960s, and has increased continuously since that time (*VS*, no. 28, 1977, p. 16).

The intelligentsia's strong interest in religious literature drove some people to photocopy religious books for the black market. In 1982 police impounded six hundred copies of the Gospels in the apartment of an individual arrested for this activity (Alexeieva 1984, p. 213).

The books and articles of Nikolai Berdiaev were probably read more than any others by those interested in religious issues. Berdiaev's publications comprised close to one third of the books belonging to VSKhON which were impounded by the KGB (twenty-three of seventy-three copies) (*VS*, no. 22, 1976, pp. 48–50). Along with Berdiaev, the Russian scholars Konstantin Leontiev, Vladimir Soloviev, Vasili Rozanov, Pavel Florenski, Nikolai Fiodorov, and Semion Frank were among the most attractive to those interested in religion and Russian tradition (for an analysis of this phenomenon, see Furman 1988). Soviet intellectuals were also able to read works published before the Revolution by these authors. Berdiaev's works, however, were primarily published in the West. Besides Russian religious philosophers, Western authors such as Søren Kierkegaard and Martin Heidegger were also popular among people with an interest in religion, as were books by other Western scholars who dealt with religious themes (Russell, Maritain, and others). Soviet intellectuals devoured anything that could enlighten them on the subject. Dostoevsky was being reread again and again, this time as a religious writer (*The Brothers Karamazov* in particular), as were other prerevolutionary Russian writers such as Nikolai Leskov and Andrei Belyi. Novels of Western writers that were devoted partially or totally to religious issues also aroused great intellectual curiosity. Among these novels, Thomas Mann's *Joseph and His Brothers* was especially popular, along with the novels of Mauriac, Marcel Dubard, and others.

Soviet intellectuals were also on the lookout for any publications containing information on the history of Christianity and other religions, or on Western attitudes toward religion. The hunger for such literature was so great that even official Soviet publications on religion became objects of interest. This was especially true of official works that appeared in the 1960s and later, when atheistic literature became more sophisticated and contained much data on religion.

Interest in religion went beyond the activity of reading and conducting private debates and began to affect other aspects of the intellectuals' lives. By the 1960s collecting ecclesiastical artifacts and old Russian icons had become a fixture in the lives of many intellectuals. The infatuation with icons soon became a new fashion, entered into by many intellectuals with no genuine interest in religion. This phenomenon of blindly jumping on the bandwagon, led by the intellectuals' leaders, is all too common.

Counteroffense against Atheism

Although most intellectuals interested in religion limited themselves to reading officially sanctioned literature, several scholars, writers, painters, and film directors tried to counter official atheistic propaganda in their works. At the least, they hoped to instill respect for religion in the mass intelligentsia, in students, and in the rest of society. Out of necessity, this was usually accomplished through elaborate techniques involving allusions, parallels, hidden ideas, and other gimmicks used to trick the censors.

For the most part, this antiatheistic propaganda was attenuated by the close connection between Russophilism, and its clear support from the Kremlin, and Orthodox religion. Intellectuals with reputations as Russophiles were able to express their religious feelings, or simply their veneration of religion, much more freely than could Westernizers, not to mention followers of Islam or, even worse, advocates of Judaism. For this reason, it is hardly surprising that the first incursion in favor of religion in legal literature was made by Vladimir Soloukhin in his famous *Letters from the Russian Museum* in 1967, just when the political leadership was beginning its offensive against the liberals. Religious motives later become a leading theme in novels and stories of the "rural prose" school. Although these authors imputed religious convictions mostly to old people, as did Rasputin in *Farewell with Matera*, the elderly were, like Rasputin's old woman Daria, invariably portrayed as models for younger generations.

Along with writers, painters such as Glazunov (also an active Russophile) began to exploit religious themes in their works, again largely indirectly. Glazunov's 1978 exhibition in Moscow was full of pictures that could be interpreted as proreligious. Russophile and religious themes continued to appear in his work in the 1980s, and his exhibitions in the latter 1980s attracted immense crowds, despite the near-unanimous contempt of the critics. (About Glazunov's exhibition in summer 1986, see *P*, July 21, 1986.)

Religious themes were then taken up simultaneously by legal philosophers, historians, and sociologists, who, being mostly liberals, wanted to confront the official ideology in this field. Levada's "Social Nature of Religion" (1965) was the first work in Soviet philosophical literature to discuss the origin of religion without official demagoguery.

Sergei Averintsev, a prominent Soviet philosopher and linguist, managed to publish a number of books that treated religion with the utmost deference and even admiration (Averintsev 1981). The authors of the five-volume *Philosophical Encyclopedia* (1965–1970), especially those of the two volumes entitled *Mythology of the Peoples of the World* (Tokarev 1980), also tried to handle issues relating to religion with due respect (see also Iablokov's *Sociology of Religion,* 1979). Of course, these publications immediately attracted the attention of the entire intellectual community.

Moreover, even some of the new generation of ideologues who, ex officio, had to carry out atheistic propaganda began to publish books in which recitation of the usual atheistic arguments could not hide the authors' deep respect for religion and religious morals (see, for instance, Sherdakov 1982).

In the 1960s practically all liberal writers and film directors, except those who openly served the current needs of Soviet propaganda (not to mention writers with Russophile tendencies, such as those of the rural prose school), ceased to attack or deride religion in any form. It is also worth noting that the extremely rich repertoire of Soviet jokes and anecdotes in the post-Stalin period contains almost nothing that could be regarded as derisive of religion or the church. Similarly, it was impossible, both in the 1960s and later, to find novels or stories in which religious people were depicted as antiheroes. Moreover, many liberals tried to include in their novels and movies episodes, dialogues, and monologues that could be interpreted as positive toward religion. Thus in the popular movie, Georgi Natanson's *All is Left to People* (1963), the main hero, a dying great scholar, challenged the faith of his cousin, a bishop, contending that religion was the lot of weak people. The bishop, who was presented as a decent person (a major departure from religious characters in previous Soviet movies) did not argue this issue with his sick relative, but very convincingly retorted that the humbled and oppressed people made up the majority, and they badly needed God. The same idea was developed simultaneously in several other movies, including the movies of Andrei Tarkovski, especially the film *Andrei Rublev.*

Underground Religious Movements

In the late 1960s some intellectuals took further steps and crossed legal lines to participate in religious activities, putting themselves in confrontation with the authorities. These intellectuals made active contacts with priests known for their nonconformism, and they attended religious ceremonies and seminars. Solzhenitsyn himself engaged in religious activity, and, in his "open letters," accused the official Orthodox hierarchy of collaboration with the state. These letters aroused heated polemics among religious and lay intellectuals (see *VS*, nos. 9–10, 1972, pp. 201–217).

Religious seminars and magazines were the most typical spheres of activity for religious intellectuals who directly challenged the state. One such seminar, with a clear bias against official ideology and the Soviet system, functioned in Leningrad and was headed by Alexander Ogorodnikov.

Following these seminars, the next event in the religious movement came in the mid-1970s with the publishing of the samizdat religious magazine, *Nadezhda* (Hope). Its publisher, the linguist Zoia Krakhmal'-nikova, was arrested in 1983, but the magazine survived (see excerpts from magazine issues 2, 3, 4, 5, and 6 in *VS*, no. 44, 1981).

More so than in other spheres of their activity, it was in the area of the defense of the people's right to a religious life that Soviet intellectuals came into close contact with the religious movement in general: not only with solitary priests who challenged the Soviet authorities and the official Orthodox hierarchy, such as fathers Dmitri Dudko and Gleb Iakunin, but also with the rank and file of this movement, such as ordinary workers, peasants, and clerks. Although the religious movement in the Soviet Union in general is extremely diversified, with numerous creeds, Orthodoxy has attracted the absolute majority of those intellectuals interested in religious issues. Other religious groups, such as Baptists, Seventh-Day Adventists, and Jehovah's Witnesses, have played no role in the lives of Soviet intellectuals (the Catholic movement in Lithuania and the Apostolic faith in Armenia are two exceptions).

The Slavic origin of most Soviet intellectuals (Russians, Ukrainians, and Bielorussians, joined in this respect by Georgians, who confess the Orthodox religion, and Armenians, who are Apostolic) is insufficient to explain this fact. Again, political factors come to the surface. To confess creeds other than Orthodoxy is much more dangerous for an intellectual, since, despite the atheistic stance of the Soviet state, Orthodoxy is regarded as more compatible with the political regime than are other religions (especially sects that are not formally recognized, such as the Pentecostals). All other national movements, in either their secular or religious manifestations, are treated by the political elite with utmost animosity.

There is no doubt that many Buriat intellectuals were very interested in Buddhism, and Uzbek intellectuals in Islam. Yet there were practically no signs of religious activity among these groups at any level similar to that of the Russians. The case of Aitmatov is typical: although he is Muslim and one of the most respected non-Russian writers, Aitmatov dared not use his novel *Executioner's Block* (1987) to express his reverence for Islam; instead he made his main hero an Orthodox priest and filled many pages of his novel with scenes involving Jesus Christ. Even Olzhas Suleimenov's *Az i Ia* (1975), with its acid attacks against Russian chauvinism and its glorification of the oriental contribution to Russian history, can be regarded as an action in favor of oriental culture, because its author did not dare, in his unbelievably un-Orthodox book, to glorify Islam as Soloukhin had done with Orthodoxy.

Since the 1930s Judaism has been a special target of the Soviet leadership's hatred. An interest in Judaism, if it became known to the authorities, has meant the immediate dismissal of an intellectual from his or her position in the establishment. The study of Jewish religion, the Talmud, or the study of Hebrew or Jewish history, even if done very privately, has been considered almost as bad as participation in the dissident movement. With such official repudiation of Judaism, it is not surprising that several intellectuals of Jewish origin who became interested in religion preferred to satisfy their religious feelings and interests through Orthodoxy, up to and including formal conversion. The Russian milieu and traditions, together with more personal reasons, strongly influenced their preference of Orthodoxy over the religion of their ancestors (see, for instance, Svetov 1978; Kolker 1985).

In the late 1980s the religious activity of Russians, and to some degree even that of non-Russians, almost totally lost its oppositional flavor. Not only did Gorbachev's regime include religion in its liberal program, but during the celebration of the one thousand year anniversary of Christianity in Russia in June 1989, the regime honored the Orthodox church with meetings between Soviet leaders and ecclesiastic dignitaries, with the return of some old church buildings to believers, with priests elected to the parliament and to various political and cultural bodies, with the permanent presence of religious themes on Soviet television, and with innumerable articles in the Soviet press supporting freedom of religion (*MN*, November 29, 1987). Along with the Russophiles, liberals were also active supporters of religion and the church (albeit to a lesser degree than the Russophiles). Minister of Culture Nikolai Gubenko, a well-known liberal, demanded the state's "cooperation with the church," and saw such cooperation as an important step in "the restoration of the spirituality and morals of the country" (*LG*, December 13, 1989).

It was no surprise that, after 1985, numerous novels and stories espoused not only open respect for religion, but a belief in religion as the only savior of the country. Among these were Rasputin's *Fire* (1985) and Astafiev (1984a). In addition, it became possible in 1989 for Soviet intellectuals to declare their deep religiosity in public, as did, for example, two writers: Grekova (the pseudonym for Elena Ventzel') and Iuri Nagibin

(*MN*, May 28, 1989; *Nedelia*, May 28, 1989, pp. 8–9). The attempt by Iosif Kryvelev, an old advocate of atheism, to attack these works from an Orthodox position was spurned and derogated by all of the leading newspapers.

THE RETREAT FROM SOCIAL LIFE: SOVIET STOICISM

The political reaction, coupled with social pessimism, also accounts for another trend among intellectuals: the rejection of any form of social activity (including religion, which assumes social communication), and absorption with the individual's own life. Three trends, each emphasizing different life goals, developed strongly in the 1970s: the separation of the individual's life from the state, unrestrained hedonism, and the "enlightened" cult of the individual's body and mind.

The first trend, which was somewhat reminiscent of stoic philosophy, supports the maximum possible separation of private life from public life. This life-style, as it was described in a samizdat magazine, was expressed in such ways as working in the second economy, educating children in private schools, organizing libraries based on private donations and used only by donors, private theaters and other entertainments, and so on (*Poiski*, no. 3, 1980, pp. 63–70).

The second trend continued a process mentioned earlier: the hunt for pleasures of any sort—drunkenness, sexual libertinism, and the systematic desire for relaxation (the oriental work *Kaif* became very popular among Moscow intellectuals in this time)—and the avoidance of hard work. This form of depravity, which in the 1970s embraced many intellectuals who had been very socially active in the previous decade, was undergirded by cynical worldviews and by the various myths discussed in chapter 4. Anatoli Makarov, complaining about the spread of drunkenness among the intelligentsia, lamented that "the moral authority of the intelligentsia, with its studied delicacy, spiritual scrupulosity, and cleanliness is, if not lost, at least diluted, and so to say transformed into pure convention. All these positive features are applauded in theater, but in life, it seems to me, other traits gain: pressure, taste for consumer goods, and conformism" (Makarov 1985, p. 12).

Along with this primitive hedonism, another trend that focused each individual's attention on him or herself became conspicuous in the 1970s. In contrast to the pleasure seekers, with their disregard for their own physical and mental health, those who represented the third trend considered fitness to be their major life goal. These intellectuals became obsessed with diet, oriental medicine, gymnastics, and in particular with aerobics, as well as with gathering and exchanging information related to health. At the same time, various forms of Eastern religions and cults emphasizing the perfecting of the human being, particularly through yoga, became extremely popular among these intellectuals. Soviet writers began to describe a new type of Soviet intellectual, who instead of becoming emotionally involved in social issues was responsive only to information that could help bring perfection, either physical or spiritual, to his or her life.

CONCLUSION

During the political reaction of the 1970s and early 1980s, most liberal intellectuals were relatively easily corrupted by the political leadership. Many intellectuals who had gained prominence as liberal activists in the 1960s participated during the political reaction in various campaigns denigrating their friends and colleagues. These turncoats often took refuge in Russophilism, which, until 1982, was mildly encouraged by the authorities.

Still, a tiny minority of liberals continued to resist the political elite and made significant progress in their confrontations with those in power by creating the intellectuals' first political organizations.

CHAPTER EIGHT

Russophile Ideology: A Trend That Rose to Dominance in the 1970s

BEGINNING in the mid-1960s, liberals—from neo-Leninists to open admirers of Western society—began to experience opposition from Russophiles, whose ideology was directed against all forms of Westernization.

EXCLUSIVENESS AGAINST UNIVERSALISM

In the tradition of the nineteenth-century Slavophiles, Russophiles challenged the two major premises of the Westernizers: the existence of universal laws of historical development, and the desirability of installing a democratic order. In combatting universalistic visions of the world (which many Russophiles referred to as "cosmopolitan" weltanschauung, given the derogatory connotation of this term in Russsia following the Stalin era), Russophiles joined the intellectual tradition that perceived the history of each people, nation, and civilization as developing according to its own specific laws.

Since the emergence of the German historical schools in the early nineteenth century (e.g., those of Roseker, Gildebrandt, Knies), which attacked the universalistic concepts advanced by the English classical economists (primarily Smith and Ricardo), debates between universalists and culturalists have raged in philosophical, sociological, economic, historical, and literary circles in almost all countries of the world. Today these debates arise most often as disputes between Westernizers (to which Marxists, in fact, belong) and nationalists of various sorts.

Soviet Russophiles, like their nineteenth-century predecessors, advanced the idea of the specific character of Russian history, based on its unique culture, traditions, and morals, and they rejected the conceptualization of Russia as only one particular case in the universal schema of world history. Although Russophiles disagree on the interpretation of some historical figures and events, they are united in attributing all post-eighteenth-century evils in Russian history to deviations from the "natural course" of Russian history.

The yearning to be different from or superior to others is a deeply rooted human feeling that plays an extremely important role at the individual, group, and societal levels. The idea of exclusiveness has been fundamental in Soviet ideology since the inception of the Soviet state. Images of the Soviet Union as the first socialist society, as the pioneer in the liberation of mankind from exploitation, and as paving the way to a radiant future for all of mankind were central to Soviet propaganda immediately following the Revolution.

With the decay of Marxist ideology, Stalin recognized the necessity of combining the concept of socialist exclusiveness with that of Russian exclusiveness. Because notions of national exclusiveness had been actively fostered by the prerevolutionary rulers of the country and by Orthodox religion, Stalin was rather successful in restoring these ideas. (About the coalescence of "socialist" and "Russian" exclusiveness, see Migranian 1989a.) After Stalin's death, the idea of Russian exclusiveness was downgraded, but it never completely vanished from official public ideology. With the defeat of the liberal movement in the 1970s, the belief in Russian exclusiveness began to spread from "below," receiving, of course, complete support from "above."

The most fully elaborated concept of Russian exclusiveness (as well as the exclusiveness of other peoples) was presented by Shafarevich in his samizdat publication of the late 1970s (Shafarevich 1989). Shafarevich resolutely rejected the notion of general patterns of historical development and lent his support to the nationalists of the past (for instance, the early nineteenth-century Germans), persistently denying that Russia had anything in common with the West, particularly in terms of political institutions. As he later wrote in a Soviet magazine, using milder terms than he had in samizdat, "I mean, the hope that our country will develop organically, on the basis of her thousand year history" (Shafarevich 1988, p. 126).

In their desire to reinforce the idea of Russian exceptionalism, some Russophiles challenged their friends' devotion to Orthodoxy and downgraded the role of Christianity and Byzantine culture, which carried Greek culture to the Kiev state. The denigration of religions other than Orthodoxy was based on the contention that the most important features of Russian culture were shaped prior to the adoption of Christianity in 988 (see, for instance, Seleznev 1986, pp. 91–92).

The Russophiles' insistence on the original character of Russian history was supported by some of the most ardent Westernizers, whom the Russophiles considered their abject enemies. The Westernizers rejected Russia's chances for democratization based on Russia's strong tradition of authoritarianism and the Russians' adverse attitudes toward individualism and freedom. With the increased freedom of expression accorded by glasnost, the liberals could point more directly toward Russian traditions, particularly the cults of power, state, and national security ("the complex of 1941"—the first very unhappy year of the war with Hitler's Germany), and the state's lack of respect for the individual as formidable and perhaps fatal obstacles to democratization (see Fadin 1988; Kliamkin 1987). Of course, the Russophiles rejected the views of the Westernizers with anger and loathing, accusing the Westernizers of Russophobia (Shafarevich 1989, pp. 3–20; about the debates regarding Russian exclusiveness, see Kheifets 1981; see also Marran 1982). Along with their insistence on the unique nature of Russia and her history, many Russophiles of the 1970s and, to a lesser extent, the 1980s also cherished the so-called Russian idea formulated by Berdiaev, which espoused Russia's moral and spiritual superiority over the world, particularly over the West, as well as Russia's mission to save the world from decadence (Berdiaev 1948).

Arguing against Russophiles in the period of glasnost, Igor Dedkov has stated: "The idea of their 'chosen-ness' emerged among almost the majority of the people. . . . Of course, this idea by itself may be encouraging. If the people are humiliated, it can arouse dignity and self-respect. But this idea can generate compassion and understanding only if it does not cross the border and become the basis for national arrogance, intolerance, or even worse" (*Iskusstvo Kino*, June 1988, p. 121).

Iuri N. Davydov was the most eloquent propagator of "the Russian idea" during Brezhnev's period. He assailed the West, its modernist philosophy, and its relativist morals and preached that, in contrast to the rest of the world, the Russian people were inclined toward sacrifices for the sake of others and were "the single bearer of the moral idea" in the world. Should the Russian people experience any feelings of "aloneness" in the moral desert, these would be "overcome with the courageous realization of their singleness" (Davydov 1982, pp. 263–271).

Davydov's sentiments were echoed by Iuri Seleznev, who presented the Russian people as the only people free of bourgeois mentality and as those who created "the literature of the nineteenth century, which solved most of the problems that Europe could not even define for itself" (Seleznev 1986, pp. 50, 65); by Fiodor Nesterov, who contended that there are no other people as patriotic as the Russians (Nesterov 1984); by Shafarevich, who asserted that the role of religion in Russia is greater than that in the West (Shafarevich 1978, p. 210); by Nikolai Fed', who saw the Russians as a people second to none in "giving the world so many great writers, musicians, scholars, artists, and thinkers" (Fed' 1989, p. 175); by Solzhenitsyn, who saw the suffering experienced by Russians under the yoke of a cruel atheistic state as the mark of the special fate of his country (Solzhenitsyn 1974; see also Krakhmal'nikova 1983); and by Anatoli Lanshchikov, who presented Russia as having saved Europe from Asia in the first five centuries of the past millennium, and Asia from Europe in the second five centuries (*Literaturnaia Rossia*, October 28, 1988, p. 5).

The idea of sacrifice as a manifestation of Russian moral superiority was central for many authors of this period (e.g., Nesterov, Kozhinov, and Bondarev) and was actively propagated in movies. This was the case with Vladimir Naumov's *Shore*, a film based on Bondarev's novel of the same title (1984), as well as with many other movies of the 1970s and early 1980s (see, for instance, Igor Talankin's *Fall of Stars*, 1982, or Pavel Kadochnikov's *I Will Never Forget You*, 1984).

A host of publications in the late 1970s and the first half of the 1980s described the West, and especially the United States, as bereft of moral values, altruism, compassion, and spiritual and cultural life (see Bondarev 1988a; Gerasimov 1985; Kondrashov 1985). In the late 1980s, however, glasnost's revelations about the moral degradation of Soviet society made it difficult to defend the thesis of the moral (or any other) superiority of the Russian people. When, in 1988, Arseni Gulyga, a former liberal philosopher of the 1960s, rejected the "trivial thesis about the backwardness of Russia in the nineteenth century" and contended that at that time Russia could "claim to be the cultural leader in Europe" and that Russian philosophy "surpassed German philosophy in various aspects" (Gulyga 1988, pp. 113–114), his statements were received as outlandish and humorless, as noted by a writer in the magazine *Voprosy Filosofii* (September 1988, p. 155).

By 1988 some Russophiles had shifted the focus of their polemics away from the idea of Russian superiority and toward the notion of the corruptive effect of the West on the morals of the Russian people. Russophiles even denied (as Palievski and Shafarevich did during the debates sponsored by *Iskusstvo Kino* [The Art of Movies]) that "the Russian idea" had ever been spread among them (*Iskusstvo Kino*, June 1988, pp. 122–123, 126–128). Renata Gal'tseva echoed Palievski and Shafarevich in her article on Berdiaev (*Literaturnaia Gazeta*, August 2, 1989).

The Rejection of Marxism and Respect for Monarchs

Russophiles bluntly reject the Marxist philosophy of history in favor of ones that emphasize the decisive role of culture, or even of the genetic makeup of a nation. With its focus on culture and ethnicity, it is not surprising that Russophile ideology was much more hostile toward Marxism than toward liberal ideology, given the former's economic determinism and its treatment of cultural, ethnic, and biological variables as of secondary importance in human history. In fact, liberal intellectuals have criticized the weaknesses of Marxist historical materialism much less intensively than have Russophiles.

Most Russophiles are consistent foes of the so-called class approach, which suggests that all significant social developments should be perceived through the prism of class conflict, and that it is impossible for intellectuals to be neutral in such conflicts. For the Russophiles, the class approach is incompatible with Russian patriotism. In the 1960s and 1970s the liberals also rejected the class approach, but with less vehemence than the Russophiles.

Russophiles insist that the patriotism and unity of the Russian people, who have always been encircled by external enemies, are their highest virtues. In challenging the class approach implanted in Soviet ideology over decades, Russophiles attempt to present the Russian tsars, their functionaries, and representatives of the Orthodox church, not as exploiters of the people (even if, especially in the 1970s, they reluctantly gave lip service to Marxist traditions in legal publications), but rather as patriots of the motherland. For example, according to Nesterov, tsarist dignitaries were preoccupied less with desires for wealth, medals, and positions than with the desire to serve Russia, "to give her all their strength, intellect, energy, blood, and life" (1984, pp. 70, 85).

With the advent of glasnost, Russophiles joined in Solzhenitsyn's glorification of Piotr Stolypin, the chairman of the tsarist government who, as a consistent defender of the Russian empire, combined his reform activities with the violent crushing of the first Russian Revolution (1905–1907). Both his name and his aggressive aphorisms aimed at the enemies of tsarism were hailed during a session of the Congress of People's Deputies and in some publications (Shipunov 1989, pp. 132–136; *Sovietskaia Kul'tura*, August 12, 1989). In 1987–1989, the Russophile "cult of Stolypin" was joined by several liberals, who emphasized Stolypin's promotion of private property and his opposition to "rural collectivism" (see Seliunin 1988c; Zyrianov 1989; see also the popular liberal television program "Vzgliad" [Outlook], September 1, 1989; and Poliakov 1989, p. 89).

Attacking the class approach meant that, with respect to Russian history, Russophiles were obliged to ignore or shrug off past social conflicts, an effort that resulted in turning official Soviet historical interpretation upside down in the 1960s and 1970s. Thus Russophile texts on the Kulikovo field battle, when Russians fought the Tartars headed by Mamai, conspicuously ignore or reduce to minor importance not only the class divisions of Russia in the Middle Ages (a fixture in official writings on this period), but even the conflicts among the Russian feudals. These omissions are meant to underscore Russia's unity against the foreign invader (see, for instance, Vladimir Vozovikov's *Kulikovo's Field*, 1982; see also Dmitri Balashov's *The Burden of Power*, 1983).

Also in rejection of the class approach, but this time in accord with official ideology, Russophiles present the foreign policy of the Russian state as always being fair and peaceful. They describe all wars conducted by the Russian government, without exception, as defensive or historically justified. Valentin Pikul' was prominent among those who sang the praises of Russian foreign policy of the past and looked for "internal enemies" undermining Russian might (Pikul' 1985a, 1985b; about Pikul's perceptions of Russian history, see Anisimov 1987).

In their radical revision of official Russian history, Russophiles are also nearly unanimous in their respect for the Russian monarchy as a political institution and as, in Vadim Borisov's words, "a religious concept" based on the "ancient spiritual culture" of the Russians.

Not only do Russophiles praise almost all the Russian monarchs, but they have created a cult of the last Russian tsar, Nikolas II, who, along with the rest of his family, was killed by the Bolsheviks in 1918. Portraying the last tsar as a martyr, Russophiles denounce his murder and try to blame this action on non-Russians, particularly on Jews. Under Brezhnev, Russophiles even managed to publish, in the Leningrad magazine *Aurora*, a poem devoted to this horrible action (see *Vol'noie Slovo*, no. 30, 1980, pp. 87–90).[1] In the period of glasnost, interest in the circumstances surrounding the killing of Nikolas II and his family increased. While liberals also spoke of this event with disgust, Russophiles demonstrated an even greater repugnance for this horrible murder. (Among the articles on this issue, see *MN*, January 28, 1990; *Nedelia*, June 25, 1989; *Ogoniok*, no. 21, 1989, pp. 4, 30–32; *Rodina*, no. 5, 1989, pp. 79–92.) At the same time, Russophiles totally ignored, as their critic Anatoli Makarov called it, "the economic backwardness of Russia, the monarchic yoke, the immorality of the caste order, the misery and degeneration of Russian villages, the perennial offenses against millions of non-Russians, the drunkeness in the terrible factory barracks, the illiteracy of millions of the Russian people, and the epidemics that destroy them" (Makarov 1985).

In 1988 Shafarevich fervently denounced Elem Klimov, the screen writer of the movie *Agony*, for his disrespectful portrayal of Russia in 1916, and especially for his "tactless portrayal" of the tsar's heir, who "was doomed to perish" within two years (Shafarevich 1988, p. 128).

Along with the class approach, Russophiles attacked with special vehemence the ideas of proletarian internationalism and world revolution, and they continued to do so into the 1980s. They argued that all such ideas, popular during the 1920s, were inimical to Russian national interests, were cosmopolitan in nature, and served Jewish interests. Leonid Borodin's 1973 samizdat article about the Russian "intelligentsia" was

---

[1] Liubomudrov, in his strong Russophile article about Soviet theater, denounced Meierkhold, a famous theater director of the 1920s, for, among other things, his disrespectful depiction of Boris Godunov, a Russian tsar, in the famous Pushkin play. He went so far as to say the intention of the director was to convey the concept of "the unfittedness of monarchic power" (Liubomudrov 1985, p. 174).

especially eloquent on this subject (Borodin 1985; see also Glazunov 1985; Kuniaev 1988b; Kuz'min 1985a, 1985b, 1987, 1988).

In the latter 1980s the Russophiles received some unexpected support from Gorbachev in their fight against the "class approach." The Soviet leader, in his determination to oblige the West, rejected this fundamental dogma of official ideology, praising, as already mentioned, "all-mankind values." In his attacks against his Marxist opponents, Kozhinov was able to cite not only Lenin's quotations but also those of Gorbachev's crusade against the class approach (Kozhinov 1987, p. 167).[2] At the same time, however, it was during glasnost that the hostility of the Russophiles toward the "class approach" significantly diminished. The logic of the struggle to defend Stalin, as well as the high praise of "all mankind values" by liberals, forced some Russophiles, even Apollon Kuz'min, to use the class approach in the polemics with their liberal opponents, trying to present them as the enemies of the Soviet system (Ivanov and Svininnikov 1988, pp. 175–176; *Nash Sovremennik*, no. 7, 1988, p. 192).

THE MORAL ISSUE: RUSSOPHILE CRITICS OF THE RUSSIAN PEOPLE

Since the early 1970s, many Russophiles have assumed that the major issue of present Soviet society is its moral degeneration. This degeneration is the leading theme in the novels of writers belonging to the "rural prose" school, such as Shukshin, Rasputin, Likhonosov, and Astafiev.

Rasputin's novel *Fire* (1985) is especially significant in this respect. In it, the author depicts the total demoralization of a Siberian village, which clearly represents the whole of Soviet society. Any form of solidarity between people, which had been so strong in the old Russian village even before the war, had completely vanished. Alcoholism, while not alien to villagers in the past, had reached unbelievably high levels. In fact, drunkards, with collusion from the authorities, had seized power in the village.

---

[2] A special kind of Russophile can be found among those Marxists who, while espousing Orthodox views on historical processes, suggest at the same time that the Russian revolutionary movement was original in its nature and free of any Western influence. For example, Militsia Nechkina, a well-known historian and member of the Academy of Sciences, asserted in the early 1980s, when Russophilism was reaching its peak, that "the Decembrist movement [the rebellion of Russian officers in 1825] grew on the soil of Russian reality." Denying the traditional analysis of this movement given in postrevolutionary Soviet historical textbooks, she added, "It was not infatuation with progressive Western European philosophy, foreign military campaigns, or the examples of Western European revolutions that begot the Decembrist movement, but the historical development of their own country, the objective tasks of the Russian historical process" (Nechkina 1982, pp. 5, 7). Only with the decline in official support for Russophilism after 1982 could Evgeni Plimak and Vladimir Khoros challenge this view, which was, as they pointed out, in stark contradiction to elementary facts (Plimak and Khoros, 1985).

Because of their intoxication and the violence it inspired, the village lost as many people as it had during the last war. Besides drunkenness, theft had also become an ordinary feature of life. People stole whatever they could from one another and especially from the state enterprises, and anyone who attempted to put an end to theft met with tragic consequences. The most terrible manifestation of demoralization seen by the hero of this novel, however, is the almost total disintegration of labor ethics. The people had lost all interest in their work and became absolutely indifferent to its social utility. As Rasputin presents it, society is deeply ill because people are not even aware of their illness, because the difference between good and evil has no importance for them anymore, and because most people are not much different than criminals.

In the period of glasnost, Astafiev (*The Sad Detective*, 1986b) and Belov (*All Ahead*, 1986) followed in Rasputin's footsteps with their novels. This time, however, it was the city rather than the countryside that was described as being in the grip of total demoralization. The disintegration of the family, the collapse of all moral values, and the burgeoning of cruelty, indifference, and rampant consumerism were presented as typical features in the life of city residents.

Although the Russophiles compete with the most critical liberals in describing life in Russia in bleak terms, there are some critical differences. For example, in their emphasis on moral issues, Russophiles differ radically from liberals, who only occasionally raise moral questions, and then mostly with relevance to the intelligentsia (as in Trifonov's novels).

While all Russophiles consider moral regeneration to be the major problem facing Russia and refuse to consider a movement toward Western life-styles as a remedy, Russophiles disagree strongly about both the causes of moral decay and the means to save Russia from its plight. This disagreement is perhaps best understood in terms of the composition of the Russophile movement.

Although the classification of Russophiles (as with liberals) is only approximate, it seems possible to separate the former into two primary categories, which I will refer to as "patriots" and "traditionalists."

RUSSOPHILE PATRIOTS: THE STATE AS THE MAJOR VALUE

Patriotism, or the worship and love of the state, forms the core of the philosophy of this first group of Russophiles. For Russophile patriots, the state is the great protector of the Russian people, and readiness to make sacrifices for the state is the highest value. The cult of the Russian state led the Russophile patriots to accept the October Revolution, Lenin, and Stalin as the creators of the Soviet empire—the natural heirs of the Russian monarchy. For this reason, the Russophile patriots are also referred to as the national Bolsheviks (see Agurski 1980; Ianov 1988).

The cult of the state and of patriotism has been incorporated into official Soviet ideology since the 1930s. Official ideology, however, links patriotism to socialism and in no way presents these values as being contradictory. Russophiles behave quite differently, and even in the legal press they directly promulgate patriotism as the highest value, absolutely independent from socialist ideals (for example, see Kuz'min 1985b, p. 186).[3]

The idea of Russian patriotism as a unique phenomenon was developed by Nesterov in a book that was awarded an official prize (Nesterov 1984). Nesterov contended that the Russians' "limitless love of the motherland" and loyalty to the state and to national leaders had no precedent in history, because "unlike any other, Russian patriotism stood out with its absolute and unconditional fealty to the state, asking nothing in reward" (pp. 66, 128). Since the Middle Ages, "Russia would demand from her sons not only personal courage, but absolute fulfillment of the military duty to vanquish or die on the field of battle." Russian patriotism, unlike any other, "made people ready to give to the state in cases of external threat as much wealth, labor, and blood as was necessary to repel it" (p. 117). This unmeasurable devotion to state and the motherland, dictated by the geographical location of Russia ("no country, at least in Western Europe, faced such a challenge to its national existence as Russia," p. 20), and by the necessity of defending the country from numerous strong enemies, is combined with a love of peace. Russians never "look for war," and "take arms only when no hopes exist for the peaceful settlement of a conflict" (pp. 68–69).

The worship of the Soviet state was also abundant in underground Russophile literature, particularly the samizdat magazine published by Osipov, an heroic figure of the Russophile movement who gradually converted from a liberal in the late 1950s to a harsh nationalist twenty years later. (About Osipov, see Kheifets 1981; Pomerants 1985a). On one hand, during the 1970s Osipov demonstrated his hostility toward the Soviet political order, and bitterly and uncompromisingly lashed out against the so-called modern patriots: individuals who speculated on Russian feelings while continuing to serve the authorities. At the same time, he rejected democracy as a political order and suggested only the "softening of dictatorship, observation of laws, and tolerance toward the differently minded." Osipov underscored his acceptance of the existing order as a

[3] Certainly, this idolization of the state is not exclusively a "Russian idea," as some authors suggest (see Ianov 1978 and 1988). The worship of the state has had long, strong traditions in major Western European countries—France, Germany, and even England—as well as in China, Latin America, Iran, and Japan. The United States, a young nation, is in this respect something of an exception, with its constitution working against a strong state.

reality, arguing that "whatever the political fate of Russia, national interests are of primary, supersocial, and eternal importance" (*VS*, nos. 17–18, 1975, pp. 13–18).

With their worship of the state, Russophile patriots assume that the solutions to all the problems that plague Russia should be looked for in the strengthening of Russian statehood. In addition, they argue that low morals in Russia, including consumerism and individualism, endanger the might of the state and of Russian national interests, both of which once again face terrible enemies.

The Russophile patriots are certain that the fulcrum of the state can only be ethnic Russians, yet ethnic Russians now have a lower standard of living than people living in the national republics. Their culture is often neglected and draws much less attention than those of other peoples, according to the Russophile patriots. Therefore, the strengthening of the state demands a radical increase in the role of Russians in the government, an increase in their material well-being, a reallocation of resources in favor of Russian regions, and drastic measures against liberal intellectuals and Jews (Seleznev 1986; Shafarevich 1989).

In line with their attitudes toward the Soviet political system, Russophile patriots of the 1970s held a rather positive view of Stalin. For them, he was the statesman who restored Russian patriotism and who deserved direct credit for creating a superpower with its capital in Moscow. For this reason, Russophiles were not, to the horror of 1960s liberals, afraid to praise the 1930s and 1940s as periods in which, in contrast to the 1920s, Russian culture flourished (see *Poiski*, no. 2, 1980, p. 66).

As Felix Chuiev said in his 1960s poem: "Let those who enter feel the dependence on motherland, on the Russian spirit. There in the middle— our generalissimo and his great marshals" (see Ianov 1988, p. 158; these lines were actively discussed twenty years later, see *Og.*, no. 52, 1988, p. 14; Ivanov and Svininnikov 1988).

RUSSOPHILE TRADITIONALISTS: SALVATION IN RELIGION

In the 1970s the Russophile traditionalists differed from the national Bolsheviks primarily in their total rejection of the October Revolution, Marxism, Lenin, and socialism. Hatred of all attributes of Soviet ideology and the state was, for instance, typical for the members of VSKhSON in Leningrad.

For the Russophile traditionalists, the main focus of Russian history has been the devotion of the Russian people to their religion, Orthodoxy. Given this worldview, traditionalists see the decline of religion as the main cause of their country's moral degeneration. In the 1970s the Russophile traditionalists were headed by Solzhenitsyn and included several leading writers of the "rural prose" movement (e.g., Rasputin, Astafiev, Shukshin, Abramov).

Of the two values—religion and the state—traditionalists clearly preferred the former in the 1970s. Solzhenitsyn's polemics against the official Orthodox church are very characteristic. He accused the patriarch of submission to the state, and set before him, by way of example, the independent behavior of church and state in other countries (Solzhenitsyn 1972).

For most Russophile traditionalists, Orthodoxy focuses not on the individual, but on *sobornost*, the unity of worshipers before God, and on the collective stance toward God and Russia. Traditionalists, with their collectivist orientations, strongly outnumber those with more liberal views who put forth the individual and Russian society as bearers of faith (see Levitin-Krasnov 1972). Unlike patriots, traditionalists are implacable foes of official ideology, which they hold to be a set of belligerently atheistic teachings. In addition, they oppose the Soviet state for its long history of religious persecution. Of course, traditionalists regard the October Revolution and dreams of world revolution as catastrophic in Russian history and as deeply inimical to the Russian soul (Blinov 1976, p. 247; Solzhenitsyn 1983b, p. 285).

Given the traditionalists' main goals, that is, the restoration of Orthodoxy's influence in the country and the liberation of the church from party tutelage, they shared a more fragmented political vision of Russia's future than did the patriots. Despite the diversity of their views, however, most traditionalists consider an authoritarian and theocratic political system to be the best way to restore the country's religious spirit, as well as to solve Russia's other problems. The negative attitudes of many traditionalists toward democracy are derived from their perceptions of the present-day West, the demoralization of which is attributed to pluralistic political systems (Solzhenitsyn 1978).

Differences between patriots and traditionalists, which were strong in the 1970s, had almost disappeared by the end of the 1980s. Rasputin's ideological evolution provides a typical example. His speeches and articles of 1988 were indistinguishable from those of such ardent and aggressive patriots as Alexander Prokhanov or Bondarev (Rasputin 1988a, 1988b, and 1988c).

THE SKETCHY SOCIAL AND POLITICAL PROGRAM IN THE 1970s

Despite serious differences in their attitudes toward the October Revolution, the Soviet state, and religion, as well as differences in the explanation of the crisis of Russian society, Russophiles in the 1970s shared a common vision of the desirable political future of their country. They rejected Western democratic institutions as riddled with organic flaws, as decaying, and as unsuitable to Russia and alien to her traditions.

Solzhenitsyn openly proclaimed that, at least in the near future, Russia needed not democratic institutions but authoritarian rule. In *From under the Rubble*, a collection of articles, Solzhenitsyn spoke with contempt about Western political freedoms, the multiparty system, and other political institutions. He clearly preferred the authoritarian order with which "Russia lived for one thousand years and which by the beginning of the twentieth century had preserved very much the health of the people" (Solzhenitsyn 1974, p. 26). Solzhenitsyn later expressed the same hostility toward Western democracy in his Harvard speech (1978).

Shafarevich proposed the Russophiles' most fully elaborated political concept, suggesting that democracy is not a political system that Russia needs to incorporate. He pointed to cases of democracy degenerating into totalitarianism, he drew attention to the fact that the road to democracy was very long and was often bloody, and he asserted that the number of opponents to democracy was growing in the West (Shafarevich 1989).

The program of the Russophiles in the 1970s, however, failed to answer one of the most essential questions of contemporary Russia: how to improve the efficiency of the economy, particularly that of agriculture, and how to raise the standard of living in the country. Of all the outstanding economic issues, Russophiles have dealt only with the allocation of resources between Russian and non-Russian regions, demanding change in favor of Russians, and with the cancelation of projects that could have deleterious effects on the natural environment in Russian regions.[4] Solzhenitsyn's economic program can essentially be reduced to the idea of mass exploitation of the Far East (Solzhenitsyn 1981b; pp. 134–167; Osipov also enthusiastically supports this idea, see *VS*, nos. 17–18, 1975, pp. 8–11).

RUSSOPHILES: CHANGING ATTITUDES TOWARD THE EMPIRE

Despite serious differences on many issues, Russophiles demonstrated a general consensus in their attitudes toward the Soviet empire and its future. Only a few of them (for instance, Solzhenitsyn; see Solzhenitsyn 1981) considered the national independence of the non-Slav people a desirable goal. Since the early 1960s program of VSKhSON, the majority

---

[4] Of the Russophiles, only the members of the All-Russian Social and Christian Alliance (VSKhON), headed by Ogurtsov, elaborated a comprehensive program of social and political change for the country. In the 1960s (when the program was developed), however, and even in the 1970s, this program was known to only a few Russians. It contemplated the creation of a theocratic state with Christianity as the only religion, and with large social functions.

of Russophiles who directly or indirectly expressed views on this issue have rejected the idea of dismantling the Soviet empire. Even such implacable a foe of the Soviet system as the "traditionalist" Shafarevich (1974, pp. 97–113) and such a moderate "patriot" as Osipov in the 1970s (1978; see also VS, nos. 17–18, 1975, pp. 19–33) wanted the empire to survive.

Like the majority of the liberals, the Russophiles continued their unqualified support of the Soviet empire in Gorbachev's period, although the members of the former group preferred to avoid the subject. Moreover, they also showed almost complete support, as mentioned before, for the official version of Russian history as shaped by Stalin in the 1940s. This version of history insisted on the specific character of the Russian empire, which almost all non-Russians joined voluntarily for protection against foreign enemies, and which, unlike other empires, treated minorities extremely benevolently (Kuniaev 1985, p. 176; Osipov 1978; Shafarevich 1974). Seleznev wrote, "There are no other countries like Russia which were joined really voluntarily by other states and nations. . . . Even those nations against which Russia fought were never considered by it as people of second rank" (Seleznev 1986, pp. 261–262).

Some authors, such as Nesterov, went even further and contended that even in prerevolutionary Russia the ethnic Russians suffered more than any other ethnic group from serfdom and bore the main thrust of the country's defense (Nesterov 1984, p. 112).

In 1986–1989, when liberals, encouraged by Gorbachev, attacked almost every episode of official Soviet history, Russophiles diligently tried to protect the old official version, ominously asserting that the denigration of Soviet history and the negative views regarding prerevolutionary Russia left the people without positive traditions and models (An. Ivanov 1987).

Beginning in mid-1989, the Russophiles' attitude toward the empire started to change. Driven by the feverish nationalism of non-Russians, the displays of open hostility toward Russia (which was blamed for the country's backwardness), the threat to Russians who were part of the minority in many regions, and the state's apparent inability to control the provinces, some Russophiles began to revise their previous positions regarding Russia as a multinational state.

Rasputin was the first to voice the new feeling emerging among the Russophiles. At a June 1989 meeting of the Congress of People's Deputies, he proposed abandoning the Russians' role as the benefactor of the people and letting the empire crumble, arguing that Russia could only gain by separating from ungrateful non-Russians, especially those in the Baltic republics (Pravda, June 7, 1988).

Interestingly, Rasputin was only repeating what Solzhenitsyn had said fifteen years earlier in "The Letter to the Soviet Leaders." Although Solzhenitsyn's view had garnered little support in 1974, many Russophiles, including those who had been bards of the empire, greeted Rasputin's restatement of it, albeit with some reservations (Prokhanov 1990; Solzhenitsyn 1975a).

Indeed, by early 1990, the empire's imminent disintegration was being taken for granted by several Russophiles, who not only elaborated various rationalizations for this process, but also took a leading role in creating pure Russian institutions—the Russian Communist party, the Russian Komsomol, the Russian Academy of Science, and Russian television, to name a few. It should be noted, however, that these actions were defensive rather than aggressive, and reflected the diminution of the idea of Russian messianism, not only for the entire world, but even for the territory once considered the Russian empire.

THE ENVY OF THE WEST

An important feature of the ideology of Russophiles, especially the patriots, is their envy of the West, its material comforts, its technological superiority, and the high prestige accorded its life-style. Russophile intellectuals often express open resentment toward the high standard of living enjoyed by their colleagues in the West, which to a great degree fuels their hatred of Western civilization. Such blatant envy is a relatively new social phenomenon and was almost unknown prior to the 1970s, when there was still a strong belief in the possibility of catching up with the West in the near future. Through their emphasis on Western society's various flaws and their denial of its positive features, many Russophiles reveal their total lack of objectivity in assessing the West (see, for instance, the spiteful speeches, articles, and novels of Bondarev, a prominent Russophile writer, for example, Bondarev 1983; see also Bondarev's article in *LG*, December 18, 1988, p. 4; Belov 1986; Seleznev 1986).

In the 1970s and early 1980s it was very easy to express this mixture of hatred and envy, since such feelings were actively fomented by official propaganda. Several former liberals of the 1960s and future perestroika activists published numerous books and articles brimming with venom toward the West (see, for instance, Korotich's book about America, *The Face of Hatred*, 1985; see also another hero of glasnost, the writer Drach [1984], and prominent journalists Gennadi Gerasimov [1985] and Kondrashov [1985]).

With Gorbachev's regime, however, came radical changes in official attitudes toward the West. The Russophiles' hatred lost its official support, and only the harshest among them (such as Bondarev) continued to express acrimony toward the West. Many intellectuals, and even some liberal Russophiles, began to move toward a more balanced and objective evaluation of the West. But envy and convictions regarding the impossibility of catching up to the West still remain fixtures in the mentality of most intellectuals, particularly Russophiles.

The Jewish Question

The most divisive issue for Russophiles, however, is not their attitude toward the West, but their attitude toward Jews. In part, the Jewish question in the Soviet Union reflects the universal law that ethnic minorities be used as scapegoats and targets of hatred in order to unite the ethnic majority. An additional facet of the Jewish issue, however, derives from the active participation of Jews in the October Revolution, the civil war, and the building of the Soviet state and its ideology, on one hand, and from their role in the liberal movement of the 1960s, on the other hand.

In the 1960s the intellectual community was generally quite well-disposed toward Jews, largely because the Jews were the primary target of Stalin's wrath toward the end of the dictator's life. Evtushenko, a sensitive barometer of the intelligentsia's mood, reflected this stance in his famous poem "Babi Yar," a passionate and bold lamentation in defense of Jews and against their persecutors. Even Kochetov's Stalinist magazine *Oktiabr'* (October), a butt of disdain for most of the intelligentsia, was almost never accused of anti-Semitic slurs. Shevtsov's book *Plant Louse* (1969) and Vasili Mishin's *Social Progress* (1970) aroused resentment due to their anti-intellectual tenor as well as their anti-Jewish insinuations. The anti-Semitic activities of some scholars, particularly mathematicians such as Anatoli Mal'tsev, Ivan Vinogradov, or Lev Pontriagin, were in no way as ostentatious as they later became.

The situation changed in the late 1960s and the 1970s, and the Soviet intellectual community began to split on attitudes toward Jews. With the Stalin era receding into the past and with relative freedom to express their genuine feelings, many intellectuals began to voice greater hostility toward Jews in general, and toward Russian Jews as an entity damaging to Russia's national interests. The Jewish emigration of the 1970s also contributed to the intellectuals' anti-Semitism in this period.

The furor surrounding Alexander Askol'dov's movie *Commissar* (1967) was indicative of feelings toward Jews at that time. The movie compassionately portrayed a Jewish family in Berdichev (a small city that symbolized Jewish settlement and was a code word for anti-Semites) as the bearers of humanistic values during the cruelty of the civil war. Not only was the movie prohibited, but the tapes were ordered destroyed. As Askol'dov recounted twenty years later in an interview in New York, the professional public (mostly filmmakers) who gathered to evaluate the movie and determine its fate not only failed to support the author against the apparatchiks but "scoffed at me, cat-called, shouted, almost spat at me—the same people who are today the activists of perestroika" (*Novoye Russskoye Slovo*, June 17, 1988).

The growing animosity toward Jews was strongly correlated with mounting Russophilism. In general, Russophiles, with their ethnic perception of the world, adopted hostile attitudes toward Jews.[5] Still, although almost all foes of the Jews came from the ranks of the Russophiles, not every Russophile harbored identical attitudes toward this minority. In the 1970s the strongest anti-Semites were found among patriots, including those with direct connections to the Soviet establishment.

Using the word "Zionist" (or "Mason," in the second half of the 1980s) as a synonym for Jew, Russophiles like Kuniaev, Palievski, Chalmaiev, Lobanov, Mark Liubomudrov, Seleznev, and Kozhinov seized every opportunity to assail the Jews and to accuse them of being committed enemies of the Russian people, Russian statehood, and Russian culture. Three major accusations were leveled against Jews by various types of Russophiles in the 1970s and 1980s. The first of these blamed the Jews for the October Revolution and the civil war, the second held the Jews responsible for the destruction of Russian culture and the mass terror of the 1920s and the 1930s, and the third blamed the Jews for the Westernization of Soviet society in the post-Stalin period.[6] In all of these cases, the Russophiles asserted that Jews were moved by their hatred of Russia in the same way that Jews have been hostile toward other Christian peoples among whom they have lived (for instance, the Germans in the nineteenth century). Russophiles painstakingly collected any statement critical of Russia made by a Jew, omitted innumerable declarations of love for Russia made by Jews in the last century, and distorted the views of Jewish authors such as Grossman whose devotion to Russia was unquestionable (see Shafarevich 1989; see also Kazintsev 1988).

Solzhenitsyn and Shafarevich were dominant in developing concepts

[5] The first clear manifestation of the Russophile movement's hostility toward Jews was probably that revealed by the Leningrad All-Russian Social and Christian Alliance, which emerged in the first half of the 1960s. The Alliance completely closed its doors to Jews, and its extremely harsh and merciless critical analysis of the Soviet system (which one quarter century later still appears very profound and well substantiated), while otherwise appearing to detail every flaw of Soviet society, failed to mention anti-Semitism. This provides a striking parallel to Khrushchev's and Gorbachev's accusations against Stalin, which also ignored Stalin's policy toward Jews. (See Osipov 1978, pp. 87–111; *VS*, no. 22, 1976; see also Borodin 1985; Ianov 1988, pp. 132–134.)

[6] Along with these major crimes against Russia, Jews were accused of several others, including cooperation with Hitler during the war and the propagation of racism. As Seleznev said, "After the defeat of Nazism, its functions almost totally were assigned to modern Zionism" (Seleznev 1986, p. 46).

regarding the pernicious role of the Jews in Russian history in the 1970s. Solzhenitsyn emphasized the role played by Jews in the October Revolution and the civil war, while Shafarevich focused on the role played by Jews in the destruction of Russian culture and the mass terror of the 1920s and 1930s. Solzhenitsyn describes Jews as comprising the core of the main revolutionary parties prior to 1917. For instance, his depiction of the activities of socialist-revolutionaries in *The Wheel* mentions almost only Jewish names. Even more remarkable is Solzhenitsyn's contraposition of the two main characters in this book: premier-minister Stolypin and his killer Dmitri Bogrov. Stolypin is portrayed as a statesman who could have saved Russia, putting her on the way to rational transformation and staving off revolution. By contrast, Bogrov, a Kiev Jew, is portrayed as the person who deprived Russia of the greatest politician in centuries and who almost single-handedly bore the responsibility for the subsequent chain of events. Bogrov is depicted as killing Stolypin not because he saw Stolypin as a class enemy, but because Stolypin was a symbol of Russian hostility toward Jewry (Solzhenitsyn 1983a, pp. 117, 120, 123, 125, 126, 135, 136, 147, 151).

In *Lenin in Zurich*, Solzhenitsyn developed the thesis that the real father of the revolution was not Lenin, a mediocre figure, but rather the energetic Parvus, a Jew obsessed with hatred for Russia and the idea of crushing it (Solzhenitsyn 1976). Some authors deny Solzhenitsyn's anti-Semitism (see *Referendum*, no. 34, 1990).

Shafarevich followed Solzhenitsyn, concentrating primarily on the civil war and the Stalin era. He suggested that the political police (Cheka and later the GPU) consisted primarily of Jews who were responsible for the execution of the last monarch and his family as well as for the organization of the gulag (Shafarevich 1989, pp. 82–88). Apparently unconcerned with inconsistency (e.g., Jews as the preachers of the proletarian dictatorship and as the advocates of democracy), Shafarevich passionately blamed Jews (both Russian and non-Russian) for their desire to impose Western institutions on Russia, seeing the actions of the Jews as a plot against the Russian people (Shafarevich 1989, pp. 14–34). With equal (and apparently genuine) vehemence, he expressed outrage that Jews were too outspoken about their personal concerns, specifically citing emigration, which, despite its minor importance for Russia and its despicable nature ("the defection from motherland"), draws the attention of world public opinion (Shafarevich 1989, pp. 54–56).[7]

[7] The position of Osipov, one of the most respected figures in the underground Russophile movement of the 1970s, is of special interest. Being more restrained than many other Russophiles, he ostensibly proclaimed himself an enemy of cosmopolitans and almost directly endorsed Stalin's anticosmopolitan campaign, whose anti-Semitic content is admitted by practically everyone.

Finally, in the second half of the 1980s, Russophiles openly declared that they held Jews (various code names were used—from Zionists to Masons) responsible for the miserable state of Russian society. Jews were held accountable for demoralization in general, for the erosion of Russian culture and the family, and for the ecological crisis. Russophiles persistently asserted that the high level of drunkenness in Russia was the result of the intentional activity of Jews and Western agents (Uglov 1987, p. 156; see also the reports about the conference at Leningrad University in November, *SK*, November 24, 1987; *NS*, no. 9, 1988, pp. 152, 169; Bondarev 1988a; Ovrutski 1988b).

During this period, Russophiles developed and propagated ideas regarding the subversive activities of Jews and Masons, accusing them, in Rasputin's words, of "the destruction of monuments, . . . the curtailment of the history of fatherland, the erosion of tradition and culture, the destruction of nature, Baikal, the rerouting of the rivers, the ruinous economic projects, the gloomy state of affairs in higher education (trained everybody but a citizen and specialist), the destruction of 'nonperspective' villages, and showoff and deception at all levels of society, since kindergarten" (Rasputin 1988a, p. 170). Jews were also accused of organizing the February (1917) Revolution, which destroyed the Russian monarchy (see Kuz'min's articles in *NS*, no. 3, 1988, and no. 7, 1988, p. 192); destroying old Moscow (*NS*, no. 2, 1988, pp. 180–185; no. 5, p. 175); creating a vanguard in the arts for the purpose of destroying Russian culture (*NS*, no. 2, 1988, p. 183); attempting to sacrifice Russia to the world revolution; leading the implementation of terror and the creation of concentration camps in the country (*NS*, no. 8, 1989, p. 168); creating Stalin's cult (albeit only partially; Kuniaev 1988b, pp. 185–189; Kozhinov 1988; and Shafarevich 1989); and encouraging the aggressive policies of the United States (*NS*, no. 7, 1988, p. 188).[8]

The theme of Masons as eternal foes of Russia, already prominent in the 1970s (see Iakovlev 1974), continued to attract Russophiles in the second half of the 1980s. Igor Karpets, for instance, described Russian history as an unremitting struggle between "Russian statehood," which embodies all that is sacred and pure, and world evil, with Satan repre-

[8] The list of crimes committed by Jews against Russia goes on to include the surreptitious dissemination of Zionist and Masonic symbols (this accusation was leveled against the director of the Sverdlovsk opera; see *NS*, no. 12, 1987, pp. 187–188; no. 5, 1988, pp. 180–184); the orchestrated persecution of some authors and the pitting of the public against them ("Zionists and Masons" were held accountable for the failure of Nikolai Burliaev's movie *Lermontov*; see *NS*, no. 6, 1987, pp. 183–184); the deaths of some of the foremost Russian intellectuals in recent times (e.g., Vampilov, Shukshin, and others) and even in the remote past (e.g., Lermontov); the denigration of such Russian geniuses as Pushkin (*NS*, no. 9, 1987, pp. 185–187); and the emergence of Lysenko's case (Kozhinov 1988, p. 175).

sented primarily by Masons, foreigners, and non-Russians inside the country (Karpets 1987; about this book see Proskurin's article, "In the Struggle with Satan," in *VF*, September 1988, pp. 148–150). Pikul', in his turn, spoke in 1989 of Masons as people "whose main goal is to conquer the world," and who "took the majority of their symbols and rituals from Judaism" (Pikul' and Zhuravlev 1989, p. 191).

For many Russophiles, particularly "patriots," hatred of the Jews has become the most important element of their credo, a sort of shibboleth that allows them to recognize one another. This hatred is, for them, a most significant social phenomenon in which they are deeply involved at an emotional level, and which could probably push them to do things against their personal interests. During the 1970s Jews, their activities, and their innumerable abject flaws were by all accounts the main topic of private communication among these Russophiles, who also tried to raise the Jewish issue at all public gatherings, either directly or indirectly. There were no public occasions that were not used by these people for the manifestation of their attitudes toward Jews, even if the ostensible subject of the occasion had no connection to them. Whatever the subject of an article or book, all of its negative personages had to be Jewish. If Russophiles discussed the problems of the theater, they would concentrate all of their rancor against Meierkhold (whom they wrongly regard as a Jew), Anatoli Efros, or Alexander Gel'man (Liubomudrov 1985).

When involved in debates on poetry, these Russophiles derided not only poets of earlier periods such as Bagritski, Mikhail Svetlov, and Alexander Bezymenski, but also contemporary poets such as David Samoilov and Iuri Levitanski. Their hatred also extended to Jewish poets who, as soldiers and officers, perished in the war against Germany (Kuniaev 1985, p. 198; about the attacks against Jewish poets who perished during the war, see Lazarev 1988). If their attention was addressed to prose, Il'f or other Jewish authors were declared guilty of damaging the Russian culture or language. When Russophiles discussed the attacks of the 1920s against the Russian classics, they named Averbakh and a few other Jews as the sole perpetrators of these actions. And in discussing the fate of Russian intellectuals after the revolution, the Russophiles of course named Grigori Zinoviev as the one man responsible for expelling the cream of the Russian intelligentsia from the country (Kuz'min 1985b, p. 186).

MILD VERSUS HARSH RUSSOPHILES

Russophiles, whether patriots or (especially) traditionalists, disagree strongly about the degree and character of the exclusiveness they attribute to Russia, the contraposition of Russians to other peoples, their degree of respect for other cultures, and their attitudes toward democratic institutions.

While recognizing Russia's uniqueness, culture, and religion, mild or liberal Russophiles tend to respect other peoples, particularly "the West" and even those Jews especially devoted to Russian culture, such as Mandel'shtam and Pasternak. Likhachev clearly took issue with the xenophobia and anti-Semitism so typical of many Russophiles, and referring to Dostoevsky, the main authority for the Russophiles, he wrote, "the Russian for Dostoevsky—the individual of high intellect, of high spiritual aspirations who accepts all European cultures, and all European history and is not at all contradictory and not so enigmatic." He added that "the deliberate love of one's own people is incompatible with the hatred of other people" (Likhachev 1987, pp. 458, 466; 1988, p. 6). In his biography, unlike those of many others, Likhachev recalls with respect and gratitude a number of his teachers and colleagues of Jewish origin (Likhachev 1985).

Averintsev, an intellectual deeply absorbed in the spirit of Russian culture ("the thousand-year anniversary of the event [the introduction of Christianity in Russia] that is so important . . . for Russian culture—moreover, for all Russian life—is *my* celebration"), wrote in 1988 when Russian chauvinism was on the rise: "Each true Russian, if only he does not violate his nature, has a mortal fear of overpraising what he has, and is doing well because it does not embellish himself" (Averintsev 1988, p. 212; see also *Iunost'*, no. 12, 1987, p. 5). A number of intellectuals with obvious Russophile sympathies (e.g., Shubkin 1979) shared the views of these two authors.

This "enlightened" Russophilism is especially strong among those for whom religion plays a key role in their worldview. Krakhmal'nikova's devotion to Russia, Russian culture, and Orthodoxy is in no way combined with hostility toward any other people, including Jews. Zoia Krakhmal'nikova had no harsh words for the West, or even for those who emigrated (Krakhmal'nikova 1983, pp. 32, 86, 87). After his release from Soviet prison, Anatoli Shcharanski recounted his close spiritual relationship in the camp with his cell mate, Vladimir Poresh, a Russian Orthodox activist (*The New York Times*, February 19, 1986, p. 4). It was likewise impossible in the 1970s to find contemptuous statements about the West in the publications of the most prominent representatives of the rural prose school. Even with their general antiurbanistic attitudes, these authors did not usually blame the West for Russian problems.

The division between the mild and harsh Russophiles was relatively strong in the early 1970s, but lost its primary significance by the early 1980s (see Ianov 1988, pp. 189–190). Given the strong polarization of the intellectual community in the period of glasnost, the unity of the majority of the Russophiles served to push the few liberal Russophiles (such as Likhachev) toward the Westernizers' camp and made them the target of insidious attacks on the part of mainstream Russophiles.

CONCLUSION

Russophilism, the dominant ideology of Russian intellectuals in the 1970s and early 1980s, was very aggressive toward the West and the Jews, contending that Russia has its own specific history, culture, and traditions that are deeply alien to Western democratic institutions. Russophiles almost unanimously see authoritative government as the best solution to Russia's problems. At the same time, Russophiles were divided into several different groups in the 1970s. Patriots tried to blend the ideas of Russian exclusiveness and socialism, while traditionalists rejected official ideology and emphasized religion instead.

CHAPTER NINE

Intellectuals Live in the Chosen Land: Gorbachev's Glasnost

As ALREADY NOTED, the Soviet intellectual community emerged from the Brezhnev era demoralized and weakened, showing no evidence of resistance against the dominant political elite, and carefully avoiding confrontations with the authorities. During the post-Brezhnev period, consumerism peaked among intellectuals, and almost all of them became involved in the aimless pursuit of material comfort—a comfort based primarily on foreign goods. Trips to the West became the most coveted of privileges, and intellectuals appeared willing to perform all manner of acts of loyalty to secure the ability to travel.

As Gorbachev began to unveil and implement his reforms, the overwhelming majority of intellectuals were deeply pessimistic and skeptical that any serious changes could occur. For most intellectuals, Brezhnev's system seemed forever indomitable. Discussing the liberalization of Soviet society in 1986–1988, Batkin wrote, "In three years, events happened in the political life of our country which, in 1985, any individual with common sense would have treated as lying outside possibility" (Batkin 1988, p. 172).

During the 1970s, the country skidded toward an economic, social, and intellectual crisis. The Soviet economy had experienced steady declines and was plagued by technological retardation. The gaps between Soviet and Western industry and science widened considerably from the 1960s to the 1980s. The USSR's continued inability to feed its own population left it dependent on food from abroad. (About the state of Soviet society by the early 1980s, see Bialer 1986; Brzezinski 1988; Byrnes 1983; see also Shlapentokh 1988).

Of particular interest for this book, however, is the intellectual crisis in Soviet society. The political elite, with its apparatus of coercion and its monopolistic control over all spheres of life, was capable of controlling the intellectuals and of bringing many of them to their knees. This task was accomplished with relatively little bloodshed, that is, with a minimal number of intellectuals incarcerated or exiled. The political elite failed, however, to counter the deleterious impact that oppression and corrupting of intellectual life have on the entire society, including the economy. The brilliant success of the party apparatus and the KGB in gradually eliminating dissent from the Soviet political scene was accompanied by drastic mediocritization within Soviet society, particularly in the areas of the sciences and culture. Brezhnev's policy toward intellectuals resulted in the loss of three or four generations of able scholars, writers, and film and theater directors. By the mid-1980s, the number of young people in various intellectual groups had become minuscule.

With glasnost, the sharp decline in intellectual performance in the 1970s was discussed in depth, rather cautiously at first, but on a full scale by 1987–1988. In his report to the Twenty-seventh Party Congress, Gorbachev all but openly acknowledged the ineffectiveness of Soviet science during the Brezhnev era (Gorbachev 1986). Alexandrov, president of the Academy of Sciences, candidly complained to the congress that Soviet managers did not trust Soviet scholars, and that all new equipment and technology was being ordered from abroad. Labeling this trend "the import plague," he argued that the practice of buying production technology from abroad "leads in many cases to stagnation in certain branches of science and technology" (*Pravda*, February 27, 1986, p. 5).

At the Nineteenth Party Conference in 1988, Guri Marchuk, the new president of the Academy of Sciences, continued to lament "the drastic decrease of the role of science in social life" and "the growing gap" between Soviet and Western science. He was seconded by Anatoli Logunov, president of Moscow University, who warned that if Soviet scientists failed to reorganize their science "we simply would stop understanding what is going on in Western science" (*P.*, July 1, 1988). Similar sentiments regarding the slowdown of Soviet science were expressed by many prominent scholars in 1987–1989 (see Frank-Kamenetski 1988a, b; Sagdeiev 1988a; Khanin 1989; see the debates on this subject in *Literaturnaia Gazeta*, June 22, 1988).

The intellectual decline was as obvious in culture and the humanities as in the natural sciences. The December 1985 Congress of Russian Writers was dominated by discussions of this decline. Of thirty-one speakers representing Russian regions at this congress, twenty-three (or 75 percent) described the quality of contemporary literature in very uncomplimentary terms, complaining of mediocrity in literature, theater, and other cultural spheres (see *LG*, December 18, 1985). Following 1985, the number and intensity of complaints regarding the mediocritization of Soviet cultural life increased monthly.

The Soviet leadership tried to neutralize this intellectual decline through imitation of Western science. The persecution and corruption of Soviet scholars in the 1970s was accompanied by a tremendous growth in the Soviet government's efforts, both legal and illegal, to collect information on Western scientific and technological developments. In all ministries, networks were created whose single task was to collect Western information. Despite these efforts, however, the resulting influx of information from the West proved insufficient to halt the retardation of technological progress and the stagnation of the economy.

The intellectual degradation of Soviet society was clearly manifested in the evolution of the Academy of Sciences during the Khrushchev and Brezhnev eras. As late as 1964, the Academy, the highest Soviet scientific institution, was a bastion of autonomy that challenged and rejected some of Khrushchev's and (until the early 1970s) Brezhnev's candidates for positions in the Academy (see the nostalgic recollection of this period in Sagdeiev's article in *Moskovskie Novosti*, January 3, 1988). During the last decade of Brezhnev's rule, however, the authorities managed to fill many open slots with obedient but untalented scholars. Under the influence of those appointed during this period, the Academy of Sciences entered the Gorbachev period as a conservative body that was inclined to support policies contradicting the new political course.

The story of Mikhail Rutkevich, the hangman of Soviet sociology in the 1970s, was typical. He was officially endorsed in December 1987 as a candidate for the position of full member of the Academy. His candidacy failed in the plenary meeting of the Academy only because of the liberals' frenetic activities toward that end (see the article of leading sociologists in *Sovietskaia Kul'tura*, December 12, 1987). Even in the face of this furious activity, however, one third of Soviet academicians voted for Rutkevich, who was a clear symbol of Stalinism.

Even more telling is another event that took place in the Academy in 1989. According to the Soviet election law adopted in 1988, the Academy of Sciences obtained the right to elect twenty-five deputies to the Congress of People's Deputies. The Presidium of the Academy was empowered to nominate candidates to be selected at the plenary meeting of academicians. Dozens of research institutes proposed the candidacies of the most authoritative scholars, such as Sakharov, Sagdeiev, Zaslavskaia, and others. Despite the angry response of the academic community, the Presidium rejected all such candidates, preferring instead to advance mediocre administrators (see *MN*, February 12, 1989; February 19, 1989).

The Academy's connection to the old regime was recently manifested in reports documenting the involvement of its various research institutes in projects now criticized as badly conceived and carried out and as serving the egotistical interests of bureaucratic bodies. As an example, these reports often cite the Academy's involvement in the rerouting of Siberian rivers to the south (see *Novyi Mir*, no. 7, 1987, and *Nash Sovremennik*, no. 1, 1987). In the 1970s, the Academy was transformed into a massive bureaucratic machine, unable to sustain a high level of research or to prevent Soviet science from slipping ever backward. (About the state of the

Academy, see, for instance, the academician Gol'danski's article in *SK*, May 28, 1988.)

Along with the Academy of Sciences, other organizations of intellectuals (e.g., unions of the creative intelligentsia) became citadels of corruption, and therefore of conservatism. Examples include the Academy of Pedagogical Science, the Academy of Medical Science, the Unions of Writers, Artists, Composers, and Actors, and several other official associations. The corruption and conservatism of these organizations has seriously hindered the entrance of talented young people into the unions. (Oleg Dmitriev spoke about the monopolistic activity of the Union of Soviet writers in *LG*, January 20, 1988; see also *P.*, March 26, 1988; about the attempt of the Union of Artists and the Union of Composers to preserve their monopoly and not allow young people to join, see *P.*, after January 22, 1988; *MN*, November 29, 1987.)

THE IDEOLOGICAL CONFLICT IN THE KREMLIN

The political establishment was deeply divided at the time of Brezhnev's death. The conservative faction wanted to continue the old policies, with hopes of maintaining the status quo for one or two more decades and of preserving both the existing political order and the country's superpower status in the national arena. They were opposed by the reformers, who were certain that immediate radical changes were necessary to save the country. In the reformers' views, Ronald Reagan's policy of rearmament, and especially his Star Wars project, based on the coordinated efforts of the major Western countries, threatened the Soviet Union's status as a major world power. Moreover, the reformers refused to consider the country's internal political stability as a given, and, in fact, predicted ensuing turmoil, should concrete changes fail to occur. They agreed that the corrupt bureaucracy was responsible for society's stagnation, that the party apparatus required serious cleaning and more effective control, and that significant resources should be directed toward accelerating technological progress so that America's military superiority might be diminished.

Still, these common beliefs notwithstanding, the reformers were divided into two major groups—neo-Stalinists and liberals. The former saw administrative measures and radical improvements in discipline (for bureaucrats and the masses alike) as the cure for the country's ills. The latter held liberalization and partial democratization to be the most efficient means by which to avert the USSR's transformation into a Third World country. These two ideologies each ascribed a different role to the intellectuals. (About the ideological struggle inside the political establishment in the 1980s, see Shlapentokh 1988.)

THE INTELLECTUAL SOURCES OF THE GORBACHEV PROGRAM

Gorbachev's program drew heavily on the liberal ideology of previous decades, most notably regarding the role of public opinion, the critical role of the mass media, and the concept of a decentralized economy. As a result, references to direct links between "glasnost and the 1960s" became a fixture in the Soviet mass media in 1987 and 1988 (see, for instance, *Znanie i Sila*, June 1988, pp. 18–25). In accordance with Shmuel Eisenstadt's concept of intellectuals as creators of blueprints for new civilizations (1987), it can be said that the role of Soviet intellectuals as authors of the transformation of Soviet society was immense.

At the same time, however, several of the most important and most specific ideas of Gorbachev's program—for example, privatization of the Soviet economy and pluralism in political activity—were almost never mentioned in samizdat during the 1960s and 1970s and probably were not discussed at private meetings as having practical relevance for the country. It can be assumed that both of these ideas—privatization and political pluralism—came to the Kremlin directly from the West, without intellectuals as intermediaries.

In their critique of Brezhnev's stagnation, neo-Stalinists also sought to enhance the intellectuals' role in society. From his first days in office, General Secretary Andropov underscored his rejection of the anti-intellectual policies of his predecessors and emphasized his plans to actively employ the nation's intellectual resources (see Andropov 1983). At the same time, however, the neo-Stalinists had no intention of relaxing their political control over the intellectuals or of offering the intellectuals any new initiatives in society.

By contrast, Gorbachev, with his aggressive liberal policy, has far surpassed Khrushchev in assigning to intellectuals an important role in his reforms. The intellectuals' standing in Gorbachev's program has been radically different from that in earlier programs. It seems Gorbachev has forgotten the legacy of contradictory relations between the intellectuals and the political elite and sees only the intellectuals' positive side.

The intellectuals have played myriad roles for Gorbachev. For example, they were the group best able to delegitimize Brezhnev's regime in general and the Stalinist model of society in particular, which Gorbachev intended to demolish at least partially in order to legitimize his regime and his sweeping reforms, which directly contradicted all of the tenets of Soviet ideology. Also of crucial importance was their support for and elaboration of reforms throughout all spheres of Soviet life. Gorbachev was convinced that without input and support from the intellectuals, the rejuvenation of society was impossible. In addition, he was convinced that they and the mass intelligentsia would be his most faithful allies, since these groups would most appreciate the dramatic reactivization of the political and cultural life that would be engendered by his liberalization efforts.

On a number of occasions, Gorbachev explicitly mentioned the leading role of the intellectuals in his programs. His meeting with the participants of the Issyk' Kul' Forum (*LG*, November 5, 1986), his December 1987 press conference in Washington (*P.*, December 3, 1987), and his speech to the Nineteenth Party Conference (*P.*, June 29, 1988) are but a few examples. He began to reveal his special admiration of intellectuals almost as soon as he came to power. He very quickly initiated contacts with prominent intellectuals of both camps—liberals and Russophiles—such as Evtushenko, Rasputin, and others.

In 1986, having strengthened his political position, Gorbachev was able to release Sakharov from exile and make several other conciliatory gestures toward the intellectuals. The full extent of his pro-intellectual feelings was not revealed, however, until 1987–1988, when he permitted the legalization of dissident scholars and allowed several emigrant figures to visit the USSR and even return permanently to their homeland.

The First Years of Glasnost: Intellectuals Look On with Mistrust

With the collapse of the first thaw still fresh in their minds, and with their renewed belief in the omnipotence and resilience of the Soviet political system, the intellectuals eyed Gorbachev's regime with mistrust. They doubted the stability of the new liberalization and were convinced that it would soon be replaced with the well-tested course of repressions and corruption. To make matters even less believable, the intellectuals received mixed messages from the Kremlin during the regime's first year.

For example, in August and September 1985, while appealing for the reactivization of intellectual and political activity, Gorbachev also lavishly praised the Stakhanov movement, a symbol of Stalin's duplicity in the minds of the Soviet people. Similarly, in 1986 Gorbachev endorsed the Stalinist law against "nonlabor income," a law directed against private initiative in the economy. Only after the January 1987 meeting of the Central Committee, when democratization was proclaimed as the core of perestroika, did the intellectual community and the mass intelligentsia begin to believe that the country had truly entered a new phase in its history.

The involvement of liberal intellectuals in the political process initiated by Gorbachev began with a number of articles and speeches made by renowned liberals. The fact that these people, and not others, were called to praise and substantiate a new policy was a clear signal regarding the character of changes to come. Evtushenko's speech at the Congress of Russian Writers in December 1985 was probably one of the first strong declarations of the liberal credo in an official public speech since the early 1960s. The poet vigorously defended real glasnost, that is, honest examination of Soviet history and current social issues (see Bondarev et al. 1987a, pp. 106–110). At almost the same time, Voznesenski, also a symbol of liberalism, published poems demanding truth and honesty in life (*P.*, September 9, 1985, and January 14, 1986). These poets were followed by several liberal authors who championed the restoration of truth and free discussions as necessary conditions for real social change (see the articles of Ganina, V. Sokolov, and Shubkin, in *LG*, August 14, 1985, January 15, 1986, and January 22, 1986; see also Zaslavskaia in *SK*, January 22, 1986; and Gel'man 1986).

Writers and scholars were energetically joined by theater figures, who were quite active in the first months of Gorbachev's regime. The play *Speak* (based on Valentin Ovechkin's book, *District Routine*), staged by Valeri Fokin, a new director, in Stanislavski's theater in Moscow, aroused enormous excitement among the Moscow public. The play depicted the actions of Stalin's regime as predestined to doom, because the rank and file were once again deprived of the freedom to "speak" (*SK*, January 23, 1989). Shatrov's play, *Dictatorship of Conscience*, staged in the Lenin Komsomol Theater, and Alexander Misharin's *Silver Wedding* were also permeated with democratic ideas. (About these plays, see *SK*, March 15, 1986; *LG*, February 12, 1986.)

Theater and movie personalities also participated in discussions of reforms in the theater and movie industries. The participants in these discussions, including such leading intellectuals as Zakharov, Tovstonogov, and Chukhrai, demanded autonomy for the theater and movie industries, limited independence from apparatchiks, and the decisive role of audiences rather than officials in evaluating theatrical performances and movies (*LG*, December 25, 1985; *P.*, February 14 and 21, 1986).

The real intellectual offensive in support of Gorbachev began in 1987. Then, as in the 1960s, writers took the lead, fiercely attacking the Stalin era. Rybakov's novel *Children of Arbat*, Anatoli Pristavkin's *The Cloudlet Spent the Night*, and Dudintsev's *People in White Robes* were major political events in 1987, strongly polarizing Soviet society.

Several outstanding scholars, such as economists Nikolai Shmelev, Gavriil Popov, and Grigori Khanin, philosopher Kariakin, and historians Afanasiev and Eidel'man, also joined the ranks of perestroika activists, despite the high probability of being blacklisted by neo-Stalinists hopeful of revenge.

In addition, a group of journalists, such as Anatoli Strelianyi, Vasili Seliunin, and a few others, began to compete successfully with scholars and writers as heralds of perestroika. In 1987 some of these journalists were even more consistent and merciless in their debunking of the Soviet system and its ideology than were scholars and writers.

In the late 1950s and the 1960s, the intellectuals constituted a serious political force able to exert pressure on the leadership, either pushing it toward liberal reforms or hindering the process of re-Stalinization. In 1987–1988, however, the major force behind liberalization was not the intellectuals, but rather the supreme leader himself—an unprecedented phenomenon in Soviet (but not Russian) history.

The intellectual community and the political leadership enjoyed unparalleled unity in 1986–1988. There was a real *entente cordiale*, which was absent even during the war with Hitler, when intellectuals, while totally supporting Stalin as the leader of a country fighting for survival, continued to be terrorized by him. Similar situations exist in recent British and French history. When the socialists came to power in London in 1964 and in Paris in 1981, intellectuals abandoned, albeit temporarily, their critique of their respective socialist governments, although they remained somewhat uncomfortable with the political elites' attempts at courting them (Ross 1987, pp. 43–44; Reader 1987, pp. 136–140).

CONFLICTS AMONG THE INTELLECTUALS: EXACERBATED BY GLASNOST

Gorbachev's regime very quickly created unprecedented opportunities for the Soviet people to reveal their true ideas and feelings, thereby arousing a level of political activity unknown in the past. The new situation made it possible for intellectuals to choose between various ideological trends in a much freer manner than had been possible in the 1970s. Ultimately, glasnost led not to the unity of the intellectuals, but to an even greater division in the intellectual community than had occurred in the 1970s.

It soon became evident that the new regime sided with the liberal intellectuals and Westernizers. Even with the Khrushchev era firmly behind them, it was a novel experience for liberal intellectuals accustomed to constant harassment and persecution to feel themselves actually protected by the leader in the Kremlin. Without an understanding of the unusual position occupied by the liberals during the first years of Gorbachev's regime, it is impossible to comprehend many of the developments within the intellectual community during this period.

The opponents of the liberals, having been bewildered for a time after Mikhail Suslov's death in January 1982 and especially after Brezhnev's demise in November 1982, quickly came to their senses, however, realizing not only that glasnost permitted them the opportunity to manifest their own ideas, but also that Gorbachev (who, with his influential wife, occasionally revealed his sympathy for Russophile ideas) had strong rivals in the Politburo who looked upon Russophile intellectuals as their allies.

Russophiles clearly enjoyed the support of some members of the Politburo (especially Ligachev, who conspicuously supported the writer Bondarev and the painter Glazunov, two aggressive Russophiles; see Bondarev's speech at the Nineteenth Party Conference, *P.*, June 2, 1988) as well as some popular support in their intensive ideological campaigns of 1987 and 1988. Thus by early 1986 the intellectual community was divided more sharply than ever into two major ideological camps—liberals and Russian nationalists—not to mention those who, with their skepticism and nihilism, tried to avoid participating in the ideological debates that ran rampant in 1986–1989.

Both Gorbachev and the Soviet mass media reluctantly recognized the schism in the intellectual community, using various terms to designate the warring factions (the liberal Anastasiev, for example, suggested that the two groups be referred to as "patriots" and "internationalists," *LG*, February 8, 1989). Passions ran so high as a result of this name calling that Gorbachev was finally obliged to publicly call on both groups to calm down (*P.*, January 10, 1989). The polemics between *Ogoniok*, *Znamia*, and *Moskovskie Novosti* on one side and *Nash Sovremennik*, *Molodaia Gvardia*, and *Moskva* on the other became major political and cultural events. Each group tried to discredit the works of the other as these works became the symbols of each group's worldviews. The liberals tried to discredit Belov's *All Ahead*, while the Russophiles spared no effort in denigrating Rybakov's *Children of Arbat* and Granin's *Aurochs*.

Despite occasional bickering for power and prestige among like-minded people, the war between the liberals and the Russophiles remained the major feature of Soviet intellectual life in the latter 1980s. This war was exacerbated during the election campaign in spring 1989. (According to the new election law, writers and scholars had the right to send their own deputies directly to the parliament.) The mutual animosity among the writers was so great that, during the election of candidates in the Writers' Union, only five writers from a list of eighteen received the required majority of votes.

BICKERING ABOUT THE PAST

With great acrimony, both camps began stirring up the past and discrediting their opponents. Liberals, for example, rebuked conservatives for their persecution of Pasternak in 1958–1960 and of Tvardovski in 1969–1970.

Pasternak's case, which had been mentioned in 1986–1987 only indirectly and without "naming names," generated great publicity in 1988.

Liberals recounted the meeting of Soviet writers where Pasternak was condemned and excluded from the Writers' Union and gave names of all those who had taken the floor to castigate the great poet (including Soloukhin and Surkov). Evtushenko and Voznesenski were especially active in resurrecting the events surrounding Pasternak during those tragic years (*MN*, June 5, 1988).

The case of Tvardovski, another liberal martyr, also became a focus of public confrontation during 1988. Most of the accusations were related to the notorious letter against the one-time editor in chief of *Novyi Mir* in *Ogoniok* (no. 30, 1969), which was signed by eleven writers, including Mikhail Alekseiev, Proskurin, Shundik, Anatoli Ivanov, and other activists of the conservative camp in the latter 1980s. (About this letter and the related polemics in the Soviet press, see the articles of various authors: Iuri Burtin in *Oktiabr'*, no. 6, 1987; Natalia Il'ina, in *Ogoniok*, no. 2, 1988; Mikhail Lobanov, in *NS*, no. 4, 1988; and Valentin Oskotski, in *Knizhnoie Obozrenie*, January 29, 1986.) Russophiles, in their turn, detailed the ways in which numerous liberals obediently served the regimes of Stalin and Brezhnev.

Apollon Kuz'min gibed Afanasiev about his past as the head of a division in the Komsomol Institution in the 1970s (*NS*, no. 3, 1988, p. 154). Kozhinov and Chalmaiev attacked the late Trifonov, recounting how this leading liberal writer of the 1960s and 1970s authored *Students* (1950; awarded the Stalin Prize in 1951), which hailed the anticosmopolitan campaign, and *The Old Man*, which denounced it (Kozhinov 1987; Lobanov 1988, p. 156). Kazintsev reminded the admirers of *Children of Arbat* that its author, Rybakov, was a sympathetic author during Stalin's times and received the Stalin Prize (*NS*, no. 11, 1988, p. 165), and Tatiana Ivanova, one the most sarcastic glasnost-era antagonists of the Russophiles, was reminded by an author from *Literaturnaia Rossia*, a tempestuous weekly which regularly blasts Westernizers, that, in the past, she had been a spirited contributor to this weekly, as well as to the like-minded *Nash Sovremennik* (*LR*, January 12, 1990).

Even more eloquent, however, was the Russophiles' 1987–1988 offensive against the revolutionary intelligentsia of the 1920s and early 1930s—a group praised by the liberals of glasnost as victims of Stalin's purges. The Russophiles recounted how the revolutionary intelligentsia (referred to by Kuniaev as "the children of Arbat" after Rybakov's novel), in their praise of world revolution, Cheka, and Stalin, remained indifferent to the genocide of Russian peasants and watched with malice the deaths of the Russian tsar and the Russian nobility, as well as tolerated the persecution of Russian intellectuals who had left close to the people (Kuniaev 1988a, pp. 26–27; 1988b).

The Ideology of the Liberals in the 1980s

In the first three years of Gorbachev's reign, when Russophile ideology remained essentially unchanged, the ideas espoused by liberal intellectuals evolved very significantly from liberal socialism to democratic market socialism. Many concepts considered irrelevant by the intellectuals of the 1960s were being defended as practical and necessary goals.

The Picture of Present Soviet Society

The liberals, prompted by Gorbachev, were quick to convey to the Soviet public their gloomy perceptions of Soviet society in the early 1980s. With opportunities for criticism gradually expanding from 1985 to 1987, liberals left practically no stone unturned. They were joined in their scathing and merciless analysis of their country and its people by some Russophiles, such as Astafiev and Rasputin, who were bent on painting the country's portrait in the blackest of colors even if the causes cited by the two groups were vastly different.

The liberals began their critique with the economy, which was described as lying in a shambles, and then proceeded to take to task the bureaucracy, which was to become the main target of their social criticism. Corruption, incompetence, privileges, and indifference to the interests of society and ordinary people were held up as the main features of Soviet apparatchiks—features that were described and subsequently denounced in detail by liberals (see, for instance, Seliunin 1988b and 1988c; Shubkin 1987, 1989).

Several authors contended that Stalin and Brezhnev, the two personalities the intellectuals despised most, were leaders advanced and supported by bureaucracies born of two coups, or counterrevolutions—one in the late 1920s and another in the mid-1960s (Butenko 1987; Migranian 1988, p. 107). They described with equal acerbity and sarcasm the moral decay of all strata of the Soviet population. Examples of this decay included such phenomena as low labor ethics, omnipresent fear, universal lying, double, triple, and even quadruple thinking, mass pilfering, alcoholism, drug addiction, prostitution, mutual indifference, and cruelty.

In 1987, and increasingly more so in 1988, the liberals increased their criticism of the Soviet political system and revealed their long-suppressed contempt for the party apparatus, censorship, the obsession with secrecy, fake elections, meaningless political rituals like "voluntary social work" or meetings "approving official policy," puppet institutions such as local governments, the Supreme Soviet, venal and unscrupulous police, and the courts. In 1988 and 1989 liberals were even permitted to malign such sacred cows of the Soviet political order as the armed forces and even (albeit to a lesser degree) the KGB.

Of course, the liberals portrayed the sorry state of culture and science in the country with special rancor and tartness, describing how, in the 1970s, mediocre and often entirely ungifted people seized leading positions in all of the institutions controlling creative activity. With this desolate and woeful picture of present-day Russia as a backdrop, the liberals began in 1985 to work intensively toward unfolding and developing their own ideology. They directly linked their ideology to views that were dominant among intellectuals in the 1960s and were convinced that they would not only be able to present almost all of their ideas, both old and new, but that this time their program would come at least to partial fruition.

Let Us Speak about Socialism

Among the debates of the 1960s that were renewed in the 1980s was the one regarding the nature of Soviet society. As was the case in the 1960s, the liberals of the 1980s were divided into four groups:

The first group, whose position was most closely linked to official ideology, was composed primarily of neo-Leninists (not a particularly large group in the age of perestroika). Members of this group insisted that, despite all of the tragic distortions, the Soviet people of the 1930s built an essentially socialist society that should now rid itself of all alien influences and move ahead toward a democratic stage in its development (Bovin, 1988; Dedkov and Latsis 1988; Kurashvili 1988; Zaslavskaia 1989).

The second group, who were the most consistent advocates of the spirit of perestroika (as believers in socialist ideals they could accurately call themselves social-democrats, and Mensheviks were certainly their predecessors), contended that the society that emerged under Lenin and Stalin's guidance was completely removed from true socialism: it was a "totalitarian" society, "barracks socialism," "feudal socialism," "state socialism," "bureaucratic socialism," "state bureaucratic socialism," a society based "on the Asian mode of production," and so on. The members of this group continued, however, to defend democratic socialism as the highest ideal for Russia as well as for other countries, and they proposed the creation of a true socialist society modeled after those envisioned in the early 1900s by European Marxists such as Eduard Bernstein and Karl Kautski (see Alexeiev 1989). They also spoke of the distortion of socialism in the USSR and the "Thermidorian" degeneration of the revolution (Afanasiev 1988a; Butenko 1988a; Karpinski 1987; Lisichkin 1989; Kisilev and Kliamkin 1989).

During this period, the social-democrats and, to some degree, the neo-Leninists popularized a theory regarding possible alternatives to historical development. They suggested that Russian history could have taken other courses following the October Revolution and Lenin's death. Shatrov, through his historical plays about the events of 1917–1924, especially *Further, further, further . . .*, was the most eloquent propagandist of this theme. His plays described the liberal (Bukharinian) and bureaucratic (Stalinist) alternatives following the October Revolution (see Shatrov 1988, and the interview with him in *Og.*, no. 45, 1988, p. 16; see also Afanasiev 1987a, 1987b, 1988a, b; Burtin 1988; Butenko 1988a; Kisilev 1988).

Members of the third group went even further than the modern social-democrats and rejected Marxist socialism completely, proposing an elaborate new concept of humanitarian socialism with the individual in the center. Alexander Zipko, a rather undistinguished philosopher, was the initial proponent of this new concept. In a series of articles in *Nauka i Zhizn'* (Science and Life), he discussed "the main truth" of the direct connection between the Stalinist system and "the Marxist project of society," which was based on unrealistic assumptions such as "a noncommodity and nonmoney economy, social property, the exaggeration of the role of theory in social development, the neglecting of democratic principles, and so on" (Zipko 1988a, 1988b, 1989; see also his article in *Nedelia*, March 19, 1989).

Zipko was joined, albeit somewhat reservedly, by Igor Kliamkin, who openly declared that socialism, as conceived by Marxists, no matter what their differences (e.g., he brilliantly showed that the ardent socialist rivals—Trotsky and Kautsky—were both wrong), could not guarantee an efficient and human society (Kliamkin 1989). In 1989 and 1990, intellectuals belonging to this group increased their use and elaboration of a non-Marxist and, of course, non-Leninist socialism, upon which they bestowed a series of adjectives, such as "democratic," "humanistic," "kind," "ethical," and "individualistic," and others (see the debates on socialism in *Pravda*, January 21, 1990).

The fourth group, composed of Western-oriented liberals who rejected socialism in general as a desirable goal for mankind, regarded the existing Soviet society as having been built according to Marxist design. They rejected even the traditional social democratic and new humanitarian concepts of socialism, contending instead, as Aitmatov stated in his speech at the Congress of Peoples' Deputies in June 1989, that "socialism," as a system able to bring comfort and a free life to the people, existed only in Northern Europe, the Netherlands, and, of course, Switzerland (*Iz.*, June 3, 1989). Moreover, another liberal went so far as to proclaim that real socialism, which prizes the welfare of the population over social production and planning, had also been built in the United States over the last three decades (Liubimov 1989).

The tendency to discard socialism as a concept was encouraged by Gorbachev's "new thinking," with its emphasis on "all-mankind values" and through the use of such notions as "the present human civilization" as the goal for Soviet society (*P.*, July 14, 1989). In 1989 and 1990, the number of liberals who rejected socialism and who praised liberal capitalism as the only "natural society" increased enormously. Similar increases occurred in the number of those who rejected Marxism not only as an obsolete teaching but as essentially incorrect and fallacious. Zipko joined this group in 1990 (*SK*, May 26, 1990).

The conflicts between the Soviet followers of Milton Friedman and Ronald Reagan on the one hand, and supporters of the social democratic model on the other hand, were exacerbated during the winter 1989 election campaign, when Larisa Mitiasheva (who had attained fame for the article she published under the pseudonym "Popkova," *NM*, no. 5, 1987) and Tatiana Koriagina vehemently denounced those who espoused the benefits of a mixed economy and a strong welfare state, most of whom were members of the semioppositional "Inter-Regional Group" in the Congress of People's Deputies.

In articles and on television, liberals actively derogated all Marxist ideas, including those about exploitation and alienation under capitalism, the superiority of public over private property, equality as the goal for social development, and so on (for example, see Burtin 1989; Shatalin 1989; Gennadi Popov's article, "About the Usefulness of Inequality," *LG*, October 4, 1989; the November 8, 1989, *Literaturnaia Gazeta* article, "Is Marxism Obsolete?" in which Georgi Smirnov, director of the Institute of Marxism-Leninism, desperately tried to defend the core of Marxist-Leninist teachings against the aggressive questions of a Moscow intellectual; Oleg Bogomolov's participation in the debates televised on October 25, 1989; and Stanislav Shatalin's statements about socialism on the television program "Vzgliad" (Outlook), February 15, 1990). It is remarkable that some Russophiles, such as Astafiev and Kuniaev, publicly expressed their hostility toward the idea of socialism per se much more openly than did the most consistent Westernizers.

THE REVISION OF HISTORY

In the 1960s liberals took the first timid steps toward the revision of official Soviet history. Novels and stories, both legal and illegal, about Stalin's concentration camps were the liberals' major contribution to this process. Inspired by Gorbachev, liberals delivered a near fatal blow to the 1986–1989 Soviet textbooks on history. The frontal attack against the official version of history was launched by Afanasiev, previously unrecognized as a historian (Afanasiev 1987b, 1988a, 1988b, and 1988c).

In 1989, with advances in liberalization and democratization, many previously taboo subjects came under scrutiny and intellectuals found themselves increasingly free to discuss Soviet foreign policy for all periods of Soviet history.

The October Revolution and Lenin: From Private to Public Rejection

Because in 1985–1988 most liberals avoided public critique of socialism and Marxism, they also skirted direct negative assessments of the October Revolution and Lenin, although many of them had, in the 1960s, privately condemned the event, Lenin, and the Revolution in general. From 1985 to 1988 these private critiques became more acerbic and more frequent. Referring to such private discussions, Boris Kurashvili declared that "statements that socialism as a social system did not pay itself off are not very rare, as well as the suggestion that February [the February Revolution] was necessary but October not" (Kurashvili 1988). Similarly, Pavel Volobuiev, a liberal party historian, wrote that "incorrect views on the Revolution had spread in the country, especially among the youth" (*Kommunist*, no. 16, 1988, p. 91).

Many prominent liberals, especially those close to the party apparatus, continued to idealize the Lenin era and ascribe to it democratic features and political pluralism—features that, despite the lack of overt repressions, clearly did not exist (Burlatski 1987, 1988c, 1988d; Medvedev 1989a; Migranian 1988, p. 100).

In 1988, however, liberals finally began to insert indirect critical comments regarding the October Revolution into their publications. For example, although Gefter declared that "there was no choice in 1917," his statement implied that the October Revolution was a forced, not necessarily a preferred, solution to the problems in Russia. He went on to say that "what happened then was an alternative to a much greater blood shuffle, to a meaningless collapse" (Gefter 1988, p. 310).

Similarly, Boris Vasiliev was the first author in an authorized periodical to denounce the dismantling of the Constitutional Assembly by the Bolsheviks in 1918 (Vasiliev 1989); Seliunin depicted the horror of the "Red terror" (Seliunin 1988c, pp. 164–167); and Zipko condemned the Revolution (specifically the October Revolution) for triggering a tragedy of mass violence (Zipko 1988b, pp. 43–44). The publication of Platonov's novels, particularly *Chevengur* (1978) and *Pit* (1987), and Vladimir Korolenko's letters to Anatoli Lunacharski about the atrocities of the Bolsheviks during the civil war dealt serious blows to the two once-inviolable icons of Soviet ideology—the October Revolution and Lenin. (The letters had been written during the war by the famous Russian liberal; *NM*, October 1988.)

Although from 1985 to 1988 liberals continued to confine their true opinions of Lenin to their private conversations (see Shatrov's interview in *Og.*, no. 45, 1988, p. 14), the number of those who believed that Stalin was truly Lenin's heir and that Lenin bore original responsibility for the cruel society created by the October Revolution clearly increased.

In 1988–1989 a few liberals began to oppose the official image of Lenin. The bravest of these liberals began the demythologization process by portraying Lenin as a leader who made mistakes. These lapses in judgment included misunderstanding the role of the state after the Revolution (Batkin 1988, p. 176) and overestimating the revolutionary potential of the working class in 1920 (*MN*, November 15, 1987). They especially criticized his devotion to the ideas of war communism and his underestimation of the market's role in the years immediately following the Revolution (Gefter 1988, p. 311; Kliamkin 1989; Seliunin 1988c; Zipko 1988b). Other authors have identified Lenin as the author of the administrative and nondemocratic model of Soviet society, despite the fact that he did not abuse his power (G. Popov 1988b). Criticism of Lenin significantly increased in late 1989 (apparently after some subtle prompting from the Kremlin). Major emphasis was placed on several developments that had occurred under Lenin's rule and with his blessing, including the suppression of two revolts (the Kronschtadt sailor's uprising in 1921 and the rebellion of peasants in Tambov in 1920–1921), mass repressions, the beginnings of privileges for the party bureaucracy, and others (Kondratiev 1990).

Still, the greatest blow to the cult of Lenin was delivered in June 1989, when *Oktiabr'* published Grossman's novel, *Forever Flowing* (written thirty years earlier), with its devastating picture of Lenin as a product of one thousand years of Russian serfdom and as an apostle of a new, Communist slavery. *Oktiabr'* then published Burtin's "The Achilles Heel of Marxism" (November 1989), which attacked both Soviet icons—Marx and Lenin—in the most caustic manner.

It is remarkable that it was the Russophiles who first dared to demonstrate publicly their rejection of the October Revolution and its progeny. Kuniaev, for example, used his poems conspicuously to denounce the Revolution and the tsar's execution (Kuniaev 1988a). Following the example set by Solzhenitsyn's "Lenin in Zurich," Soloukhin denounced Lenin with extraordinary hatred in his article, "Reading Lenin." Regularly citing Lenin's works, Soloukhin described the founder of the Soviet state as the creator of a new despotism far more terrible than tsarism—one that had used its monopolistic control over bread and hunger as its main means of coercion. Soloukhin even accused Lenin of the genocide of the Russian people (Soloukhin 1989). A number of intellectuals, primarily those from the older generations, continued to profess their allegiance to the October Revolution and its ideals (see, for example, the article by Alexandrov [1987], the famous mathematician and active social figure, calling for more regular referral to the works of revolutionary era authors).

The Appraisals of the Stalin Era

Despite disagreement regarding the possibility that another course of events could have followed 1917, as well as dissension about the attitudes of Stalin's contemporaries and his regime, liberals unanimously portrayed the Stalin era as horrifying and barbarous. They fiercely dismissed the views of their political opponents who suggested that, despite its flaws, it was a heroic era in Soviet history (see Kazutin's article against Mialo in *MN*, June 5, 1988).

As mentioned earlier, liberals began unmasking and debunking collectivization in the 1960s. With the advent of glasnost, liberals and Russophiles alike radically increased the intensity of their attacks, particularly in 1988 (see Mozhaiev's novel *Muzhiks and Old Women*, 1988; Burlatski 1987; Chernichenko 1988; Tikhonov 1987). Still, even in 1988, most liberals dared not publicly condemn collectivization per se, confining their denunciations instead to Stalin's version and presenting themselves as advocates of Lenin's cooperative plan, which supposedly lured peasants to collectives only on a voluntary basis. This was especially true for those liberals who linked the cooperatives with Russian prerevolutionary rural communes (see, for instance, Antonov 1987b, 1988; see also Burlatski 1987). By 1989, however, all liberals condemned collectivization, referring to it as a crime, as genocide, and as the installation of serfdom (see, for example, Popov and Shmelev 1989).

Liberals unanimously condemned not only Stalin's version of collectivization, but his industrialization as well. They even characterized the postcollectivization Soviet order in the countryside as "feudalistic" or as a return to serfdom (Medvedev 1988).

In response to those who defended industrialization as a necessary condition for winning the war against Hitler, the intellectuals pointed out that Russia's economy would have developed rapidly even without Stalin, and that the majority of the factories built before 1941 were in territories occupied by the Germans within the first two months of the war (Aitmatov 1988b). And, of course, the intellectuals detailed the hardships and suffering experienced by the Soviet people who worked on accelerated and often ill-designed industrial projects such as the Moscow subway (see Antonov's novel *Vas'ka*, 1987).

As soon as conditions permitted, the liberals seized every opportunity to debunk any and all myths about Stalin (e.g., "Stalin as commander," "Stalin as an economist," "Stalin as philosopher," "Stalin as linguist," etc.) to uncover his crimes, and to rehabilitate his victims (see Dzokaieva's article in *P.*, May 6, 1988; see also Gorbanevski 1988; Kondratiev 1987a, 1987b; Volkogonov 1987, 1988; Volkov 1988). In 1987–1988 portrayals of the gulag horrors that rivaled even those described by Solzhenitsyn were published. Zhigulin's documentary novel *Black Stones*, about his tribulations in the camps, is no less eloquent than *The Gulag Archipelago* (Zhigulin 1988). Prompted by Gorbachev, liberals moved from characterizing Stalin as a despot and a tyrant to labeling him a criminal and a vampire, equating him with Hitler, and referring to him as a madman and a paranoiac (see Moroz 1988; Ambartsumov 1988b; Kapustin 1989). Finally, Stalin was reduced to being called "insignificant and colorless" (Batkin 1989b, p. 50), and "a comedian" (Antonov-Ovseienko 1989, p. 110).

Liberals advanced various theories to explain the Stalin phenomenon. These theories overlapped somewhat, contrasting with the "pure" personalistic explanation developed, for example, by Rybakov in *Children of Arbat* (1987) and by Medvedev in *Stalin and Stalinism* (1989a). Theories advanced by the liberals included:

The Miscalculation Theory. The Lenin guard may have underestimated Stalin and his perfidy. If the Politburo had followed Lenin's wishes regarding Stalin (the dying leader had proposed transferring him from the position of General Secretary to a less influential post), history would have taken a radically different course (Butenko 1989; Dzarasov 1988; Latsis 1989).

The Peasants Theory. Stalin was able to build up his system because of the support he received from uneducated peasants and unskilled workers (Butenko 1988a, p. 126; Furman 1988, p. 25; Kliamkin 1987, pp. 173–184; Vodolazov 1989, pp. 25–28).

The Social-Democrat Theory. The nondemocratic character of the October Revolution, war communism (especially under Lenin, who had no time to correct his mistakes), and blind "revolutionary romanticism," with its desire to build "a pure communist society tomorrow," combined to permit Stalin to act as he did (Gefter 1988, p. 311).

The Bureaucratic, Thermidorian Counterrevolution. The apparatchiks managed to confiscate the power of the proletariat and create a "military-feudal" society under their own rule (Afanasiev 1988a; Alexeiev 1988; Butenko 1988a).

The Cultural Theory. The Russian tradition, with its cult of the tsar-leader and its xenophobia, coupled with the low educational level of the population and the antibourgeois character of the Russian intelligentsia and its yearning for a missionary role in the world, enabled Stalin to turn the newly transformed socialist society into a despotic state (Frolov 1988; Zlobin et al. 1988, pp. 34–35; see also Kisilev and Kliamkin 1989, pp. 76–77).

The Great National State Theory. Regardless of the various descriptions given Stalin's rule ("barracks socialism," "feudal socialism," etc.), he was merely answering the nation's demands for order and a strong state (Grossman 1980; Kapustin 1988, pp. 189–190).

It is noteworthy that none of these theories challenges socialism as a great goal for Russia—they merely suggest why the goal was not attained following the October Revolution.

The most resolute critic of theories that suggested the possibility of alternatives to Stalin was Zipko, who, as mentioned earlier, defying recently shaped dogma, declared Stalin a representative of Marxism as it was interpreted at the time (about "possible alternatives to Stalin"—one of the most popular phrases in the political lexicon of the Gorbachev era—see Kisilev and Kliamkin 1989; and Popov and Shmelev 1989). Zipko suggested that Stalin's "ideas about socialism were typical for Marxists of that time," and that his understanding of the ultimate goals of the socialist transformation of the economy diverged from neither that of other party leaders such as Lev Trotsky, Zinoviev, or Lev Kamenev or even from that of his mortal enemy, the opportunist and revisionist Karl Kautsky (Zipko 1988a, p. 50). Even such a liberal as Lev Karpinski could not accept the core of Zipko's article—that Stalinism stemmed "from Marxism" (*MN*, April 16, 1989).

Ideas similar to those of Zipko were espoused by Igor Kliamkin who, in 1987, contended that, under the existing historical conditions, both Stalin and his policy in the city and the countryside were unavoidable in one form or another. Those who shared this view often pointed to the lack of democratic traditions in Russian history as a decisive factor predetermining Stalinism (see Gal'tseva 1988; Gordon and Klopov 1989; Kliamkin 1987, 1989). Certainly, these views rang true for those liberals who considered the October Revolution to be a national disaster that led inexorably to further unfortunate developments and who rejected ideas that Stalin or his equivalent could have been avoided (Ovrutski 1988a).

The Controversial Rehabilitation of Stalin's Victims

In the 1960s, even consistent liberals, with the legacy of Lenin and the Bolsheviks in mind, having little accurate knowledge of the past, and prompted by their hatred of Stalin, maintained that almost all prominent people killed by Stalin had been honest and decent (the only exceptions being Iagoda and Ezhov, both of whom were consecutive chiefs of the political police).

Similar positive feelings toward Stalin's victims continued through the early years of glasnost, when the official rehabilitation of each new name was received with great jubilation. Moreover, intellectuals were active in creating new myths regarding Stalin's opponents (primarily Bukharin, but also Kirov), presenting them as leaders who could have created socialism with a human face (see, for instance, Burlatski, who presented Bukharin and Kirov, as well as Rykov and Rudzutak, as "advocates of democratization"; Burlatski 1988a, p. 425).

Liberals had other heroes as well, such as Fiodor Raskol'nikov, a prominent revolutionary and diplomat, who, after defecting, published his "Open Letter to Stalin" abroad (Raskol'nikov 1939/1988). Others whom the liberals held in high regard included Martemian Riutin and Alexander Kuznetsov. Riutin, a prominent party official, wrote a bold manifesto in 1932, which, like Raskol'nikov's "Letter," contained accusations against Stalin very similar to those leveled in 1986–1988. Kuznetsov, a secretary of the Leningrad party committee, is said to have plotted against Stalin in the aftermath of the war (Raskol'nikov 1939/1988; Razgon 1988; Vaksberg 1988a; *Komsomolskaia Pravda*, January 15, 1988, and April 25, 1988).

Around 1988, however, intellectuals began to develop more sophisticated and multifaceted views of Stalin's victims. For example, Sergei Kirov, who was presented by Rybakov in *Children of Arbat* in 1987 as a Lancelot-like character, was, in less than a year, being presented by Anatoli Butenko in a much more critical light. Butenko was aware that Kirov had belonged to Stalin's inner circle and was also responsible for the tragic developments since the late 1920s (Butenko 1988b).

Others of Stalin's victims, such as Sergo Ordzhonikidze and Mikhail Kol'tsov, also came under much more balanced scrutiny as writers became less willing to overlook their role in Stalin's political machine (*LG*, June 15, 1988). A few critical, albeit very reserved, reflections on Nikolai Bukharin (for instance, as an ideologue of war communism) also appeared in *Moskovskie Novosti* and in other periodicals (*MN*, January 3, 1988).

The Soviet generals, also victims of Stalin, came under fire for acting as judges in fake trials on the eve of their arrests (e.g., Vasili Blukher) and for slandering dozens of their colleagues during interrogations (e.g., Vitali Primakov; see Viktorov's article, "The Conspiracy in the Red Army," in *P.*, April 29, 1988). Liberal authors also reminded their readers that, in the early 1920s, Mikhail Tukhachevski resorted to "unjustified cruelties during the punitive expeditions" against the peasant rebellion in Tambov (Voskresenski 1988).

244 · Chapter Nine

Russophiles actually played a positive role in this process when, in their fervent defense of Stalin, they objected to the idealization of Stalin's victims, such as Bukharin or Kirov (see Kozhinov 1987; see also the polemics of Sarnov with Kozhinov about Bukharin in *LG*, March 22, 1989).

Yet in 1988 liberals were still unable to provide multifaceted analyses of figures such as Trotsky, who, despite having admittedly made some useful contributions in the Revolution and contributing to victory in the civil war, were presented primarily as "The Demons of the Revolution" (the title of Volkogonov's article in *P.*, September 9, 1988; see also Vasetski's article on Trotsky in *KP*, May 19, 1989.

The Historical Taboos in 1987–1988

In 1987–1988, at the height of glasnost, liberals did not yet dare discuss certain historical events, particularly those relating to Soviet international and ethnic relations, and most liberals did not seek out opportunities to begin discussing such topics in public. These events included the suppression of the national movements during the civil war and the formation of the USSR, the Soviet occupation of the Baltic republics in 1940, the invasion of Czechoslovakia in 1968, and many others. In addition, in 1988 many liberals produced articles and documentary movies that deliberately misrepresented the past (see, for instance, *MN*'s orthodox treatment of the history of the Soviet invasion of Czechoslovakia, August 22, 1988; also see the article about Borshchevski's highly acclaimed movie *Risk* [1987], which rudely distorted Soviet foreign policy after the war but nonetheless pleased many intellectuals because of its anti-Stalinist barbs, in *LG*, November 4, 1987).[1]

Besides such historical events, liberals in 1987–1988 were also unable to discuss publicly the democratic movement of the 1970s or to mention its main heroes. Burlatski, for instance, in explaining the factors that prevented Brezhnev's leadership from openly restoring Stalin's reputation in the late 1960s, totally ignored the protest letter campaign as well as other oppositional actions (Burlatski 1988b).

It was not until 1989 that liberals, apparently with the permission of the Kremlin, began to reveal publicly their attitudes regarding the Czechoslovakian invasion of 1968 and to talk about the few Soviet intellectuals who had protested against the suppression of the Prague Spring at the time. (These disscussions were particularly frequent following the

[1] Eidel'man was among the few historians to risk breaking taboos, such as that surrounding the Katyn massacre, when, in 1940, Soviets killed thousands of Polish officers. In an interview with a Polish magazine, this historian unequivocally backed the Western and Polish versions (*NRS*, August 23, 1988).

"velvet revolution" in Czechoslovakia in fall 1989; see, for example, Viktor Sheinis's article in *Iz.*, October 13, 1989.)

THE REVENGE OF THE INTELLECTUALS

Glasnost provided the first opportunities for intellectuals to speak openly about themselves and their detractors. Very few active liberals failed to participate in this campaign of revenge.

The Cult of Intellectuals as Heroes

The intellectuals' growing public participation in glasnost manifested itself first in their attempts to find heroes among their ranks. They initially looked to those who had resisted official pressure and corruption in the 1950s and 1960s, and especially to those who had done so in the 1970s. One of the first to be elevated to the hero's pedestal was Vysotski. The bard, who had been officially ignored in Russia in the 1970s, became the object of growing idolatry, promoted by the liberal intelligentsia and eagerly supported by the entire Soviet population. The numerous articles on Vysotski published during this period were considered a form of revenge to the detractors of the intelligentsia in the 1970s, as well as a direct challenge to the conservatives and Russophiles, all of whom held the bard in great contempt (Bestuzhev-Lada 1988).

Along with Vysotski, the public elevated numerous other figures, both dead and alive, to prominence, including Nikolai Vavilov, Tvardovski, Platonov, Tarkovski, Pasternak, Grossman, Sakharov, Dudintsev, Chukovskaia, and Viacheslav Ivanov. In addition, the intellectuals created a pantheon of highly refined scholars, artists, and other creative people who had been killed or harassed, and were practically unknown to the public. This list included the philosopher Florenski, the scholar Mikhail Bakhtin, the artist Filonov, the theater director Meierkhold, and the psychologist Lev Vygotski (Ivanov 1988; *SK*, May 7, 1988).

It is only natural that liberals, glasnost's earliest and most vocal proponents, would exploit the unique opportunities afforded by it to speak about their past, particularly about the perennial harassment and persecution of intellectuals during Stalin's reign. In 1987 and 1988 the first accounts of the major campaigns against intellectuals were made available to the public. They detailed the persecution of writers during all periods of Soviet history, of agrarian economists in the early 1930s, geneticists in the 1930s and 1940s, physiologists in the early 1950s, and philosophers in the 1930s (see Dudintsev 1987a, 1987b; Granin 1987; *MN*, August 12, 1987, and December 20, 1987).

Squaring Up with the Enemies

While praising their heroes, liberals also cautiously began assailing those authors regarded as pillars of official ideology, such as Maxim Gorky, Sholokhov, Vladimir Maiakovski, and Vsevolod Vishnevski (*LG*, May 18, 1988; *MN*, August 9, 1987, June 4, 1989; *Moskovskaia Pravda*, March 5, 1989).

Both of these actions elicited strong opposition from the Russophiles, who, acting as defenders of Soviet ideology, accused the liberals of idealizing authors who perished in the gulag or were harassed in the past (Pasternak was named most often in this regard, along with Mandel'shtam, Tsvetaieva, and Akhmatova), as well as of intentionally denigrating the Soviet classics. The Russophiles also hinted that the liberals were concerned only with the posthumous glory of authors with either Jewish backgrounds or emigrant or oppositional pasts, ignoring purely Russian writers of peasant origin such as Nikolai Kliuev or Pavel Vasiliev, who also perished in the gulag (Glushkova 1988; see also *LG*, January 1, 1988).

With very few, if any, highly regarded Soviet writers on their side, the Russophiles were especially exuberant in praising Sholokhov, portraying him not only as a great author, but also as a hero who defended the peasants against the cruelty of collectivization (see, for instance, Khvatov 1987).

Along with their attacks on official Soviet writers, liberals also exploited the opportunities presented by glasnost to settle old scores with hack social scientists who, over several decades, had dominated the scene, stifling any evidence of free thought. Soviet readers were offered, for instance, a colorful portrait of Piotr Fedoseiev in Afanasiev's collection of articles entitled "There Is No Other Way" (Vodolazov 1988). As vice president of the Academy of Sciences, Fedoseiev controlled the social sciences in the USSR for fifteen years and faithfully supported mutually exclusive ideas for every regime since the 1940s.

One privilege denied the liberals in 1986 and 1987, but finally granted in 1988, was the ability to name past tormentors other than Stalin. Andrei Zhdanov was the first to be offered up to the liberals for the settling of scores. The oppressive role played by this myrmidon of Stalin in the sadistic and degrading persecution of Akhmatova and Mikhail Zoshchenko in 1946 constituted the core of several articles (see Kariakin's "Zhdanov's Liquid or Against Denigration," 1988; see also *MN*, June 19, 1988). Liberals championed the drive to rename cities, districts, and colleges that bore Zhdanov's name, a campaign that met with strong resistance from the apparatchiks. After Zhdanov, the liberals targeted Suslov, who had controlled Soviet ideology over three decades.

The Reunion with Emigration

With the gradual evolution of glasnost, intellectuals adopted a new attitude about emigration from the country and toward their former colleagues working abroad. Once again the political leadership set the tone, moving from the harsh evaluation of all emigrants as traitors to labeling some of those who left the country as patriots who could not tolerate the stagnation of the Brezhnev years.

Having first obtained support from Gorbachev's people, the liberals immediately moved ahead with plans to rehabilite several of their former colleagues. Among the first emigrants to be rehabilitated were poets Brodsky and Galich, painter Mikhail Shemiakin, theater director Liubimov, writers Viktor Nekrasov, Voinovich, Korzhavin, and Sasha Sokolov, literature experts Efim Etkind, Kopelev, and Orlova, and the musician Mstislav Rostropovich. Some liberals, primarily Evtushenko, considered the destigmatization of emigrants, as well as others subjected to past persecutions, their major task (see, for instance, Evtushenko's impassioned article about Oleg Tselkov, an emigrant painter, in *LG*, August 10, 1988).

By late 1988 liberals were even using television for the rehabilitation of emigrants, particularly the program "Vzgliad" (Glance), which competed during this time with *Ogoniok* for the boldest acts of bravery. Liberals gleefully broadcast programs and organized meetings and parties in order to honor and praise emigrants as heroes of resistance to Brezhnev's regime, even though they were still being depicted by conservatives and Russophiles as traitors of the motherland. Liberals enthusiastically supported the idea of cultural cooperation with emigrants, citing a precedence already established by other countries, primarily China (Gozman and Etkind 1988, pp. 37–38).

Along with the emigrants of the "third wave" of the 1970s, a number of emigrants of the first (after the Revolution) and even of the second (during the war with Germany) waves were also "rehabilitated" in 1987–1988 (a few, such as Bunin, Shaliapin, Rakhmaninov, and Stravinski were reinstated to official culture in the 1960s). Among the old emigrants to return home posthumously were the writers Vladimir Nabokov and Boris Zaitsev and the actor Mikhail Chekhov.

The restoration of the emigrants' good names in the Soviet press drew extremely angry reactions from conservatives, particularly Russophiles, who regarded this development as one of the worst manifestations of decadent liberalism. Fury over the exculpation of some emigrant intellectuals, as well as the permission granted them to visit the USSR, was one of the main themes of Andreieva's letter in March 1988 (Andreieva 1988; see also Rasputin 1988a, p. 171).

Encouraged by the liberalization of the official policy toward emigrants, Soviet intellectuals started to meet their old colleagues during their trips abroad, as well as inviting the emigrants to their homes in Moscow when they visited their motherland. Intellectuals strictly followed the evolution of official policy in these matters, however, and practically never outpaced it.

SOLZHENITSYN'S TRIUMPH

Solzhenitsyn's rehabilitation in 1989, which was supported by intellectuals of all persuasions, was probably the last and most momentous episode in this process. Since he had not emigrated (in fact, he had condemned the emigration of true Russian intellectuals from Brezhnev's Russia) but rather had been deported by force, even the most arduous "patriots" were constrained to withhold the accusations they usually leveled against emigrants and defectors.

Moreover, Solzhenitsyn was the single person respected in one way or another by every faction of the intellectual community. Whereas glasnost-era liberals openly praised him for *Gulag* and for other works of the 1960s that contributed immensely to debunking Stalin, Lenin, socialism, and Communism (see, for instance, Adamovich 1989), Russophiles emphasized his writings and speeches of the 1970s, with their strong nationalism and their rejection of Western values (see Bondarenko 1989). In the race to praise Solzhenitsyn, the Russophiles had the upper hand, since they were able to refer to works far more recent than those cited by the liberals.

In any case, 1989 was truly the "year of Solzhenitsyn" in the USSR. Not only did almost every Moscow and Leningrad magazine publish some work by Solzhenitsyn (with *Novyi Mir* emerging as the champion, publishing *The Gulag Archipelago* in volume numbers 8 and 11), but many provincial magazines (such as *Don*, *Volga*, and others) did so as well.

In the absence of any direct contact with his motherland, with no public statement since 1985 about his attitudes toward contemporary historical processes in Russia, and with no clear information about his intentions to visit Russia, Solzhenitsyn became an invisible guru in Moscow. His hypothetical opinions were used to influence developments in the country, and even a Soviet television anchorman deemed it appropriate to cite Solzhenitsyn when discussing most convincing arguments against political extremism (see the program "Seven Days," February 25, 1990).

In 1989–1990, it was almost impossible to criticize Solzhenitsyn, his behavior, or his works. When Vladimir Lakshin tried to do so, accusing Solzhenitsyn of having been unfair to Tvardovski in his memoirs, he was attacked caustically by the Russophiles, who claimed that Solzhenitsyn had acted as a saint (see *Argumenty i Fakty*, January 5 and 26, 1990). It is remarkable that, in a discussion about the old argument between Sakharov and Solzhenitsyn in the mid-1970s, even such liberal Russophiles as Rodnianskaia and Gal'tseva took Solzhenitsyn's side and suggested that it was Sakharov who had shifted his views on major issues toward those of Solzhenitsyn—a suggestion that blatantly ignored not only the radical differences between the authors regarding the role of democratic values for Russia, but the fact that perestroika, as it evolved between 1987 and 1989, was a triumph for Sakharov's liberal program, and not for Solzhenitsyn's authoritarianism (even though the latter was strongly anti-Communist; see *LG*, March 7, 1990; see also Chuprinin's angry response in *LG*, May 9, 1970).

POLITICAL VIEWS OF LIBERALS IN 1986–1989

It is widely acknowledged that a democratic system requires at least two dimensions: political pluralism (or public contestation) and the involvement of the masses in government, usually comprised of the right to participate in elections and hold office (Dahl 1971).

During the 1960s, when serious political change in the country seemed very improbable, liberals had the luxury of being vague and even irresponsible in their views on the political order they desired for Russia. But when, in January and June 1987, their new and energetic leader proclaimed his goal to be the true democratization of the country (Gorbachev 1987, 1988), liberals were forced to specify, on very short notice, the political system they would recommend and for which they were ready to fight. It is noteworthy that an intellectual and emotional consensus was achieved almost immediately regarding the first dimension—political pluralism—but was much less quickly forthcoming regarding the second.

A New Concept: Civil Society

In 1987–1988 liberals quickly learned the elementary concepts of democracy and began to champion the idea of a civil society, which was almost unknown even in 1985. Suddenly, destatization became the main focus of their efforts. For example, Evgeni Ambartsumov contended that "socialism had exhausted its potential in the state" and that the "state should be absorbed by society" (Ambartsumov 1988a, p. 86). And with even greater passion, Batkin demanded "the maximal destatization of Soviet life" (Batkin 1988, p. 176).

In 1988 liberals began assaulting the cornerstone of Soviet paternalistic ideology—that the state provides its citizens with the means for subsistence—and declared that, in reality, exactly the opposite was true: that, in fact, society creates the state and furnishes it with the means to function (Nuikin 1988a).

During this period, liberals published innumerable articles in support of civil society, although some authors did not use this term. They insisted on the separation of the state and the party and demanded the introduction of parallel social structures, supporting so-called informal organizations, including those that could be regarded as a prototype of the party, such as the Popular Front in the Support of Perestroika (Kurashvili 1988; see also Ambartsumov 1988b, pp. 88–89; Maliutin 1988; Rumiantsev 1988, pp. 23–25; Zaslavskaia 1988, p. 43).

Along with the idea of a civil society, liberals also discovered that ideas regarding the division of power were also directly relevant and began to work feverishly along these lines from 1987 to 1989 (Migranian 1988, p. 104).

The Multiparty System: The Long Way to Public Support

The liberals' gradual mastery of the concept of civil society was accompanied by their inexorable examination of the party's role in Soviet society. Some suggested recognizing the monopoly of the party as a historical fact, but one that should not preclude the formation of civil society and political pluralism (Batkin 1988, pp. 187–189; Migranian 1988, p. 120). Most intellectuals during this period, however, were more inclined to look for ways to criticize the party's monopoly.

As Gorbachev more clearly expressed his intention to curtail the party's interference in many spheres of social life, intellectuals began to include the party itself in their list of targets for critique. Despite their public recognition in 1987–1988 of the "leading role of the party," liberals tried to move beyond the official line at least somewhat, using terms that implicitly assumed a multiparty system (Gel'man 1988).

Still, even those who were quite bold in their analyses of the Soviet system in 1987–1988 avoided direct endorsement of the multiparty system as the single antidote to the "deformations" in Soviet political history that were being discussed with such verve. Some liberals avoided such endorsements because of censorship (in 1985–1988 glasnost did not extend to direct critiques of the party) and reserved their opinions on this issue for private communications. Others remained silent on the issue of multiparty systems because they did not pay much attention to political pluralism, and still others did so because they considered the formation of a multiparty system unrealistic and therefore undeserving of serious consideration.

Those who were most outspoken about the deleterious effects of the party's political monopoly usually resorted to suggestions that implicitly led readers to the realization that the one-party system represented a major obstacle to the country's progress. Burlatski's article, "Brezhnev and the End of the Thaw" (1988b), is typical of this type of argument. He suggested that a new political system, headed by outstanding people, could be created out of "socialist pluralism." For Burlatski, "socialist pluralism" included "the freedom to think, speak, write, and look for the truth and seek its recognition," "the autonomy of the minority in the framework of the dominant order," and the elimination of "flattery from political life." Apparently Burlatski placed all his hopes on the goodwill of the leadership of the party, which he hoped would understand the usefulness of political freedom (Burlatski 1988e; see also Migranian 1989a).

Alexander Iakovlev, a well-known expert on Soviet law, vehemently defended the idea of "a law-abiding state" and identified two major impediments to its establishment: "the lack of economic self-respect of the Soviet people" and "the circumstance that economic power in the USSR belongs not to whom it should belong" (meaning the excessive economic role of the state). Iakovlev failed, however, to discuss any institutions able to prevent the central powers from infringing on the law, except to suggest that this role could be fulfilled by the newspapers, provided that their editorial boards could be independent of the local party apparatus (Iakovlev 1988).

Finally, in 1989 intellectuals engaged in a more open dialogue in favor of the multiparty system. Kliamkin's brilliant article, "Why It Is Difficult to Tell the Truth," was a significant factor in this dialogue. Kliamkin was one of the first to attack the idea of "unity" as the basic tenet of the party and society and to demonstrate that, without real political institutional pluralism (and not just pluralism of opinions, which is at the center of Gorbachev's political program) and protection of the minority view, society is doomed to despotism and mass repression (Kliamkin 1989).

Besides the dialogue of Kliamkin and others, the most radical change in the public's attitude toward the multiparty issue was occasioned by the election campaign in spring 1989 for positions in the Soviet parliament. The importance of political institutional pluralism as a condition for the genuine democratization of society became a leading slogan in the Soviet public mind. This idea, however, was promoted during the campaign not so much by the intellectuals, but by young members of the mass intelligentsia, with the clear support of party mavericks such as Boris El'tsin.

Liberals were in a hurry to catch up with the new mood in the country, and during the session of the Congress of People's Deputies (May–June 1989), a few intellectuals, such as former sportsman and writer Iuri Vlasov, economist Alexei Emel'ianov, and others bravely challenged the party's dominance in the country (*Iz.*, May 26 through June 9, 1989). By late 1989, with the spectacular collapse of Communist regimes throughout

Eastern Europe and with the imminent implementation of multiparty systems in East Germany and Czechoslovakia (events which the liberals had expected even less than the party's defeat in the March 26, 1989 election), liberals rushed to voice publicly their objections to the Communist party's monopoly on power. In doing so, they presaged Gorbachev's official call for the elimination of the infamous Article Six from the Soviet Constitution (which declares "the leading role of the Communist party") by only one or two months (Gorbachev's announcement came in February 1990; see *P*, February 6, 1990).

The Masses: An Ambivalent Variable

As mentioned earlier, the liberals of the 1960s, despite being great admirers of Western democracy, were very skeptical about the role of the masses in Soviet political life. With the advent of glasnost, new information came to light about the activities of the people in the 1930s, including their support of both Stalin's regime and mass repressions; the army of voluntary informers numbered in the millions. This new information, combined with the resistance of the masses to Gorbachev's reforms—for instance, the popular discontent with private cooperatives and with the 1986–1988 attacks against Stalin—merely reinforced the intellectuals' old views toward the masses. So, when Gorbachev proposed including the masses in the governmental process (his degree of sincerity and consistency being another issue), it quickly became evident that not all liberals were ready to support this idea.

Three groups of intellectuals can be identified depending on their attitudes toward the democratization of Soviet society: realists, elitists, and democrats. In most cases, individual liberals did not fit neatly into any one of these categories. Rather, they fit into one category fairly well and shared at least a few of the views held by those in the other two categories.

It is also important to note that with the process of democratization, and especially with the unexpected political activity of the masses during the election campaign in the winter of 1989, the number of intellectuals who could label themselves "democrats" strongly increased.

Realists

Realists, who were very influential in the first years of Gorbachev's regime, regarded the genuine democratization of Soviet society as virtually impossible. These intellectuals were convinced that the political leadership would never permit a multiparty system, without which true elections were meaningless. The realists doubted there could be even a limited choice of candidates, since they felt sure that the apparatchiks would never expose themselves to the risk of an election. Therefore, the realists argued that intellectuals should concern themselves only with the promotion of the accoutrements typical to an "enlightened monarchy"—the active role of the mass media, polls, and the autonomy of the intellectuals. Burlatski was a typical realist, spurning those colleagues who naively took Gorbachev at his word when he spoke of the participation of the masses in government (Burlatski 1988d).

Elitists

While the realists considered the party to be a major and probably insurmountable impediment to democratization, quite a few liberals revitalized in 1986–1987 a position they had taken during the 1960s and actually supported party officials who were opposed to the idea of the true participation of the masses in governmental processes. These intellectuals insisted that, based on Russian history and the lack of any democratic experience, Russians and other Soviet people were just not prepared for democracy, and only in the distant future could real steps be taken toward establishing a truly competitive political order.

The elitist liberals were very concerned about the animosity of the masses toward Gorbachev's reforms ("perestroika does not have wide and specific mass support"; Batkin 1988, p. 157), and were afraid not only of polls, but especially of actual elections, which they feared would favor only the conservatives. Moreover, the elitists considered the party to be the one force capable of gradually leading society toward liberalism or democracy while simultaneously combatting the threat of anarchy.

Natan Eidel'man clearly expressed the elitists' position in his praise of "the revolution from above," suggesting that the involvement of the masses in the political process is fraught with many dangers for political stability. Citing and explicitly applying the ideas of Alexander Herzen to the situation at hand, Eidel'man went so far as to declare that "there are cases when power is better than society." Given these views, it is not surprising that in his long article on perestroika, Eidel'man almost completely ignored the issues of democratic political institutions and elections (Eidel'man 1988, p. 4; see also Eidel'man 1989).

Batkin expressed his elitist views with equal candor in his brilliant and lengthy article in *There Is No Other Way* and, like Eidel'man, almost totally avoided the issue of mass participation in government (Batkin 1988; see also Migranian 1988, p. 109; see also the critique of the "advocates of the enlightened monarchy" in Vinogradov 1988, pp. 294–295).

Democrats

Finally, at the very beginning of perestroika, a significant number of liberals adopted a clear stance in favor of the immediate introduction of democracy in the country. They believed that true elections with competing political forces were the essence of political reform, and that without such elections, any reforms, economic or otherwise, would be impossible (Burtin 1988; Vinogradov 1988, pp. 292–293). These intellectuals were very sensitive to official statements regarding elections and their implementation. Liberals in this group were strongly critical of inconsistencies and hypocrisy in Gorbachev's political reforms, particularly in relation to free elections.

Democrats, of course, received the results of the March 26, 1989, election with delight. These results demonstrated an expected level of political activity among the masses and revealed strongly democratic popular attitudes toward the existing political system. (About fifty high party officials were defeated, primarily because they were the only ones on the ballot.)

Of course, the election results provided democrats with powerful arguments in their debates with their liberal opponents—the realists and the elitists. Having been influenced by the election results, many of them (e.g., Batkin) changed their views.

However, as the country's economic and political situations deteriorated drastically in late 1989, the influence of the elitist view increased once again. Two prominent liberals—Igor Kliamkin and Andranik Migranian—initiated a heated debate throughout the country by insisting that an "iron hand" was the single remedy for the wavering course of reforms and that, in the past, liberalism and democracy were successful only if assisted by an absolutist state (LG, August 16, 1989; see also LG, September 26, September 27, and December 27, 1989; Migranian 1989b).

THE SOVIET EMPIRE AND DEMOCRACY: THE DEEP CONFLICT OF VALUES

With the onset of the anti-Stalinist campaign, most liberals vehemently condemned the persecution of ethnic groups, particularly those who were the victims of Stalin's terror, such as the Checheno-Ingush, the Kalmyks, the Crimean Tartars, and others. Pristavkin's novel, already mentioned, stood as a symbol of the liberals' disgust with the Stalinist, chauvinistic policy toward small ethnic groups. Still, most liberal intellectuals followed Gorbachev's evolving national policy and stayed well within the official course.

In the first years of glasnost, Russian liberals almost never discussed the integrity of the Soviet empire or the economic or cultural autonomy of the national republics and numerous ethnic groups, nor did they manifest any initiative in this most sensitive area of Soviet politics. From 1985 to 1987, few of them—including Evtushenko and Voznesenski, who regularly wrote about "the internationalist issue"—raised their voices against Russian chauvinism or dared even mention that Russians might be harboring unjust attitudes toward non-Russians. When, in 1986, Astafiev published stories that rudely derogated Georgians and other non-Russians, no prominent liberal rebuked him publicly. At the June 1986 Congress of Soviet Writers, where Georgian writers organized a protest demonstration, Astafiev was criticized only by Sergei Mikhalkov; even then, the criticism was extremely mild and offset by words of reverence. He was vehemently defended by Rasputin (see Bondarev 1988b, pp. 25, 396).

The passivity of the Russian liberals regarding Russian chauvinism was especially noticeable in 1987 when, in the aftermath of the Alma-Ata riot, *Pravda* launched a strong offensive against the national republics and against teaching non-Russian languages and preserving non-Russian culture and religion (*P.*, February 11 and 13, March 28, 1987; see also *LG*'s aggressive articles against Islam, May 20 and 27, 1987; see also *Komsomol'skaia Pravda*'s article accusing Aitmatov of Kirgiz nationalism, January 16, 1988).

It is typical that Afansiev's famous *There Is No Other Way*, a collection of thirty-five articles by the most prominent liberals published in 1988 when ethnic conflicts had already spread across the country (e.g., the Kasakh riot in Alma-Ata in December 1986, the Armenia-Azerbaijan conflict in 1987–1988, the strong nationalist demonstrations in the Baltic republics in 1987, particularly that on August 23, and several others), did not contain a single paper devoted to the ethnic issue.

In his paper, Sakharov briefly discussed two issues: the fate of the Crimean Tartars banished by Stalin to Central Asia, mainly in connection with the right of people to live in the country of their own choosing; and the Nagorno-Karabakh region, an administrative entity in Azerbaijan whose Armenian majority demanded unification with the Armenian republic. (Later, Sakharov's positions espoused the radical reform of the Soviet empire, giving greater autonomy to all ethnic groups; see *Og.*, no. 31, 1988, pp. 26–27; see also his draft for a new Soviet Constitution, *Dos'ie*, January 1990, pp. 9–10.) Other authors, including such leading theorists of perestroika as Zaslavskaia, Batkin, Seliunin, Alexander Bovin, Butenko, and Gavriil Popov, in their long articles about the past, present, and future of Soviet society, were unable to find room for even a very short analysis of the ethnic variable or of the desire of non-Russians, which comprise 50 percent of the population, for real autonomy and independence. No liberal, including the contributors to Afanasiev's book, even indirectly voiced support of each nation's right to self-determination (see Afanasiev 1988a; see also Afanasiev 1988d). Similarly, the three collections of articles published in 1989, with a total of seventy-seven liberal authors (Kobo 1989; Borodkin, Kosals, and Ryvkina 1989; Vishnevski 1989), produced only two articles on ethnic issues, and neither contained any profound analysis of the country's ethnic conflicts. The articles in these collections also totally ignored such crucial questions as the fate of the Soviet empire, self-determination for the major ethnic groups, Russian chauvinism, and anti-Semitism. Only one author supported the idea of self-determination, and even then only in passing and only within the USSR (Sheinis 1989, pp. 380–381).

In 1987–1988 Russian liberals could be credited for publicly defending only the Crimean Tartars. The article in *Pravda* (July 24, 1987) signed by Pristavkin, Okudzhava, Evtushenko, and Sergei Baruzdin was among the few actions in support of an ethnic minority. Although sympathetic to the Armenians, especially after the Sumgaiti carnage in December 1988, prominent liberals (Sakharov once again being an exception) in no way publicly expressed their views regarding the ethnic conflicts in the Caucasus region. In 1989 the Kremlin gradually started to change its national policy, recognizing, under pressure from increasing ethnic conflict, the necessity of meeting at least some of the nationalists' demands. When the restraints regarding debates on ethnic issues were relaxed, liberals were able to express almost all of their views on this subject. This was especially true during the session of the Congress of People's Deputies.

In defining, for the first time in their lives, their public attitudes, Russian liberals were influenced by several somewhat mutually exclusive factors. The main question they had to answer for themselves and for the public concerned the compatibility between the Russian empire as it stood at the end of the nineteenth century and democratic ideas, which imply the right of the ethnic groups to self-determination.

By 1989 the majority of the liberals contended that the preservation of the multinational Soviet state and the democratization of Soviet society was not only possible, but even necessary for the success of Gorbachev's reforms. They argued that any secession movement in the USSR would only encourage the neo-Stalinists to take the offensive and might thereby lead to the failure of Gorbachev's regime (see the exposition of these views in Migranian 1989). This position seemingly satisfied any feelings of Russian patriotism still associated with the Russian empire without compromising the liberals' allegiance to democratic ideals or aggravating the strong chauvinism of the masses. Of course, it is impossible to determine the extent to which each of these ingredients accounts for the imperial orientation of the Russian liberals in the late 1980s.

In any case, during the session of the Congress of People's Deputies, almost none of the liberal members of the so-called Moscow Group came to the direct and open support of the delegates from the Baltic republics, who valiantly defended the right of their countries to sovereignty. In the most valiant speeches of the congress—those of Vlasov, Sakharov, Popov, and Emel'ianov—very little was said in favor of self-determination in general or in support of the Baltic delegates in particular. The speeches that reported the plight of non-Russians in various regions of the country were also mostly ignored by Russian liberals, with the exception of Galina Starovoitova, a Leningrad ethnographer, who passionately defended the interests of Armenians (*Iz.*, May 26–June 10, 1989). The same problem was ignored by the prominent liberals who analyzed the session of the congress (see the analytical articles in *MN*: Batkin, June 11, 1989; Viasheslav Ivanov, June 18, 1989; Kliamkin, July 2, 1989; see also Zakharov's article in *Iz*, July 5, 1989).

The situation in Georgia was the only exception to the rule. The cruel and bloody quenching of the peaceful meeting in Tbilisi on April 9, 1989, aroused the anger of the liberal intellectuals, who sensed, as writer B. Vasiliev put it, a rehearsal for the suppression of the whole democratic process. Still, while denouncing the Soviet repressive apparatus and, indirectly, Gorbachev, for this action, liberals never expressed their support for the Georgian independence movement that had inspired the ill-fated meeting (see the articles of leading Moscow liberals—B. Vasiliev, Gel'man, Egor Iakovlev, and others—in *MN*, April 23, 1989; see also *LG*, May 24, 1989; *Argumenty i Fakty*, June 2, 1989).

At the same time, however, democratic ideas significantly influenced the attitudes of liberals toward individual ethnic regions. The Baltic republics, where nationalism was combined with a strong democratic movement (the so-called Popular Front), enjoyed great support from the intellectual circles in Moscow and Leningrad. Support for these republics was qualified, however, since many Russian liberals had difficulty accepting the new laws passed in these republics in 1989, which restrained the rights of Russians who did not know the native language or who had not lived long enough in the republics to participate in election of local officials (see, for instance, noted liberal journalist Irina Ovchinnikova's article on discrimination against Russians in Estonia, *Izvestia*, June 2, 1989).

At the same time, nationalism in Central Asia, which thrived on deep corruption, Islamic religious fanaticism, and Middle Age traditions, was shunned in the same intellectual circles. The Uzbek riots in Fergana (June 1989), which were directed against local Turks, served only to strengthen the diffident attitudes of Russian liberals toward Muslim nationalism.

While most liberal intellectuals were unwilling in 1987–1989 to sacrifice one value (the preservation of the Soviet empire) for the sake of another (democracy), some of them, especially the young, took the opposite

258 · Chapter Nine

position and were ready to support the idea of national self-determination. For example, the scholars of the Central Economic and Mathematical Institute endorsed a resolution that demanded "guarantees of real, and not formal, sovereignty for the republics" (*LG*, June 22, 1989; see also Galina Starovoitova's consistent defense of national self-determination in her interview on Soviet television, September 9, 1989). It was not until late 1989, when the secession of Lithuania and two other Baltic republics was imminent and when the Kremlin itself began to accommodate this idea, that the majority of liberal intellectuals also began to support the idea of self-determination.

THE CLOSING OF EYES ON ANTI-SEMITISM

During the 1960s the major ethnic concern for Russian liberals was the Jewish issue, and liberals considered it their duty to fight state anti-Semitism, a remnant of Stalin's heritage. In the 1970s, under pressure from both Russophiles and the authorities, liberals almost totally abandoned this issue, and some of them even drifted toward their own mild forms of anti-Semitism.

With the advent of glasnost, liberals cautiously reintroduced the battle against anti-Semitism into their political agenda. Their activity was strongly tempered, however, by the fear of being labeled Zionists and being discredited and thereby rendered unfit to promote perestroika. As a result, even in 1985 and 1986 it was almost impossible to find evidence of the liberals' opposition to the anti-Semitism that was rife in state policy and in the ideology of the Russophiles. For the most part, liberals (along with their leader, Gorbachev) pretended that there was no Jewish issue in Soviet society. During that period, they failed to respond to numerous anti-Semitic jabs from the Russophiles and from other anti-Semites who were especially active in the Bielorussian capital of Minsk, which clearly replaced Kiev as a center for the dissemination of anti-Semitic literature. For example, Voznesenski's poem "Ditch," about diggers looking for gold teeth and other jewels in a ravine where Nazis had killed Jews, identified the victims very timidly, in stark contrast to Evtushenko's "Babi Iar" of the 1960s (Voznesenski 1986). It was not until 1987–1988 that liberals again began to address the Jewish issue in their publications and in other works. Even then, they acted only after being prompted from above, and in a very defensive style.

Mention of the famous anticosmopolitan campaign of 1948–1952 did not appear in Soviet magazines until 1988, and even then its anti-Semitic character was often left unrecognized. The historian Iuri Poliakov wrote about this campaign and mentioned its victims (almost all of whom had Jewish names) but remained silent about the anti-Semitism that clearly underlay its ideological operation (*MN*, February 7, 1988; September 4, 1988). The same omission was made by the author of the first article discussing "the doctors plot" (*MN*, February 7, 1988). Not until mid-1988 did some liberals (mostly the victims of this campaign) begin to discuss the anti-Semitic background of these events (for instance, Borshchagovski 1988; Rapoport 1988; Rudnitski 1988). Even then these liberals maintained almost absolute silence not only about discrimination against Jews in the economy, education, science, and culture during Brezhnev's era and in the present, but even about such discrimination in the 1940s and 1950s.

Grossman's novel *Life and Fate*, which was published in the USSR in 1988, correctly portrayed the Jewish question in Stalin's Russia and represented a major breakthrough in the application of glasnost to this burning problem. Still, nearly all of the reviews in praise of the novel remained silent on the question of Soviet anti-Semitism. This silence was maintained even by Viktor Lakshin, a leading Russian liberal, as well as other reviewers (Lakshin 1988; see also Zolotusski 1988; see also *P.*, July 4, 1988).

Eventually, escalation of the political struggle between the supporters and the opponents of Gorbachev's policy of modernization forced several intellectuals (such as Ales Adamovich, Vasili' Bykov, and Mikhail Ulianov) who had remained rather neutral on the Jewish question to take a stand against the society "Pamiat' " (Memory) and its supporters (see, for instance, Adamovich 1987; Bykov 1988; Kondratiev 1989). Still, among the "legal" liberals of high status—the activists of perestroika—none fought anti-Semitism with the perseverance and fervor exhibited by their grandparents before the Revolution or even in the 1960s.

In 1988 it finally became possible to show (albeit to a limited audience) the film *Commissar*, discussed in an earlier chapter. Although liberals received this film favorably, and some, like Evtushenko, did so with great enthusiasm, almost none of their reviews recounted the real history of the movie and the atmosphere surrounding it (*SK*, February 13, 1988).

Even by the end of 1988, the only publications to approach the Jewish issue honestly, fearlessly, and with a readiness to compare anti-Semitism in the USSR with that in Hitler's Germany were those by the late Vladimir Tendriakov and the ethnographer Natalia Iukhneva. Tendriakov's story, "Hunting," described the hunt for Jewish intellectuals during the anticosmopolitan campaign (Tendriakov 1971/1988). Iukhneva presented a paper at a June 1988 meeting at the Institute of Ethnography in which he defended Zionism and Judaism, denounced the ostracism of Jews in Soviet society, and castigated attempts to suppress information about the holocaust and about the history of Jews in general. Only the Estonian magazine *Raduga* dared publish this paper (Iukhneva 1988).

The reluctance of the liberals to adopt a clear stance against anti-Semitism as a general social issue in present society as well as in the past was revealed not only in the absence of analytical publications on this subject in even the most vanguard periodicals, but also in the liberals' silence at the first session of the Congress of People's Deputies in summer 1989. As mentioned above, the unprecedented freedom of speech at this congress permitted speakers to raise any issue and to stand up to the critique of the General Secretary, the KGB, and the Communist party. Although heated debate arose regarding the plight of almost every ethnic group, none of the liberal intellectual deputies that took the podium even mentioned the existence of the Jews in the country. By all accounts, the liberals, mindful of their sharp conflicts with the conservatives at the Congress, wanted to avoid being labeled Zionists—a label that would have certainly given the conservatives an extra edge in public opinion, considering the persistent anti-Semitic feelings of the masses. A similar line of thinking also partially explains why liberal Russian deputies ignored the plight of all non-Russian groups.

It is remarkable, however, that almost all of the liberal deputies (with a few exceptions, such as Sakharov and Evtushenko) were willing to sign a petition to the congress regarding anti-Semitism. The petition, prepared by Grigori Kanovich, a Jewish writer from Lithuania, was totally disregarded by Gorbachev, the chairman of the congress, who refused even to mention the petition in his numerous speeches at the session (about the developments surrounding this petition, see the interview with Kanovich in *Sovietskaia Litva*, June 7, 1989).

LIBERAL ECONOMIC PROGRAM

The concept of liberal socialism cherished by the liberals in the 1960s assumed the drastic decentralization of the economy as well as the legalization of existing private economic activity. This early conceptualization, however, stopped far short of the privatization of the Soviet economy. The liberals of the 1960s also believed that radical improvements in the material rewards of state industry and collective farms would substantially raise productivity, even without significant reforms in management or changes in property relations.

By the late 1980s the economic views of the liberals had changed significantly. Following the Twenty-seventh Party Congress, Gorbachev significantly expanded on the idea of private business, encompassing not only services and industry, but including the new concepts of private cooperatives and tenant, or lease, contracts. The latter involve the transformation of state enterprises or collective farms into federations run by groups of tenants (see Gorbachev 1988).

With Gorbachev's encouragement, the economic philosophy of the liberals underwent radical changes in 1987 and 1988. Because of their radical reassessment of the roles of social production, private property, and private initiative in Soviet history, they began to consider almost all of the party's postrevolution economic actions as disastrous for the economy. Similarly, although the liberals of the 1960s had accepted the economic model created in the late 1920s and early 1930s as more or less well suited to the requirements of an underdeveloped country, they were able, in the late 1980s, to declare the "command-administrative system" (the term coined by Gavriil Popov) ill-fated from its very inception (G. Popov 1987; see also Seliunin 1988a; Shmelev 1987).

The liberals not only supported Gorbachev's ideas of private business, but, with his blessing, expanded them considerably, declaring that only the maximal privatization of the Soviet economy could save the country from disaster. They strongly supported the dismantling of collectives and state farms and were confident that only private farming could save Soviet agriculture. And they exuberantly hailed Sivkov, the "Arkhangelsk Muzhik," who, working as a private farmer, exceeded the efficiency of his state farm many times over (Ananiev 1988; Chernichenko 1989; Mozhaiev 1987; Sakharov 1989a, pp. 8–9; Strelianyi 1987; Tikhonov 1988a, 1988b; Vershinin 1988).

In the late 1980s liberals finally dared to voice, both publicly and loudly, their opinions on a subject about which they had remained silent during the 1960s: the necessity of allowing people to earn as much as they could from an honest job. Some liberals were even ready to adopt Louis Philipp's slogan, "enrich yourselves" (Lisichkin 1988; Nuikin 1988a; Sakharov 1989a). At the same time, liberal economists, in alliance with journalists, engaged in a radical reassessment of planning as the basis of economic regulation. In the 1960s even advocates of a market economy dared not cast doubt on the positive role of central planning. By contrast, in the 1980s, the most authoritative economic thinkers, such as Nikolai Petrakov (1987), Gavriil Popov (1988c), Seliunin (1988a), and Shmelev (1987; Popov and Shmelev 1988), almost totally dismissed Soviet planning as inefficient and irrational and came out in favor of open-market regulation of economic activity. These economists insisted that enterprises should answer only to the laws of supply and demand, adjusting their production plans and prices accordingly.

In general, the mid-1989 program shaped by the liberal intellectuals assumed the highest level of Westernization possible. Liberals accepted practically all of the elements of Western economic and political models, although they understood that existing conditions would prohibit the realization of many of these elements in the foreseeable future (and perhaps forever). While retaining many socialist ideals that show concern for the weak and disaffected, liberals generally assumed that the modern state, with its welfare programs, would perform the "socialist function" quite well.

Nikolai Amosov, a famous Soviet surgeon and social figure, was probably the only liberal to present an entire program of economic transformation in 1987–1988. He appeared confident in explicitly discussing several items that other liberals seemed to avoid (Amosov 1988). He explicitly based his program on the assumption that "individualism, even egotism," and not collectivism, are the real stimulators of progress, which accounts for why "capitalism, having a good biological footing, is so vigorous and dynamic." He also insisted that "inequality is also a strong stimulator for progress," although it should be tempered to loosen "the discontent of weak people." Summarizing the views of all liberals, Amosov presented himself as a staunch advocate of "the democratic procedures of the West," including the division of power, secret balloting, freedom of association, and so on (he stopped short of supporting the multiparty system). Finally, he demanded the restoration of religion as the basis for a good moral life and as an effective means for relieving the suffering of the people.

Amosov's economic program presupposes the free market regulation of economic activity, the autonomy of enterprises, the restoration of private initiative under state control, and the existence of unemployment. As a typical Soviet liberal, he wants to preserve certain elements of socialism in his society but recognizes that this can be accomplished only by sacrificing efficiency for the sake of "moral goals." It is remarkable that, on the strength of his program, Amosov defeated his rivals in Kiev and was elected to the Soviet parliament in March 1989. In 1989–1990, a multitude of liberals openly joined Amosov and declared that Western society should serve as the ideal for the USSR. "To become like Europe" (as Leonid Batkin proclaimed in his article with this title, see *Vek XX i Mir*, no. 8, 1989) became a rallying cry among liberals in 1989–1990 (see also Sheinis 1989; and Kondratiev 1990).

THE LIBERAL ARMY

The army of liberal intellectuals active in the first years of Gorbachev's regime consisted of five rather disparate detachments.

The Old Guard

Despite the demoralization of the 1970s, the core of the liberal camp in 1986–1988 was comprised of the older generation of intellectuals, that is, those who had gained prominence in the 1960s. This was especially true for the first two years of glasnost.

The intellectuals of the 1960s who went on to become leading figures in the late 1980s survived the repression and the corruption of the 1970s in very different ways. These intellectuals can be divided into three groups, depending on their activities in the 1970s: total opportunists, partial opportunists, and resisters.

The total opportunists were officially recognized figures who weathered the 1970s rather comfortably. Although they tried to publicize liberal ideas between the lines, they also adjusted quite well to Brezhnev's times and made various concessions to the regime, including (as mentioned earlier) participation in various political campaigns sponsored by the government. Among the total opportunists were writers such as Korotich, Zalygin, Evtushenko, and Granin and social scientists such as Burlatski. Some, like Korotich, wrote very nasty books (see, for instance, Korotich's *The Face of Hatred*, a rude, propagandistic book aimed at America) as late as 1985 and 1986, and published articles rife with old ideological material only a few months before their "radical turn to the left" (see Korotich 1986).

The partial opportunists were not favored by the authorities but nonetheless remained relatively active on the public scene, carefully avoiding participation in any ignoble political actions. This group included social scientists such as Zaslavskaia, Kariakin, and Shubkin; writers such as Shatrov, Baklanov, and Bykov; critics such as Rassadin; historians such as Eidel'man; film directors such as Riazanov; and theater directors such as Oleg Efremov.

Resisters were practically excluded from public life during the 1970s and rarely ever published their works. They lived rather difficult lives and lacked decent incomes but did not compromise with the authorities. Some of them took part in illegal actions (e.g., writers such as Dudintsev and Iskander, critics such as Sarnov, and journalists such as Karpinski).

In 1987 and 1988 the liberals of the 1960s who had left the country during the 1970s also gradually joined the struggle for change through their publications in Soviet periodicals (these liberals included Voinovich and Korzhavin). Only in 1987 did new names begin to surface on the political scene, comprising the remaining four types of new liberal activists.

Dead Liberals

This group was composed of dead authors whose novels and poems had come out in the West years ago but were not published in the USSR until 1986–1988. Among these authors, who became some of the most influential figures of perestroika, were Platonov with *Pit* (1987) and *Cheven-gur* (1987), Grossman with *Life and Fate*, Varlam Shalamov with *Kolym Stories* (1982), and a few others. While these works significantly expanded the Soviet people's knowledge of Stalin's times and especially of life in the gulag, many of these works bewildered Soviet readers with their descriptions of Soviet society as deeply inhuman and morally perverted from its very inception. The revelations in these works were shocking, despite glasnost and the new political and psychological climate in the country. Russophiles and Stalinists were outraged with these publications, and tried not only to diminish their artistic and civic values, but to denigrate them as well (see, for instance, Urnov's article about *Doctor Zhivago* in *P.*, April 27, 1988).

By contrast, liberals received these works with enthusiasm and euphoria and wrote brilliant articles inspired by them. Some of these articles, such as Gavriil Popov's essay on Bek's *Appointment* (G. Popov 1987) or Evtushenko's reflections on Platonov (Evtushenko 1988), became great cultural and political events.

Old Authors Become Liberals in 1986–1988

Rybakov is a good example of the group of writers who were transformed. Having published only trivial and official novels in the past (some of them addressed to children, such as *The Adventures of Krosh* and *Dirk*), Rybakov published *Children of Arbat* in 1987. This novel, with its strong anti-Stalinist orientation, became one of the great political events of the year.

Previously Unknown Old Works and Authors

These intellectuals, now in their fifties and sixties, were previously unable to surface in public life, primarily because of their liberal convictions. Members of the third group included writers such as Andrei Bitov (whose novel, *Pushkin's House*, recounted the tribulations of the true intellectuals of the 1970s) and Venedict Erofeiev (whose satirical novel, *Moscow—Petushki*, depicted drunkenness in Russia), economists such as Shmelev (who also gained popularity as a writer) and Gavriil Popov, journalists such as Seliunin and Egor Iakovlev, the historian Mikhail Gefter, the film directors Alexander Sokurov and Alexei German, and the critics Iuri Burtin, Natalia Il'ina, and Tatiana Ivanova. Also included in this group are intellectuals in their thirties and forties, who were too young during the 1960s to become visible.

The "Young" Generation

Finally, the liberal camp recruited a number of middle-aged intellectuals, such as writers Sergei Kaledin (who gained recognition with his novel about Soviet lumpenproletarians who earned their living in cemeteries; Kaledin 1987), Liudmila Petrushevskaia, and Tatiana Tolstaia; film director Marina Goldovskaia (with her movies advocating privatization, such as "The Arkhangelsk Muzhik," and about Stalin's terror, such as "The Solovetsk Power"); and historians Afanasiev and Igor Nuikin; and law expert Anatoli Sobchak, who became popular in 1989 for his fight against conservatives in the new Soviet Parliament.

INFLUENCING THE MASSES

The result of the liberals' activities was amazing—in a short period, with the support of the central mass media, they managed to radically change the ideological atmosphere in the country. In fact, it took less than one hundred liberal intellectuals to effect a change in viewpoints of the mass intelligentsia and of the politically active part of the rest of the population. Substantial data indirectly demonstrate the success of the joint efforts of the mass media and the intellectuals in destroying Soviet myths and gaining sympathy for liberal reforms among the intelligentsia.

Of course, the liberal intellectuals and the mass media also had a much more modest, but no less remarkable, effect on the masses. The representative, nationwide survey carried out in early 1989 by the Center of Public Opinion Studies revealed that while only 15.6 percent of the respondents ascribed the crisis in society to "declines in the belief in socialist ideals" and only 1.9 percent to "the policy of imperialist countries," 41.4 percent pointed to "the power of the bureaucracy," 12.7 percent to "the Stalinist heritage," and 22.7 percent to "egalitarianism and the suppression of initiative."

The popularity of liberal versus conservative periodicals is also indicative of the numbers of those ascribing to each viewpoint. The average growth coefficient for liberal periodicals between 1985 and 1989 was 4.69, while the corresponding coefficient for conservative and Russophile periodicals was 1.35 (Izvestia TsK KPSS, January, 1989, p. 139). Similar subscription data clearly indicate that liberal publications enjoyed tremendous popularity during this period, while Russophile and other conservative publications gained only a small fraction of the huge Soviet audience. The growth coefficients of *Ogoniok* (5.17) and *Znamia* (6.32), two of the most vigorous advocates of democratization and Westernization, is especially illustrative. The triumph of liberal ideas were especially impressive during the first session of the Congress of People's Deputies.

The majority of the population criticized the congress—and Gorbachev as its chairman—for violating democratic procedures.

BASKING IN OFFICIAL SUPPORT

In 1987 and 1988, for the first time in Soviet history, liberals finally understood what it meant to be on the good side of the political leadership. Still, their promotions to state and party positions were very modest at first, and took place primarily among those in the mass media. Along with Korotich and Iakovlev, who were among the first liberals to be appointed editors of periodicals (*Ogoniok* and *Moskovskie Novosti*, respectively), Zalygin became the editor of *Novyi Mir*, Baklanov of *Znamia*, and Gavriil Popov of *Voprosy Ekomomiki* (Questions of Economics). The appointments of Zaslavskaia as director of the Center of Public Opinion and Iadov as provisional director of the Sociological Institute were also included in the liberals' roster of administrative achievements.

And yet, no liberal found himself or herself in the highest echelons of power. During these years, even the most eloquent defenders of perestroika and party members with experience in the party apparatus, such as Burlatski, Bovin, and Genadi Lisichkin, remained where the new regime had found them. None secured a position at the Central Committee or in a governmental institution, including those controlling television, culture, and ideology.

By mid-1989 a few true intellectuals finally gained positions in the government (but not in the party). For example, Leonid Abalkin was appointed as a deputy chairman of the government, and Nikolai Vorontsov, who was not even a party member, was appointed head of the State Committee in Defense of Nature. In late 1989, Nikolai Gubenko, a famous actor and film director and a committed liberal (for example, he maintained his relationship with Liubimov, his mentor and the director of the Theater On Taganka, despite Liubimov's defection to the West, and he was the first to invite Liubimov to come back to the USSR) was appointed Minister of Culture. Moreover, following his election as president in 1990, Gorbachev included in his presidential council (a body of the size and importance of the Politburo) five intellectuals, three of whom (Aitmatov, Rasputin, and Shatalin) were quite prominent.

In addition, liberals finally began to receive the official prizes that had previously been awarded only to hack intellectuals or Russophiles. Among those to receive state prizes in 1989 were such Westernizers as Akhmadullina, Iskander, and Strelianyi, as well as the late famous film director and defector Andrei Tarkovskii (*P.*, November 9, 1989).

During this same time, however, liberals were securing free access to travel abroad (many of them for the first time in their lives) as members of numerous delegations to the West, where they praised glasnost and Gorbachev. They also tried to scare Western audiences with the possibility that perestroika and glasnost might collapse and demanded the support of Western leaders.

1988: The First Sign of Disagreement with the Leaders

In 1986–1989 liberal intellectuals were Gorbachev's committed advocates, and even the slightest rebukes directed against him immediately met with rebuttals.

When Nina Popkova published a short article in *Novyi Mir* that cast doubt on the future of Gorbachev's economic reforms and asserted the impossibility both of being "a little pregnant" and of uniting a market and planned economy, she was immediately refuted by Otto Latsis, who ridiculed her timing, saying that she "spoke in inappropriate moment" (Latsis 1987; Popkova 1987). Similarly, when Gorbachev surrendered El'tsin, his lieutenant, to the conservatives for reprisal, Gavriil Popov quickly justified this action, suggesting that "left radicals" had become dangerous to perestroika (*MN*, November 12, 1989).

Karpinski came to Gorbachev's defense during the election campaign when a candidate accused the leader of "the deception of the people" (*MN*, May 21, 1989), and Kariakin reprimanded the Congress of People's Deputies because speakers "too often are rude" to the General Secretary (*Iz.*, June 3, 1989). All laudatory records were broken, however, by Aitmatov, who, as the main speaker proposing Gorbachev's foreclosed candidacy for the position of president, outdid himself with a pathetic ode in honor of the leader. He presented him as a hero who decided, out of altruistic motives, to save the country, a man "with striking flexibility," a person "who more than any other recognizes the importance of the rebirth of the people," and so on (*P.*, May 26, 1989). These statements sounded outlandish even when coming from the mouth of a liberal advocate of democratization.

In accordance with official policy, the liberal intellectuals were extremely cautious with their political activities during this period and avoided any confrontation with the leadership. Even in the matter of creating a memorial for Stalin's victims (the decision to do this was raised at the Twenty-second Party Congress in 1961 and then "forgotten"), the intellectuals comported themselves rather timidly. Early in 1988 young educated people (not prominent intellectuals) started gathering signatures for an appeal to the Kremlin about building the monument. Only after the formal approval of the idea at the Nineteenth Party Conference did leading intellectuals flock to support it publicly (*LG*, July 6, 1988).

Despite the backdrop of caution, the first signs of dissent were seen in

1988. The first clash between Gorbachev and the liberals in the establishment developed during the Nineteenth Party Conference, when Gorbachev supported the conservative majority in its rude attacks against intellectuals and the mass media. In late 1988, however, following the conference, almost all leading liberals kept silent on this development as well as on the draft of the new electoral law. Despite significant improvements, the draft was disappointing in its contrivances. For example, although the new electoral law represented major progress, it was still designed to guarantee the party's control over the election. While a few intellectuals criticized the law only mildly (G. Popov 1988d; N. Popov 1988), Sakharov dared to air strong grievances publicly, both in the USSR and during his first trip abroad (Sakharov 1988, 1989b).

It is important to note that most prominent liberal intellectuals avoided participating in the activities of the informal groups and organization that mushroomed in 1987–1988. For the most part, they avoided all such organizations that demanded real democratization, such as Democratic Alliance (led by Novodvorskaia), Democratic Perestroika (led by Oleg Rumiantsev), the All Union Social and Political Club (led by Kagarlit;ki), and others (see Maliutin 1988; Rumiantsev 1988, p. 9). Likewise, no prominent intellectuals participated in the August 1987 meeting of several informal organizations with political interests (about this meeting see *KP*, January 31, 1988). Only in June 1988 did Afanasiev, for example, take part in a meeting of "autonomous organizations sharing socialist principles" (*MN*, June 19, 1988). In April 1989 A. Rumiantsev mockingly referred to these liberals as "Messrs. liberals," "status liberals," "foremen of perestroika," and "rebels of the creative unions and the liberal-democratic periodicals" who avoided participating "in the real struggle of the democratic movement" (Rumiantsev 1989, p. 5).

Later in 1988 intellectuals started to play active roles in the informal organization, Memorial, and then in Moscow Tribune. In spring 1989, liberal writers created their own alternative club, April, which challenged the official Union of Soviet Writers. Several prominent intellectuals were active in both groups (e.g., Afanasiev, Adamovich, Kariakin, Sakharov, Batkin, Sagdeiev, and Vadim Sokolov).

In contrast to the 1960s, none of the liberals (with the exception of Sakharov), even those belonging to the vanguard, dared raise their voices in support of prisoners, refuseniks, or those held in psychiatric hospitals. The activities of former prisoners Sergei Grigoriants and Lev Timofeiev received no support from activists of perestroika (see Grigoriants's article in *The New York Times*, February 23, 1988, and May 10, 1988).

The *entente cordiale* between Gorbachev and the liberal intellectuals finally ended during the first session of the Congress of People's Deputies. Once again, Sakharov openly and defiantly challenged the leader and the whole congress, accusing them of self-deception and a willingness to leave the existing political order intact while using glasnost as a sort of cosmetic. The final minutes of the congress dramatically revealed several things: Gorbachev's duality, the deep hostility of the majority of the deputies picked by the party apparatus toward the liberal intelligentsia, and the determination of the bravest intellectuals to continue as an oppositional force in their struggle for democracy.

Despite the stormy objections of the audience, Gorbachev followed his self-congratulatory speech by permitting Sakharov to take the podium. However, when Sakharov did not stop directing accusations against Gorbachev and his "compliant aggressive majority," Gorbachev switched off Sakharov's microphone (*Iz.*, June 11, 1989). Along with Sakharov, a few other intellectuals, mostly writers (e.g., Drutse, Adamovich, Chernichenko) and also a few scholars (e.g., Afanasiev, economists Emelianov and Popov) bravely opposed the booing and heckling of the official majority.

In late 1989, as the country's political and economic situations continued to worsen, increasing numbers of liberals began to defy Gorbachev, casting doubt on both his real intentions and on his ability to lead the USSR toward a new society. In 1990 Gorbachev, preoccupied with trying to halt the country's slide toward chaos, abandoned his role as an innovator. Liberals, having lost all hope in the party's ability to act effectively, began setting the agenda for the democratization and privatization of Soviet society.

RUSSOPHILE IDEOLOGY IN THE PERIOD OF GLASNOST

Glasnost permitted Russophiles (as well as their opponents) to publicly develop their views on crucial social and political issues. Moreover, the exacerbation of the ideological struggle of the late 1980s forced them to define more clearly their positions on subjects they had ignored in the 1970s.

The most significant event in the evolution of the Russophiles in the latter 1980s was the transformation of xenophobia and anti-Semitism into central tenets of their credo. Since 1986 they have launched increasingly belligerent broadsides against Western culture, life-style, and political and economic order.

The Expansion of Xenophobia and Anti-Semitism

The dominant feature of the Russophile movement in 1985–1989 was its increasingly radical and hostile stance toward the West and the Jews. The major figures took the lead in the xenophobic and anti-Semitic campaigns. In the late 1980s, Bondarev and P. Proskurin became the most fervent detractors of the effects of Western mass culture on Russia. Russian culture, along with the Russian national character, were, according to Proskurin, the main targets "for the most aggressive forces that try to undermine our state foundation" (*Literaturnaia Rossia*, October 16, 1987; see also Bondarev 1987a).

Attacks on rock music were typical among Russophiles during this period. Rock music was declared the devil incarnate, a weapon in the West's war against Russia. Leading figures in the Russophile movement such as Iuri Bondarev, Rasputin, Astafiev, and others were preoccupied with the denunciation of rock music (see the speeches at the Congress of Russian Writers in December 1985; Bondarev 1987a; Rasputin 1988a, p. 171; *NS*, no. 10, 1988, with three articles against rock music).

Xenophobic ideas were developed by Russophiles such as Belov, who, in his novel *All Ahead*, portrayed the demoralizing role played by Moscow's Westernized intellectuals in Russian society (Belov 1986), and by other authors as well (see Vykhodtsev 1988; for an analysis of the anti-Western tendencies of Russophile literature, see T. Ivanova 1988, pp. 27–28).

Still, the main target of the Russophiles in the late 1980s was not the West as such, but rather the Jews. As discussed in earlier chapters, anti-Semitism was a leading theme in the Russophile publications of the 1970s. Some of these publications, however, stopped short of shifting universal responsibility for practically every flaw of Soviet society to the "alien" or "nomadic" (as opposed to "settled," i.e., Russian) elements in Soviet society.

Moreover, many intellectuals with great sympathy for Russophilism remained silent on the Jewish issue in the 1970s, no matter what their feelings toward Jews. None of the representatives of the "rural prose" school, such as Rasputin or Astafiev, ever hinted to their liberal admirers, including Jews (such as myself), that in the next decade they would spout the most rabid anti-Semitic invectives (for a sad reflection on this issue, see Pomerants 1988, p. 28).

The start of the strong anti-Semitic campaign came in 1986, when the public learned, through samizdat, about the correspondence between Eidel'man and Astafiev that had been provoked by Astafiev's anti-Semitic slurs in *Sad Detective* (1986b) and his *The Catching of Gudgeons in Georgia* (1986a), which ridiculed Georgians. Astafiev's response to Eidel'man's rebukes was replete with comments suggesting a passionate loathing of Jews; he characterized Eidel'man's letter as "filled with the overboiled pus of Jewish high intellectual arrogance." This response startled the intellectual community, which had respected Astafiev as a high moral authority in the country, and led to the escalation of anti-Semitism among the Russophiles (see the correspondence between the two authors in *SiM.*, December 1986, pp. 54–58).

Fueled by their hatred of the Jews, Russophiles regularly inveighed against Jews, demanding their expulsion from their positions in Soviet society (for example, writer Vladimir Gorbachev did so at a meeting in Moscow; about this meeting, see Evtushenko's article in *MN*, June 12, 1987). Some Russophiles, such as Vladimir Lichutin in Riasan in December 1988, even called for the creation of reservations for Jews and other minorities (*Og.*, no. 4, 1989, p. 31).

The litmus test for the Russophile community was its attitude toward the group Pamiat (Memory), an openly anti-Semitic organization founded in 1986. Some Russophiles, such as Rasputin (1988a, p. 170), Kuniaev (1989, *NS*, no. 6, pp. 157–159), and the economist Mikhail Lemeshev, openly sided with this organization (*SK*, November 24, 1987), while others, like Astafiev or Glazunov, did not openly express their support of Pamiat, but nevertheless failed to condemn it.

In 1987–1988, Russophiles organized a number of meetings, conferences, and seminars designed to propagate their anti-Semitic views (for instance, at Leningrad University in November 1987, see *SK*, November 24, 1987; in Riasan, December 1988, see *LG*, December 23, 1988, and *Og.*, no. 4, 1989, p. 31; in Moscow, January 1989, see *MN*, March 26, 1989). As of March 1990, the peak of the anti-Semitic campaign was attained with *Nash Sovremennik*'s publication of Shafarevich's book *About Russophobia*, a genuine Soviet version of *Mein Kampf* (*NS*, no. 6 and 11, 1989), and with a November 1989 meeting of the board of the RSFSR Writers' Union, at which a number of speakers (including Belov, Tatiana Glushkova, Anatoli Builov, and others) dropped all pretenses, abandoned the use of the term of Zionist, and openly denounced Jews as a dangerous minority (see *Nedelia*, November 26, 1989).

This meeting was followed soon after by a pogrom against members of the liberal organization, April. On January 18, 1990, members of this organization, including writers such as Okudzhava, Kurchatkin, and others, were physically attacked during a meeting at the Moscow Club of Writers by Pamiat' storm troopers shouting anti-Semitic slogans (about this attack, see *Og*, no. 5, 1990, pp. 2–3; see also *MN*, January 28, 1990).

In the 1980s Russian nationalists extended their hostility to many ethnic Russian authors—especially if the authors were suspected of having less than 100 percent pure Russian blood—who were either friendly to the nationalists' enemies or praised by them. Their enmity toward Vysotski, Okudzhava, Korotich, Evtushenko, and El'dar Riazanov stemmed from the "impurity" of these authors' bloodlines (Kazintsev 1987; Kuniaev 1985).[2] Even Dmitri Likhachev, a liberal Russophile intellectual,

---

[2] The hatred of Korotich reached its peak during the election campaign of winter 1989,

was targeted in several attacks because he was considered too tolerant of Western culture and Jews, particularly of Marc Chagall (see Vykhodtsev 1988, pp. 167–168).

In late 1989, Russophiles were particularly fervent in their attacks on Anatoli Ananiev, accusing him of promoting Russophobia through the publication of Grossman's novels and Andrei Siniavski's essay "The walks with Pushkin" in *Oktiabr'* (no. 4, 1989), and insisting that he be dismissed as the journal's editor (*MN*, January 14, 1990). The Leningrad Writers' Union was also targeted by the Russophiles, who claimed that it was controlled by Jews (see *Moskovski Literator*, December 22, 1989; *LR*, January 12, 1990); similar accusations were leveled against the association April.

For the most part, Russophiles showed no favor for those Jewish authors, such as Irina Rodnianskaia, who, since the 1970s, had in various ways demonstrated their respect for Russophile ideology and its followers (see the invectives hurled at Rodnianskaia in Tatiana Glushkova's article, *Nash Sovremennik*, no. 7, 1989, pp. 169–170).

But, of course, the Russophiles of the 1980s assailed with special hatred those Jews whom they considered the main heralds of Perestroika, such as Shatrov, Gel'man, and Rybakov.

The Defense of Stalin

The next most prominent subject in the Russophile ideology of the late 1980s was socialism, as it had been constructed by Stalin. As mentioned earlier, Russophiles, particularly "patriots," tried to fuse their advocacy of Russian exceptionalism with both socialism and the cult of Stalin, while traditionalists combined their nationalism with the rejection of all elements of official ideology. In the late 1980s, however, bound by the logic of their struggle against the Westernizers, most traditionalists became such ardent advocates of Stalinism that they forgot, as some of them had in the 1970s, their hatred of official Marxist ideology.

Anatoli Ivanov clearly expressed this fusion of Russophilism and Stalinism, arguing that liberals "treated all of the prerevolutionary history of Russia as total obscurantism" and "described all of postrevolutionary history as negative" (Ivanov 1987b, p. 6). An author in *Nash Sovremennik* equated "anti-Sovietism" with "Russophobia," clearly demonstrating the

---

when his candidacy for the Congress of People's Deputies was advanced in Moscow. Shouting anti-Semitic slogans (e.g., "death to kikes"), about seventy demonstrators disrupted a meeting at which Korotich had an excellent chance of being nominated as a candidate (*Og.*, no. 3, 1989, p. 31).

way in which Russophiles incorporate Stalinism into their ideology (*NS*, no. 1, 1987, p. 185).

Several Russophiles were actively repressing the growing avalanche of information about Stalin's heinous deeds and about the major developments of the Stalin era, such as industrialization, collectivization, and the conduct of the war against Hitler. Their defense of Stalin centered primarily around justifying his deeds as a necessary evil in the preparation for the inevitable war with the West (see Alexeiev's article in *LG*, 1987, p. 11; Chalmaiev's and other authors' articles in *Moskva*, no. 4, 1988; Rosliakov's article in *LG*, August 28, 1987; Kulikov 1988, p. 145).

At the same time, in order to save Stalin's name, Russophile patriots who had condemned the atrocities of the civil war or collectivization intensified their efforts to attribute these atrocities to Jews such as Trotsky, G. Zinoviev, Kamenev, Volodarski (whose real name was Mikhail Gol'dstein), Iakov Iakovlev (whose real name was Epstein, the Minister of Agriculture in the 1930s), Lazar' Kaganovich, and Grigori Kaminski (Belov 1983, pp. 274–275; Kozhinov 1988, p. 174; Kuniaev 1988a, pp. 182–183; Pikul' and Zhuravlev 1989; see Anatoli Ivanov's interview in *NS*, no. 5, 1988, p. 175).

Some peculiar evidence used by patriots in their defense of Stalin included positive references to Stalin in the memoirs of his contemporaries and political partners such as Sir Winston Churchill, Theodore Roosevelt, and Charles de Gaulle (Andreieva 1988), as well as the wide admiration for Stalin among Western intellectuals of the 1930s, such as that depicted in Barbuse's *Stalin* (Kozhinov 1988, p. 163; Lanshchikov 1988, p. 128; *Molodaia Gvardia*, no. 3, 1988).

Ironically, Russophiles found themselves somewhat in agreement with the most radical liberals in their criticism of the emphasis several authors, especially Rybakov and Shatrov, put on the dictator's personal qualities. They countered these remarks by characterizing Stalin as "a great state leader who turned our country into a powerful industrial state in a short period and gained in the war against Nazism" and insisting that some of Stalin's misdeeds were dictated by historical necessity, that "history is being written not only with ink but also with blood" (Baigushev 1988, pp. 188–189; Kozhinov 1988; Lanshchikov 1988, pp. 126, 133; see also *Molodaia Gvardia*, no. 12, 1989, pp. 170–203).

In the late 1980s, as in the 1970s, a significant number of traditionalist Russophiles, such as Astafiev and Soloukhin, were still unable to reconcile themselves with Marxism, the October Revolution, and many of Stalin's deeds. As they had in the 1970s, many of them continued to present the October Revolution as a plot by non-Russians (particularly Jews) against the Russian people, and to see Stalin as an agent of Masonry and Jews (Shafarevich 1989).

An Almost Open Hatred of Gorbachev's Program

Being unaccustomed to opposing the authorities, Russophiles pretended at first to be loyal to Gorbachev and to support perestroika. By 1987 and especially 1988, however, it had become clear that Russophiles were strongly opposed to the major elements of Gorbachev's program, which essentially assumed the Westernization of Soviet society. During these years, the Russophiles were generally outspoken in their dissatisfaction with perestroika and its destructive impact on Russia. Although direct attacks on Gorbachev were avoided at first, Russophiles did criticize all the leading supporters of perestroika, such as Korotich or A. N. Iakovlev (see, for instance, Bondarev's article in *SR*, March 25, 1987).

Beginning in 1987, when Bondarev compared the state of affairs in the country with that before the victory in Stalingrad during the war, Russophiles began raising alarms and predicting the collapse of society unless liberals, Westernizers, and Jews were deprived of power (see A. Ivanov 1987b; Kazintsev 1988, pp. 167–168; *LR*, December 23, 1988). As A. Ivanov put it, "The party loses control over society, permitting the free way to the forces of destruction" (*NS*, no. 5, 1988, p. 174).

The 1988 meeting of the secretaries of the Russian Writers' Union in Riasan provided a noteworthy example of Russophile sentiment, as the participants of the meeting—all leading Russophiles—openly assailed Gorbachev's policy as leading to chaos and moral degradation (see *LG*, 1988, p. 43; see also *Og.*, no. 52, 1988, pp. 13–15).

During 1989–1990, as the country's political polarization increased, Russophiles moved toward open, undisguised attacks against Gorbachev and blatantly accused him of the destruction of Russia, Russian culture, Russian statehood, and the morals of Russians. Moreover, they accused him of staging a new, post-1917 revolution and shattering the basis of Russian society, destroying its morals, traditions, and historical continuity, and plunging it into chaos once again (see the gloomy description of the situation in the country in Prokhanov 1990; see also Oleg Mikhailov's article in *LG*, October 11, 1989).

Opposition to Open Markets and Privatization

As mentioned earlier, the Russophiles of the 1970s lacked even an elementary economic program of their own. With the advent of perestroika and the liberals' proposal of radical economic reforms, they began to develop their own vision of the Russian economy as well as search for arguments against the vision of the liberals.

The Russophiles were divided, however, in their views on economic matters. The Russophile patriots gravitated toward justifying the state's control over the economy and underscoring the role of collectivism in the lives of prerevolutionary peasants and craftsmen. By contrast, the traditionalists, with their hatred of the Soviet system, were inclined, with some reservations, to support privatization in the countryside but not in the city. Given the dominance of the patriots in the 1980s, their economic views were supported by the majority of the Russophiles.

Like the populists of the late nineteenth century, many (but not all) Russophile patriots rejected the privatization of the Soviet economy, arguing that privatization was alien to Russian traditions and to socialist ideals, both of which argue against social differentiation and place social justice and moral values above purely economic considerations (see, for instance, the report about the meeting of Russian writers in Riasan, *LG*, December 23, 1988, pp. 3–4; Salutski 1988, pp. 148–152, 156–160).

Again harking back to the Russian populists and their adulation of Russian *obshchina* (rural collective communities) and *arteli* (teams of workers), the Russophiles presented collectivism and mutual support as the most valuable features of Russian tradition—features which, in their opinion, were required for the revitalization of Russian villages (Antonov 1986, pp. 17; Kozhinov 1987, pp. 168–169).

Mikhail Antonov, a leading Russophile economist, went so far as to assert that there was a Russian political economy which, reflecting "our national character and Russian mind," rejected material wealth as the highest value (a value typical, according to Antonov, of Western economies since Adam Smith) and placed moral values at the center of economic activity (Antonov 1986, pp. 15–17). In his opposition to a free-market economy, he offered a concept of Russian socialism that does not tolerate a "satisfied life, one not enlightened by the highest ideals regarding national historical goals," and that is also concerned with ecological problems (Antonov 1989, p. 149). To counter the protests raised in the 1920s against Stalin's industrialization (particularly those from the famous Nikolai Kondratiev, who "defended market economy" and was "indeed anti-Marxist and counterrevolutionary in the eyes of the party"), Antonov contended that during this period "it was possible to arouse the Russian people, who had accomplished the greatest revolution and won the civil war, only for heroic work, with an extraordinary task set before them—to build a powerful state, a model of social justice for all mankind. However, it would have been impossible to excite them with the perspective of slow everyday life and an increase of only five kopecks on each ruble of salary every five years" (Antonov 1989, p. 137).

While liberals, in the person of Strelianyi, attacked *obshchina* as "coerced collectivism," "beneficial only for unable, inert, and submissive people" (Strelianyi 1987, p. 245), Russophiles, in the person of Salutski, rejected Strelianyi's arguments, passionately defending *obshchina* as an effective economic mechanism (Salutski 1988, pp. 144–148).

Most Russophiles were inimical to all aspects of privatization—market regulation of the economy (flexible and equilibrium pricing, profit as a major criterion of economic performance, etc.), private farms and cooperatives, and, of course, intensive cooperation with the West and joint enterprises that depended on foreign capital. The Russophiles clearly opposed "the capitalistic way of development" in agriculture as well as in other branches of the economy (Antonov 1988, p. 5; Ivanov and Svininnikov 1988, p. 178; Kulikov 1988, p. 156; Ochkin 1987; Salutski 1987, 1988).

Unlike "patriots," most traditionalists, with their ardent hatred of collectivization, were very supportive of privatization in the countryside. These Russophiles, like Belov (see his speeches at the Congress of People's Deputies on June 1 and December 20, 1989; *Iz.*, June 2, 1989; *LG*, December 20, 1989), had little faith in the collectivistic spirit of the Russian peasants, recognized the demoralization of the peasants following collectivization, and realized that only the independent peasants, as the masters of the land they tilled, could save the country from its impending food crisis. As a result, these Russophiles considered the peasants to be the single hope for resurrecting the countryside. But even the Russophiles usually avoided praising private farmers, choosing instead to underscore the role of the peasants' mutual support (Astafiev 1988; Vasiliev 1988).

In general, Russophile ideology in the late 1980s was very close to Soviet ideology in the late 1940s, when Stalin combined Russian chauvinism with Marxist dogmas, clearly emphasizing the former ingredient. Like Stalin's propagandists fifty year earlier, the average Russophile praised the uniqueness and superiority of Russia and the leading role of Russians in the Soviet empire, fomented hatred of foreign countries and Jews, and presented the October Revolution and the socialist society built by Stalin as the Russian challenge to the decaying Western world. While in the 1970s Russophile ideology fought on two fronts—against official Marxist ideology and against liberals—in the latter 1980s it had only one adversary.

THE RUSSOPHILES IN ACTION

Although the Russophiles' activities from 1985 to 1989 were far less visible than those of the liberals, they remained far from defeat and vigorously promoted their ideas.

Like the liberals, the old guard of Russophiles (those from the late 1960s and the 1970s) made up the core of the Russophile camp in 1986–

1989. This group included Kozhinov, Sergei Vikulov, Proskurin, and Anatoli Ivanov.

In addition to the old-guard Russophiles, a significant number of intellectuals shifted their alliances toward the Russophile camp. Included in this group were old liberals such as Bondarev and Gulyga, as well as new names such as historian Apollon Kuz'min, writers Vladimir Krupin, Iuri Kuznetsov, and Vladimir Lichutin, critics Piotr Vykhodtsev, Tatiana Glushkova, and Vladimir Bondarenko, and theater expert Liubomudrov.

In 1985–1989 the Russian nationalists seized every opportunity to challenge the liberals. With their significant influence in the Writers' Union, they usually outnumbered their opponents at the podium, particularly from 1985 to 1986 (see Bondarev 1987a). They energetically attacked the liberals at the Nineteenth Party Conference, enjoying the clear support of the majority of the conference participants. For example, Bondarev's extremely aggressive speech was received with a near-ovation by the same delegates who had tried to use catcalls to remove Baklanov from the platform (*P.*, July 2, 1988; see also Soviet TV, June 26, 1988). As People's Deputies, Rasputin and Belov also exploited opportunities to denounce their enemies, who "impose moral pluralism on the country along with the propaganda of sex and violence in the mass media" (*Iz.*, June 8, 1989).

As mentioned before, the liberal intellectuals and the liberal mass media clearly had a strong influence on the mentality of the Soviet people. Similarly, Russophiles can point to data collected in 1988–1989 which suggest that they, too, have a solid constituency in Soviet society, and that those who today espouse liberal ideas may tomorrow become ardent supporters of Russian chauvinism. For example, 50.4 percent of the respondents in the late 1988 nationwide survey conducted by the Center of Public Opinion Studies endorsed the "necessity of restoring order in the country" as the major way to improve life in the country.

Similarly, when asked to indicate "who profits most from the changes [supposedly liberal reforms] in the country," 39.6 percent of the respondents pointed to members of private cooperatives, 20.7 percent to "crooks, tricksters," and 13.6 percent to "private businessmen," while only 30 percent mentioned "those who work honestly" and 15.2 percent identified those "who work in the self-supporting enterprises." It is also remarkable that 21.6 percent of all respondents (many of whom were non-Russians) thought that "the next year would bring more actions in favor of the Russian people," and that 37 percent indicated that "newspapers and magazines do not publish enough material about the fate of the Russian people."

In addition to the "negative" activities of the Russophiles from 1985 to 1988 (e.g., the propagation of chauvinistic and xenophobic views, the defense of Stalin, etc)., "positive" efforts were concentrated in three spheres: the preservation of nature, the battle against drunkenness, and the maintenance of Russia's cultural heritage.

The Salvation of Russia's Ecology

As mentioned earlier, Brezhnev's regime created catastrophic ecological situations in many regions of the country. Russophiles, especially writers such as Rasputin, Belov, and Krupin, comprised the vanguard of the intellectual community's efforts to improve the country's ecological situation.

Given their worship of both the past and the countryside, it was only natural that by the 1970s Russophiles had declared themselves enemies of unrestrained technological progress, which they considered a threat to nature. In his marvelous *Farewell Matera* in 1976, Rasputin was probably the first to defy Soviet dogma espousing the beneficial role of technological progress.

In the late 1980s, Russophiles transformed a number of congresses and meetings of writers into battles against bureaucrats whom they considered guilty of destroying nature (for instance, the meeting of Russian writers in December 1985, and the eighth meeting of the Soviet writers in 1986; see *LG*, December 18, 1985; see also Belov 1988; Markov et al. 1988, pp. 32, 35, 399, 403). In addition, *Nash Sovremennik* became one of the most active fighters in the ecological movement.

The Devotion to Russian Cultural Heritage

Throughout the latter 1980s the Russophiles remained the group that was most concerned with the protection of historical monuments and other elements of the Russian cultural heritage. Having created, in the 1960s, a society for the preservation of historical monuments, they intensified their activities in the late 1980s, enjoying the direct support of Gorbachev's regime. The new policy toward religion bolstered the Russophiles' campaign to save old churches and monasteries, as well as buildings connected with major figures of Russian history and culture (see Rasputin 1988a). With equal fervor, Russophiles championed the preservation of the purity of the Russian language, folklore, and forgotten figures in literature and the arts (Markov et al. 1988, pp. 83, 143–144).

The Struggle against Drunkenness

Claiming that drunkenness in Russia is foisted on Russians by Jews and other forces inimical to Russia, Russophiles presented their anti-alcoholic campaign as a major responsibility.

One of Pamiat's first centers was created in Academic Town in Novosibirsk, its major goal being the struggle against drunkenness and its Jewish sponsors. A few other Pamiat centers were created following the Novosibirsk model, particularly in Karelia.

The fight against alcoholism became a dominant topic in magazines with Russophile tendencies (see, for instance, *NS*, no. 7, 1987, and no. 3, 1988).

CONCLUSION

For liberal intellectuals in the Soviet Union, Gorbachev's glasnost was the happiest period in all Soviet history. For the first time, the political elite considered liberal intellectuals its allies and encouraged their political activism. Intellectuals responded with almost unrestrained support of the regime, and performed many important tasks, including the denunciation of the country's Stalinist past and the present bureaucracy, and the elaboration of various projects for the political leadership. At the same time, intellectuals almost completely abandoned their role as critics of the current regime, only partially returning to this role in 1990.

The liberal intellectuals were actively challenged by the Russophiles, who declared themselves opponents of liberal reforms and the Westernization of society. The conflict between liberals and Russophiles, which drew the combative energy of the intellectuals, was the center of the intellectual community in 1985–1989. The outcome of this conflict will be inextricably intertwined with the future of Gorbachev's experiment.

Conclusion

THE HISTORY of the Soviet intellectuals in the post-Stalin era contains many elements typical not only to the life of the creative intelligentsia (i.e., scholars, writers, film directors, and other professionals engaged in creative work) in socialist countries but also to that in any other country with a powerful state.

Those studying the lives of intellectuals will find numerous similarities between the sufferings of writers or scholars in the USSR (or Poland or China) and those of intellectuals in France in the eighteenth century, in prerevolutionary Russia, in Latin American countries ruled by military juntas, or in any other country or at any other time when the intellectuals' main employer is the state.

By contrast, outside of a few commonalities, the lives of intellectuals in socialist societies are radically different from those in capitalist societies, especially the United States. Here, the intellectuals, the professionals, and the mass intelligentsia are, as a group, not distinctly different from any other part of the middle class. Only at the height of McCarthyism did the lives of American intellectuals compare to those of their colleagues in socialist societies.

To summarize briefly, in this book we have examined the role of the Soviet intellectual community in the country's arduous transition from a socialist society shaped in the 1920s and 1930s (whatever one may call it: Stalinist, administrative-command, hegemonic, authoritarian, totalitarian, etc.) to a Western-type society, complete with Western economic and political institutions, or, as Gorbachev's theorists refer to it, "the present human civilization," which in their interpretation resembles the United States or Western Europe.

During the post-Stalin era, Soviet intellectuals traversed three periods—Khrushchev's thaw, Brezhnev's mild repressions and corruption, and Gorbachev's spring. These periods, each a special experiment, revealed various qualities of the creative intelligentsia, especially their relationship with the political elite.

In the two periods when Soviet society took steps toward liberalization, the intellectual community was a major political actor. In general, the Soviet intellectual community conveyed a Western blueprint for the transformation of the country, although it was almost completely unable to produce its own economic, social, or political conceptualization of the society it desired. Ironically, the Stalinists were much more original in the 1920s and 1930s, inventing several institutions unknown in the past.

Soviet intellectuals played a much more important role in transforming their society during the first period of modernization (the 1960s) than during the second period (the late 1980s).

The intellectuals of the 1960s were:

1. The only source of ideas for transforming Soviet society;
2. The only group to provide society with a model of moral virtue;
3. The only mouthpiece of the masses; and
4. The only political force to prompt the leadership to modernize the country.

In the late 1980s, the intellectuals' role in the modernization of Soviet society remained crucial, if somewhat more modest:

1. The intellectuals lost their monopoly as a source of ideas regarding modernization and shared the creation of social projects with members of the political elite, who were directly influenced by the West, as well as with the mass intelligentsia, the youth, and the rest of the population.

2. The role of the intellectuals as moral standard-bearers for the country significantly changed in the 1980s. The role of the intellectuals as moral standard-bearers for the country significantly changed in the 1980s. Although the opinions of intellectuals such as Sakharov and Likhachev remained extremely important for the Soviet population, the number of intellectuals who were considered moral authorities was much smaller in Gorbachev's time than in the 1960s, and much smaller than the number in Poland or Czechoslovakia in the late 1980s.

To a very great extent, the decline of the intellectuals' moral prestige had its genesis in the 1970s. This period, while free of mass repressions, demonstrated how successful the political elite in a nondemocratic society can frighten and corrupt the intellectuals, driving them to participate in the most contemptible ideological and political actions, including cooperation with the secret police.

3. Glasnost, with its relatively free mass media, almost totally deprived writers and movie directors of their role as the only conduit for public opinion. Comparatively free public discussions, torrents of genuine letters to the editors published in newspapers and weeklies, and access by ordinary people to television all served to radically diminish the political role previously played in the forms of poetry, films, and paintings.

4. Liberal Russian intellectuals also appeared far less active in the 1980s than was the case in the 1960s. Soviet experience suggests that the intellectuals are most active as an oppositional force when the regime is moving from mass terror to limited repressions. When the political elite radically liberalizes society, as was the case in the Soviet Union, Poland, Hungary, and elsewhere in the 1980s, the opposition became much larger and more heterogeneous.

Moreover, with the liberalization of society, other political actors, such as the youth (particularly young professionals), members of the mass intelligentsia, workers, and nationalists, become much more aggressive toward the old political and economic structures than do the intellectuals. The mass strikes in the USSR in July 1989 are very telling in this respect. Although spurred primarily by economic discontent, the strikers in many cities (especially the coal miners' strikes in Kuzbass) also made several purely political demands with clear democratic overtones (e.g., autonomy for their enterprises, the immediate democratic election of local authorities, the creation of independent trade unions). Never did the intellectuals or even the mass intelligentsia defy the authorities as did the workers in the strikes of summer 1989.

Intellectuals in the national republics also turned out to be much more daring than were Russian liberals. Inspired by the ideas of national survival and independence, intellectuals in the Baltic republics, Armenia, Moldavia, and Georgia demonstrated in 1987–1989 a level of valor that clearly surpassed that exhibited by their colleagues in Moscow or Leningrad.

Still, even in the extremely liberal climate of 1985–1989, prominent intellectuals continued to be important for being the most consistent in their support of modernization and for being the most able to expose the past to deep critical analysis and to create new social projects and a new ideology.

The political struggle surrounding the Congress of People's Deputies—including the election campaign and the polemics at sessions of the congress (January–June 1989)—proved liberal intellectuals to be the leading power challenging the system during this period. For example, intellectual deputies created the first oppositional group in the new Soviet parliament (The Moscow Group, which then was transformed into the Interregional Group).

At the same time, however, developments in 1985–1989 continued to indicate that the threshold for the intellectuals' cooperation with the political leadership is relatively low. A leader demonstrating sympathy for the intellectuals and taking steps on the road toward liberalization can, as Soviet experience suggests, relatively easily gain the uncritical support of the intellectual community.

Unity with a supreme political power that encourages and respects creative work is the realization of the wildest dreams of the intellectuals of the past. Under these conditions, it becomes possible to relish an intimacy with power and official privilege without feeling the compunctions of conscience, as was the case in the 1970s. This situation is so comfortable that many intellectuals prefer to relinquish their role as the oppositional force in society in order to become the leader's troubadours and even join his apparatus. These intellectuals persuade themselves (and not without reason) that, under the circumstances, it makes more sense to back the leader in his fight with conservatives (even if, in fact, the leader occasionally allies with apparatchiks against the liberal intellectuals, as was the case with Gorbachev at the Nineteenth Party Conference in the summer of 1988 and the Congress of People's Deputies in the summer of 1989) than to be critical of him and push him, through his irritation with the ingratitude of liberal intellectuals, into the embrace of the political right.

Status and age differences between intellectuals are manifested quite clearly during liberal periods such as Gorbachev's. Older intellectuals holding high official positions and enjoying a relatively high standard of living are particularly inclined to confine themselves to the role of the leader's lieutenants, even if they occasionally appear more radical than their superior. Young professionals behave much more aggressively toward the regime than do "status intellectuals," joining semi-legal organizations and engaging in critiques of the liberal leader.

An *entente cordiale* between the leader and the intellectual community in a Soviet-type society cannot survive if it fails to transform quickly into "a normal civilized society," to use the terminology of perestroika. It is likely, however, that, for present socialist societies, the transformation into normal civilized societies will be quite long and of a necessarily cyclical character, as has been the case for other societies on their way to democratic order. The regimes of Khrushchev, Brezhnev, and Gorbachev are but initial stages in a long process of Westernization that began in Russia early in the eighteenth century.

The first draft of this book was finished in 1983, when Brezhnev's regime, as well as its anti-intellectual policy, appeared unshakable. At that time, it seemed as though "the betrayal of the clerks," in this case the Soviet intellectuals and their ideals, would continue indefinitely. Yet, being confident of the cyclical character of Westernization as well as of the dynamics in the relationship between the political elite and intellectuals, I was sure that the persecution and corruption of the intellectuals would not last forever, and that a new phase of political evolution would occasion the courting of the creative intelligentsia by the political leadership.

Now, alas, I envision yet another phase, but, in this case, one far more gloomy.

Gorbachev's liberal regime is, by definition, unable to live up to its promises, as is any regime in the process of transition. By early 1990, numerous developments threatened the maintenance of order in the country. These developments included an increase in violent crime, countless interethnic conflicts, increased feudalization in the country (with regions refusing to sell deficit goods to one another), a total demoralization throughout all levels and all spheres of society, increasing social envy and cruelty, and loss of respect for all Soviet institutions (from the party and the central government to the army, police, and courts, not to mention the trade unions, Komsomol, and other official public organizations).

All of these destructive processes were fueled by, and in turn stimulated, the decline in the economy, the destruction of the consumer market, and the deterioration of the population's standard of living. Therefore, it is very likely that Gorbachev's regime will be followed by one characterized by "counter-reforms," although not all his achievements will be eradicated, even if Gorbachev then leads society back to his original goals, as was the case with Alexander II in the 1860s.

In the aftermath of glasnost, the liberals and the mass media will be the first to be blamed for the failures of the previous regime, and the confrontations between the political leadership and the intellectual community will thus be renewed.

Once again, history will witness the public betrayal of liberal ideas by a number of prominent intellectuals, including the heroes of perestroika, whom the new regime will no doubt be especially interested in recruiting. These heroes will find many arguments, some of them relatively new, for justifying their collaboration with the new regime, and will abandon the colleagues and friends who will be persecuted by the new administration.

As has happened in the past, Russophiles, in alliance with Stalinists, will be used by the political elite to defy the majority of the intellectuals. And, as in the past, especially during the 1970s, the distance between the public and private lives of the intellectuals, as well as those of the rest of the population, will again be widened drastically.

Still, a significant number of intellectuals (probably more than in the 1970s, although only the scope of repressions will determine how many) will, at very great risk, publicly defend their convictions of the previous phase and will become models for subsequent generations. By and large, these will be people in their thirties and forties. The protests of their more aged colleagues will be manifested only in silence and in the refusal to publicly justify changes in official policy.

Several elements of the civil society born in the 1980s will probably survive the conservative offensive, and a number of intellectuals, especially among the young, will find refuge in abandoning their work for the state and preserving their integrity and their allegiance to democratic ideals. Still others will flee the country. Civil society, even in its fledgling form, will prevent the gap between natural scientists and humanitarians from reaching the proportions seen in the 1960s and 1970s.

The liberals' defeat will have the same deleterious effect on the morals of the intellectuals as did the political reaction of the 1970s. The gradual but strong increase in cynicism that occurred during the Brezhnev era will be even stronger following the collapse of glasnost.

At the same time, however, the process of emancipation from the influence of socialist ideals will continue throughout the next period, as will the further decline of the ideals of Soviet or Russian exclusiveness. The average Russian intellectual will increasingly feel himself or herself to be a member of the world democratic community, and will in no way differ from his or her Western colleagues in attitudes toward major political or social issues. Only some catastrophic event able to propel the state, with its extraordinary dictatorial measures, into the position of savior of the nation would be able to counteract the Westernization of Russian intellectuals and return the ideas of Russian patriotism to the forefront of the intellectuals' conscience.

The cohesiveness of the intellectual community, so strong in the first decade following the cessation of the mass terror, has been declining since that time and will continue to do so in the future. The discontinuation of democratization can only exacerbate the conflicts between Westernizers and Russophiles. In the next stage, however, with the support of the mass intelligentsia and the politically active workers, the liberals will continue to dominate the intellectual community.

Of course, the intensity of the conflict between the Westernizers and the Russophiles will depend on many facets of the transitional process, particularly its social costs—the degree of deprivations suffered by the masses, the scope of social and ethnic conflicts, the frequency of strikes and riots, and others. The higher the costs, the stronger will be the Russophile faction in the intellectual community.

Whatever successes and failures await Soviet intellectuals in the future, it is clear that they will continue to play a very important role in the process of modernizing their society.

Epilogue

The final touches are being put on this manuscript in March 1990—a time when the Soviet people, including the intellectuals (the heroes of this book, many of whom are among my personal friends), by now accustomed to hearing one piece of bad news after another, face the future with apprehension and are afraid of civil war, the collapse of order in the country, the expansion of violence, or worse. Still, even during this period, they cling to the hope that the process of modernization and democratization that started in 1985–1987 will continue unabated. It is also my deepest wish that the gloomy prognosis I delineated a few lines earlier not come to pass (even at the expense of my scholarly pride) and that Russia and its cream—the intellectuals—continue their journey toward a "normal" and "civilized" society.

References

Abel, L. 1984. *The Intellectual Follies: A Memoir of the Literary Venture in New York and Paris*. New York: Norton.

Abovin-Egides, P. 1984. Filosof v kolkhoze. *Kontinent* 42:199–239.

Abovin-Egides, P., and Podrabinek, P. 1980. Nekotyryie aktual'nyie voprosy demokraticheskogo dvizhenia v nashei strane. *Poiski* 2:5–40.

Abramov, F. 1973. *Bratia i Sestry: Dve Zimy a Tri Leta*. Leningrad.

Abramov, F. 1982. *Trava-Murava. Povesti i Rasskazy*. Moscow: Sovremennik.

Adamovich, A. 1989. Tikhoie imia. *Literaturnaia Gazeta*, October 18, 1989.

Adamovich, A. 1987. Poslednia li Pastoral'. *Literaturnaia Gazeta*, September 30, 1987.

Adzhubei, A. 1988. Te desiat' let. *Znamia* 6; 7:80–133.

Afanasiev, Iu. 1987a. Nelepo boiatsia samikh sebia. *Moskovskie Novosti*, September 13, 1987.

Afanasiev, Iu. 1987b. Sotsial'naia pamiat' chelovechestva. *Nauka i Zhizn'* 9:56–60.

Afanasiev, Iu., ed. 1988a. *Inogo ne Dano*. Moscow: Progress.

Afanasiev, Iu. 1988b. Otvet istorika. *Pravda*, July 26, 1988.

Afanasiev, Iu. 1988c. Perestroika i Istoricheskoie znanie. *Literaturnaia Rossia*, June 17, 1988.

Afanasiev, Iu. 1988d. Deistvovat' dostoino nashego vremeni. *Sovietskaia Estonia*, September 29, 1988, p. 3.

Aganbegian, A., ed. 1972. *Metodicheskie Polozhenia Optimal'nogo Otraslevogo Planirovania V Promyshlennosti*. Novosibirsk: Nauka.

Aganbegian, A. 1987. Chelovek i ekonomika. *Ogoniok*, July 29, 1987, pp. 2–5.

Aganbegian, A. 1988a. *Sovietskaia Ekonomika-Vzgliad v Budushcheie*. Moscow: Ekonomika.

Aganbegian, A. 1988b. Ekonomika dolzhna byt' ekonomnoi. *Komsomol'skaia Pravda*, April 23, 1988.

Aganbegian, A. 1989. Lekarstvo ot defizita. *Pravitel'stvennyi Vestnik*, September 13, 1989.

Aganbegian, A., and Belkin, V., eds. 1961. *Primenenie Matematiki i Elektronnoi Tekhniki v Planirovanii*. Moscow: Ekonomicheskaia Literatura.

Aganbegian, A., and Kazakevich, D., eds. 1969. *Optimal'noie Territorial'no-proizvodstvennoie Planirovanie*. Novosibirsk: Nauka.

Aganbegian, A., Kozlov, L., and Kazakevich, D., eds. 1974. *Planirovanie Otraslevykh Sistem. Modeli i Metody Optimizatsii*. Moscow: Ekonomika.

Agisheva, R. 1987. Poteriannoie pokolenie. *Moskovskie Novosti*, September 6, 1987.

Agurski, M. 1980. *Ideologia Natsional—Bol'shevisma*. Paris: YMCA Press.

Aitmatov, Ch. 1987. *Plakha Roman*. Moscow: Molodaia Gvardia.

Aitmatov, Ch. 1988a. Speech at the Committee of the Supreme Soviet. *Pravda*, February 14, 1988.

Aitmatov, Ch. 1988b. Podryvaiutsia li osnovy. *Izvestia*, May 4, 1988.

Aitov, N. 1983. *Rabochie Khoroshie i Plokhie*. Moscow: Mysl'.

Akhmatova, A. 1987. Listki iz dnevnika. *Iunost'* 9:72–74.

Aksenov, V., ed. 1982. *Metropol*. New York: Norton.

Aksenov, V. 1985. *Skazhi Izium*. Ann Arbor: Ardis.

Alexandrov, A. 1987. Ishchite istinu. *Komsomol'skaia Pravda*, August 25, 1987.

Alexeiev, P. 1988. Pogrom v khrame nauki. *Nedelia* 31:6–7.

Alexeiev, S. 1989. Vlast' i Ekonomika. *Literaturnaia Gazeta*, December 6, 1989.

Alexeieva, L. 1984. *Istoria Inakomyslia v SSSR. Noveishi Period*. Benson, Va.: Khronika Press.

Alexeieva, L., and Chalidze, V. 1985. *Mass Rioting in the USSR*. Silver Springs, Md.: Foundation for Soviet Studies.

Altaiev [pseudonym]. 1970. Dvoinoie soznanie intelligentsii i psevdo kul'tura, *Vestnik RKhD* 97:9–32.

Amalrik, A. 1978. *SSSR i Zapad v Odnoi Lodke*. London: Overseas Publishing Interchange.

Amalrik, A. 1982. *Notes of a Revolutionary*. New York: Knopf.

Ambartsumov, E. 1988a. O putiakh sovershenstvovania politicheskoi sistemy sotsializma. In Iu. Afanasiev, ed., *Inogo ne Dano*, pp. 77–98. Moscow: Progress.

Ambartsumov, E. 1988b. Iadovityi tuman rasseivaietsia. *Moskovskie Novosti*, June 19, 1988.

Amosov, N. 1988. Real'nosti, idealy i modeli. *Literaturnaia Gazeta*, October 5, 1988.

Ananiev, A. 1988. Sovietski fermer. *Literaturnaia Gazeta*, September 21, 1988.

Andreiev, S. 1988. Prichiny i Sledstvia. *Ural* no. 1.

Andreieva, N. 1988. Ne mogu postupat'sia printsypami. *Sovietskaia Rossia*, March 13, 1988.

Andrisani, P., Appelbaum, E., Koppel, R., and Miljus, R. 1977. *Work Attitudes and Labor Market Experience: Evidence from the National Longitudinal Studies*. Philadelphia: Temple University Press.

Andropov, Iu. 1983. *Izbrannye Rechi i Stat'i*. Moscow: Politizdat.

Anisimov, E. 1987. 'Phenomen Pikulia' glazami istorika. *Znamia* 11:214–223.

Antonov, M. 1986. Uskorenie: Vozmozhnosti i pregrady. *Nash Sovremennik* 7:3–20.

Antonov, M. 1989. Nechustvuiushchie liudi. *Nash Sovremennik* 2:125–151.

Antonov, S. 1987a. Vas'ka. *Iunost'* 3:4.

Antonov, S. 1987b. Puti cherez ovragi. *Moskovskie Novosti*, December 20, 1987.

Antonov, S. 1988. Ovragi. *Druzhba Narodov* nos. 1, 2.

Antonov-Ovseenko, A. 1989. Teatr Iosifa Stalina. In X. Kobo, ed., *Kul't Stalina* pp. 81–111. Moscow: Progress.

Arbatov, G. 1987. Vospominania o voine. *Moskovskie Novosti* 25:4.

Arbatov, G. 1988. *Nedelia*, March 27, 1988.

Arnol'dov, A. 1980. *Sotsialisticheskaia Intelligentsia i Kul'turnyi Progress*. Moscow: Nauka.

Aron, R. 1955. *L'opium des intellectuelles*. Paris.

Arutiunian, Iu. 1968. *Opyt Sotiologicheskogo Izuchenia Sela*. Moscow: Izdate'l-stvo MGU.

Arutiunian, Iu. 1971. *Sotsial'naia Structura Sel'skogo Naselenia SSSR*. Moscow: Mysl'.

Ashkenazy, V. 1985. *Beyond Frontiers*. London: Collins.

Astafiev, V. 1984a. *Rasskazy*. Moscow: Sovietskaia Rossia.

Astafiev, V. 1984b. *Tsar'-Ryba. Povestvovanie v Raskazakh*. Moscow: Molodaia Gvardia.

Astafiev, V. 1986a. Lovlia peskarei v Gruzii. *Nash Sovremennik* 5:123–141.

Astafiev, V. 1986b. *Pechal'nyi detektiv. Zhizn' Prozhit'*. Moscow: Sovremennik.

Astafiev, V. 1988. Ob'edinitsia obshchim ustremleniem. *Izvestia*, September 13, 1988.

Averintsev, S. 1981. *Religia i Literatura*. Ann Arbor: Ermitazh.

Averintsev, S. 1988. Vizantia i Rus': Dva tipa dukhovnosti. *Novyi Mir* 7:210–220.

Babanski, Iu. 1985. *Obraztsovyie Shkoly Moskvy*. Moscow: Pedagogika.

Babenyshev, A., ed. 1981. *Sakharovski Sbornik*. New York: Khronika Press.

Babenysheva, S. 1981. Tsena prozrenia. In *Vnutrennie Protivorechia*, vol. 2. New York: Chalidze.

Baigushev, A. 1988. Letopis' pokoleni. *Nash Sovremennik* 21:185–191.

Balashov, D. 1983. *Bremia Vlasti Roman*. Moscow: Sovremennik.

Barrett, W. 1982. *Truants: Adventures among the Intellectuals*. Garden City, N.Y.: Anchor Press.

Batkin, L. 1988. Vozobnovlenie Istorii. In Iu. Afanasiev, ed., *Inogo ne Dano*, pp. 154–191. Moscow: Progress.

Batkin, L. 1989a. Dissident. *Znanie i Sila*, November, pp. 45–47.

Batkin, L. 1989b. Son razuma. O sotsio-kul'turnykh mashtabakh lichnosti Stalina. In X. Kobo, ed., *Kul't Stalina*, pp. 9–53. Moscow: Progress.

Belinkov, A. 1976. *Sdacha i Gibel' Sovietskogo Intelligenta, Iuri Olesha*. Madrid: Belinkov.

Bell, D. 1973. *The Coming Post-Industrial Society*. New York: Basic Books.

Bellah, R. 1985. *Habits of the Heart*. Berkeley: University of California Press.

Belov, V. 1971. *Sel'skie Povesti*. Moscow: Molodaia Gvardia.

Belov, V. 1983. *Izbrannyie Proizvedenia v Trekh Tomakh*, vol. 1. Kanuny M: Sovremennik.

Belov, V. 1986. Vse vperedi. *Nash Sovremennik* 7:29–106; 8:59–110.

Belov, V. 1988. Remeslo otchuzhdenia. *Novyi Mir* 6:152–181.

Benda, J. 1927. *La trahison des clercs*. Paris: Grasset.

Benn, S., and Gaus, G. 1983. *Public and Private in Social Life*. New York: St. Martin's.

Berberova, N. 1983. *Kursiv Moi: Avtobiografia*, vols. 1 and 2. New York: Russica.

Berdiaev, N., ed. 1909. *Vekhi*. Moscow.

Berdiaev, N. 1948. *The Russian Idea*. New York: Macmillan.

Berg, R. 1983. *Sukhovei. Vospominania Genetika*. New York: Chalidze.

Berg, R. 1984. Varvary na oblomkakh tsivilizatsii. *Kontinent* 41:219–252.

Besançon, A. 1977. *Les origins intellectuals du Leninism*. Paris: Colman-Levy.

Bestuzhev-Lada, I. 1988. Poeta otkryvaia. *Nedelia* 29:16–17.

Bialer, S. 1986. *The Soviet Paradox*. New York: Knopf.

Biddulph, H. 1972. Soviet Intellectual Dissent As a Political Counterculture. *Western Political Science Quarterly* 25(3).

Bliakhman, L., and Shkaratan, O. 1973. *NTR: Rabochi Klass i Intelligentsia*. Moscow: Politizdat.

Blinkova, M. 1983. Volkhonka 14—Dmitria Ul'ianova 19. *Kontinent* 38:221–256.

Blinov, Iu. 1976. Griadushchi grad. *Vestnik RKhD* 119:240–253.

Bodin, L. 1964. *Intellectuals*. Paris: Presse Universitaires de France.

Bondarenko, V. 1989. Sterzhnevaia slovesnost'. *Nash Sovremennik* 12:165–178.

Bondarev, Iu. 1983. *Mgnovenia*. Moscow: Molodaia Gvardia.

Bondarev, Iu. 1986. *Bereg Vybor: Romany*. Minsk: Belarus'.

Bondarev, Iu., ed. 1987a. *Shestoi S'ezd Pisatelei RSFSR Stenograficheski Otchet*. Moscow: Sovremennik.

Bondarev, Iu. 1987b. Istina mnogolika. *Sovietskaia Kul'tura*, July 18, 1987.

Bondarev, Iu. 1988a. Bol' i nadezhda. *Literaturnaia Gazeta*, June 22, 1988.

Bondarev, Iu. 1988b. S Liuboviu i boliu. Kritika-kategoria istiny? In I. Posvirov, ed., *Pisatel' i Vremia*. Moscow: Sovietski Pisatel'.

Bonner, E. 1986. *Alone Together*. New York: Knopf.

Borisova, I. 1988. Andrei Platonov. *Pravda*, May 9, 1988.

Borodin, L. 1985. O Russkoi intelligentsii. *Vestnik RKhD* 1:106–146.

Borodkin, F., Kosals, L., and Ryvkina, R., eds. 1989. *Postizhenie*. Moscow: Progress.

Borshchagovski, A. 1987. O chuvstve viny. *Moskovskie Novosti*, October 11, 1987.

Borshchagovski, A. 1988. Zapiski balovnia sud'by. *Teatr* 10:163–178; 11:153–169; 12:160–170.

Bovin, A. 1988. Perestroika: Pravda o sotsializme i sud'ba sotsializma. In Iu. Afanasiev, ed., *Inogo ne Dano*, pp. 519–550. Moscow: Progress.

Brezhnev, L. 1972. *Leninskim Kursom, Rechi i Stat'i*, vol. 3. Moscow: Politizdat.

Brown, A. 1982. Political Power and the Soviet State: Western and Soviet Perspectives. In N. Harding, ed., *The State in Socialist Society*. Albany: State University of New York Press.

Brym, R. 1980. *Intellectuals and Politics*. New York: Allen and Unwin.

Brzezinski, Z. 1989. *The Grand Failure: The Birth and Death of Communism in the 20th Century*. New York: Scribner's.

Bukovski, V. 1978. *To Build a Castle: My Life as a Dissenter*. New York: Viking Press.

Bukovski, V. 1979. *I Vozvrashchaietsia Veter*. New York: Khronika Press.

Bulgakov, M. 1983. *Master i Margarita. Izbrannoie*. Moscow: Khudozhesvennaia Literatura.

Burlatski, F. 1970. *Lenin Gosudarstvo Politika*. Moscow: Nauka.

Burlatski, F. 1979. *Mao Dze Dun i Iego Nasledniki.* Moscow: Mezhdunarodnyie Otnoshenia.

Burlatski, F. 1987. Politicheskoie zaveshchanie. *Literaturnaia Gazeta,* July 22, 1987.

Burlatski, F. 1988a. Krushchev. Shtrikhi k portretu. In Iu. Afanasiev, ed., *Inogo ne Dano,* pp. 424–441. Moscow: Progress.

Burlatski, F. 1988b. Khrushchev. *Literaturnaia Gazeta,* February 24, 1988.

Burlatski, F. 1988c. Kakoi sotsialism nam nuzhen. *Literaturnaia Gazeta,* April 20, 1988.

Burlatski, F. 1988d. Posle Stalina: Zametki o politicheskoi ottepeli. *Novyi Mir* 10:153.

Burlatski, F. 1988e. Brezhnev i krushenie ottepeli. *Literaturnaia Gazeta,* September 14, 1988.

Burtin, Iu. 1988. Vozmozhnost' vozrazit'. In Iu. Afanasiev, ed., *Inogo ne Dano,* pp. 468–490. Moscow: Progress.

Burtin, Iu. 1989. Akhillesova piata istoricheskoi teorii Marksa. *Oktiabr'* 11:3–25.

Butenko, A. 1987. Mekhanizm tormozhenia: Chto eto takoe i kak s nim borot'sia. *Moskovskie Novosti,* October 25, 1987, p. 8.

Butenko, A. 1988a. O revolutsionnoi perestroike gosudarstvenno-administrativnogo sotsializma. In Iu. Afanasiev, ed., *Inogo ne Dano,* pp. 551–568. Moscow: Progress.

Butenko, A. 1988b. Pered sudom pokoleni. *Sovietskaia Kul'tura,* February 4, 1988.

Butenko, A. 1989. Byl li Stalinism neizbezhen. *Nedelia,* October 15, 1989.

Bykov, V. 1988. Vazhno ne ostanavlivatsia. *Izvestia,* March 10, 1988.

Bykov, V. 1989. Pod znakom peremen. *Literaturnaia Gazeta,* January 18, 1989.

Byrnes, R., ed. 1983. *After Brezhnev.* Bloomington: Indiana University Press.

Camp, R. 1985. *Intellectuals and the State in Twentieth-Century Mexico.* Austin: University of Texas Press.

Campbell, A., Converse, P., and Rogers, W. 1976. *The Quality of American Life: Perceptions, Evaluations, and Satisfactions.* New York: Russell Sage Foundation.

Carey, J. 1972. *Proceedings of the Moscow Human Rights Committee.* New York: The International League for the Rights of Man.

Chalidze, V., ed. 1972. *Dokumenty Komiteta Prav Cheloveka.* New York: The International League for the Rights of Man.

Chalidze, V. 1974. *Prava Cheloveka i Sovetski Souz.* New York: Khronika Press.

Chalidze, V., ed. 1981. *Otvetstvennost' Pokoleni.* New York: Chalidze.

Chalidze, V. 1982. *Khel'sinskoie Dvizhenie.* New York: Chalidze.

Chalmaiev, V. 1968. Neizbezhnost'. *Molodaia Gvardia* 9.

Cherednichenko, G., and Shubkin, V. 1985. *Molodezh Vstupaiet v Zhizn'.* Moscow: Mysl'.

Chernichenko, Iu. 1988. Dve tainy. *Literaturnaia Gazeta,* April 13, 1988.

Chernichenko, Iu. 1989. Predvybornaia platforma. *Moskovskie Novosti,* February 5, 1989.

Chernovolenko, V., Ossovski, V., and Paniotto, V. 1979. *Prestizh Professi i Problemy Sotsial'noiprofessional'noi Orientatsi Molodezhi*. Kiev: Naukova Dumka.

Chubar'ian, O. 1979. *Chelovek i Kniga*. Moscow: Nauka.

Chukovskaia, L. 1976. *Otkrytoie Slovo*. New York: Khronika Press.

Chukovskaia, L. 1976, 1980. *Zapiski ob Anne Akhmatovoi*, vols. 1 and 2. Paris: YMCA Press.

Chukovskaia, L. 1979. *Protsess Iskliuchenia*. Paris: YMCA Press.

Chukovskaia, L. 1981. *Opustelyi Dom*. Paris: Alagante.

Churchward, L. G. 1973. *The Soviet Intelligentsia*. London: Routledge.

Clark, K., and Holquist, M. 1984. *Mikhail Bakhtin*. Cambridge, Mass.: Belknap Press of Harvard University Press.

Cohen, S., ed. 1982. *An End to Silence*. New York: Norton.

Coser, L. 1965. *Men of Ideas: A Sociologist's View*. New York: The Free Press.

Dahl, R. 1971. *Polyarchy*. New Haven and London: Yale University Press.

Davydov, Iu. N. 1963. *Trud i Svoboda*. Moscow: Vyshaia Shkola.

Davydov, Iu. N. 1975. *Estetika Nigilizma*. Moscow: Nauka.

Davydov, Iu. N. 1977. *Kritika Sotsial'no-Filosofskikh Vozzreni Frankfurtskoi Shkoly*. Moscow: Nauka.

Davydov, Iu. N. 1978. *Begstvo ot Svobody*. Moscow: Khudozhestvennaia Literatura.

Davydov, Iu. N. 1982. *Etika Liubvi i Metafizika Svoevolia*. Moscow: Molodaia Gvardia.

Davydov, Iu. N., and Rodnianskaia, I. 1979. *Sotsiologia Kontr-Kul'tury*. Moscow: Nauka.

Davydov, Iu. V. 1970. *Glukhaia Pora Listopada*. Moscow: Molodaia Gvardia.

Dedkov, I., and Latsis, O. 1988. Put' vybran. *Pravda*, July 31, 1988.

Degtiarova, R. 1985. *O Deiatel'nosti KPSS po Formirovaniu Politicheskoi Kul'tury Nauchno-Technicheskoi Intelligentsii v Usloviakh Razvitogo Sotsializma*. Leningrad: Izdatel'stvo Leningradski Universitet.

Dementiev, A. 1969. O traditsii i narodnosti. *Novyi Mir* 4.

Dmitriev, Iu. 1988. Segodnia v perestroike ochen' nuzhdaietsia i nashe tvorcheskoie i zhitieiskoie povedenie. *Literaturnaia Gazeta*, January 20, 1988.

Dmitriev, O. 1988. Kto pisatel'? Pokazhis'. *Literaturnaia Gazeta*, January 20, 1988.

Dolmatovski, E. 1988. *Bylo. Zapiski Poeta. Novyie Stranitsy*. Moscow: Sovietski Pisatel'.

Drach, I. 1984. *Amerikanskaia Tetrad': Stikhi, Dramaticheskaia Poema*. Moscow: Sovietski Pisatel'.

Drobnitski, O. 1977. *Problemy Nravstvennosti*. Moscow: Nauka.

Drozd, V. 1987. Tak vernetsia li ikh vremia. *Literaturnaia Gazeta*, September 30, 1987.

Druze, I. 1987. Zelenyi list, voda i znaki prepinania. *Literaturnaia Gazeta*, July 29, 1987.

Dudinstev, V. 1987a. Genetika sovesti. *Sovietskaia Kul'tura*, February 17, 1987.

Dudintsev, V. 1987b. Tsvet istiny i nadezhdy. *Pravda*, May 10, 1987.

Dudintsev, V. 1988a. Tsvet nashikh odezhd. *Literaturnaia Gazeta*, August 17, 1988.

Dudintsev, V. 1988b. *Belyie odezhdy*. Moscow: Knizhnaia Palata.

Dzarasov, S. 1988. Partinaia demokratia i burokratia: K istokam problemy. In Afanasiev, Iu., ed., *Inogo ne Dano*, pp. 324–342. Moscow: Progress.

Edlis, Iu. 1986. Antrakt. *Novyi Mir* 4:6–77; 5:84–151.

Efimov, B. 1988. Ia sozhaleiu. *Ogoniok* 43:3.

Efros, A. 1985. *Prodolzhenie Teatral'nogo Rasskaza*. Moscow: Iskusstvo.

Ehrenburg, I. 1954. *Ottepel'*. Moscow: Sovietski Pisatel'.

Ehrenburg, I. 1960. Liudi, gody, zhizn'. *Novyi Mir* 8–10.

Ehrenburg, I. 1962. *Chekhov, Stendhal, and Other Essays*. Moscow: Sovietski Pisatel'.

Ehrenburg, I. 1987. Liudi, gody, zhizn'. *Ogoniok* 25:22–24.

Eidel'man, N. 1988, 1989. Revolutsia sverkhu v Rossii. *Nauka i Zhizn'*. 1988, 10:97–105; 11:109–121; 12:102–112; 1989, 1:108–123; 2:80–87; 3:101–108.

Eisenstadt, S. 1987. Intellectuals and Political Elites. In A. Gagnon, ed., *In Liberal Democracies*, pp. 157–166. New York: Praeger.

Emmanuel, N. 1982. Sotsialisticheskoie sorevnovanie i povyshenie effektivnosti nauchnykh issledovani. In R. Ianovski, ed., *Ideino-Politicheskoie Vospitanie Nauchno-Tekhnicheskoi Intelligentsi*. Moscow: Nauka.

Esakov, V. 1971. *Sovietskaia Nauka v Gody Pervoi Piatiletki*. Moscow: Nauka.

Evtushenko, E. 1985. Fuku. Poema. *Novyi Mir* 9:3–58.

Evtushenko, E. 1988. Partia bezpartinykh. *Moskovskie Novosti*, June 12, 1988.

Fadin, A. 1988. Prokliatyie sily. *Vek XX i Mir* 10:27–32.

Fed', N. 1989. Poslanie drugu ili pis'ma o literature. *Nash Sovremennik* 5:169–189.

Fediukin, S. 1983. *Partia i Intelligentsia*. Moscow: Gospolitizdat.

Feuer, L. 1969. *The Conflict of Generations: The Character and Significance of Student Movements*. New York: Basic Books.

Fomicheva, I., ed. 1978. *Literaturnaia Gazeta i Ieie Auditoria*. Moscow: Izdatel'stvo MGU.

Frank-Kamenetski, M. 1988a. Mekhanizmy tormozhenia v nauke. In Iu. Afanasiev, ed., *Inogo ne Dano*, pp. 634–647. Moscow: Progress.

Frank-Kamenetski, M. 1988b. Pochemu molchat uchenyie. *Literaturnaia Gazeta*, March 16, 1988.

Frolov, V. 1988. Chtoby eto ne povtorilos'. In Iu. Afanasiev, ed., *Inogo ne Dano*, pp. 392–411. Moscow: Progress.

Furman, O. 1988. Nash put' k normal'noi kul'ture. In Iu. Afanasiev, ed., *Inogo ne Dano*, pp. 569–580. Moscow: Progress.

Gabrilovich, E. 1987. Tragedii i dramy shchastlivogo kontsa. *Moskovskie Novosti*, October 11, 1987.

Gagnon, A. 1987. *Intellectuals in Liberal Democracies*. New York: Praeger.

Gai, D. 1988. Konets 'dela vrachei. *Moskovskie Novosti*, February 7, 1988.

Gal'tseva, R. 1988. The Participation in the Discussion "Istoria—protsess? Istoria—drama." *Znanie-Sila*, July 23, 1988.

Gasster, M. 1972. *China's Struggle to Modernize.* New York: Knopf.

Gefter, M. 1979. Est' li vykhod. *Poiski* 1:215–252.

Gefter, M. 1988. Stalin umer vchera. In Iu. Afanasiev, ed., *Inogo ne Dano*, pp. 297–324. Moscow: Progress.

Gella, A. 1976. An Introduction to the Sociology of the Intelligentsia. In A. Gella, ed., *The Intelligentsia and the Intellectuals: Theory, Method, and Case Study.* Beverly Hills, Calif.: Sage.

Gel'man, A. 1986. Vremia sobirania sil. *Sovietskaia Kul'tura*, April 9, 1986.

Gel'man, A. 1988. Posledni, reshitelnyi. *Moskovskie Novosti*, June 5, 1988.

Geluta, A., and Staroverov, V. 1977. *Sotsial'nyi Oblik Rabochego Intelligenta.* Moscow: Mysl'.

Gerasimov, G. 1985. *Semeinyie Romany.* Moscow: Sovietski Pisatel'.

German, Iu. 1988. Pust' laiet sobaka. *Pravda*, May 6, 1988.

Gershkovich, A. 1984. Ispovied' Andreia Tarkovskogo. *Kontinent* 42:385–406.

Gidoni, A. 1980. *Solntse Idet s Zapada Kniga Vospominani.* Toronto: Sovremennik.

Ginzburg, E. 1979. *Krutoi Marshrut*, vol. 2. Milan: Mondadori.

Ginzburg, E. 1985. *Krutoi Marshrut*, vol. 1. New York: Posev.

Ginzburg, L. 1988. V poiskakh tozhdestva. *Sovietskaia Kul'tura*, November 12, 1988.

Gladilin, A. 1980. Zagadka Valentina Kataieva. *Novoye Russkoye Slovo*, October 5, 1980, pp. 10–15.

Glazer, N. 1984. New York Intellectuals: Up from Revolution. *New York Times Review of Books*, February 26, 1984.

Glazunov, I. 1985. Chto pomnish? Chem gordishsia. *Pravda*, June 11, 1985, p. 3.

Gleba, Iu. 1988. Prioritet-talantu. *Izvestia*, May 24, 1988.

Glezer, A. 1981. Iubilei neoffitsial'nogo iskusstva. *Novoye Russkoye Slovo*, August 28, 1981.

Glezer, A. 1984. Desiatiletie posle bul'dozernoi vystavki. *Novoye Russkoye Slovo*, September 8, 1984, p. 10.

Glikman, G. 1983. Shostakovich kakim ia znal iego. *Kontinent* 38:319–354.

Glushkova, T. 1988. Kuda vedet Ariadnina nit'. *Literaturnaia Gazeta*, March 23, 1988.

Gnedin, E. 1982. *Vykhod iz Labirinta.* New York: Chalidze.

Gol'danski, V. 1988. Iskusstvo razvivat' nauku. *Sovietskaia Kul'tura*, May 28, 1988.

Gol'denberg, I. 1969. Chitateli Literaturnoi Gazety. In V. Shlapentokh, ed., *Chitatel' i Gazeta. Itogi Izuchenia Chitatel'skoi Auditorii Tsentral'nykh Gazet*, vol. 2. Moscow: Institut Konkretnykh Sotsial'nykh Issledovani.

Gol'dshtein, M. 1970. *Zapiski Muzykanta.* Frankfurt: Posev.

Goliakhovski, V. 1984. *Russian Doctor.* New York: St. Martin's.

Golod, S. 1977. Sotsial'no-psykhologicheskie i nravstennyie tsennosti sem'i. In D. Valentei, ed., *Molodaia Sem'ia.* Moscow: Statistika.

Gorbachev, M. 1986. Politicheski Doklad Tsentral'nogo Komiteta KPSS XXVII

S'ezdu Kommunisticheskoi Partii Sovietskogo Soiuza. *Pravda*, February 26, 1986, pp. 2–10.

Gorbachev, M. 1987. *Izbrannyie Rechi i Stat'i*, vol. 3. Moscow: Politicheskaia Literatura.

Gorbachev, M. 1988. *Perestroika i Novoie Myshlenie*. Moscow: Politizdat.

Gorbanevskaia, N. 1985. Interview s Iuriem Petrovichem Liubimovym. *Kontinent* 44:411–443.

Gorbanevski, M. 1988. Konspekt po korifeiu. *Literaturnaia Gazeta*, June 25, 1988.

Gorbovski, G. 1985. *Odnazhdy na Zemlie*. Moscow: Molodaia Gvardia.

Gorlov, A. 1977. *Sluchai na dache*. Paris: YMCA Press.

Gouldner, A. 1979. *The Future of the Intellectuals and the Rise of the New Class*. New York: Seabury Press.

Gozman, L., and Etkind, A. 1988. Pochemu my ne uiezzhaiem. *Vek* 9:32–38.

Graham, L. 1987. *Science, Philosophy, and Human Behavior in the Soviet Union*. New York: Columbia University Press.

Granin, D. 1954. *Iskateli*. Moscow: Sovietski Pisatel'.

Granin, D. 1956. Sobstvennoie mnenie V. *Literaturniaia Moskva*, vol. 2, Sovietski Pisatel'.

Granin, D. 1962. *Idu na Grozu*. Moscow: Sovietski Pisatel'.

Granin, D. 1987. Ekho dal'neie i blizkoie. *Literaturnaia Gazeta*, May 27, 1987.

Granin, D. 1988a. Kak stat' dobreie. *Nedelia* 3:11.

Granin, D. 1988b. Mimoletnoie videnie. *Ogoniok* 6:9–29.

Granin, D. 1988c. Doroga k zdravomu smyslu. *Pravda*, August 3, 1988.

Grigorenko, P. 1982. *Memoires*. New York: Norton.

Grinberg, A., and Frenkel', V. 1984. *Igor' Vasil'evich Kurchatov v Fiziko-Technicheskom Institute (1925–1943 gg.)*. Leningrad: Nauka.

Grossman, V. 1980. *Zhizn' i Sud'ba*. Lausanne: L'age d'homme.

Grossman, V. 1989. Vse techet. *Oktiabr'* 6:30–108.

Grushin, B. 1968. *Mir Mneni i Mnenia o Mire*. Moscow: Politizdat.

Gudkov, L., and Dubin, B. 1988. Literaturnaia kul'tura: Protses i ratsion. *Druzhba Narodov* 2:168–189.

Gudkov, L., Levada, Iu., Levinson, A., and Sedov, L. 1988. Burokratizm i Burokratia: Neobkhodimost' utochnenia. *Kommunist* 12:73–84.

Gulyga, A. 1987. Poiski absoluta. *Novyi Mir* 10:245–253.

Gulyga, A. 1988. Stat' zerkalom dushi naroda. *Voprosy Filosofii* 9:113–115.

Hayek, F. 1960. The Intellectuals and Socialism. In Q. Huszar, ed., *The Intellectuals*. Glencoe, Ill.: The Free Press of Glencoe.

Heller, M., and Nekrich, A. 1982. *L'Utopie au Pouvoir*. Paris: Calman-Levy.

Hellman, L. 1976. *Scoundrel Time*. Boston: Little, Brown.

Hofstadter, R. 1963. *Anti-Intellectualism in American Life*. New York: Knopf.

Hollander, P. 1981. *Political Pilgrimage: Travels of Western Intellectuals to the Soviet Union, China, and Cuba*. New York: Oxford University Press.

Howe, E. 1982. *A Margin of Hope: An Intellectual Biography*. San Diego: Harcourt.

Hruby, P. 1980. *Fools and Heroes: The Changing Role of Communist Intellectuals in Czecholsolvakia*. New York: Pergamon.

Hughes, S. 1988. *Sophisticated Rebels: The Political Culture of European Dissent, 1968–1987*. Cambridge, Mass.: Harvard University Press.

Iablokov, Iu. 1979. *Sotsiologia Religii*. Moscow: Mysl'.

Iadov, R., ed. 1979. *Samoreguliatsia i Prognozirovanie Sotsial'nogo Povedinia Lichnosti*. Leningrad: Nauka.

Iadov, V., et al., eds. 1967. *Chelovek i Iego Rabota*. Moscow: Mysl'.

Iadov, V., Rozhin, V., and Zdravomyslov, A., eds. 1970. *Man and His Work*. White Plains, N.Y.: Sharp.

Iakovlev, A. M. 1988. Otverzhenie i utverzhdenie. *Ogoniok* 43:14–30.

Iakovlev, N. 1974. *I Avgusta 1914*. Moscow: Molodaia Gvardia.

Iakovlev, N. 1984. *CIA Target—The USSR*. Moscow: Progress.

Ianov, A. 1978. *The Russian New Right: Right Wing Ideologues in the Contemporary USSR*. Berkeley: Institute of Internationial Studies.

Ianov, A. 1988. *Russkaia Ideia i 2000 God*. New York: Liberty Publishing House.

Ianovski, R. 1979a. *Formirovanie Lichnosti Uchenogo v Usloviakh Razvitogo Sotsializma*. Novosibirsk: Nauka.

Ianovski, R. 1979b. Sotsial'nyie i politicheskie problemy vospitania lichnosti uchenogo. In Okladnikov, ed., *Nauka, Organizatsia, i Upravlenie*. Novosibirsk.

Ianovski, R., ed. 1982a. *Ideino-Politicheskoie Vospitanie Nauchno-Tekhnicheskoi Intelligentsii*. Moscow: Nauka.

Ianovski, R., ed. 1982b. *Problemy Sorevnovania Nauchnykh Kollektivov*. Moscow: Vysshaia Shkola.

Ianovski, R., ed. 1986. *Sotsial'noie Razvitie Sovietskoi Intelligentsii*. Moscow: Nauka.

Il'ina, N. 1987. Ob Akhmatovoi. *Ogoniok* 38:28–30.

Iskander, F. 1983. *Sandro of Chegem: A Novel*. New York: Random House.

Iskander, F. 1988. *Sozvezdie Kozlatura. In Izbrannoie*. Moscow: Sovietski Pisatel'.

Iukhneva, N. 1988. Aktual'nyie voprosy mezhnatsional'nykh otnosheni (ob usilienii agressivno-shovinisticheskikh i antisemitskikh nastroeni v sovremennom russkom obshchestve). *Raduga* 11:86–92.

Iutkevich, S. 1988. My s uvlecheniem nachali s'iemki. *Iskusstvo Kino* 2:94–108.

Ivanov, Al. 1987. Nadeius. *Moskovskie Novosti*, June 26, 1987.

Ivanov, An. 1987. Dvizhenie vremeni, dvizhenie literatury. *Ogoniok* 46:6–7.

Ivanov, A., and Svininnikov, V. 1988. Chestnyi khleb iskusstva. *Nash Sovremennik* 5:171–179.

Ivanova, L. 1980. *Formirovanie Sovietskoi Nauchnoi Intelligentsii 1917–1927*. Moscow: Nauka.

Ivanova, L., ed. 1987. *Sovietskaia Intelligentsia*. Moscow: Politizdat.

Ivanova, T. 1988. Na chiei storone uspekh. *Ogoniok* 8:26–28.

Ivinskaia, O. 1978. *A Captive of Time: My Years with Pasternak*. New York: Doubleday.

Jha, A. 1977. *Intellectuals at the Crossroads*. New Delhi: Vikas.

Johnson, P., ed. 1973. *Khrushchev and the Arts: The Politics of Soviet Culture, 1962–1964*. Cambridge, Mass.: MIT Press.

Johnson, P. 1988. *Intellectuals*. London: Weidenfeld and Nicolson.

Kadushin, C. 1974. *American Intellectual Elite*. Boston: Little, Brown.

Kagarlitski, B. 1988. *The Thinking Reed*. London and New York: Verso.

Kaidalov, D. 1976. *Zakon Peremeny Truda i Vsestoronneie Razvitie Cheloveka*. Moscow: Ekonomika.

Kaledin, S. 1987. Smirennoie kladbishche. *Novyi Mir* 5:39–85.

Kalistratova, S. 1989. Takoie bylo tiazhkoie vremia. *Moskovskie Novosti*, August 6, 1989.

Kaminskaia, D. 1984. *Zapiski Advokata*. Benson, Va.: Khronika Press.

Kapustin, M. 1988. Ot kakogo nasledstva my otkazyvaemsia? *Oktiabr'* 4:176; 5:149.

Kapustin, M. 1989. K fenomenologii vlasti. Psikhologicheskie modeli avtoritarisma: Groznyi-Stalin-Hitler. In X. Kobo, ed., *Kul't Stalina*, pp. 372–401. Moscow: Progress.

Kariakin, Iu. 1988. Zhdanovskaia zhidkost' ili protiv ochernitel'stva. In Iu. Afanasiev, ed., *Inogo ne Dano*, pp. 412–424. Moscow: Progress.

Karpets, V. 1987. *Muzh Otechestvoliubimyi*. Moscow: Molodai Gvardia.

Karpinski, L. 1972. Novaia rabochaia arena. *Novyi Mir 5*.

Karpinski, L. 1987. Ne vredno posmotret' na sebia so storony. *Moskovskie Novosti*, October 11, 1987.

Kataiev, V. 1981. *Almaznyi Moi Venets*. Moscow: Sovietski Pisatel'.

Katsenelinboigen, A. 1980. *Soviet Economic Thought and Political Power in the USSR*. Elmsford: Pergamon.

Kaverin, V. 1985. *Pis'mennyi Stol: Vospominania i Razmyshlenia*. Moscow: Sovietski Pisatel'.

Kaverin, V. 1987. Literator. *Znamia* 8:80–121.

Kaverin, V. 1988. Uzhe napisana pervaia fraza. *Literaturnaia Gazeta*, June 15, 1988, p. 5.

Kazintsev, A. 1987. Litsom k istorii: Prodolzhateli ili potrebiteli. *Nash Sovremennik* 11:166–175.

Kazintsev, A. 1988. Istoria-obediniaiushchaia ili razobshchaiushchaia. *Nash Sovremennik* 11:163.

Kelle, V., Kugel', S., and Makeshin, N. 1978. Sotsiologicheskie aspekty organizatsii truda nauchnykh rabotnikov. In J. Kelle, ed., *Sotsiologicheskie Problemy Nauchnoi Deiatel'nosti*. Moscow: Nauka.

Khanin, G. 1989. Pochemu probuksovyvaiet sovietskaia nauka. In F. Borodkin, L. Kosals, and I. Ryvkina, eds., *Postizhenie*, pp. 140–168. Moscow: Progress.

Khansen, Kh. 1977. Struktura chitatel'skikh interesov v sovremennykh usloviakh. In L. Kogan and E. R. Rannik, eds., *Problemy Razvitia Kul'tury v Usloviakh Industrial'nogo Regiona*. Tallin: Akademia Nauk SSSR.

Kharchev, A. 1964. *Brak i Sem'ia v SSSR*. 1st ed. Moscow: Mysl'.

Kheifets, Io. 1987. O druziakh-tovarishchakh. *Sovietskaia Kul'tura*, October 20, 1987.

Kheifets, M. 1978. *Mesto i Vremia (Evreiskie Zamietki)*. Paris: Tretia Volna.

Kheifets, M. 1981. Russki Patriot Vladimir Osipov. *Kontinent*, vol. 28, 27–28.

Khrushchev, N. 1970. *Khrushchev Remembers*. Vol. 1. New York: Random House.

Khvatov, A. 1987. Gumanizm Mikhaila Sholokhova. *Nash Sovremennik* 9:163–171.

Kiesler, A., and Kiesler, S. 1969. *Conformity*. Reading, Mass.: Addison-Wesley.

Kisilev, V. 1988. Skol'ko modelei sotsializma bylo v SSSR? In Iu. Afanasiev, ed., *Inogo ne Dano*, pp. 354–369. Moscow: Progress.

Kisilev, V., and Kliamkin, I., eds. 1989. *Sotsializm Mezhdu Proshlym i Budushchim*. Moscow: Progress.

Kliamkin, I. 1987. Kakaia ulitsa idiot k khramu? *Novyi Mir* 9:150.

Kliamkin, I. 1989. Pochemu trudno govorit' pravdu. *Novyi Mir*, vol. 2.

Klimov, E. 1988. Vlast'-vot v chem vopros. *Moskovskie Novosti*, June 19, 1988.

Kobo, X., ed. 1989. *Osmyslit' Kul't Stalina*. Moscow: Progress.

Kochetov, V. 1969. *Chego Zhe Ty Khochesh*. Moscow: Sovietski Pisatel'.

Kohn, M. 1969. *Class and Conformity: A Study of Values*. Homewood, Ill.: Dorsey Press.

Kolker, Iu. 1985. Ostrova blazhennykh. *Strana i Mir* 1–2:104–114.

Kol'man, E. 1982. *My Tak Ne Dolzhny Byli Zhit'*. New York: Chalidze.

Kon, I. 1967. *Sotsiologia Lichnosti*. Moscow: Politizdat.

Kondrashov, S. 1985. V chuzhoi stikhii. *Novyi Mir* 11:5–130.

Kondrashov, S. 1989. Chelovek u tribuny. *Moskovskie Novosti*, June 9, 1989.

Kondratiev, V. 1987a. Po goriachim sledam pamiati i pravdy. *Nedelia* 50:11.

Kondratiev, V. 1987b. Kogda soldaty vozvrashchaiutsia domoi. *Moskovskie Novosti*, August 30, 1987.

Kondratiev, V. 1989. Pogovorim o svobode. *Literaturnaia Gazeta*, May 24, 1989.

Kondratiev, V. 1990. Pogovorim ob idealakh. *Literaturnaia Gazeta*, January 17, 1990.

Konrad, G., and Szelenyi, I. 1978. *The Intellectuals on the Road to Class Power*. New York: Harcourt.

Kopelev, L. 1978. *Sotvorim Sebe Kumira*. Ann Arbor: Ardis.

Kopelev, L. 1982a. *Der'zhava i narod*. Ann Arbor: Ardis.

Kopelev, L. 1982b. *O Pravde i Terpimosti*. New York: Khronika Press.

Kornilov, V. 1988. Pol'za vpechatleni. *Literaturnaia Gazeta*, July 13, 1988, p. 7.

Korotich, V. 1985. *Litso Nenavisti*. Moscow: Sovietski Pisatel'.

Korotich, V. 1986. My-tol'ko kapli, a reka—narod. *Sovietskaia Kul'tura*, August 8, 1986.

Koval'chuk, A., and Naumova, T. 1983. Sotsial'nyie problemy vosproizvodstva sovietskoi intelligentsii. In A. Amvrosov, ed., *Problemy Nauchnogo Kommunizma*, vol. 17. Moscow: Mysl'.

Koval'chuk, A., and Naumova, T. 1984. Mesto intelligentsii v sotsial'noi strukture sotsialistcheskogo obshchestva. In A. Amvrosov, ed., *Problemy Nauchnogo Kommunisma*, vol. 18. Moscow: Mysl'.

Kozhinov, V. 1978. *Kniga o Russkoi Liricheskoi Poezii XIX Veka: Razvitie Stilia i Zhanra*. Moscow: Sovremennik.

Kozhinov, V. 1980. *Aktual'nyie Problemy Metodologii Literaturnoi Kritiki: Printsipy i Kriterii*. Moscow: Nauka.

Kozhinov, V. 1987. My meniaiemsia? Polemicheskie zametki o kul'ture, zhizni i ieie deiateliakh. *Nash Sovremennik* 10:160–174.

Kozhinov, V. 1988. Pravda i Istina. *Nash Sovremennik* 4:160–175.

Kozlova, T. 1983. *Vozrastnyie Gruppy v Nauchnom Kollektive*. Moscow: Nauka.

Krakhmal'nikova, Z. 1983. *Blagovest*. Zollikon: GZW-Verlag.

Krasil'nikov, S., and Soskin, V. 1985. *Intelligentsiia Sibiri v Period Bor'by za Pobedu i Utverzhdenie Sovietskoi Vlasti*. Novosibirsk: Nauka.

Krasin, V. 1983. *Sud*. New York: Chalidze.

Kugel, S. 1983. *Professional'naia Mobil'nost' v Nauke*. Moscow: Mysl'.

Kugel, S., and Nikandrov, O. 1971. *Molodyie Inzhenery*. Moscow.

Kulikov, B. 1988. Kak zhe vesti dom. *Nash Sovremennik* 7:144–158.

Kuniaev, S. 1985. O 'vselenskikh drovakh' i traditsiakh otechestvennoi poezii, polemicheskie zametki. *Nash Sovremennik* 2:170–181.

Kuniaev, S. 1988a. Vremia. Razmyshlenia na starom Arbate. *Nash Sovremennik* 7:26–27.

Kuniaev, S. 1988b. Vse nachinalos' s iarlykov. *Nash Sovremennik* 9:180–189.

Kurashvili, B. 1985. Perspektivy sovietskogo sotsializma. *Vek XX i Mir* 5:18–23.

Kurashvili, B. 1988. Vremia politicheskikh resheni. *Moskovskie Novosti*, June 5, 1988.

Kuz'min, A. 1985a. V prodolzhenii vazhnogo razgovora. *Nash Sovremennik* 3:182–190.

Kuz'min, A. 1985b. Neozhidannyie priznania. *Nash Sovremennik* 9:182–190.

Kuz'min, A. 1987. Meli v eksterritorial'nom potoke. *Nash Sovremennik* 9:173–179.

Kuz'min, A. 1988. K Kakomu khramu ishchem my dorogu. *Nash Sovremennik* 3:154–164.

Lakshin, V. 1977. *La réponse à Solzhenitsyn*. Paris: Albin Michel.

Lakshin, V. 1980. *Solzhenitsyn, Tvardovski, and Lakshin*. Cambridge, Mass.: MIT Press.

Lakshin, V. 1988. Narod i liudi. *Izvestia*, June 25, 1988.

Lanshchikov, A. 1988. My vse gliadim v Napoleony. *Nash Sovremennik* 7:106–142.

Latsis, A. 1987. Molebnov lesti ne poiu. . . . *Novyi Mir* 1:168.

Latsis, O. 1989. Stalin protiv Lenina. In X. Kobo, ed., *Kul't Stalina*, pp. 214–246. Moscow: Progress.

Latyshev, A. 1988. Bukharin Izvestnyi i Neizvestnyi. *Nedelia* 51:6–7.

Lavrov, K. 1986. Chelovecheski faktor. *Nedelia* 11:6.

Lazarev, L. 1988. A ikh povybilo zhelezom. *Znamia* 2:215–225.

Lee, A. 1984. *Russian Journal*. New York: Vintage Books.

Le Goffe, J., and Köpeczi, B., eds. 1985. *Intellectuelles français, Intellectuelles hongrois, XII–XX siècles*. Paris: Editions du CNRS.

Lel'chuk, V., ed. 1988. *Istoriki Sporiat*. Moscow: Gospolitizdat.

Levada, Iu. 1965. *Sotsial'naia Priroda Religii*. Moscow: Nauka.

Levada, Iu. 1969. *Lektsii po Sotsiologii*. 2 vols. Moscow: Institut Konkretnykh Sotsial'nykh Issledovani.

Levada, Iu., and Sheinis, V. 1988a. 1953–1964: Pochemu togda ne poluchilos'. *Moskovskie Novosti* 18:8–9.

Levada, Iu., and Sheinis, V. 1988b. Pogruzhenie v triasinu. Akt pervyi: 1964–1968. *Moskovskie Novosti*, November 13, 1988, pp. 8–9.

Levada, Iu., and Urlanis, B., eds. 1968. *Kolichestvennyie Metody v Sotsial'nykh Issledovaniakh*. Moscow: Institut Konkretnykh Sotsial'nykh Issledovani.

Levitin-Krasnov, A. 1972. *Stromaty*. Frankfurt am Main: Posev.

Liberman, E. 1971. *The Economic Method and the Effective Economy*. New York.

Likhachev, D. 1985. *Proshloie-Budushchemu. Stat'i i Ocherki*. Leningrad: Nauka.

Likhachev, D. 1987. Ot pokaiania k deistviu. *Literaturnaia Gazeta*, September 9, 1987.

Likhachev, D. 1988. Rossia. *Literaturnaia Gazeta*, October 12, 1988. pp. 5–6.

Likhonosov, V. 1985. *Liubliu Tebia Svetlo*. Moscow: Sovietski Pisatel'.

Lipset, S. M. 1959. *Political Man: The Social Basis of Politics*. Garden City, N.Y.: Anchor Books.

Lisichkin, G. 1976. *Plan i Rynok*. Moscow: Ekonomika.

Lisichkin, G. 1988. Liudi i veshchi. *Druzhba Narodov* 1:207–239.

Lisichkin, G. 1989. Mify i real'nost'. In X. Kobo, ed., *Osmyolit' Kul't Stalina*, pp. 247–283. Moscow: Progress.

Litvinov, P. 1976. O dvizhenii za prava cheloveka. In P. Litvinov, M. Meerson-Aksenov, and B. Shragin, eds., *Samosoznanie. Sbornik Statei*. New York: Khronika Press.

Liubarski, K. 1984. Stena kotoraia ne dolzhna nas razdeliat'. *Strana i Mir* 11.

Liubimov, L. 1989. Kakoi sisteme prinadlezhat SShA? *Literaturnaia Gazeta*, June 28, 1989.

Liubomudrov, M. 1985. Teatr nachinaetsia s rodiny. *Nash Sovremennik* 6:168–178.

Liubomudrov, M. 1989. Izvlechem li uroki? O russkom teatre i ne tol'ko o nem. *Nash Sovremennik* 2:170–183.

Lobanov, M. 1968. Obrazovannyie lavochniki. *Molodaia Gvardia* 4.

Lobanov, M. 1988. Posleslovie. *Nash Sovremennik* 4:154–159.

Lubrano, L. L., and Solomon, S. G. 1980. *The Social Context of Soviet Science*. Boulder, Colo.: Westview Press.

Machajski, J. 1968. Umstvennyi rabochi. In A. Sokolov, ed., *Umstvennyi Rabochi*. New York: Mezhdunarodnoie sodruzhestvo.

Makarenko, M. 1974. Iz moei zhizni. *Vol'noie Slovo* 12.

Makarov, A. 1985. Piushchi intelligent? *Nedelia* 20.

Maksudov (pseudonym). 1981. Chto vy dumaiete o Sakharove. In A. Babenyshev, R. Lert, and E. Pechuro, eds., *Sakharovski Sbornik*. New York: Khronika Press.

Maliutin, M. 1988. Neformaly v perestroike: Opyt i perspektivy. In Iu. Afanasiev, ed., *Inogo ne Dano*, pp. 210–227. Moscow: Progress.

Mandel'shtam, N. 1970. *Vospominania*. Paris: YMCA Press.

Mandel'shtam, N. 1972. *Vtoraia Kniga*. Paris: YMCA Press.

Mannheim, K. 1949. *Ideology and Utopia*. New York: Harcourt and Brace.

Marchenko, A. 1981. Otkrytoie pis'mo akademiku Kapitse P.L. In Babenyshev et al., eds., *Sakharovski Sbornik*. New York: Chalidze.

Mar'iamov, A. 1985. Prozrenie. Istoria dvukh khudozhnikov. *Kontinent* 43:303–322.

Markov, G., Karpov, V., Verchenko, Iu., et al., eds. 1988. *Vos'moi S'ezd Pisatelei SSSR*. Moscow: Sovietski Pisatel'.

Marran (pseudonym). 1982. Liki Russkoi idei. *Vremia i My* 63.

Medvedev, R. 1975. *On Socialist Democracy*. New York: Norton.

Medvedev, R. 1988. Bez Vyrvannykh Stranits. *Komsomol'skaia Pravda*, August 25, 1988.

Medvedev, R. 1989a. O Staline i Stalinizme. *Znamia* 1:159–210; 2:174–223; 3:144–192.

Medvedev, R. 1989b. 33 goda spustia. *Nedelia*, April 30, 1989, pp. 10–13.

Medvedev, Zh. 1973. *Ten Years After Ivan Denisovich*. London: Macmillan.

Meerson-Aksenov, M., and Shragin, B., eds. 1977. *The Political, Social and Religious Thought of Russian Samizdat: An Anthology*. Belmont: Norlan.

Merton, R. 1949. *Social Theory and Social Structure*. Glencoe, Ill.: Free Press.

Migranian, A. 1988. Mekhanizm tormozhenia v politicheskoi sisteme i puti iego preodolenia. In Iu. Afanasiev, ed., *Inogo ne Dano*, pp. 97–121. Moscow: Progress.

Migranian, A. 1989a. *Demokratia i Nravstvennost'*. Moscow: Znanie.

Migranian, A. 1989b. Dolgi put' k evropeiskomu domu. *Novyi Mir* 7:166–184.

Migranian, A. 1989c. Populizm. *Sovietskaia Kul'tura*, June 24, 1989.

Milosz, Cz. 1953. *The Captive Mind*. New York: Knopf.

Milton, D., and Milton, N. 1973. The Great Cultural Revolution. In M. Coye and J. Livingston, eds., *China: Yesterday and Today*. New York: Bantam Books.

Mironova, M., and Menaker, A. 1984. *V Svoiem Repertuare*. Moscow: Iskusstvo.

Mishin, V. 1970. *Obshchestvennyi Progress*. Gorky: Viatskoie Izdatel'stvo.

Moiseiev, N. 1988. Oblik Rukovoditelia. *Novyi Mir* 4:176–188.

Moore, B. 1984. *Privacy: Studies in Social and Cultural History*. Armonk, N.Y.: M. E. Sharpe.

Moroz, O. 1984. Fizikoi ocharovannyi. *Literaturnaia Gazeta*, April 4, 1984.

Moroz, O. 1988. Posledni diagnoz. *Literaturnaia Gazeta*, December 28, 1988.

Mozhaiev, B. 1987. Khleb nash nasushchnyi. *Sovietskaia Kul'tura*, November 14, 1987.

Mozhaiev, B. 1988. *Muzhiki i Baby*. Moscow: Sovremennik.

Natalushko, S. 1981. *Povyshenie urovnia sotsial'nogo razvitia trudovogo kollektiva kak faktora rosta effektivnosti truda. Planirovanie i Upravlenie v Nauchnykh Kollektivakh*. Moscow: Institut Sotsiologicheskikh Issledovani.

Naumova, N. 1984. *Piotr Kapitsa*. Leningrad: Soviestki Pisatel'.

Nechkina, A. 1982. *Dekabristy*. Moscow: Nauka.

Neizvestnyi, E. 1984. *Govorit Neizvestnyi*. Frankfurt: Posev.

Nesterov, F. 1984. *Sviaz' Vremen*. 2d ed. Moscow: Molodaia Gvardia.

Nuikin, A. 1988a. O tsene slova i tsenakh na produkty. *Ogoniok* 22:6–27.

Nuikin, A. 1988b. Pchela i kommunisticheski ideal. In Iu. Afanasiev, ed., *Inogo ne Dano*, pp. 509–519. Moscow: Progress.

Obraztsov, S. 1987. Nauchitsia liubit'. *Ogoniok* 45:12–14.

Ochkin, A. 1987. Naguliaiet li tsena pribyl'. *Nash Sovremennik* 12:154–161.

Okudzhava, B. 1984. *Stikhotvorenia*. Moscow: Sovietski Pisatel'.

Ol'shanski, V. 1966. In G. Osipov, ed., *Sotsiologia v SSSR*, vol. 1. Moscow: Mysl'.

O'Neill, N. 1982. *A Better World. The Great Schism: Stalinism and the American Intellectuals*. New York: Simon and Schuster.

Orlov, Iu. 1976. Vozmozhen li sotsializm ne totalitarnogo tipa. In P. Litvinov, M. Meyerson-Aksenov, and B. Shragin, eds., *Samosoznanie*. New York: Khronika Press.

Orlova, R. 1982. Frida Vigdorova. *Vnutrennie Protivorechia* 3.

Orlova, R. 1983. *Memoirs*. New York: Random House.

Orwell, G. 1984. *Nineteen Eighty-Four*. New York and Oxford: Clarendon Press.

Osipov, V. 1978. *Tri Otnoshenia k Rodine*. Frankfurt: Posev.

Ovrutski, L. 1988a. Istoria v uslovnom naklonenii. *Sovietskaia Kul'tura*, February 4, 1988.

Ovrutski, L. 1988b. Tupiki otrezvlenia. *Sovietskaia Kul'tura*, July 16, 1988.

Palievski, P. 1978. *Literatura i Teoria*. Moscow: Nash Sovremennik.

Pankin, B. 1988. Vozdukh 6–go etazha. *Komsomol'skaia Pravda*, May 5, 1988.

Panova, V. 1975. *O Moei Zhizni, Knigakh i Chitateliakh*. Leningrad: Lenizdat.

Papernyi, D. 1983. *Zapiski Moskovskogo Pianista*. Ann Arbor: Ermitazh.

Parkin, F. 1972. System Contradiction and Political Transformation. *European Journal of Sociology* 13:45–62.

Pashaiev, S. 1984. *Nauka i Nravstvennoie Vospitanie*. Moscow: Vysshaia Shkola.

Pastukhova, M. 1987. Iarche liuboi legendy. *Ogoniok* 49:18–23.

Pells, B. 1985. *The Liberal Mind in a Conservative Age: American Intellectuals in the 1940's and 1950's*. New York: Harper and Row.

Perevedentsev, V. 1975. *Metody Izuchenia Migratsii Naselenia*. Moscow: Nauka.

Perry, L. 1984. *Intellectual Life in America: A History*. New York: F. Watts.

Petrakov, N. 1971. *Khoziastvennaia Reforma*. Moscow: Ekonomika.

Petrakov, N. 1987. Zolotoi chervonets vchera i segodnia. *Novyi Mir* 3:205.

Petrushevskaia, L. 1988. V svoiem kruge. *Novyi Mir* 1:116–130.

Phillips, W. 1983. *A Partisan View: Five Decades of the Literary Life*. New York: Stein and Day.

Pikul', V. 1985a. *Favorit*. Vols. 1 and 2. Leningrad: Lenizdat.

Pikul', V. 1985b. *Tri Vozrasta Okini-San. Sentimental'nyi Roman*. Moscow: Sovremennik.

Pikul', V., and Zhuravlev, S. 1989. Chest' sobstvennogo imeni. *Nash Sovremennik* 2:184–192.

Pimenov, R. 1973. Odin politcheski protses. *Vol'noie Slovo* 8.

Pimenov, R. 1979, 1980. Vospominania. In *Pamiat' vypusk* 2 (1979); *Vypusk* 3 (1980). Paris: YMCA Press.

Pischel, E. 1977. The teacher. In D. Wilson, ed., *Mao Tse-tung in the Scale of History*. Cambridge, Eng.: Cambridge University Press.

Plakhov, A. 1987. Khochetsia zhit' i zhit'. *Moskovskie Novosti*, December 13, 1987.

Platonov, A. 1978. *Chevengur*. Ann Arbor: Ardis.

Platonov, A. 1987. Kotlovan. *Novyi Mir* 6:50.

Plimak, E., and Khoros, V. 1985. Problemy dekabristskogo dvizhenia. *Voprosy Filosofii* 12:96–109.

Pliushch, L. 1979. *Na Karnavale Istorii*. London: Overseas Publications.

Podhoretz, N. 1979. *Breaking Ranks: A Political Memoir*. New York: Harper and Row.

Poliakov, I. 1989. Apofigei. *Iunost'* 5:11–30.

Polikanov, S. 1983. *Razryv. Zapiski Atomnogo Fizika*. Frankfurt: Posev.

Pomerants, G. 1981. Tsena otrechenia. In A. Babenyshev et al., eds., *Sakharovski Sbornik*. New York: Khronika.

Pomerants, G. 1985a. Za povorotom. *Strana i Mir* 1–2:95–103.

Pomerants, G. 1985b. Zhazhda dobra. *Strana i Mir* 9:83–96; 10:66–79.

Pomerants, G. 1988. Po tu storonu zdravogo smysla. *Is. K.* 10:25–32.

Popkova, L. 1987. Gde pyshneie pirogi? *Novyi Mir* 5:139–241.

Popov, G. 1987. Tochki zrenia ekonomista. *Nauka i Zhizn* 4:54–65.

Popov, G. 1988a. Dat' vziatku gosplanu. *Strana i Mir* 4:35–49.

Popov, G. 1988b. Samyi khudshi vnutrenni vrag. *Sovietskaia Kul'tura*, July, 21, 1988.

Popov, G. 1988c. Perestroika upravlenia ekonomikoi. In Iu. Afanasiev, ed., *Inogo ne Dano*. Moscow: Progress.

Popov, G. 1988d. Tol'ko pri neskol'kikh kandidatakh. *Moskovskie Novosti*, November 27, 1988.

Popov, G. 1989. O pol'ze neravenstva. *Literaturnaia Gazeta*, October 4, 1989.

Popov, N. 1988. Kto vyshe vlasti. *Sovietskaia Kul'tura*, April 26, 1988.

Popov, V., and Shmelev, N. 1988. Anatomia defitsita. *Znamia* 5:158–183.

Popov, V., and Shmelev, N. 1989. Na razvilke dorog. Byla li al'ternativa Stalinskoi modeli razvitia. In X. Kobo, ed., *Kul't Stalina*, pp. 284–326. Moscow: Progress.

Popova, I. 1984. Tsennostnyie Predstavlenia i "paradoksy" Samosoznania. *Sotsiologicheskie Issledovania* 4:29–36.

Popovski, M. 1983. *Delo Akademika Vavilova*. Ann Arbor: Ermitazh.

Prokhanov, A. 1986. Speech at the VIII Congress of Soviet Writers. *Literaturnaia Gazeta*, July 2, 1986.

Prokhanov, A. 1988. Raduisia, blagodatnaia. *Literaturnaia Gazeta*, April 13, 1988.

Prokhorov, A., ed. 1987. *Sovietski Entsiklopedicheski Slovar'*. Moscow: Sovietskaia Entsiklopedia.

Prokhanov, A. 1990. Tragedia tsentrizma. *Literaturnaia Rossia*, January 5, 1990.

Puchkovski, M., and Zakharov, N., eds. 1985. *S Chuzhogo Golosa*. Moscow: Moskovski Rabochi.

Pukhov, S. 1981. Otnoshenie Moskvichei k profsoiuzu "Solidarnost." In V. Chalidze, ed., *SSSR: Vnutrenie Protivorechia*. New York: Chalidze.

Radaiev, V., and O. Shkaratan. 1990. Vozvrashchenie k istokam. *Izvestia*, February 16, 1990.

Rapoport, Ia. 1988. Vospominania, o 'dele vrachei. *Druzhba Narodov* 4:222–245.

Raskol'nikov, F. 1939/1988. Otkrytoie pis'mo Stalinu. *Nedelia* 26:6–7.

Rasputin, V. 1978. *Proshchanie s Materoi*. Povesti. Moscow: Sovietskaia Rossia.

Rasputin, V. 1980. *Povesti*. Moscow: Molodaia Gvardia.

Rasputin, V. 1985. Pozhar. In *Vek Zhivi—Vek Liubi*. Moscow: Izvestia.

Rasputin, V. 1988a. Zhertvovat' soboi radi pravdy. *Nash Sovremennik* 1:169–172.

Rasputin, V. 1988b. Esli po sovesti. *Literaturnaia Gazeta*, January 1, 1988.

Rasputin, V. 1988c. Znat' sebia patriotom. *Pravda*, June 24, 1988.

Razgon, L. 1988. Nakonets. *Moskovskie Novosti*, June 26, 1988.

Reader, K. 1987. *Intellectuals and the Left in France since 1986*. New York: St. Martin's.

Reddaway, P., ed. 1972. *Uncensored Russia: Protest and Dissent in the Soviet Union*. New York: American Heritage Press.

Reshetovskaia, N. 1977. *Sania: My Life With Alexander Solzhenitsyn*. London: Hart-Davis.

Reznikov, M. 1984. *Vospominania Starogo Muzykanta*. London: Overseas Publications.

Ross, P. 1987. The Decline of the Left Intellectuals in Modern France. In A. Gagnon, ed., *Intellectuals in Liberal Democracies*, pp. 43–66. New York: Praeger.

Roziner, F. 1981. *Nekto Finkel'maier*. London: Overseas Publications.

Rubinstein, L. 1983. Rasskaz o Viktore Shklovskom. *Novoye Russkoye Slovo*, October 15, 1983.

Rudnitski, K. 1988. Krushenie teatra. *Ogoniok* 22:10–14.

Rumiantsev, A. 1965. Narod i intelligentsia. *Pravda*, February 21, 1965.

Rumiantsev, A. 1969. Maoizm i antimarksistskaia sushchnost' iego filosofi. *Kommunist* 2.

Rumiantsev, A. 1970. *V. I. Lenin i Sotsiologia*. In: *Lenin i Sovremennaia Nauka*, vol. 1. Moscow: Nauka.

Rumiantsev, O. 1988. *O Samodeiatel'nom Dvizhenii Obshchestvennykh Organizatsi*. Moscow: Institut Ekonomiki Mirovoi Sotsialisticheskoi Sistemy.

Rumiantsev, O. 1989. *Ob Avtoritarnoi Modernizatsi i Sotsial-Demokraticheskoi Al'ternative*. Moscow: Manuscript.

Rybakov, A. 1987. *Deti Arbata*. Moscow: Sovietski Pisatel'.

Sagdeiev, R. 1988a. Gde my poteriali temp. *Izvestia*, April 28, 1988.

Sagdeiev, R. 1988b. Akademia nauk na perelome. *Moskovskie Novosti*, January 3, 1988.

Sakharov, A. 1970. *Progress, Coexistence, and Intellectual Freedom*. New York: Norton.

Sakharov, A. 1974. *Sakharov Speaks*. New York: Knopf.

Sakharov, A. 1978. *Trevoga i Nadezhda*. New York: Khronika Press.

Sakharov, A. 1981. The Responsibility of Scientists. *The New York Review of Books*, June 25, 1981.

Sakharov, A. 1982. Letter to My Foreign Colleagues. *The New York Review of Books*, January 21, 1982.

Sakharov, A. 1988. Sakharov Assails Threats to Perestroika. *New York Times*, November 8, 1988.

Sakharov, A. 1989a. Za mir i progress. *Moskovskie Novosti*, February 5, 1989.

Sakharov, A. 1989b. Ia aktivno podderzhivaiu perestroiku. *Izvestia*, February 6, 1989.

Salutski, A. 1987. Sil'nyie i slabyie. *Nash Sovremennik* 12:100–119.

Salutski, A. 1988. Umozrenie i real'nosti. *Nash Sovremennik* 6:136–162.

Sarnov, B. 1989a. Skol'ko vesit nashe gosudarstvo. In X. Kobo, ed., *Kul't Stalina*, pp. 160–194. Moscow: Progress.

Sarnov, B. 1989b. Kto vinovat? *Literaturnaia Gazeta*, March 8, 1989.

Sats, N. 1984. Novelly moei Zhizn'i. *Kniga pervaia, vtoraia*. Moscow: Iskusstvo.

Scammell, M. 1984. *Sozhenitsyn: A Biography*. New York: Norton.

Schaff, A. 1962/1970. Marxism and the Human Individual. In R. S. Cohen, ed., *Marxism and the Human Individual*. New York: McGraw-Hill.

Schram, S. R. 1969. *The Political Thought of Mao Tse Tung*. London: Penguin.

Sedletski, R. 1976. Uzuchenie zritelia i praktika teatra. In N. Khrenov, ed., *Teatr i Nauka: Sovremennyie Napravlenia v Issledovanii Teatra*. Moscow: Vserossiskoie Teatral'noie Obshchestvo.

Selden, M. 1979. *The People's Republic of China: A Documentary History of Revolutionary Change*. New York: Monthly Review Press.

Seleznev, Iu. 1986. *Glazami Naroda*. Moscow: Sovremennik.

Seliunin, V. 1988a. Planirovat' ili upravliat'. *Moskovskie Novosti*, May 1, 1988.

Seliunin, V. 1988b. Revansh burokratii. In Iu. Afanasiev, ed., *Inogo ne Dano*, pp. 192–210. Moscow: Progress.

Seliunin, V. 1988c. Istoki. *Novyi Mir* 5:162.

Sennett, R. 1977. *The Fall of Public Man*. New York: Knopf.

Sevastianov, A. 1988. Intelligentsia: Chto vperedi. *Literaturnaia Gazeta*, September 21, 1988.

Shafarevich, I. 1974. Sotsializm. In M. Agurski et al., eds., *Iz-Pod Glyb*. Paris: YMCA Press.

Shafarevich, I. 1978. Ar'ergardnyie boi marksizma v rabotakh R. A. Medvedeva. *Vestnik RKhD* 125:160–181.

Shafarevich, I. 1988. Logika istorii. *Moskovskie Novosti*, June 12, 1988.

Shafarevich, I. 1989. O rusofobii. *Vremia i My* 104:145–172.

Shalamov, V. 1982. *Kolymskie Rasskazy*. Paris: YMCA Press.

Shanov, D., and Kuznetsov, A. 1977. Opyt sotsiologicheskogo analiza problemy sotsial'nogo planirovania v nauchnom kollektive. In A. Zvorykin, ed., *Problemy Sotsial'nogo Planirovania v Nauchnom Kollektive*. Moscow.

Shatalin, S. 1989. Izderzhki neizbezhny, no . . . *Literaturnaia Gazeta*, October 11, 1989.

Shatrov, M. 1988. I dal'she . . . dal'she . . . dal'she. *Znamia* 1:3–53.

Shcherbakov, A. 1975. *Sotsial'no-Ekonomicheskie Problemy Effektivnosti Nauchnogo Truda*. Novosibirsk: Nauka.

Sheinin, Iu. 1980. Uslovia nauchnogo truda. In L. Bazhenov and A. Akhundov, eds., *Nauka v Sotsial'nykh, Gnoseologicheskikh i Tsennostnykh Aspektakh*. Moscow: Nauka.

Sheinis, V. 1989. Perestroika na novom etape: Opasnosti i problemy. In F. Borodkin, L. Kosals, and I. Ryvkina, eds., *Postizhenie*, pp. 357–388. Moscow: Progress.

Shelestov, D. 1988. Piat' konvertov. *Nedelia*, June 26, 1988.

Sherdakov, V. 1982. *Illiuzia Dobra*. Moscow: Politicheskaia Literatura.

Shevtsov, I. 1988. *Vo imia otsa i syna. Izbrannyie Proizvedenia*. Vol. 2. Moscow: Voennoie Izdatel'stvo.

Shils, E. 1972. *The Intellectuals and the Powers, and Other Essays*. Chicago: University of Chicago Press.

Shipler, D. 1983. *Russia: Broken Idols, Solemn Dreams*. New York: Times Books.

Shipunov, F. 1989. Velikaia zamiatnia. *Nash Sovremennik* 11:132–139.

Shkaratan, O. 1982. Peremeny v sotsial'nom oblike gorozhan. In T. Riabushkin and G. Osipov, eds., *Sovietskaia Sotsiologia*, vol. 2. Moscow: Nauka.

Shklovski, V. 1928. *Gamburgski Schet*. Leningrad: Izdatel'stvo Pisatelei.

Shlapentokh, V. 1968. O sootnoshenii obshchikh i individual'nykh tselevykh funktsi. In Iu. Levada and B. Urlanis, eds., *Kolichestvennyie Metody v Sotsial'nykh Issledovaniakh*. Moscow: Institut Konkretnykh Sotsial'nykh Issledovani.

Shlapentokh, V., ed. 1969a. *Chitatel' i Gazeta: Chitateli Truda*. Moscow: Institut Konkretnykh Sotsial'nykh Issledovani.

Shlapentokh, V., ed. 1969b. *Chitatel' i Gazeta: Chitateli Izvesti i Literaturnoi Gazety*. Moscow: Institut Konkretnykh Sotsial'nykh Issledovani.

Shlapentokh, V. 1973. *Problemy Dostovernosti Statisticheskoi Informatsii v Sotsiologicheskikh Issledovaniakh*. Moscow: Statistika.

Shlapentokh, V. 1975. *Kak Segodnia Izuchaiut Zavtra*. Moscow: Sovietskaia Rossia.

Shlapentokh, V. 1980. Essays in Sociology. *International Journal of Sociology* 10 (Spring, special issue).

Shlapentokh, V. 1982. The Study of Values as a Social Phenomenon: The Soviet Case. *Social Forces* 61 (2):403–418.

Shlapentokh, V. 1984. *Love, Marriage and Friendship in the Soviet Union: Ideals and Practices*. New York: Praeger.

Shlapentokh, V. 1986. *Soviet Public Opinion and Ideology*. New York: Praeger.

Shlapentokh, V. 1987. *The Politics of Sociology in the Soviet Union*. Boulder and London: Westview Press.

Shlapentokh, V. 1988. *Soviet Ideologies in the Period of Glasnost*. New York: Praeger.

Shlapentokh, V. 1989a. *Public and Private Life of Soviet People*. Oxford: Oxford University Press.

Shlapentokh, V. 1989b. Stalin, Simonov as drugie. *Vremia i My*, 102:137–148.

Shmelev, N. 1987. Avansy i dolgi. *Novyi Mir* 3:142.

Shragin, B. 1977. *Protivostoianie Dukha*. London: Overseas Publications.

Shreider, L. 1969. Nauka-istochnik znani i sueveri. *Novy Mir* 10.

Shtein, A. 1987. Moie pokolenie. *Sovietskaia Kul'tura*, May 23, 1987.

Shtein, A. 1988. I ne tol'ko o nem. *Teatr* 3:169–187.

Shtromas, A. 1981. *Political Change and Social Development: The Case of the Soviet Union*. Frankfurt: Verlag Peter Lang.

Shturman, D. 1985. Ne mne meda tvoiego, ni uksusa tvoiego. *Novoye Russkoye Slovo*, September 26, 27, 1985; October 2, 3, 1985.

Shubkin, V. 1970. *Sotsiologicheskie Opyty*. Moscow: Mysl'.

Shubkin, V. 1978. Predely. *Novyi Mir* 2:188–217.

Shubkin, V. 1979. *Nachalo Puti: Problemy Molodezhi v Zerkale Sotsiologii i Literatury*. Moscow: Molodaia Gvardia.

Shubkin, V., ed. 1984. *Trudiashchaiasia Molodezh: Obrazovanie, Professia, Mobil'nost'*. Moscow: Nauka.

Shubkin, V. 1987. Odin den' voiny. *Literaturnaia Gazeta*, September 18, 1987.

Shubkin, V. 1989. Trudnoe proshchanie. *Novyi Mir* 4:165–184.

Shul'zhenko, K. 1985. *Kogda Vy Menia Sprosite*. Moscow: Molodaia Gvardia.

Simis, K. 1982. *USSR: The Corrupt Society*. New York: Simon and Schuster.

Simone, V., ed. 1968. *China in Revolution: History, Documents, and Analyses*. Greenwich, Ct.: Fawcett Publications.

Simonov, K. 1988. Glazami cheloveka moiego pokolenia. *Znamia* 3:3–66; 4:49–121; 5:69–96.

Sirotkin, V. 1990. Neformaly—za pechatnym stankom. *Nedelia*, January 21, 1990.

Skrinski, A., ed. 1988. *Akademik G. I. Budker*. Novosibirsk: Nauka.

Slutski, B. 1987. Stikhi raznykh let. *Iunost'* 11:78–79.

Smekhov, V. 1988. Skripka mastera. *Teatr* 2:97–115.

Smilga, V. 1987. Trebuiutsia bystryie razumom Niutony. *Literaturnaia Gazeta*, June 24, 1987.

Smith, G. 1984. *Song to Seven Strings: Russian Guitar Poetry and Soviet Mass Song*. Bloomington, Ind.: Indiana University Press.

Smith, H. 1976. *The Russians*. New York: Ballantine.

Soifer, V. 1988. Gor'ki plod. *Ogoniok* 1–2:4–31.

Sokirko, V. 1981. O vozmozhnosti i zhiznennoi neobkhodimosti dialoga mezhdu "stalinistami" i dissidentami. *Posev 5*.

Sokirko, V. 1983a. Radi Rossii. *Poiski* 5–6:106–142.

Sokirko, V. 1983b. Posleslovie k knige A. Kuznetsova. *Bednost' Narodov*, 189–197.

Soloukhin, V. 1989. Chitaia Lenina. *Rodina* 10:66–70.

Solov'ieva, N., ed. 1978. *Kniga i Chtenie v Zhizni Sovietskogo Sela: Problemy i Tendentsii*. Moscow: Kniga.

Solzhenitsyn, A. 1968. *The First Circle*. New York: Harper.

Solzhenitsyn, A. 1972. *A Lenten Letter to Pimen, Patriarch of All Russia*. Minneapolis: Burgess.

Solzhenitsyn, A., ed. 1974. *Iz-Pod Glyb*. Paris: YMCA Press.

Solzhenitsyn, A. 1975a. *Letter to the Soviet Leaders*. New York: Harper and Row.

Solzhenitsyn, A. 1975b. *The Gulag Archipelago, 1918–1956*. New York: Harper and Row.

Solzhenitsyn, A. 1975c. *Bodalsia Telenok s Dubom*. Paris: YMCA Press.

Solzhenitsyn, A. 1976. *Lenin in Zurich*. New York: Farrar, Straus, Giroux.

Solzhenitsyn, A. 1978. *A World Split Apart: Commencement Address Delivered at Harvard University*. New York: Harper.

Solzhenitsyn, A. 1981a. Nashi pliuralisty. *Vestnik RKhD* 139:133–160.

Solzhenitsyn, A. 1981b. *Publizistika*. Paris: YMCA Press.

Solzhenitsyn, A. 1983a. *Krasnoie Koleso, Usel 1. August Chetyrnadtsatogo*. Paris: YMCA Press.

Solzhenitsyn, A. 1983b. Vystuplenie v Itone. *Vestnik RKhD* 140:281–289.

Srivastava, H. 1978. *Intellectuals in Contemporary India*. New Delhi: Heritage Publishers.

Stalin, J. 1945. *O Velikoi Otechestvennoi Voine*. Moscow: Politizdat.

Stalin, J. 1952. *Voprosy Leninizma*. Moscow: Politizdat.

Stepanian, Z., ed. 1983. *Sovietskaia Intelligentsia i Ieie Rol' v Stroitel'stve Kommunizma*. Moscow: Nauka.

Strelianyi, A. 1987. Dva umozrenia. *Novyi Mir* 2:234.

Strelianyi, A. 1988a. Strel'ba vzlet. *Druzhba Narodov* 6:3–49.

Strelianyi, A. 1988b. O sukhariakh i gazetakh. *Moskovskie Novosti* 18:3.

Strizhov, G., ed. 1984. *O Reforme Obshcheobrazovatel'noi i Professional'noi Shkoly. Sbornik Dokumentov i Materialov*. Moscow: Gospolitizdat.

Suleimenov, A. 1975. *Az i Ia*. Alma-Ata.

Sumbaiev, O., ed. 1985. *Akademik B. P. Konstantinov: Vospominania, Stat'i, Dokumenty*. Leningrad: Nauka.

Svetov, F. 1978. *Otverzi mi Dveri*. Paris: Les Editeurs Reunis.

Svininnikov, V. 1985. *Sotsialism i Svobodnoie Vremia. Pravo na Otdykh*. Moscow: Vysshaia Shkola.

Swirski, G. 1979. *Na Lobnom Meste*. London: Novaia Literaturnaia Biblioteka.

Sysoiev, V. 1983. *Khodite Tikho, Govorite Tikho*. Paris: Tret'ia Volna.

Taratuta, E. 1987. Chestnaia zhizn', tiazhkaia sud'ba. *Ogoniok* 40:22–23.

Tendriakov, V. 1971/1988. Okhota. *Znamia* 9:87–124.

Tendriakov, V. 1988. Na blazhennom ostrove kommunizma. *Novyi Mir* 9:20.

Tikhonov, V. 1987. Tak kuda zhe nas zovut. *Literaturnaia Gazeta*, April 8, 1987.

Tikhonov, V. 1988a. Pora zemel'noi reformy. *Moskovskie Novosti*, August 7, 1988.

Tikhonov, V. 1988b. Chtoby narod prokormil sebia. *Literaturnaia Gazeta*, March 8, 1988.

Timofeiev, L. 1982. Tekhnologia Chernogo Rynka ili Krestianskoie Iskusstvo Golodat'. *Grani*, no. 120.

Titma, M., ed. 1973. *Sotsial'no-Professional'naia Orientatsia Molodezhi*. Tartu: Tartuski Universitet.

Tokarev, S., ed. 1980, 1988. *Mify Narodov Mira*. 2 vols. Moscow: Sovietskaia Entsiklopedia.

Tokes, R. 1975. Introduction. In R. Tokes, ed., *Dissent in the USSR: Politics, Ideology, and People*. Baltimore: Johns Hopkins University Press.

Tolstaia, T. 1988. Somnambula v tumane. *Novyi Mir* 7:8–26.

Trifonov. Iu. 1973. *Neterpenie*. Moscow: Sovietski Pisatel'.

Trifonov, Iu. 1982. Vremia i Mesto. Postcriptum, 1982.

Trifonov, Iu. 1983a. *Izbrannoie*. Minsk: Vysshaia Shkola.

Trifonov, Iu. 1983b. *Dom na Naberezhnoi*. Ann Arbor: Ardis.

Trifonov, Iu. 1984. Starik. In *Vechnyie Temy*. Moscow: Sovietski Pisatel'.

TsSU SSSR. 1987. *Narodnoie Khoziastvo SSSR za 70 Let*. Moscow: Finansy i Statistika.

Tugarinov, V. 1960. *O Tsenostiakh Zhizni i Kul'tury*. Leningrad: Nauka.

Turchenko, V., ed. 1969. *Sotsiologicheskie i Ekonomicheskie Problemy Obrazovania*. Novosibirsk: Nauka.

Turchin, V. 1978. *Inertsia Strakha*. New York: Khronika Press.

Turgenev, I. S. 1859/1963. *Dvorianskoie Gnezdo*. Moscow: Gospolitizdat Khudozhestvennaia Literatura.

Tvardovski, A. 1974. *O Samom Glavnom*. Moscow: Sovietski Pisatel'.

Tvardovski, A. 1985. *Pis'ma o Literature*. Moscow: Sovietski Pisatel'.

Tvardovski, I. 1988. Stranitsy perezhitogo. *Iunost'* 3:10–32.

Uglov, F. 1987. Gliadia pravde v glaza. *Nash Sovremennik* 7:150–157.

Ulanovskaia, V. 1966. *Formirovanie Nauchnoi Inteligentsii v SSSR, 1917–1937*. Moscow: Nauka.

Ulanovskie, N., and M. 1982. *Istoria Odnoi Sem'i*. New York: Chalidze.

Vail, B. 1980. *Osobo Opasnyi*. London: Overseas Publications.

Vaksberg, A. 1988a. Kak zhivoi s zhivymi. *Literaturnaia Gazeta*, June 29, 1988.

Vaksberg, A. 1988b. Kost' mamonta. *Literaturnaia Gazeta*, May 18, 1988.

Vasiliev, B. 1989. Liubi Rossiu v nepogodu. *Izvestia*, January 16, 17, 18, 1989.

Vasiliev, I. 1987. Ochishchenie. *Nash Sovremennik* 8:3–80.

Vasiliev, I. 1988. Bumerang. *Pravda*, October 2, 1988.

Vasilieva, L. 1988. Otkroi cheloveka. *Literaturnaia Gazeta*, July 27, 1988.

Vatai, F. 1984. *Intellectuals in Politics in the Greek World*. London: Croom Helm.

Vein, A., and Vlasov, N. 1985. *Nikolai Ivanovich Grashchenkov*. Moscow: Nauka.

Venzher, V. 1966. *Kolkhoznyi Stroi na Sovremennom Etape*. Moscow: Ekonomika.

Vershinin, V. 1988. Iskusstvo khoziastvonania. *Sovietskaia Kul'tura*, October 1, 1988.

Vinogradov, I. 1988. Mozhet li pravda byt' poetapnoi? In Iu. Afanasiev, ed., *Inogo ne Dano*, pp. 277–298. Moscow: Progress.

Vishnevskaia, G. 1984. *Galina*. New York: Random House.

Vishnevski, A., ed. 1989. *V Chelovecheskom Izmerenie*. Moscow: Progress.

Vladimov, G. 1980. Lik vsego naroda? O protsesse Aleksandra Ginzburga. *Poiski* 12:225–227.

Vladimov, G. 1983. *Ne Obrashchaite Vnimanie Maestro*. Frankfurt: Posev.

Vodolazov, G. 1988. Kto vinovat, chto delat' i kakoi schet? In Iu. Afanasiev, ed., *Inogo ne Dano*, pp. 441–467. Moscow: Progress.

Vodolazov, G. 1989. Lenin i Stalin. *Oktiabr'* 9:3–29.

Voinovich, V. 1985. *Antisovietski Sovietski Soiuz*. Ann Arbor: Ardis.

Volkogonov, D. 1987. Fenomen Stalina. *Pravda*, December 18, 1987.

Volkogonov, D. 1988. Triumf i tragedia. Politicheski portret L. V. Stalina. *Oktiabr'* 10:3; 11:16; 12:46.

Volkov, G. 1988. Voznesenie. O tom kak Stalin sdelalsia velikim filosofom. *Sovietskaia Kul'tura*, June 7, 1988.

Volkov, S. 1979. *Testimony: The Memoirs of Dimitri Shostakovich*. New York: Harper and Row.

Volkov, V. 1975. Teatr i televidenie: Sotsiologicheski aspekt vzaimodeistvia. In L. Kogan and A. Sharova, eds., *Issledovanie i Planirovanie Razvitia Dukhovnoi Kul'tury Trudiashchikhsia Urala*. Sverdlovsk: Ural'ski Nauchnyi Tsentr.

Vooglaid, Iu., ed. 1967. *Metodologicheskie Problemy Issledovania Massovoi Kommunikatsii*. Tartu: Tartu Universitet.

Vooglaid, Iu., ed. 1968. *Tsennostnyie Orientatsii Lichnosti i Massovaia Kommunikatsia*. Tartu: Tartu Universitet.

Vooglaid, Iu., ed. 1969. *Lichnost' i Massovaia Kommunikatsia*. Tartu: Tartu Universitet.

Voskresenski, L. 1987. Znaite, tovarischi. *Moskovskie Novosti*, December 6, 1987.

Voskresenski, L. 1988. Pora nachat'. *Moskovskie Novosti*, January 3, 1988.

Voslenski, M. 1980. *La nomenclature: Les privilèges en URSS*. Paris: Pierre Belfon.

Voznesenski, A. 1984. Proraby dukha. *Literaturnaia Gazeta*, March 7, 1984, p. 5.

Voznesenski, A. 1986. Rov. Poema. *Iunost'* 6:28.

Voznesenski, A. 1988a. Otvet moiemu chitateliu. *Sovietskaia Kul'tura*, June 11, 1988.

Voznesenski, A. 1988b. Pis'mo A. Voznesenskogo v redaktsiu gazety Novoye Russkoye Slovo. *Novoye Russkoye Slovo*, April 30, 1988.

Voznesenski, A. 1988c. Pervyi god komissii. *Nedelia* 3.

Voznesenski, A. 1988d. Svecha i mietel'. *Pravda*, June 6, 1988, p. 3.

Vozovikov, V. 1982. *Pole Kulikovo Roman*. Moscow: Sovremennik.

Vykhodtsev, P. 1988. O mode i vechnykh tsennostiakh. *Nash Sovremennik* 5:161–170.

Weber, M. 1968. *Economy and Society*. 3 vols. New York: Bedminster Press.

Wolter, U., ed. 1980. *Rudolf Bahro: Critical Responses*. White Plains, N.Y.: Sharp.

Zalygin, S. 1987. Povorot Uroki odnoi diskussi. *Novyi Mir* 1:3–18.

Zaslavskaia, T., ed. 1970. *Migratsia Sel'skogo Naselenia*. Moscow: Mysl'.

Zaslavskaia, T. 1988. O Strategii sotsial'nogo upravlenia perestroikoi. In Iu. Afanasiev, ed., *Inogo ne Dano*, pp. 9–50. Moscow: Progress.

Zaslavskaia, T. 1989. Perestroika i sotsialism. In F. Borodkin, L. Kosals, and I. Ryvkina, eds., *Postizhenie*, pp. 217–240. Moscow: Progress.

Zaslavski, V., and Z. (pseudonym). 1981. Adult Political Socialization in the USSR: A Study of Attitudes of Soviet Workers to the Invasion of Czechoslovakia. *Sociology* 15 (August):407–423.

Zhadov, L., Karaganov, S., and Katzeva, E. eds. 1984. *Konstantin Simonov v Vospominaniakh Sovremennikov*. Moscow: Sovietski Pisatel'.

Zhigulin, A. 1988. Chernyie kamni, autobiograficheskaia povest'. *Znamia* 7:10–75; 8:48–119..

Zimin, A. (pseudonym). 1981. *Sotsializm i Neostalinizm*. New York: Chalidze.

Zinoviev, A. 1976. *Ziaushchie Vysoty*. Lausanne: L'age d'homme.

Zinoviev, A. 1978. *Svetloie Budushcheie*. Lausanne: L'age d'homme.

Zinoviev, A. 1982. *Homo Sovieticus*. Paris: L'Age d'Homme.

Zinoviev, A. 1985. Ne vse my dissidenty. O sotsial'noi oppositsii v Sovietskom obshchestve. *Kontinent* 44:175–190.

Zipko, A. 1988a. O zonakh zakrytykh dlia mysli. *Nauka i Zhizn'* 11:45–55.

Zipko, A. 1988b. Prevratnosti chistogo sotsializma. *Nauka i Zhizn* 12:40–48.

Zipko, A. 1989. Egoizm mechtatelei. *Nauka i Zhizn'* 1:46–56.

Zlobin, N., et al. 1988. Filosofia i istoricheskaia nauka. *Voprosy Filosofii* 10:33–35.

Zolotusski, I. 1988. Voina i svoboda. *Literaturnaia Gazeta*, June 8, 1988.

Zudilova, T. 1975. Zritel'skie orientatsii v sfere teatra. In L. Kogan and V. Volkov, eds., *Issledovanie i Planirovanie Razvitia Dukhovnoi Kul'tury Trudiashchikhsia Urala*. Sverdlovsk: Akademia Nauk Ural'ski Nauchnyi Tsentr.

Zykina, L. 1984. *Na Perekrestke Vstrech*. Moscow: Sovietskaia Rossia.

Zyrianov, P. 1989. O Stolypine i ne tol'ko o nem. *Nedelia*, September 22, 1989.

Name Index

Subject Index